T0316269

Chinese Management in the 'Harmonious Society'

Whither Chinese management? The Middle Kingdom has come a long way since the economic reforms were introduced after 1978. As ownership has opened up and has become more fragmented, the state-owned firms no longer dominate the scene, nor does their management model. Managing has also become more complex and diversified, as well as more professional. This book asks what the next steps are likely to be and will assess the current directions in which Chinese managers are developing, as its economy slows down in the face of global uncertainty. It aims to update previous works in the field covering business and management in these countries. It covers a wide range of topics, including banking, competition, employee satisfaction, expatriates, industrial relations, HRM, organization, SMEs, social responsibility, strategic sourcing, trust and so on. The book also asks in which future directions management may be moving in this important part of the international economy. The authors are all experts in their fields and are all based in universities and business schools in countries such as Australia and the UK, among others.

The work is aimed at undergraduate and postgraduate students in business administration especially those on MBA programmes, as well as those studying development economics, management studies and related courses, including lecturers in those subjects.

This book was previously published as a special issue of *Asia Pacific Business Review*.

Malcolm Warner is Professor and Fellow Emeritus, Wolfson College, Cambridge and Judge Business School, University of Cambridge. He was the Editor-in-Chief, of the *International Encyclopedia of Business and Management* [IEBM] latest edition, 8 vols, 2002. He is currently Co-Editor of the *Asia Pacific Business Review*.

Chris Rowley is a Professor and Director of the Centre for Research on Asian Management, City University, London, UK and Director of Research and Publications, HEAD Foundation, Singapore. His most recent book (as editor) is *The Changing Face of Chinese Management* (with Fang Lee Cooke) (Routledge, 2010). He is currently co-editor of *Asia Pacific Business Review*.

Chinese Management in the 'Harmonious Society'

Managers, Markets and the Globalized Economy

Edited by
Malcolm Warner and Chris Rowley

Routledge
Taylor & Francis Group

LONDON AND NEW YORK

First published 2011
by Routledge
2 Park Square, Milton Park, Abingdon, Oxon, OX14 4RN

Simultaneously published in the USA and Canada
by Routledge
711 Third Avenue, New York, NY 10017

Routledge is an imprint of the Taylor & Francis Group, an informa business

© 2011 Taylor & Francis

This book is a reproduction of *Asia Pacific Business Review*, vol. 16, issue 3. The Publisher requests to those authors who may be citing this book to state, also, the bibliographical details of the special issue on which the book was based.

Typeset in Times New Roman by Taylor & Francis Books

All rights reserved. No part of this book may be reprinted or reproduced or utilised in any form or by any electronic, mechanical, or other means, now known or hereafter invented, including photocopying and recording, or in any information storage or retrieval system, without permission in writing from the publishers.

British Library Cataloguing in Publication Data
A catalogue record for this book is available from the British Library

ISBN13: 978-0-415-57242-2

Disclaimer
The publisher would like to make readers aware that the chapters in this book are referred to as articles as they had been in the special issue. The publisher accepts responsibility for any inconsistencies that may have arisen in the course of preparing this volume for print.

Contents

CONTENTS

Notes on contributors

John Benson is a Professor and Head of the School of Management at the University of South Australia, Australia. He has published many books, book chapters and journal articles in the areas of management and HRM in Japan and China, trade unions, unemployment and labour markets in Asia.

Fang Lee Cooke is Professor of Human Resource Management and Chinese Studies at the School of Management, RMIT University, Australia. Her research interests are in the area of employment relations and management. She is the author of *HRM, Work and Employment in China* (2005) and *Competition, Strategy and Management in China* (2008).

Li Xue Cunningham is a RCUK Research Fellow, as well as Deputy Director, of Centre for Research in Asian Management, Cass Business School, City University. Before she embarked on her research career, she worked as a manager for several large Chinese corporations in international business. Dr. Cunningham's research interests include international and comparative human resource management, small and medium enterprise business and development, especially in China.

Angus Duff is a Professor of Accounting and Finance at the University of the West of Scotland and Research Advisor to the Institute of Chartered Accountants of Scotland. He has published extensively in academic and professional journals. His current interests lie in accounting education, the accounting profession, credit rating agencies and credit markets.

Xin Guo is a Lecturer in Accounting and Finance at the Business School of the University of the West of Scotland. His main research interests include banking relations, service quality measurement, accounting education, structural equation modelling, and accounting and finance in China.

Mario Hair is a Lecturer in Statistics at the University of West of Scotland and is also an active researcher and consultant within the Statistics Consultancy Unit based at the university. His research interests and publications are mainly in this field.

Qiaoling He graduated from Manchester Business School, University of Manchester, UK in 2008 with a Masters in Chinese Business and Management. She is currently working as a manager in a privately-owned commercial business in China.

Neng Jiang is a PhD candidate at the Judge Business School, University of Cambridge, UK. His thesis is on 'Profitability Dynamics in the Emerging Markets'. He earned two Masters' degrees in operational research and accounting and financial management respectively from Lancaster University Management School.

Paul A. Kattuman is Reader in Economics at Judge Business School, University of Cambridge, UK, and Fellow in Economics and Management Studies at Corpus Christi College, Cambridge. He has published extensively in the field of economics.

Byron Keating is Associate Professor of Service Management, Faculty of Business and Government, University of Canberra, Australia. He received his PhD in services management from the University of Newcastle, and carries out research in the impact of culture, technology and ethics on service firm strategy. His work has been published, or is forthcoming, in the *Journal of the Academy of Marketing Science, Supply Chain Management: An International Journal,* the *International Journal of Tourism Research*, and others.

Anton Kriz is a Senior Lecturer in the Newcastle Business School, Australia. His PhD investigated the nature of trust and business relationships in China. He is currently completing research as part of a Winston Churchill fellowship into the regional variations in China. His work has been published, or is forthcoming, in the *China Review International*, the *Journal of Hospitality and Tourism Management*, the *International Journal of Hospitality & Tourism Administration*, and others.

Jane Nolan is a Senior Research Fellow and Director of Studies at Magdalene College, University of Cambridge, UK. Her current research is focused on the role of Western banks in the reform of financial institutions in mainland China. Her research interests include economic sociology, comparative analysis, globalization and institutional change.

Chris Nyland is the Professor of International Business in the Faculty of Business and Economics, Monash University, Australia. His primary research interest is the association between globalization and human security and has published extensively in this field.

Chris Rowley is a Professor and Director of the Centre for Research on Asian Management, City University, London, UK and Director of Research and Publications, HEAD Foundation, Singapore. His most recent book (as editor) is *The Changing Face of Chinese Management* (with Fang Lee Cooke) (Routledge, 2010). He is currently co-editor of *Asia Pacific Business Review*.

Jie Shen is Associate Professor of International Human Resource Management, School of Management, University of South Australia, Australia. His main research interests are international human resource management, human resource management and industrial relations. His most recent book on China was *Labour Disputes and Their Management in China* (Chandos Publishing, 2007).

Malcolm Warner is Professor and Fellow Emeritus, Wolfson College, Cambridge and Judge Business School, University of Cambridge, UK. He has published extensively on Asian management. His most recent book (as editor) is 'Making Sense' of HRM in China (Routledge, 2010). He is currently co-editor of *Asia Pacific Business Review*.

NOTES ON CONTRIBUTORS

Michael Webber is a Professorial Fellow in the Department of Resource Management and Geography, the University of Melbourne, Australia. He has a large number of publications covering issues such as economic geography, Asian development, environmental protection and rural migrant workers in China.

Mingqiong Zhang obtained his PhD in Sociology and now is pursuing his second PhD in Management at the Department of Management, Monash University, Australia. His research interests include institutionalism, social security, multinational corporations, HRM and Chinese studies.

Cherrie Jiuhua Zhu (PhD) is an Associate Professor of Human Resource Management (HRM) and Chinese studies in the Department of Management, Monash University, Australia. Her research areas cover cross-culture management, especially HRM; the impact of international business/globalization on social protection systems; and HRM policies and practices in emerging economies such as China. Her book entitled *HRM in China: Past, Current and Future HR Practices in the Industrial Sector* was published by Routledge in 2005.

Ying Zhu is an Associate Professor and Director of Master of HRM in the Department of Management and Marketing, the University of Melbourne, Australia. He has published books, book chapters and journal articles in the areas of international HRM, employment relations and labour regulations in Asia.

Chinese management at the crossroads: setting the scene

Malcolm Warner[a] and Chris Rowley[b]

[a]Judge Business School, University of Cambridge, UK; [b]Centre for Research on Asian Management, City University, London, UK; Head Foundation, Singapore

The 'Middle Kingdom' has come a long way in the last few decades, its economy has burgeoned and its prosperity has flourished. Chinese management has evolved greatly too but is now at the 'crossroads', as the People's Republic of China celebrates the 60th anniversary of the 'Liberation' led by Mao Zedong and the 30th anniversary of the economic reforms launched by his successor, Deng Xiaoping. In this symposium, we review its past legacy, its evolution to date, as well as its options, covering a wide range of management topics. As ownership of its enterprises has opened-up and has become more fragmented, state-owned firms arguably no longer dominate the scene, nor does their management model. Being a manager has also become more complex and diversified, as well as more professional. The Party has proclaimed the 'Harmonious Society' as the route to reconciling economic performance with social justice. This edited collection asks what are the next steps and will assess the current directions in which Chinese managers are developing, as its economy now has to cope with a slowdown in the face of global uncertainty.

Introduction

Whither Chinese management, we may well ask? The 'Middle Kingdom' has come a long way since market-driven economic reforms were introduced in 1978 and after (Child 1994, Rowley and Wei 2009c, Warner 2009). Has the modernization of its management gone far enough? Are its managers professional enough? Where does it go from here? Chinese management is now indeed at the 'crossroads', as the People's Republic of China (PRC) celebrates the 60th anniversary of the 'Liberation' of 1949 led by Mao Zedong and the 30th anniversary of Deng Xiaoping, his successor's, reforms, the latter described as based on socialism 'with Chinese characteristics' and in this way seeking to reflect the national culture (Child and Warner 2003). More recently, the new leader Hu Jintao has proclaimed the 'Harmonious Society' as the route to reconciling economic performance with social justice (Warner 2009).

Background

Today, the PRC is increasingly seen as an 'economic superpower' (World Bank 2009). China's Gross Domestic Product (GDP) in 2008 was said to be over US$4.4 trillion, somewhat smaller than Japan's but predicted to overtake it in 2010, if as yet only a third of that of the US. The outward investment of China was around US$56 million in 2008. Some see the PRC as umbilically linked to the US in a relationship called '*Chi-merica*' (Ferguson 2009), constituting what has been dubbed the 'G2'; it has now become the biggest lender to the US and the RMB *(yuan),* if possibly overvalued, is predicted to become a 'reserve currency' at a future date (The Economist 2009a, pp. 1–2). Its massive financial stimulus policy of US$586 billion to counteract the current economic crisis has been praised by the International Monetary Fund (IMF 2009) to better compensate for the fall in exports and the rise in unemployment at the end of 2008 (China Economic Review 2009). Even so, it has indeed become the new Asian 'giant' economy (Bergsten *et al.* 2008, World Bank 2009), and we can here clearly see China's achievement, in a comparative context, for example its high rate of economic growth, *vis-à-vis* its neighbours, one 'socialist' (Vietnam) and the other two 'capitalist' (Japan and South Korea), in Table 1.

Table 1. Comparative contextual factors – China *vis-à-vis* its neighbours, one 'socialist' and the other two 'capitalist' (2009, est.).

	China	Vietnam	Japan	South Korea
Geography				
Size (sq km)	9,596,961	331,210	377,915	99,720
People				
Population (million)	1338.61	86.96	127.08	48.51
Age structure (%) 0–14 yrs	19.8	24.9	13.5	16.5
15–64	72.1	69.4	64.3	72.3
65+	8.1	5.7	22.2	10.8
Median age (years)	34.1	27.0	44.2	37.3
Growth rate (%)	0.655	0.977	−0.191	0.266
Birth rate (per 1000 pop.)	14.00	16.41	7.64	8.93
TFR* (children per woman)	1.79	1.83	1.21	1.21
Urban population (%)	43	28	66	81
Education expenditure (% GDP)	1.9 (2006)	1.8 (1991)	3.5 (2005)	4.6 (2004)
Economy				
GDP ppp** (US$ 2008)	7973 trillion	241.7 billion	4329 trillion	1335 trillion
Real growth rate (% 2008)	9.0	6.2	−0.7	2.2
Per capita ppp (US$ 2008)	6000	2800	34,000	27,600
By sector (% 2008)				
Agriculture	11.3	22	1.5	3.0
Industry	48.6	39.9	26.3	39.5
Services	40.1	38.1	72.3	57.6
Inflation (CPI % 2008)	5.9	24.4	1.4	4.7
Labour market				
Labour force (million 2008)	807.3	47.41	66.5	24.35
By occupation (%)				
Agriculture	43.0	55.6	4.4	7.2
Industry	25.8	18.9	27.9	25.1
Services	32.0	25.5	66.4	67.1
	(2006)	(2005)	(2005)	(2007)
Unemployment official figures (% 2008)	4.0	4.7	4.0	3.2

Notes: * total fertility rate; ** purchasing power parity.
Source: adapted from CIA (2009) and miscellaneous statistical reports.

This table is also of interest as it shows some interesting contrasts, such as in terms of size (geographical, population and labour force) and relative importance (employment and contribution) of sectors. For instance, in terms of (1) population structure, 8.1% of the population is over the age of 65 in China, in Japan, 22.2%; (2) birth rate, 14.0 in China, 7.6 in Japan; (3) urban, 43% in China, 66% in Japan. Similarly, in terms of percentages of the labour force in different sectors, in China 43% are in agriculture, 26% in industry and 32% in services, while in Japan the figures are 4.4%, 27.9% and 66.4% respectively. Even more telling is the percentage of GDP each provides; for example, in China 11.3% comes from agriculture, 49% from industry and 40% from service, while in Japan the figures are 1.5%, 26.3% and 72.3% respectively.

In this symposium, we review the evolution of management in the PRC over recent years, which we see as having been modernized *pari passu* with the transformation of its economy. As ownership has now opened-up and has become more fragmented, the state-owned enterprises (SOEs) that once dominated its industrial landscape are no longer as prominent as they were (Garnaut *et al.* 2005, Zeng 2005, Warner 2009, 2010a, 2010b). Markets now drive the economy and management has also become more complex and diversified, as well as more professional and less ideological (Chen 2008). Even so, the state still plays a key role in orchestrating the score (Huang 2008, The Economist 2009b, Scissors 2009). Right now, the Party is said to be attempting to blend Marxist-Leninism with traditional notions of Confucianism (Bell 2008) as it seeks to cope with the growing contradictions in Chinese society, such as relate to inequalities of wealth and income, and more fairly deal with its labour–management relations by promoting the 'Harmonious Society'. This edited collection asks what are the next steps to take and will assess the current directions in which Chinese managers are developing as the economy slows down in the face of global uncertainty (see the variety of areas of management in Rowley and Cooke [2010]). We can see the range of the contributions in the symposium in the overview of contents in Table 2 below. This is in terms of main themes, organizations and sectors and locations covered.

Contributions to this symposium

We now present a summary of each of the contributions to this symposium, in the following section. First up is a study by Warner and Zhu, which looks at the relations in the workplace between labour and management. It examines the challenges now facing China's increasingly complex ways of managing people in the new economic, political and social environments of the twenty-first century and how managers are adapting to the new concept of a 'harmonious society' to which the new Chinese leadership currently aspires. The authors hypothesize that this search for harmony, built on Chinese cultural values, represents what amounts to what can be conceptualized as a 'coping mechanism' to deal with the existing and potential conflicts now facing Chinese society. Labour–management relations in the workplace are accordingly now changing fast. The older ways of people management are being replaced with newer ones. Notions of human capital and human resources (HR) are now increasingly *de rigueur.* The more 'human resources management' (HRM) replaces 'personnel management' in China, the more of the old people management ethos of the planned economy goes out of the window. HRM is now more typical of the non-state sector.

However, it might be argued that this new way of managing may be more often found in most of what have been called 'learning organizations', such as those more 'open' Sino–foreign joint venture (JV) enterprises or multinational companies (MNCs)

Table 2. Overview of content: themes, sector/organization and locations.

Authors	Themes	Organizations/Sectors	Locations
Warner and Zhu	Labour–management relations; Harmonious Society	SOE, JV, SME, POE, FEI, MNC	PRC
Kriz and Keating	Interpersonal trust; *xinren*	SOE, JV, SME, POE, FEI, MNC	Beijing, Shanghai, Xiamen, Taipei, Hong Kong
		Trading, insurance, R&D, PR, information, education, petrol	
Cunningham and Rowley	HRM	SME	PRC
Shen	Employee satisfaction; HRM	POE, SOE, TVE	Jiangsu province
		Manufacturing: luggage production, electrical wires and cables, liquor, cereal and feed machinery	
Cooke and He	HRM; CSR	Textiles and apparel	Guangdong province
Zhang *et al.*	Socially embedded HRM;	POE, SOE, JV, WFOE	Jiangsu province Shanghai
	hukou system	Auto spares, electric motors, real estate, house decorations, photo-electric displays, yarn, electronic devices, aluminium pigments, cocoa products, house appliance fittings	
Guo *et al.*	Exchange relationships; corporate relations; commitment	Banking	Beijing
Nolan	Corporate governance; institutional theory	Banking	Beijing Hong Kong Shanghai
Zhu *et al.*	Intangible management; Employee satisfaction; organizational performance	SOE, DPE, FIE, COE, SME, LF Textiles, clothing and footwear; electronics	Beijing and Hangzhou Harbin and Kunming Lanzhou and Wuhan
Jiang and Kattuman	Market competition; firm profitability	Chinese listed companies	PRC

operating in China. In such firms, we are likely to find new management practices that have been initially transplanted when the JV was initially founded, for example, by the overseas partner from its home base to, say, Beijing or Shanghai.

This contribution concludes that the changes in the relations between labour and management reflect the impact of globalization on economic restructuring and enterprise diversity, as well as the changing role of trade unions and their efforts to protect workers' rights and interests in the light of these developments. Yet, the authors believe that there will indeed have to be another 'Long March' for the Party/state and unions, as well as other civil groups in China, before the partners can reach a new social equilibrium.

In the next contribution included in this collection, Kriz and Keating examine interpersonal trust which they argue may be identified as a critical issue for Western firms attempting to do business in China. To go 'within' Chinese culture and what some refer to as 'inside-out' or 'bottom-up', their study adopts a grounded interpretive approach, employing mainly qualitative techniques. These include using 'rich' and 'thick' descriptions and 'in-depth' semi-structured interviews.

Initially pilot interviews were conducted with Chinese individuals resident in Australia and this was later followed up with 'face-to-face' interviews in Beijing, Shanghai and Xiamen, as well as the non-Mainland Chinese markets of Taipei and Hong Kong. A key goal of this research was to offer a more indigenous or native Chinese definition for trust. After coding, processing and analysing the data, it became evident that Chinese defined trust (*xinren*) as the 'heart-and-mind' confidence and belief that the other person will perform, in a positive manner, what is expected of him or her, irrespective of whether that expectation is stated or implied.

Another important strand of the study was to pin-point potential antecedents of trust, as well as a conceptual framework. The study identified that what the Chinese refer to as trust or *xinren* is reserved for a minority of people and is erected on several important elements, like honesty, sincerity, help, reciprocity and performance over time. The relationship between *xinren* and its associated construct in Chinese business is called *guanxi*. The tag *xinren* is really reserved for a few select relationships, whereas *guanxi* is built around more extended connections and a larger network. The study suggests that lower forms of trust can of course be built from initial connections and *guanxi*, but 'deep trust' or *xinren* does not occur until a threshold is achieved. At this level, the bonds become very strong.

This finding is, the contributors believe, an important addition to the literature on the subject, as those business people operating in China and relying on *guanxi* may be over-estimating the depth of their potential connection's commitment. Crucially, deeper levels of trust, they argue, are built on both *cognitive* and *affective* aspects and are not simply instrumental or emotional as reported in recent literature. They believe that what they calls an *emic* approach to understanding *xinren* is a timely contribution to the growing importance of doing business in Chinese markets and has important implications for both theory and practice.

After this, Cunningham and Rowley, in their study of small and medium-sized enterprises (SMEs) in China, discuss the importance of HRM. As the importance of SMEs there has increased, they see it as critical to review research on HRM in such firms, in order to identify the 'gaps' or areas that may exist in current coverage. Therefore, the aim of the current study is to provide an *overall* examination of the research on HRM in SMEs in China. The authors begin with a discussion of the literature addressing HRM in this category of firms by looking at the nature of HRM in SMEs and the importance of *contextual* factors on its 'take-up' in enterprises. Then, research methods and data collection processes are presented; after this, the findings of the research are set out. Finally, the study draws together some conclusions and outlines possible future directions.

While the results of this review suggest that *informality* is the key feature of HRM in SMEs in China, the findings of the current study illustrate that *two* key factors contribute to the informality of the HRM approach in such firms in China. One relates to the specific characteristics of SMEs (that is, external uncertainty and the 'dictatorship' of the owner-manager), and the other is the market environment. In other words, this review confirms that HRM practices in SMEs in China are rather more informal than those formalized and systematic procedures prescribed in the concepts of Western HRM 'best practices'. The findings of this review also demonstrate that traditional Chinese culture limits the applicability of HRM in non-Western settings, while institutional factors create barriers to effective management practices.

Although China provides a *dynamic* environment for SMEs to grow and the evidence suggests a linkage between HRM and organizational performance, the current study implies that it is clear that contextual influences restrain the pace and depth of HRM changes in SMEs. Even though the progress of SME-related HRM studies is promising, this review suggests that the research on this in China is sparse and limited, as well as geographically biased and concentrated.

Next, Shen's contribution investigates levels of employees' satisfaction with HRM practices in Chinese privately owned enterprises (POEs) in manufacturing and differences in satisfaction between different employee groups. In China, he argues, HR is managed 'differently' according to the type of pragmatic and market-oriented firms, resulting in a significant growth in labour disputes. However, little is known about how employees in this sector perceive HRM policies and practices.

This study posits that the levels of employees of POEs satisfied with HRM ranged from low to high. Employees were relatively more satisfied with performance appraisal, particularly appraisal criteria and appraisal execution, than other HRM policies and practices. Employees were moderately satisfied with contract-based employment relations, the two-way selection process and performance-based rewards and compensation (see also Rowley and Wei [2009a, 2009b]), except for signing labour contracts and welfare and benefits. Employees were very dissatisfied with training provision and management development opportunities, and with the poor level of organizational support being offered for personal and management development.

This author concludes that during the past three decades the economic reforms have eroded Chinese employees' sense of having a truly 'socialist-egalitarian' ideology. Employees' satisfaction with the HRM reform varied significantly according to their own personal characteristics and experiences. The study points out that the 'inequality' in HRM practices is the key reason for variations in levels of satisfaction with HRM.

After this, in the next contribution, Cooke and He examine issues related to corporate social responsibility (CSR) which has been the subject of growing debate across an increasingly wide range of disciplines in social sciences and business and management studies. China's manufacturing-based economy, producing a large share of world trade, they note, has been facing mounting pressure to take CSR issues seriously, with particular reference to environmental protection and labour standards. However, issues related to CSR and HRM remain under-explored, and existing studies on the topic focus primarily on labour standards in value chains. While research interest on CSR has grown significantly in China in recent years, few empirical studies have been undertaken to identify how companies, particularly those in the private sector, perceive CSR issues, what actions they are taking, if any, and what implications these may have for institutional bodies that seek to promote CSR in the country. This study addresses this research gap by investigating the current situation of CSR, of which HRM is an integral part, in China. The study specifically focuses on the textile and apparel industry, which is highly export-oriented and cost-sensitive and where labour standards are often reported to be low.

Based on evidence from interviews with senior Chinese managers in a wide range of firms, the authors found that the Chinese are beginning to realize the importance of adopting CSR. This apparent *demarche* exists in spite of the fact that many of the enterprises do not have a written CSR policy and that the majority of enterprises have *not* obtained CSR standards. The main reasons for firms to implement CSR practices are to enhance their reputation, improve customer satisfaction and reduce operating costs. In other words, a business 'case study' approach is adopted. In addition, companies believe that *legal* and *economic* responsibilities are more important than ethical and voluntary responsibilities. This fact implies that legal compliance remains the main source of pressure for adopting CSR activities and that a firm's public statement of their commitment to CSR may be little more than lip-service. Firms are also more likely to respond to pressures from the government.

The findings of this study suggest that external bodies and value chains are not the main drivers for firms' CSR activities in China. The majority of companies have not yet developed a working relationship with other companies to share experience and information related to CSR. They have not received sufficient pressure in the value chain to engage in CSR activities. Nor have they become a source of pressure for other firms in the value chain to do the same.

Whilst many of Cooke and He's findings reflect those found in other studies outside China, suggesting some universal patterns in the adoption of CSR activities, their findings also reveal a number of unique characteristics and institutional weaknesses specific to the Chinese context. These include, for example, the role of the government and the types of incentives that may prove effective to motivate firms and their employees to engage in CSR activities. The limited power of non-government-led pressure groups is evident and a voluntary approach to CSR is unlikely to have much effect in the current business environment.

Further, Zhang, Nyland and Zhu, in the study that follows, note that HRM research has been dominated by a 'managerialist-determined HRM' perspective; this assumes that the pattern of HRM in a firm is determined by managers based on their chosen business strategies. However, a 'managerialist-determined HRM without institutional context' they find problematic – because empirical findings have demonstrated that HRM policy and practice are primarily based on local labour regulations. Advocates of a 'socially embedded HRM', by contrast, believe that HRM policy and practice are reflections of or responses to organizations' larger institutional environments and can be understood only in relation to the institutional contexts in which they are embedded. Drawing on a 'socially embedded HRM' perspective, the study hypothesizes that HRM in China would probably be *hukou*-based, dependent on residence registration, given the long-lasting rural–urban separation this may involve.

Based on a number of case studies, this research documents how the system examined here in contemporary China informs six major HRM functions. It shows how the system has generated a division between urbanites as core employees and rural migrants as peripheral workers. Rural workers tend to suffer from job and wage discrimination and have less access to training, welfare benefits, social insurance and promotion than urban-*hukou* holders. The hierarchical nature of this division reflects the fact that HRM policy and practice in China is a product of the larger institutional environment and lends support to the theoretical notion of 'socially embedded HRM'.

This study claims to be among the first to examine the influence of the *hukou* system on HRM in China. The research provides rich first-hand evidence, which facilitates a better understanding of HRM and management in the context. The findings here have important implications. First, the findings indicate a close linkage between HRM and the institutional context, and lend support both to the argument that the *hukou* system is still a powerful institution controlling Chinese society and to the 'socially embedded HRM' perspective. The study is designed to evoke discussion and to stimulate further HRM studies that embrace the perspective of 'socially embedded HRM'. The research suggests that Chinese HRM studies should pay more attention to the institutional environment. Second, the work has implications for workforce diversity management. It shows that managing rural migrants has become a challenging issue in contemporary China as rural workers become the main body of the Chinese workforce. Third, the research also has implications for the ongoing debate regarding the dual pressures of localization and standardization faced by subsidiaries of MNCs. The findings show that the forces of local isomorphism tend to be more powerful than the forces of standardization, and consequently MNC subsidiaries tend to share similar behavioural characteristics with local firms in response to institutional environments.

Next, Guo, Duff and Hair in their contribution investigate markets for corporate banking in China. Such services are now facing intensified competition in a new deregulated environment. A review of the extant literature identified that empirical studies in financial services marketing generally focus on the conceptualization of relationship banking and its associated costs and benefits; however, little is known of what motivates corporate customers to continue their relationships with their banking service providers. Particularly, few researchers offer empirical data in the Chinese banking sector. The dearth of research is unexpected here, given the rapid economic development of China. More importantly, the opening of the Chinese banking market in accordance with the WTO requirements provides both Chinese domestic and foreign banks with huge challenges and opportunities. Therefore, investigating bank–corporate relations in the Chinese banking sector is significant to practitioner audiences, allowing both Chinese domestic and foreign banks to incorporate relationship banking issues into their strategic planning.

This study attempts to draw on the exchange relationships literature to create a model of what motivates corporate customers to continue their relationships with their primary banking services providers. By reference to the exchange relationships literature in the West, the research proposes a conceptual model by hypothesizing positive or negative relationships between the constructs relating to commitment. The model was tested using a research instrument specifically designed for the purpose, and data collected from a wide sample of financial managers in China.

The results show that sufficient evidence exists to support the hypothesized positive relationships between the antecedents of commitment and the two types of commitment (that is, affective commitment and calculative commitment). Notably, service quality is found to be a significant antecedent of affective commitment, which in turn leads to cooperation and continuance intentions. The final model is found to be more parsimonious than the hypothesized conceptual model.

A number of policy implications are made for bank management and treasury practitioners. For example, the creation of trust in the relationship should be a focus for both bankers and financial managers. Banks' managements should carefully target the market and gain access to those customers who genuinely wish to engage in relationships with their bankers. Banks will benefit economically from focusing their efforts on improving service quality, for example, regularly visiting corporate customers, providing adequate training for bank staff, and recruiting staff with social skills that assist the development of long-standing customer relationships. Banks' managements should also try to avoid those relationships where corporate customers only demonstrate calculative commitment, as the results identify calculative commitment is positively associated with opportunistic behaviour and negatively associated with cooperation, reducing expectations of relationship continuation. Without a genuine attempt to develop affective commitment, banks' efforts to develop their relationships with corporate customers will be ineffective.

After this, Nolan looks at the influence of Western banks on corporate governance in China. In 2006, the Chinese financial sector was opened to Western banks. As well as meeting certain WTO obligations, the move was partly based on a belief by the Chinese authorities that Western banks could enhance the corporate governance of local institutions, both directly (through JVs and acquiring shareholdings in Chinese banks) and indirectly (through creating competitive pressures by setting up their own branch networks). However, the distinctive institutional and organizational environments of Western and Chinese banks means that cooperation and technical assistance in this area is likely to be formed by *path-dependent* processes. The aim of this study is to investigate the institutional forces which affect the adoption of Western corporate governance mechanisms in Chinese banks.

The theoretical framework draws on 'institutional theory' which categorizes institutions according to their regulatory, normative and cognitive characteristics. The regulatory level is the most formal and includes legal rules and other forms of codified sanctions. Normative institutions are somewhat less formal and can be identified as the authority systems or principles that guide behavioural goals and legitimate ways to achieve them. Cultural-cognitive institutions are the most informal and represent taken-for-granted assumptions about reality and the way in which it is perceived.

The data are drawn from in-depth qualitative interviews with senior managers across China, who were either employed in Western banks with stockholdings in Chinese institutions, held non-executive directorships of Chinese banks, or had participated in other financial advisory roles. The data are analysed using a 'grounded theory' approach where the emphasis is placed on concept and thematic development and an examination of the conditions and consequences which influence perceptions.

The results show that while there has been relatively rapid change in the formal legislative environment in which banks operated, the informal normative and cultural-cognitive realms are changing at a much slower pace. Components of Western models of corporate governance such as the board of directors, diversified ownership structures, and technical assistance in areas such as credit rating and risk management have been widely adopted. However, the over-riding perception was that the motivation for these changes was legitimacy-seeking by Chinese banks in the global financial environment. Enduring cognitive and normative institutions including a 'who you know' credit culture and the importance of informal institutions, such as *guanxi*, mean that the influence of foreign banks on corporate governance reforms in China is perceived by informants as usually ineffective. Given the serious failures of Western credit-rating systems in the sub-prime crisis, it is likely that this perception will increase in the future.

Further, Zhu, Webber and Benson's study focuses on three questions about the role of management within a transitional economy like the PRC. First, does the degree of intangible aspects of management, such as organizational culture, management structures and management systems, affect enterprise output and productivity? Second, do the various elements making up intangible management directly affect enterprise success, or do they work indirectly through other critical factors such as employee satisfaction? Third, what is the relative role of intangible management and other contextual conditions (such as market competition, ownership form, age of the enterprise and location) in determining the success of enterprises? The central theme is to examine the inter-relationships between these three important factors that may determine enterprise success: management actions; employees' responses; and contextual conditions.

The study is organized as follows. First, it reviews the theoretical underpinnings of the Western management literature on the role of intangible elements and related empirical research on the adoption of 'modern management systems' in China. The research framework and hypotheses are defined in this section. The next section identifies the research methods, sample selection and analytical procedures. This is followed by a results section that links intangible management practices, various dimensions of employee satisfaction and a range of structural contextual variables with enterprise performance. Based on the results of the data analysis, the penultimate section interprets the findings in terms of the central hypotheses of this research. The theoretical and practical implications of the results are considered in the conclusion.

To sum up, the research leads to the following findings. The forms of management in China have changed substantially since the beginning of the economic restructuring period and most of the innovative management practices, the forms of organizational culture, management structures and systems that are common in advanced economies are now present, at least to a fair degree, in Chinese enterprises. The research also confirms that the success of Chinese enterprises owes much to similar kinds of intangible management variables, employee satisfaction and contextual variables that appear to drive the success of Western enterprises. In fact, the impact of changing intangible management elements on employees' satisfaction is significant. In addition, the effect of the internal-oriented clan culture is more profound than that of the external-oriented market culture. Furthermore, employees' satisfaction is more associated with autonomy and individual rights than benefits, though both components are important. The effects of changing managerial intangible elements and employee satisfaction on overall organizational survival/performance were also significant. Managerial intangible elements including certain aspects of management culture, such as references to cooperation and unity, and open and decentralized management structures, were found to have a significant effect on sales. In addition, employees' satisfaction as measured by their level of responsibility was found to have a positive effect on sales in enterprises.

Thus, the study has significant practical and theoretical implications. In practice, the results provide an improved understanding about which intangible elements have significant impact on employee satisfaction and how both intangible management and employee satisfaction work together to influence the success of organizations. These findings, the authors believe, also contribute significantly to the literature. The major contribution of this study, they feel, is to offer an evaluation of the role of *intangible* elements in enterprise performance in the context of the emerging economy of China.

Next, Jiang and Kattuman look at market competition in the PRC, which they argue tends to equalize returns across economic activities. Abnormally high rates of return, they say, are competed away by entry and the threat of entry. Firms making lower than normal profits are subject to the disciplining force of the market, which catalyzes restructuring (if not exit). Firms, they argue, are driven to various measures, such as reducing slack and costs and re-organizing more efficiently.

Although there is a large literature covering both developed and developing countries on profitability dynamics, there has been, notably, no empirical study of the intensity of competition in China, despite its significance as an important, large, emerging market with a limited market history. This investigation seeks to redress this gap, exploring China's competitive process with a research question focused on the degree of mean reversion in profitability among Chinese listed companies. They see it as useful to understand the extent to which competition is a force in this important 'socialist-market' economy.

Developing and applying the 'Fama–MacBeth' approach, the study uses a simple partial adjustment model to examine the extent to which deviations from their expected values of profitability (individual conditional profitability) tend to be corrected among listed companies in China. China's entry into the WTO in 2001, the study concludes, opened out the Chinese market in a gradual way to global competition. That has not, the authors conclude, had a significant impact in terms of further intensifying competition faced by Chinese listed companies. In addition, they confirm that profitability mean reversion is pivotal to the predictability in earnings, notably reversion from negative deviations in profitability.

Last, an Epilogue by the editors concludes this collection of studies and comments on the contributions which have been presented by the authors involved in this symposium.

Concluding remarks

To sum up, the research studies summarized above, we believe, cover an illustrative range of topics *vis-à-vis* the 'new' Chinese management that is now emerging in the 'Harmonious Society'. The contributions presented, in turn, deal with banking, competition, corporate governance, employee satisfaction, financial expatriates, industrial and labour relations, HRM, organizational structure, SMEs, social responsibility, trust-relations, and so on. They ask in their respective ways in which future directions management may be evolving in this important linchpin of the international economy, given the *future* path of globalization in the long-run as well as the *current* instability of the financial system in the short-run (World Bank 2009). We believe, however, that whatever the challenges, a revitalized managerial synthesis will emerge in the next decade!

References

Bell, D., 2008. *China's new Confucianism*. Princeton, NJ: Princeton University Press.
Bergsten, C.F., *et al.*, 2008. *China's rise: challenges and opportunities*. Washington, DC: Peterson Institute of International Economics.

Chen, S.J., 2008. The adoption of HR strategies in a Confucian context. *In*: J.J. Lawler and G. Hundley, eds. *The global diffusion of human resource practices: institutional and cultural limits, advances in international management*. Amsterdam: Elsevier, 145–169.

Child, J., 1994. *Management in China during the era of reform*. Cambridge: Cambridge University Press.

Child, J. and Warner, M., 2003. Culture and management in China. *In*: M. Warner, ed. *Culture and management in Asia*. London and New York: Routledge, 24–47.

China Economic Review, 2009. The worst is yet to come [online]. China Economic Review. Available from: http://www.chinaeconomicreview.com/perspective/philip_bowring/2009-02/The_worst_is_yet_to_come.html [Accessed 23 November 2009].

CIA, 2009. *The world factbook* [online]. Available from: https://www.cia.gov/library/publications/the-world-factbook/ [Accessed 21 November 2009].

Economist, The, 2009a. A special report on China and America. *The Economist*, 24 October, pp. 1–16.

Economist, The, 2009b. China's state-owned enterprises: nationalization rides again. *The Economist*, 14 November, pp. 73–74.

Ferguson, N., 2009. *The ascent of money: the financial history of the world*. London: Penguin Books.

Garnaut, R., *et al.*, 2005. *China's ownership transformation*. Washington, DC: IFC.

Huang, Y., 2008. *Capitalism with Chinese characteristics: entrepreneurship and the state*. Cambridge: Cambridge University Press.

IMF, 2009. IMF backs continued Chinese stimulus, economic rebalancing [online]. International Monetary Fund, 17 November. Available from: http://www.imf.org/external/pubs/ft/survey/so/2009/NEW111709A.htm [Accessed 23 November 2009].

Rowley, C. and Cooke, F., eds, 2010. *The changing face of management China*. London: Routledge.

Rowley, C. and Wei, Q., 2009a. Pay for performance in China's non-public sector enterprises. *Asia Pacific journal of business administration*, 1 (2), 119–143.

Rowley, C. and Wei, Q., 2009b. Changing patterns of rewards in Asia. *Asia Pacific business review*, 15 (4), 489–506.

Rowley, C. and Wei, Q., 2009c. China. *In*: C. Wankel, ed. *Encyclopaedia of business in today's world*. London and Thousand Oaks, CA: Sage, 320–325.

Scissors, D., 2009. Deng undone: the costs of halting market reform in China. *Foreign affairs*, 88, 3.

Warner, M., 2009. "Making sense" of Chinese human resource management: setting the scene. *International journal of human resource management*, 20, 1–25.

Warner, M., 2010a. Labour markets in China: coming to terms with globalization. *In*: J. Benson and Y. Zhu, eds. *The dynamics of Asian labour markets: balancing control and flexibility*. London and New York: Routledge.

Warner, M., ed., 2010b. *'Making sense' of HRM in China: economy, enterprises and workers*. London and New York: Routledge.

World Bank, 2009. Crisis talk: emerging markets and the financial crisis [online]. World Bank, 24 September. Available from: http://crisistalk.worldbank.org/2009/09/chinas-crisis-response-goes-global.html [Accessed 22 November 2009].

Zeng, D.Z., 2005. China's employment challenges and strategies after the WTO accession [online]. Working paper, World Bank. Available from: http://papers.ssrn.com/sol3/papers.cfm?abstract_id=667861 [Accessed 10 April 2009].

Labour and management in the People's Republic of China: seeking the 'harmonious society'

Malcolm Warner[a] and Ying Zhu[b]

[a]Wolfson College, Judge Business School, University of Cambridge, UK; [b]Department of Management and Marketing, University of Melbourne, Australia

This study examines the challenges facing China's increasingly complex labour-management relations system vis-a-vis the new economic, political and social environment it faces and how it is adapting to the new concept of the 'harmonious society' – to which the new Chinese leadership now aspires. The contribution concludes that the changes in the labour-management relations system reflect the impact of globalization on enterprise diversity as well as the increasing important position of trade unions to coordinate labour relations and protect worker's rights and interests. There will be another 'Long-March' needed for both party/state and other civil groups in China to reach a new social equilibrium.

Introduction

In this study, we undertake an in-depth qualitative overview of the changing labour-management relations system in the People's Republic of China (PRC) vis-a-vis the new economic, political and social environment it faces and how it is adapting to the new concept of the 'Harmonious Society' – to which the new Chinese leadership aspires.

Economic reform has been an important factor in shaping the labour-management relations system. The Chinese economy has now been transformed dramatically since 1978. The State now runs much less of economic life than it did in the past. The share of state-owned enterprises (SOEs) in productive output has fallen from around 80% in 1978 to around 30% now, a veritable 'sea-change'. The so-called 'dinosaur' SOEs no longer dominate the economy, either by share of output or employment (see Nolan 1998, 2003, ADB 2006, World Bank 2008).

Given the impact of globalization and the membership of China in the World Trade Organisation (WTO) signed and sealed in late 2001 (see Wang 2006), it is not surprising that there appears to be a tension between the market forces now endemic and the institution that seeks to protect Chinese workers against these forces (WTO 2008, p. 1).

By taking on these commitments, the government, enterprises, management and trade unions now have to face a wide range of challenges from further opening up the economy with increasing pressures such as external competition and internal instability of a growing *imbalance of income-distribution* and conflict of different interests in Chinese society. The Gini coefficient which measures how unequal a nation is, has veered in the direction of greater inequality, up to around 0.47 from 0.25 in Mao's day (Shue and Wong 2007);

the higher the value of the coefficient, the more unequally household income is distributed. The PRC is probably becoming one of the most unequal societies in East Asia compared with other developed and developing economies in the region, such as Japan with 0.38, South Korea with 0.35, India with 0.37 and Vietnam with 0.37 (CIA 2008). This seems rather odd for a country officially characterizing itself 'socialist', we may note in passing.

Therefore, this contribution attempts to explore the historical, organizational and policy contradictions of the ongoing reform process in general and changing labour-management relations, in particular. The Chinese leadership has sought to promote a policy of seeking a 'harmonious society' in order to better accommodate these conflicts and potential instability in the society and we hope to explore the implications of this notion.

The authors hypothesise that this search for 'harmony', built on Chinese cultural values, blending Confucianism with Marxist-Leninism, represents what amounts to what we may conceptualize as a 'coping-mechanism' to deal with the existing and potential conflicts now facing Chinese society (see Warner 2010).

The impact of the above changes has caused a backlash in Chinese society amongst certain sections of the population, particularly the 'losers' are opposed to the 'winners' vis-a-vis the economic reforms. The Party leadership has become particularly sensitive to labour protest and the recent wave of strikes more than justifies these fears (see Chan 2001, Cheng 2004, Cai 2006, Chan 2010).

The 'harmonious society'

In 2006, the Central Committee of the Communist Party of China published a resolution on the 'Building of a Harmonious Socialist Society' (*jianshe hexie shehui*), building on Hu Jintao's 'harmonious society' vision announced the previous year. This demarche is said to be the driving ideology behind China's broad strategy, with the deadline for achievement set at 2020. The Plenum even enshrined this policy as the 'intrinsic nature of socialism with Chinese characteristics', giving it historical backing as a social aim pursued ever since the Chinese Communist Party was founded. This report, 'A resolution on the major issues concerning the building of a socialist harmonious society', as its full title, adopted at the Sixth Plenum of the Sixteenth CCP Central Committee, 11 October 2006, sets out as follows: 'Social harmony is the intrinsic nature of socialism with Chinese characteristics and an important guarantee of the country's prosperity, the nation's rejuvenation, and the people's happiness'. The building of a socialist harmonious society is an important strategic task, which was put forward partly under the guidance of Marxism-Leninism, Mao Zedong Thought, Deng Xiaoping Theory, and the important thinking on the 'Three Represents'. It continues further: 'No society can have no contradictions. Human society has been developing and progressing amid movements of all kinds of contradiction. The building of a socialist harmonious society is a sustained process during which social contradictions are resolved'. Such reasoning presents a series of ideological somersaults which attempt to reconcile the ongoing economic and social changes with past beliefs and values (see Quarterly Chronicle and Documentation 2007, p. 261ff).

Building such a 'harmonious society' covers a wide range of goals: Hu described the outcome broadly as achieving '*democracy*, the rule of law, equity, justice, sincerity, amity and vitality' (see Quarterly Chronicle and Documentation 2007, p. 261ff). This policy is understood to mean a renewed emphasis on *extra-economic* challenges such as tackling rural poverty, income inequality and environmental degradation. These three issues are clearly of considerable importance vis-a-vis the government's agenda of never ending economic expansion. A national policy of this kind appears to raise these anxieties to the same level of importance as economic growth, reflecting the priority the Party attaches to the threat posed to China's stability by such worries. The Chinese have traditionally feared disorder (*luan*) and this concern has by no means been absent in recent history; it surfaced once again in 1989 when student dissatisfaction fused with popular resentment against corruption and maladministration.

After dealing with ideological and institutional issues, the text moves on to propose the possibilities of ensuring social equality and improving the income distribution system, for example: 'We should strengthen regulation and control over enterprise wages, increase guidance in this regard and bring the guiding role of information about the wage guiding-line, labour-market price, and industrial labour cost into play in the wage level'. It goes on to specify how the Party can act out a greater role in the building of a socialist harmonious society. It continues: 'They should step up the improvement of the party's leadership over trade unions, the *Communist Youth League* (CYL), women's federations, and other mass organisations and support them in playing their role in maintaining close ties with the masses, serving and educating, and protecting their legitimate rights and interests' (see Quarterly Chronicle and Documentation 2007, p. 261ff). We can see from this quotation that the Party would like to see that the other mass organizations, including the trade unions, are seen as playing a key role in linking the top and bottom sections of Chinese society to re-create such a balance.

It is now necessary to have an overview of the evolution of the Chinese labour-management relations system and the development of the trade union movement in order to understand the current relationships among the key players, namely the Party/State, the firms and the trade unions in general, and the tensions and possible obstacle factors for maintaining harmony in society, in particular.

Labour-management relations

The Chinese labour-management relations system has, *grosso modo*, evolved through several guises in the twentieth century. However, since the Communists took power in China in 1949, it has been 'part and parcel' of the official power-structure, formerly more authoritarian and now less so, as market socialism has become *de rigueur*. Once 'unitarist', the system if not quite 'pluralist', now hinges on an evolving tripartite relationship involving the Party/state, the enterprises and the trade unions (see Ng and Warner 1998).

In the past, one of these key actors in the labour-management relations system, namely the All China Federation of Trade Unions (ACFTU) unambiguously conformed to the Leninist 'transmission belt' model, given the revolutionary provenance from which it emerged. From the 1950s onwards, the Chinese labour-management relations system had been anchored in the 'command economy', adopted after the takeover of power in 1949, with its Soviet-inspired state-owned enterprises (SOEs) and their distinctive 'iron rice bowl' (*tie fan wan*) cradle-to-grave employment system and, relatively egalitarian wage configuration (Child 1994). This enterprise-based employment system may be even seen as a paternalistic hangover from pre-communist times and Japanese Occupation (see Warner 1995). It was characterized by what were called the 'three old irons' (*jiu santi*), that is to say, the pillars of lifetime employment (the 'iron rice bowl', *tie fan wan*), centrally administered wages (the 'iron wage', *tie gongzi*), and ministry-based appointment and promotion of managerial staff (the 'iron chair', *tie jiaoyi*). It was a system which was to dominate Chinese economic life for many years, with all its ups-and-downs, until the death of Mao Zedong in the mid-1970s. It consolidated employment, provided job security and ensured the welfare of all those working within its confines (Taylor *et al.* 2003). However, only a minority of Chinese workers were to be sheltered in the urban 'state-owned enterprise' (SOE) sector where such a system was endemic. Many others were employed in 'collectively-owned enterprises' (COEs) and the majority of the rest worked the land. They did not occupy the privileged positions of those in the SOEs, the latter being regarded as the '*avant-garde* of the working class' and the 'masters of society', with a relatively high percentage in the larger enterprises being trade union members, at least on paper (see Ng and Warner 1998).

Such a system provided rock-solid security for those who were fortunate to be employed within it. One popular saying current at the time was 'the managers pretended to pay us and we pretended to work'. Once hired, workers kept their jobs for life; dismissals were infrequent. The industrial system was highly bureaucratic and hierarchical, formalized and standardized (see Child 1994). Top-down Party and managerial power was, however, mitigated by varying forms of worker representation at different times but it was always an uneasy balance. The 1960s even appeared to put 'worker-power' further to the fore in the throes of the 'Cultural Revolution', but the experimentation fizzled out. After this period of social turbulence, the Chinese trade unions tried to 'put their house in order' so to speak and revive their own original organizational role (Taylor *et al.* 2003).

After Mao Zedong died, Deng Xiaoping introduced a wave of economic reforms in the late 1970s, in line with the 'Four Modernisations' (*sige xiandaihua*) and the 'Open Door' (*kaifang*) policies that were set to transform a wide range of hide-bound institutions, and encourage them to be more efficient and learn from the West and Japan (see Child 1994). Even so, afraid of a Polish *Solidarity*-style reaction, Deng tried to sweeten the sometimes bitter pill of reform by encouraging worker councils, parallel to the unions, even as he was creating a 'nascent' labour market that heralded the demise of the 'iron rice bowl' (*tie fan wan*). However, in 1992, managers were finally allowed to manage, hire and fire and so on. This step clearly took years to 'come to pass', given the travails of the preceding decades (Zhu and Warner 2004a, 2004b, 2008).

Since Deng's economic reforms were introduced, the enterprise-based system of 'lifetime employment' and 'cradle-to-grave' mini-welfare state (*xiao shehui*) has been gradually cut back: in 1986, for example, the authorities experimented with the introduction of labour contracts for new workers (see Korzec 1992, Warner and Ng 1999, Zhu 2005). In 1992, another important step was the 'three personnel reforms' (*san gaige*), this inaugurated labour contracts, performance-linked rewards systems, and contributory social insurance (Warner 1995). *Pari passu*, access to healthcare eventually became less and less equitable. By this time, the labour-management relations system had already become a 'hybrid' one, mixing what remained of the old one with the newer features (see Warner 2008b). Once the system hinged on the notion of personnel management (*renshi guanli*) but this was superseded by a new demarche, to be known as '*renli ziyuan guanli*' quite literally meaning 'labour force resources management', having the same characters in Chinese as in Japanese, being used as a synonym for (what is in effect) human resource management (HRM). Labour-management relations are more often simply referred to as '*laodong guanli guanxi*', being part of the wider Employment Relations (*jioye or guyong guanxi*) System. Books began to appear in Chinese in the 1990s using this terminology (see Cooke 2005, Zhu 2005).

The Chinese Communist Party (CCP) continued to dominate the trade unions and the ACFTU, in turn, sought ways to survive in the changing socio-political climate of the 1980s and 1990s. The philosophy behind the new shift in orientation came to be known in the early 2000s as the 'harmonious society', which represents an attempt by the current

Chinese dual-leadership (that is Hu Jintao as President, as well as Wen Jibao, as Premier) to present an ideological formula which might help to rectify perceived inequities and tensions among the different interest groups. In fact, the role of trade unions in this new order has become very important in recent years and it is now necessary to review the evolution of the trade union movement in China up until the recent changes.

Trade unions

Since the Republican Revolution of 1911, which overthrew the Imperial regime which had previously ruled the country for millennia, China has tried to evolve its own political and social institutions appropriate to 'modernisation'. Trade unions were to be among these but did not formally appear until the First World War had run its course. The Party had already emerged in the turmoil of those turbulent years but did not formally set itself up until July 1921. The ACFTU was founded a little later, in May 1925 making it now an 'octogenarian', and was established as an organization to 'represent' the emergent Chinese 'working-class', concentrated at the time mainly in a few industrialized centres and the major sea-ports, like Canton (now Guangzhou) and Shanghai. Remember, China was not significantly industrialized until the late 1950s and had no significantly large industrial working class until the end of the decade. The union movement was soon suppressed by the Nationalist (*Kuomintang*) authorities and went underground in 1927, when the Communists and Nationalists were locked in open inter-factional conflict.

Organized labour was not to surface prominently again until after the Second World War, and in 1948 it assembled its Sixth National Congress. It then was institutionalized as the nation's sole trade union fulcrum after the 1949 'Liberation', with the Trade Union Law 1950, later updated at the Seventh National People's Congress in 1992, and amended at the Ninth National People's Congress in 2001. This legislation worked in parallel with several other key laws shaping both labour-management relations and trade union activities. In this context, the ACFTU has enjoyed a 'monopoly' of representation, as it brooks no rival, even in the new millennium, having been the official mainland labour movement for over half a century, as in Vietnam and North Korea but unlike Hong Kong SAR. There may be sporadic outbursts of independent trade union activity from time to time but these are soon suppressed. The PRC does not, for instance, comply with ILO Convention No.87 (Freedom of Association and Protection of the Right to Organise 1948), nor ILO Convention No.98 (Right to Organise and Collective Bargaining) as it has not ratified these Conventions. Even if the Trade Union Law (1950, 1992, rev. 2001) creates a right to form trade unions (Article 3), and to provide a defined degree of union security (see Articles 3, 11, 17, 18, 50–55), it does not allow independent unions to be organized. The 2001 revisions of the legislation confirm that all unions must be subordinated to the ACFTU (Article 2) according to the principle of 'democratic centralism'. According to this formula, it is laid down that 'trade union organizations at a lower level shall be under the leadership of trade unions organizations at a higher level'.

The ACFTU is the world's largest national trade union body in terms of its formal membership, by far, although some say much of its adherence is 'on paper' only. It has more members than the entire population of many European states. By the mid-1980s, the ACFTU membership exceeded 80 million workers, covering some 15 national industrial unions, over 22,000 local trade union organizations and more than 460,000 enterprise unions, employing around 300,000 full–time union officials. By 1990, there were over 89 million members, in 15 national industrial unions, 30 provincial or municipal union councils and more than 560,000 grassroots trade union organizations. By the end of the last century, the size of its

Table 1.   Trade unions in China (end of 2009).

General statistics	
Number of unions	15 national industrial unions in single federation
Number of union:	
Members (end of 2009)	230 million
Male	64%
Female	36%
Migrant workers	24%
Level of collective bargaining	Low to medium
Main union type	Party/state control
Main union structure	ACFTU – official union body
Extent of unity of peak organization	High to medium

Source: State Statistical Bureau 2009; ACFTU 2008; *People's Daily*, 25 December 2008.

membership stood at over 133 million, while the number of grassroots trade unions registered some 1.7 million. By its eightieth anniversary, at the end of 2004, the ACFTU was said to have around 137 million members, covering nearly 2 million enterprises. By the end of 2006 (see Table 1), it had even exceeded these numbers. The membership of the ACFTU now totals around 230 million (of which over 36% of the total number of union members are women, with migrant workers (*mingong*), accounting for 24% of the total), with a membership rate, on paper at least, of around three out of four in enterprises where workers are eligible to join, a figure of which we must be cautious. This figure was mostly found in large SOEs in past years but these are now less numerous, as the Chinese industrial ownership has become more diverse.

The Chinese trade unions organize on *industrial* lines, as well as recruiting on a *locality* basis. There are currently 31 federations of trade unions in all, based respectively on provinces, autonomous regions and municipalities, directly under the Central ACFTU Government and 10 national industrial unions, as set out in Table 2.

The organization of workers in the Chinese enterprise remains more bureaucratic than in the capitalist West. It was laid down by legislation, hence dependent neither on 'custom and practice' on the one hand, nor on 'collective bargaining' on the other. Article 10 of the Trade Union Law proposed that:

> A basic-level trade union committee shall be set up in an enterprise, an institution or a government department with a membership of twenty-five or more; where the membership is less than twenty-five, a basic-level trade union committee may be separately set up, or a basic-level trade union committee may be set up jointly by the members in two or more work units, or an organizer may be elected, to organize the members in various activities. Where female workers and staff members are relatively large in number, a trade union committee for female workers and staff members may be set up, which shall carry out its work under the leadership of the trade union at the corresponding level; where they are relatively small in number, there may be a member in charge of the female workers and staff members on a trade union committee. (Trade Union Law 1950, 1992, rev. 2001)

Of the total members, just under half were to be found in state-owned enterprises, accounting for 45% of the workforce; those in the private sector, making up 54%. Chinese official statistics are however often unreliable and it is hard to have impartial confirmation of the numbers and percentages cited above. These numbers appear problematic in that the state sector, where it was more likely to find ACFTU membership,

Table 2.   The organization of the ACFTU.

1. National Committee of the Chinese Educational, Scientific, Cultural, Medical and Sports Workers Union
2. National Committee of the Chinese Seamen and Construction Workers Union
3. National Committee of the Chinese Energy and Chemical Workers Union
4. National Committee of the Chinese Machinery, Metallurgical and Building Material Workers Union
5. National Committee of the Chinese Defense Industry, Postal and Telecommunications Workers Union
6. National Committee of the Chinese Financial, Commercial, Light Industry, Textile and Tobacco Workers Union
7. National Committee of the Chinese Agricultural, Forestry and Water Conservancy Workers Union
8. All-China Federation of Railway Workers Unions
9. National Committee of the Chinese Aviation Workers Union
10. National Committee of the Chinese Banking Workers Union

Source: ACFTU 2008.

had shrunk proportionately along with dominance of the SOEs over the last two decades and because the unions had experienced great difficulties in expanding their base in the non-state sector, which had mushroomed in recent years. Under the new Party/State leadership, the shift towards encouraging union establishment at traditional non-union enterprises, such as foreign-owned and domestic private-owned enterprises, was evident with the example of union branches formed at all Wal-Mart stores in China. Multiple reports indicated that such changes resulted from direct intervention of Party leader Hu, as he ordered: 'Do a better job of building Party organizations and trade unions in foreign-invested enterprises' (see China Labour Bulletin 2006). This support from top leadership created a new and opportune moment for union establishment in foreign-owned enterprises.

In order to implement the Party's call to 'establishing harmonious society', the leadership of the trade unions have developed some initiatives. At the Fifth Session of the 14th ACFTU Executive Committee that was held in Beijing on 12–14 December 2007, the ACFTU Chairman Wang Zhaoguo emphasised that 'the broad masses of workers and union cadres should make greater contributions to scientific development and social harmony'. He called on trade unions at all levels to earnestly perform their duty of protecting workers' legal rights and interests, heighten the sense of workers as masters of the country, upgrade the ideological and ethical standards as well as the scientific and cultural qualities of the entire workforce and encourage them to play a major role in the socialist economic, political, cultural and social construction. He also called on trade unions to carry out the principle of 'organize the unorganized and fight for labour rights' in real earnest, focus their attention on adjusting labour relations, and try all out to solve issues of immediate interest to workers such as employment, income distribution, social welfare and work safety' (ACFTU 2007, p. 1). Whilst the rhetoric is somewhat vague, we can however see the direction of policy intent.

Yet labour-management relations in China are fast changing (Ding *et al.* 2001, 2002, 2004, Warner 2005, 2008a, 2008b). The older ways of people-management are now being replaced with newer ones. Notions of human capital and human resources are now increasingly *de rigueur*. The more 'human resource management' replaces 'personnel management' in China, the more that the old ethos of the planned economy goes out of the window. HRM is now more typical of the non-state sector and the trade unions have found it less compatible with their rationale. However, it might be argued that this new mode of people-management may be more frequently found in what have been called 'learning organizations', such as those more 'open' Sino-foreign enterprises or multinational corporations (MNCs). In such firms, we are likely to find new management practices that have been initially transplanted, for example by the overseas partner, when the joint ventures (JVs) were initially founded. Also in a number of former SOEs, HRM soon appeared in a number of guises, both token and substantial. Leading companies the present writers encountered over the years, like the steel-giant Shougang Group (*Shougang Jituan*) (see Nolan 1998 for its history) had already formally introduced HRM departments by the mid-1990s.

Yet, even in such cases, the kind of HRM to be found was often concerned with short-term issues like wages, welfare and promotion rather than long-term strategic ones. A knowledgeable scholar in the field, for example, bemoans the lack of research that systematically explores in detail topics such as appraisal, compensation, planning and staffing (Zhu 2005, p. 34). Broadly speaking, it is now fairly well-established that it is mainly in larger business enterprises, whether they are former SOEs, joint ventures (JVs) or wholly owned foreign enterprises (WOFEs), that we find the most definitive forms of *strategic* HRM in Chinese enterprises, as is also the case in Vietnam. There is, however, less research on this *corporate* or *strategic level* of HRM than one would expect but this may be changing (see Gadiesh *et al.* 2007). A good deal of investigation in the field is still nonetheless concerned with HR practices relating to *workplace-level* areas, such as life stress, organizational commitment, supervisor-employee bonds, psychological contracts and the like (see Zhu 2005).

Pari passu with the above there was a State Council initiative to introduce 'corporate culture' (*qiye wenhua*) in large Chinese state-managed corporations. In a recent study, Hawes (2008) has shown how these were urged to take on board such foreign concepts in order to improve their performance and to keep the firms in line with government policy priorities. Such developments (Hawes 2008, p. 39) are said to directly link into the drive for a more 'harmonious society'.

In fact, the State often feels the need to compromise with enterprises, mainly due to its desire to minimize discontent and promote economic growth. It has succeeded in that, so far, economic development in China has encouraged its managers and workers to support the regime since it offered a better standard of living and has so far delivered. Due to this pragmatic approach, when the government recognizes that a policy is not working well, it tries to act quickly to adjust the policy to minimize enterprises', as well as workers' grievances coming to a head but does not always succeed. When firms have needed more flexibility in recruiting and training workers, the government has boosted reforms in these areas to give the enterprises more freedom. Sometimes what is conceded to firms does not always benefit employees. From the enterprises' point of view, firms are more likely to comply with government policy and even compromise their economic interests − if and when the cultural or ideological values embodied in the policy matches their own beliefs.

In more recent years, the government's emphasis on reducing workplace conflict by addressing the importance of respecting workers' rights and improving working conditions has been as one of the approaches towards 'social harmony' under the current leadership. This new shift towards more 'pro-labour' policies may have an influence on how Chinese enterprises implement their human resources policies. The new Labour Contract Law might be seen as a good example of the government's efforts to create a reinvigorated 'social contract', by enhancing job security and so forth, of which more later.

Corporate citizenship

The Party leadership hope that the move to a more harmonious set of social relationships will meaningfully change not only labour-management relations but also China's business environment, and that CEOs and top managers who wish to prosper in contemporary China will now need to make sure where they stand on 'corporate citizenship'. The 'harmonious society' policy will eventually, they hope, influence businesses in China in the guise of 'corporate citizenship' concepts. The goals sought by Hu's clarion call potentially appear to link closely to the objective of corporate citizenship as understood in the West. A bolder emphasis on the impact of extra-economic concerns can be viewed as a parallel goal in corporate citizenship, where companies are urged to consider the wider impact of their economic activities on stakeholders, be they workers or customers (Hawes 2008).

However, the role of the business community in contributing to a 'harmonious society' has yet to be made more precise, limiting the influence of the changes so far. Building 'this society' is still viewed as the specific responsibility of the State and an official high-level policy explicitly linking corporations and 'harmonious society' is yet to be enunciated, nor has the role of the trade unions been robustly defined and spelt out in detail. The precise actions that social actors involved should take to contribute to this vision have yet to be agreed upon and made public by the government. Chinese managers have, for example, mentioned that the lack of measurement tools tracking their contributions, or clearer guidelines about their roles, result in bounded actions on their part. With the lack of clarity, many organizations, whether public or private, have taken to dubbing any and all corporate actions as contributing to a 'harmonious society'. Yet one spelt-out route to greater harmony has been in the labour legislation sphere to which we now turn.

New labour legislation

The most important changes in the labour management architecture in recent years potentially leading to the 'harmonious society', include the introduction of new legislation, such as the Labour Contract Law, which was passed in June 2007 and which became effective in January 2008 (see Brown 2010). This demarche provides a highly detailed regulatory framework in eight chapters and 98 sub-articles (Labour Contract Law 2007). The eight chapters of the law cover the issues of general provisions, establishment of labour contracts, implementation and amendment of labour contracts, termination and ending of labour contracts, special provisions (including collective contracts, labour hire and dispatch, and non full-time labour contracts), monitoring inspections, legal liability, and supplementary provisions (see Labour Contract Law 2007). Under the general provisions, the fundamental principles were stipulated, such as the proposal to improve the labour contract system, to specify the rights and obligations of the parties to labour contracts, to protect the lawful rights and interests of workers and *to build and develop harmonious and stable employment relationships* (Article 1, Labour Contract Law 2007). In many respects, the Labour Contract Law is a distinct improvement on the existing legal framework regulating employment relations. Security of employment is now reinforced, much to the consternation of employers in foreign-owned firms and their Chamber of Commerce spokespersons but to the relief of the unions. As the International Hong Kong Liaison Office (IHLO) for the worldwide trade union movement claimed:

> As many know, the ACFTU, while not playing a particularly strong role in defending worker rights to say the very least, has had a history of some success in terms of legislative influence (both the Labour Contract Law and the Trade Union Law show this clearly). It has had a strong input into the drafting of the new Labour Contract Law. While the final version

> certainly watered down many more pro-union aspects, it remains a potential tool for both ACFTU internal goals of strengthening its footing within companies and for the ACFTU to help campaign rights such as collective bargaining and the drafting of (good) collective contracts. (IHLO 2008, p. 1)

The new law is being hailed as a breakthrough in labour legislation in the PRC context but, it can certainly not be regarded as a panacea for all of China's labour ills (details of the final draft of the Labour Contract Law have been translated in full into English and is available on the IHLO website, http://www.ihlo.org/LRC/W/290607.html).

In fact, the process of establishing this new Labour Contract Law demonstrates how to move towards civil society and citizenship, with different voices representing different interests. It may be also seen as a good example of how to use legislation to manage conflict in order to create the so-called 'harmonious society'. In March 2006, for example, the Standing Committee of China's National People's Congress published a draft of the Labour Contract Law on its website and asked for feedback. The level of public response was unprecedented (see Cooney *et al.* 2007, p. 789). Around 200,000 people are said to have sent in comments and contributions. Participants in the arguments over the first official draft of the Law were said to include individual workers, union leaders, NGOs, management of SOEs, officials from labour bureaux, academics in the labour law and industrial relations areas, owners of domestic private enterprises and representatives of MNCs, including the American Chamber of Commerce in Shanghai, amongst others. If it works as intended, the legislation will greatly enhance employee rights across a range of issues but approving laws is one thing, enforcement is quite another matter. Labour inspection in China very often leaves a great deal to be desired. As Wu and Yongniang (2008) point out:

> Compared with former Chinese President *Jiang Zemin*, who emphasised economic growth, efficiency and political participation by newly rising social classes, especially private entrepreneurs or capitalists, the new leadership of *Hu* and *Wen* since 2002, have been trying to improve the livelihoods and basic rights of Chinese farmers and workers. Amongst others, the new labour contract law is a key battlefield for China's new leadership as it is closely tied to the country's poor labour standards. Without the change of leadership in Beijing the new law would not have been passed within such a short period of time, with such a high rate of agreement and without demand for further compromises. (Wu and Yongniang 2008, p. 1)

The major argument from a business perspective was underlined by opposition to measures which would limit the capacity of corporations to structure their employment arrangements as they chose (Cooney *et al.* 2007). They targeted, for example, the provisions requiring union or employee representative consent to changes to general working conditions, articles requiring interpretations in favour of the employee in the event of ambiguity, clauses restricting dismissals and requiring substantive severance payments, and provisions converting fixed-term contract to permanent employment after the passage of certain time periods (Cooney *et al.* 2007). In opposition, workers and union organizations see these criticisms as simply designed to further business interests at the expense of workers. These debates had been ongoing, in particular at the recent National People's Congress with representatives of both employer and employee arguing for further amendment of this new Labour Contract Law. There have been reports of many firms packing up and leaving the PRC for cheaper south east Asian economies. Hard evidence of this on any significant scale has yet to be presented, however.

More recently, a new, less controversial Labour Arbitration Law has been passed into law and implemented in early 2008. The draft bill aims to strengthen the system of mediation and arbitration, so as to help fairly resolve labour disputes – without going to the courts and thus protect employees' legitimate rights and help promote social harmony.

A labour mediation committee may be set up in enterprises to tackle the labour disputes, so as to resolve disputes at grassroots level. The corporate labour mediation committee should consist of both employees and representatives of managerial levels (see *China Daily* 2007). However, numerous problems that remain in China's labour arbitration and court system confront workers seeking redress for violations of their rights. A recent report by China Labour Bulletin (2008) identifies major problems such as arbitration committees being ill-equipped to deal with the recent dramatic rise in the number of labour disputes; are influenced by powerful corporations and individuals in their decision making; and have become overly bureaucratic.

Discussion

Trade unions in emerging economies in East Asia, as elsewhere, carry the legacy of the past on their shoulders (see Zhu *et al.* 2007). The historical background of these trade unions has been closely linked with the history of the Communist Party in fighting against 'capitalist exploitation' in China, and 'Western domination' in Vietnam. The unions therefore, on paper at least, share the State's view vis-a-vis the role of a socialist government in protecting working class interests from 'capitalist exploitation' (see Warner 2008a). Even in the new business environment, union leaders' ideological beliefs still remain the same, so they do not see any need to replace the traditional union model and are happy to cooperate with the government, as is the case with the All-China Confederation of Trade Unions (ACFTU) or its Vietnamese counterpart, the General Confederation of Labour (GCL). In addition, management has found that the 'socialist' union-structure serves the businesses well in terms of maintaining harmony and minimizing conflict and bargaining at the workplace. It, in turn, makes the labour force easier to control. They, therefore, support this type of union structure and role.

Since the original Soviet stereotype has now been largely diluted, the main Leninist 'transmission-belt' unions that remain are to be found in residual 'hard-line' communist regimes such as in Cuba, North Korea and so on, compared with the few 'soft-line' 'transitional' economies such as China and Vietnam. Here, trade unions are on a 'longer leash', although not as much as in the Overseas Chinese community. By the term 'longer leash', we mean where unions that have been part of the reform process have been given enhanced, but still limited, 'devolved powers' and new roles that enable them to better adjust to the market forces now driving the economy. Trade union roles have changed during the transitional economic phase, some faster than others. Nonetheless, most worker representative institutions have undergone a process of renewal (see Warner 2008b).

The ACFTU has been no exception to this general proposition: 'With the socialist market economy surging ahead in China, trade unions have made every effort to protect workers' labour and economic rights and interests, democratic and political rights, spiritual and cultural needs as well as social rights and interests, participated in adjusting labour relations and regulating social contradictions in a bid to boost economic growth and ensure long-term social stability', as its official website has recently noted (ACFTU 2008). Yet, it is clear from the evidence available that Chinese trade unions have exercised a mainly 'reactive' rather than 'proactive' role vis-a-vis the economic reforms they have had to face.

The recent effort to manage existing and potential conflict and crisis through building a 'harmonious society' by the new Party/state leadership may be the first steps towards a 'civil society' model, through engaging in public debate on new regulations and legislations (as in the case of the establishment of a new Labour Contract Law). It is no longer taboo that either capitalist representatives or worker/union organisations feel restrained in raising their concerns on behalf of their classes' interests, but the right to strike or form independent unions is another matter. We can see, on the other hand, that at the recent National People's Congress, representatives were elected with multiple social and economic backgrounds, including Party members and non-Party members, capitalists, intellectuals and workers, even migrant workers' representatives. Certainly, after three decades of economic reform, the 'winners' have gained huge benefits from the fruits of economic development. In order to reconcile a so-called 'socialist' market economy with a vaguely Confucian 'harmony' in society, it is the time to think, they might argue, about how to do something for the 'losers' and to help the 'poor' to 'get rich' – by following the initial reform path designed by Deng in 1978 and continued by his successors. Only time will tell if the contradictions of contemporary Chinese society may be played out both constructively and peacefully.

Conclusion

China's 30 years of economic reforms have passed quickly; the PRC is no longer the same society it was in 1978. Whilst not a 'pluralist' society, there is more 'social space' than there was a few decades ago. Once a 'command economy', it is now a 'socialist market' one, even becoming a 'consumer society'.

China's rapid development however, has generated a more unequal society and the sources of potential conflict and crisis may be hard to dampen down (see Whyte 2010). Therefore, developing a 'harmonious society' to become a 'coping mechanism' as we initially hypothesised, has become a priority, in particular to enhance 'harmony' between different interest groups, between human and natural environments, between China and the international community and between current and future generations.

On the labour-management relations front, much has changed (see Brown 2010, 3–22), reflecting the impact of globalization on enterprise diversity, as a nascent labour market emerged and matured (see Taylor *et al.* 2003, Warner 2005, Warner 2010). As the ACFTU official website states:

> Chinese trade unions are committed to establish a new socialist labour-management relationship that is standardized, equitable, mutually beneficial and harmonious, urge enterprises of all types to establish and improve the labour contract system, equal consultation and collective contract system and various other democratic management and supervision systems with the workers' congress as their basic form. These systems are an important means through which trade unions coordinate labour relations and protect workers' rights and interests. (ACFTU 2008)

On this, we must, however, retain an open mind but at the same time a critical, even sceptical stance given the recent wave of strikes in Guangdong Province and the Shenzen Special Economic Zone. Clearly, it will be another 'Long March' for both Party/state and other civil groups in China to reach a new social equilibrium – one which will do justice to all parties involved.

References

ACFTU, *See* All-China Federation of Trade Unions.

ADB, *See* Asian Development Bank.

All-China Federation of Trade Unions, 2007. Fifth session of 14th ACFTU executive committee [online]. Available from: http://www.acftu.org.cn/template/10002/file.jsp?cid=47&aid=389 [Accessed 21 January 2008].

All-China Federation of Trade Unions, 2008. A brief introduction of the All-China federation of trade unions [online]. Available from: http://english.acftu.org/template/10002/file.jsp?cid=63& aid=156 [Accessed 26 March 2008].

Asian Development Bank, 2006. Privatization and reform [online]. *ADB review*, April-May. Available from: http://www.adb.org/Documents/Periodicals/ADB_Review/2006/vol38-1/ privatization-reform.asp [Accessed 22 June 2007].

Brown, R., 2010. *Understanding labor and employment law in China*. Cambridge: Cambridge University Press.

Cai, Y., 2006. *State and laid-off workers in reform China*. London and New York: Routledge.

Central Intelligence Agency, 2008. *World factbook* [online]. Available from: https://www.cia.-gov/library/ publications/the-world-factbook/ [Accessed 21 January 2008].

Chan, A., 2001. *China's workers under assault: the exploitation of labour in a globalizing economy*. Armonk, NY: M.E. Sharpe.

Chan, A., 2010. Labour unrest and the role of unions. *China Daily*, 18 June, p. 1.

Cheng, Y., 2004. The development of labour disputes and the regulation of industrial relations in China. *International journal of comparative labour law and industrial relations*, 20 (2), 277–295.

Child, J., 1994. *Management in China during the era of reform*. Cambridge: Cambridge University Press.

China Daily, 2007. China to enact law on labor disputes arbitration [online]. 27 August. Available from: http://www.chinadaily.com.cn/china/2007-08/27/content_6058495.htm [Accessed 2 February 2008].

China Labour Bulletin, 2006. *Wal-mart unionisation drive ordered by Hu Jintao in March – a total of 17 union branches now set up* [online]. Available from: http://iso.china-labour.org.hk/en [Accessed 15 August 2006].

China Labour Bulletin, 2008. *Labour arbitration law welcome but systemic change, investment needed up* [online]. Available from: http://iso.china-labour.org.hk/en/node/100244 [Accessed 1 May 2008].

CIA, *See* Central Intelligence Agency.

Cooke, F.L., 2005. *HRM, work and employment in China*. London and New York: Routledge.

Cooney, S., Biddulph, S., Li, K., and Zhu, Y., 2007. China's new labour contract law: responding to the growing complexity of labour relations in the PRC. *The University of New South Wales law journal*, 30 (3), 786–801.

Ding, D.Z., Ge, G., and Warner, M., 2004. Evolution of organizational governance and human resource management in China's township and village enterprises. *International journal of human resource management*, 15 (4/5), 836–852.

Ding, D.Z., Goodall, K., and Warner, M., 2002. The impact of economic reform on the role of trade unions in Chinese enterprises. *International journal of human resource management*, 13 (3), 431–449.

Ding, D.Z., Lan, G., and Warner, M., 2001. A new form of Chinese human resource management? Personnel and labour-management relations in Chinese TVEs. *Industrial relations journal*, 32, 328–343.

Gadiesh, O., Di Paola, P., Caruso, L., and Oi, C.L., 2007. Preparing for China's next great leap. *Strategy and leadership*, 35 (1), 43–46.

Hawes, C., 2008. Representing corporate culture in China: official and academic perspectives. *The China journal*, 59 (1), 31–62.

IHLO, *See* International Hong Kong Liaison Office.

International Hong Kong Liaison Office, 2008. Available from: http://www.ihlo.org/LRC/W/ 101207.html [Accessed 1 May 2008].

Korzec, M., 1992. *Labour and the failure of reform in China*. London and New York: Routledge.

Labour Contract Law, 2007. Beijing: State Publishing House.

Ng, S.H. and Warner, M., 1998. *China's trade unions and management*. Basingstoke: Macmillan and New York: St Martins Press.

Nolan, P., 1998. *Indigenous large firms in China's economic reform: the case of Shougang iron and steel corporation*. London: Contemporary China Institute.

Nolan, P., 2003. *China at the crossroads*. New ed. Oxford: Blackwell Publishers.

Quarterly Chronicle and Documentation, 2007. *China quarterly*, 189 (March), 232–285.

Schram, S., 1989. *The thought of Mao Tse-Tung*. Cambridge: Cambridge University Press.

Shue, V. and Wong, C., eds., 2007. *Paying for progress in China: public finance, human welfare and changing patterns of inequality*. London and New York, NY: Routledge.

State Statistical Bureau, 2007. *China labour statistics yearbook*. Beijing: State Statistical Bureau.

Taylor, B., Chang, K., and Li, Q., 2003. *Industrial relations in China*. Cheltenham: Edward Elgar.

Trade Union Law, 1950, 1992, rev. 2001. Beijing: ACFTU Publishing House.

Wang, Y., 2006. China in the WTO: a Chinese view [online]. *China business review online*. Available from: http://www.chinabusinessreview.com/public/0609/yong.html [Accessed 12 July 2007].

Warner, M., 1995. *The management of human resources in Chinese industry*. Basingstoke: Macmillan and New York: St Martin's Press.

Warner, M., 2008a. Trade unions in China: towards the harmonious society. *In*: J. Benson and Y. Zhu, eds. *Trade unions in Asia*. London and New York: Routledge.

Warner, M., ed., 2008b. *Human resource management 'with Chinese characteristics'*. London and New York: Routledge.

Warner, M., ed., 2010. *Making sense of Chinese HRM*. London and New York: Routledge.

Warner, M., Edwards, V., Polansky, G., Pucko, D., and Zhu, Y., 2005. *Management in transitional economies: from the Berlin wall to the great wall of China*. London and New York: Routledge-Curzon.

Warner, M. and Ng, S.H., 1999. Collective contracts in Chinese enterprises: a new brand of collective bargaining under 'market socialism'. *British journal of industrial relations*, 37 (2), 295–314.

Whyte, M.K., 2010. *Myth of the social volcano: perceptions of inequality and distributive injustice in contemporary China*. Stanford, CA: Stanford University Press.

World Bank, 2008. China and the World Bank [online]. Available from: http://web.worldbank.org/WBSITE/EXTERNAL/COUNTRIES/EASTASIAPACIFICEXT/CHINAEXTN/0,, menuPK: 318958 ~ pagePK:141132 ~ piPK:141121 ~ theSitePK:318950,00.html [Accessed 29 April 2008].

World Trade Organization website, 2008. Available from: http://www.wto.org/english/news_e/pres01_e/pr243_e.htm [Accessed 2 March].

WTO, *See* World Trade Organisation.

Wu, B. and Yongniang, Z., 2008. *A long march to improve labour standards in China: Chinese debates on the new labour contract law*. Briefing series – issue 39, April. Nottingham: Nottingham University China Policy Institute.

Zhu, C.J., 2005. *Human resource management in China: past, current and future HR practices in the industrial sector*. London and New York: RoutledgeCurzon.

Zhu, Y. and Warner, M., 2004a. HRM in East Asia. *In*: A.W. Harzing and J.V. Ruysseveldt, eds. *International human resource management*. 2nd ed. London: Sage, 195–220.

Zhu, Y. and Warner, M., 2004b. Changing patterns of human resource management in contemporary China. *Industrial relations journal*, 35 (4), 311–328.

Zhu, Y. and Warner, M., 2008. Organizational literature, Asian. *In*: S. Clegg and J. Bailey, eds. *International encyclopaedia of organization studies*. London and New York: Sage, 1108–1112.

Zhu, Y., Warner, M., and Rowley, C., 2007. Human resource management with Asian characteristics: a hybrid people management system in East Asia. *International journal of human resource management*, 18 (5), 44–67.

Business relationships in China: lessons about deep trust

Anton Kriz[a] and Byron Keating[b]

[a]Newcastle Business School, University of Newcastle, Australia; [b]The Australian National University, Canberra, Australia

Trust is acknowledged as a central tenet of business relationships. Yet for all the attention it receives, rarely has trust been investigated in the Chinese business setting. This study uses an emic approach to unearth some within-culture 'truths' about Chinese notions of trust in business exchange. The findings of this research suggest that deep trust (*xinren*), which is driven by reciprocal help and emotional bonding, is critical for doing business in China. A conceptual framework is provided to assist Western businesspersons to better understand the Chinese concept of trust as well as the interplay between its key antecedents.

Introduction

One day a man took his grandson to meet his childhood friend, Deng Xiaoping, former Paramount Leader of the PRC. The young child was in awe of Deng and hid himself behind his grandfather. Surprised by the behaviour of his usually friendly and talkative grandson, the man asked Deng if he could give the child an apple from a nearby fruit bowl. The child quickly took the apple from Deng's outstretched hand and immediately began to talk as if he had known Deng all his life. When the man was asked by Deng why his grandson had changed his behaviour so quickly, he simply replied that reputation seems to matter little to children. Deng agreed, suggesting that to build trust it is first necessary to offer some positive gesture. Deng and the grandfather then both chuckled as they remembered their first meeting in the playground at their old school in Xiexing. They then agreed that children probably realize more than most that courtesy demands reciprocity and that such actions open the door for a relationship to grow.

This Chinese fable illustrates a major challenge confronting many Western firms wishing to do business in China – how do they move from a simple, instrumental relationship to build a deep sense of trust? This situation is further complicated by concerns that Western definitions of trust may lack resonance in China (Kriz and Flint 2003), and observations that having a well-known and successful brand in the West does not always guarantee success in the East (Doctoroff 2005). In response, Western firms frequently engage Chinese locals, or business partners, to advise them on how best to navigate this unfamiliar terrain. While such partnerships may facilitate short-term outcomes and provide valuable introductions, as the above fable highlights with Deng and the grandfather, they are no substitute for developing a first-hand relationship that is based on deep trust.

The scholarly literature frequently eludes the importance of strong interpersonal relationships for success in Chinese business (Wong 1996, Buttery and Leung 1998, Wong *et al.* 1998, Herbig and Martin 1998, Wong and Tam 2000, Yau *et al.* 2000, Pearce and Robinson 2000, Fang 2001, Fang 2004). However, for many Western firms the rules that govern Chinese interpersonal relationships may seem complicated, often leading to perceptions of nepotism, deception and corruption (Pye 1992, Blackman 2000). But this lack of understanding is not a function of research effort, as research in the area of Chinese business relationships has steadily increased over the past decade (Wong 1996, Wong and Tam 2000, Fang 2004, Gu *et al.* 2008). We see that trust is emerging as a critical issue in need of more empirical research (Fukuyama 1995, Tong and Yong 1998, Child and Möllering 2003, Leung *et al.* 2005). However, recent studies that have considered the concept of trust in the Chinese business setting are far from conclusive, highlighting that there is still much to be learnt, particularly with regard to cross-cultural business relationships.

For instance, while Leung *et al.* (2005) attempt to examine the interplay between a range of business relationship constructs in China, including *guanxi*, defined in our study as connections and/or relationships, and personal trust (*xinyong*); some methodological issues cast a shadow over their findings. Despite providing a good rationale for the importance of interpersonal trust in strengthening business relations with Chinese firms, a closer inspection of the items used to measure trust appear to be unrelated to how they define the construct (i.e. focus on business trust rather than personal trust). Further, there are even basic questions regarding their use of the word *xinyong,* which most Chinese dictionaries define as credit-worthy. Though the authors reported a strong and statistically significant relationship between their measure of trust and *guanxi*, the problems with their measurement model limit the contribution and reinforce the need to better define trust in the Chinese context.

This point is also underscored by a recent study investigating differences in trust patterns between Chinese and American managers. Chua *et al.* (2009) highlight that the business networks of Chinese managers are more dominated by emotional, affect-based trust than the instrumental, cognitive-based trust that characterizes the business networks of American managers. While their study is valuable in that it is the first to empirically test key cultural differences, confirming that trust is a complex construct with at least two dimensions; we see two fundamental problems with their work. First, like the Leung *et al.* study, Chua *et al.* use established theoretical frameworks to conceptualize trust. This presumes that trust is essentially a universal construct with a common definition across cultures. In other words, what we already understand about trust in the West is believed to have a direct relationship with what we are yet to understand about trust in China. Second, both Chua *et al.* and Leung *et al.* opted for a deductive, positivist approach. While this approach has obvious merits when investigating constructs that are mature and well understood, we would argue that the issue of trust in Chinese business relationships does not fit this description, and that the topic would benefit from more inductive empirical research to better define the nature and boundaries of the construct.

Research questions

Our study seeks to add to the body of knowledge by investigating the Chinese concept of trust using an emic approach that emphasizes an indigenous, within-culture perspective.

To achieve this aim, we use a grounded theory approach (Corbin and Straus 1990, Liang and Whiteley 2003) to resolve four principal research questions:

(1) What is the Chinese emic definition of trust?
(2) What are the antecedents of trust in China?
(3) What is the difference between the Chinese view of trust and *guanxi*?
(4) Can we advance a conceptual framework to assist Western firms wanting to develop a deeper sense of trust in their Chinese business relationships?

Addressing these questions makes a valuable and timely contribution to the international business literature. Specifically, the findings of this study will assist non-Chinese to understand the role of trust within the broader context of Chinese business relationships. This is important because prior research has yet to fully appreciate the importance of trust; choosing, rather, to concentrate on related aspects of interpersonal relationships such as *guanxi* (Wong 1996) and stratagem (Fang 1999). Recent research suggests that trust is critical and may actually be the most important construct influencing the development of strong and enduring business relationships in China (Pearce and Robinson 2000, Leung *et al.* 2005).

A better understanding of how the key relationship constructs interact in the Chinese business setting also makes an important practical contribution, given the continued growth of the Chinese economy and the growing dependence of the West on China to provide economic stability at a time of uncertainty in international markets. While the growth of the Chinese economy may have slowed, it is still expected to exceed the OECD average over the next decade (International Monetary Fund 2009). Indeed, the IMF reports that many developed nations are pinning their hopes on China's continued prosperity. Accordingly, Western firms with a good understanding of Chinese business relationships, and of trust in particular, are expected to enjoy significant competitive advantage and be in a better position to exploit the continuing opportunities available (Fang 2006).

By investigating trust in China, this research will also stimulate a richer understanding of trust in non-Eastern contexts. To this end, Blois (1999) asserts that there is still no commonly accepted definition for trust [in the West], and that the construct is frequently confused conceptually with related constructs such as confidence and mutual dependence. Furthermore, the emphasis on instrumental, cognitive-based relationships in the West (Chua *et al.* 2009) also raises questions about whether such relationships *really* exhibit trust at all (Williamson 1993, Sako 1998, Blois 1999). While this is not to say that social bonding is not an important issue for Western firms (e.g. Morgan and Hunt 1994), we believe that an explication of the Chinese concept of trust may also provide some interesting insights for interpreting interpersonal relationships, and trust in particular, beyond China.

To achieve these collective aims, this study is organized as follows. The next section develops the theoretical background as it applies to our understanding of trust in the cross-cultural context, and China in particular. We then describe our methodology, which is based on a grounded theory and an exploratory emic approach. Finally, we discuss the results and the implications of this work to academics and practitioners.

Background theory

Trust in the international business setting has received significant attention over the years (Young and Wilkinson 1989, Moorman *et al.* 1993, Morgan and Hunt 1994, Cowles 1997, Blois 1999, Svensson 2001). Though Fukuyama (1995) asserts that trust is universally significant, and a critical component of relationships in international business markets, he did not endorse a common definition of trust across cultures. What does appear common to most definitions of trust, however, is a form of reliance on another party and exposure to some form of vulnerability (Blois 1999).

To this end, a general definition of business trust has been proposed by Sako (1998), who suggests that trust in business should be defined in terms of three main elements – contractual compliance, competence and goodwill. Germane to this conceptualization of trust is the recognition that firms require their trading partners to be competent and meet expectations; and as they do, goodwill and trust will increase. However, this is only one such definition. Curran *et al.* (1998) contend that there are many conceptualizations of trust, with the authors identifying no fewer than 33 possible dimensions of trust from a review of the literature. Likewise, a bibliometric analysis of 22 papers submitted to a recent special issue of the *European Journal of Marketing* on trust highlighted 336 unique trust-related citations (Arnott 2007). The most popular definition cited was that of Morgan and Hunt (1994), who define trust in terms of a partner's reliability, integrity and competence. In common with Sako, Morgan and Hunt assert that businesspeople desire business partners that they can trust because it reduces the risks associated with doing business.

Trust in the Chinese context

Trust has been translated in Chinese markets as '*xin*' (Luo 2000), '*xinren*' (Chua *et al.* 2009) and '*xinyong*' (Wong 1996, Wong *et al.* 1998, Leung *et al.* 2005). In the case of this research, we focus on *xinren* which is believed to characterize a deeper form of trust. While this variation in translation illustrates the need for clarification, it is notable that Leung *et al.* (2005) emphasize the difference between Chinese notions of trust in people and the Western notions of trust in systems. This point is further articulated by Chua *et al.*'s (2009) dissection of trust into an affective- and cognitive-based trust. However, as mentioned previously, these conceptualizations, and the distinctions inherent within them, have been drawn from secondary research. A major contribution of this study lies in testing these conceptualizations empirically.

Importantly, any such examination needs to recognize the contextual nature of trust in China, and that the construct is associated with many other Chinese characteristics. For instance, Fang (1999) highlights the interplay between trust and philosophy, politics, family obedience and corporate style as part of what he called the PRC condition (*guoqing*). Much of the research on *guanxi* also mentions trust; however, very few of these studies go on to explicitly examine the construct in any detail (e.g. Yeung and Tung 1996, Xin and Pearce 1996, Lovett *et al.* 1999, Tsui *et al.* 2000, Dunfee and Warren 2001, Fan 2002a).

Though studies specifically investigating trust in China are rare, there are a few notable contributions that deserve attention. In addition to the research of Leung *et al.* (2005) and Chua *et al.* (2009) that has been discussed previously, Lui (1998) provides a comprehensive review of trust in Chinese business at a conceptual level. In particular, he suggests that trust is critical to cooperation and acts to facilitate transactions. Child and Möllering (2003) also highlight the importance of developing strategies to build trust, and the significance of relationship context for Hong Kong firms doing business in China. However, unlike our research, all of this prior work has derived the meaning of key constructs from previous literature, rather than from empirical investigation. Several other articles and texts (Chan 1995, Wank 1996, Bian 1997, Buttery and Wong 1999) also allude to the importance of trust, but these studies only provide marginal benefit as they do not specifically explore the role of trust within Chinese business relations.

Another key issue for consideration relates to the interplay between trust and other relational constructs in the Chinese business setting. As already mentioned, there are two core aspects that consistently appear in the context of trust and Chinese business relationships – guanxi (Wong 1996, Buttery and Leung 1998, Buttery and Wong 1999) and stratagem (Cleary 1988, Fang 1999). Guanxi refers to personal connections, and is thought to have origins in Confucian hierarchical relationships (Wong et al. 1998). The principles of guanxi have been adapted over time and modified to include a wider social and business guanxi, and is often used in commercial exchange to describe connections that vary from instrumental transactions to relational bonds (Kipnis 1997). Stratagem (ji), on the other hand, is the antithesis of trust and is based on the use of military-like tactics to pursue an objective even if it is at the expense of a third party. Master Sun's writings on the Art of War have been identified as a key treatise of stratagem that has since been embedded into 36 key business strategies (Fang 2004).

The Confucian ideal of building trust based on guanxi may seem at odds with the military doctrine of stratagem, where victory requires tactics of deceit that can actually promote distrust. However, this apparent contradiction is key to why an understanding of trust in China is so elusive. This is referred to by Fang (1999, 2006) as the Chinese paradox, and is embedded in cultural values such as yin-yang, where two opposing views can combine synergistically to create a richer composite. In practice, this fundamental difference has been the source of much frustration for Western people attempting to do business in China (Blackman 2000).

Our research strives to provide Western businesspeople with a better understanding of the relationship-orientation of the Chinese. In contrast to the rule-based orientation of the West (Redding and Witt 2007), trust in China is not embedded in a legal, rule-based system that provides protection to, and imposes restrictions upon, the nature of commercial exchange. While Western firms often put their confidence in formal contracts to guide business decisions (Wank 1996), the Chinese have used trust like a 'social credit rating' (Tong and Yong 1998). That is, Chinese businesspeople will assess risk by seeking to understand the social connectedness of another party, wherein low risk perceptions are afforded to an individual that has established ties with known individuals that are perceived as credible. This has important implications for Western firms doing business in China, with suggestions that the oft-cited failure of Western firms in China may stem, in part, from an inability to appreciate and enhance their own social credit rating (Bjorkman and Kock 1995, Luo 2000).

Despite an increased focus on relational variables such as guanxi and stratagem in the literature on Chinese business relationships, it is acknowledged that there is still a lack of clear direction for how best to manage such variables in the development of trust within Chinese commercial settings (Chen 2001, Graham and Lam 2003). Further, we were not able to identify any prior research that has sought to inductively define trust using a grounded, emic approach. We take up this challenge in the present study.

Methodology

This study was informed by the Straus approach to grounded theory. Building on the original premises of grounded theory, as developed by Glaser and Strauss (1967), we used a systematic qualitative approach to generate theory from data rather than building hypotheses from secondary research. We started first with data collection using semi-structured interviews. From the interview data, we used open (or substantive) coding to extract the key issues from the text. Selective coding was then used to delimit the findings and aid in the identification of key concepts. These concepts were categorized using memos within the Nvivo qualitative research software package, from which concept trees and the eventual theory were developed (Patton 2001).

A grounded approach is considered appropriate for an emic cultural study of this nature. Our method seeks to investigate the nature of Chinese business relationships and has been recommended for the study of cultural issues in countries such as China (Redding 1990, Fang 1999). In undertaking their studies of foreign cultures, Malhotra *et al.* (1996, p. 14) noted that, in the initial stages of cross-cultural research, qualitative research can provide insights into the problem and help in developing an understanding of relevant research questions, identifying hypotheses and conceptualizing models. The use of an interpretive approach is also considered appropriate where only a few *a priori* ideas exist (Perry and Gummesson 2004) and where theory generation is complex and may not follow a prescribed linear process (Gioia and Pitre 1990).

The present research complies closely with Berry's (1980) first step of an exploratory emic research process, where interpretations of a culture are driven from within the respective culture and from the bottom-up. This method helps build a theory about trust from the Chinese perspective, rather than imposing a Western theoretical framework and viewing the research questions through a Western lens (Malhotra *et al.* 1996, Morris *et al.* 1999).

Our study also complies closely with a similar methodologically grounded piece of research on China (Liang and Whiteley 2003, p. 42) that used 'a non-standardized, non-directive, semi-structured and open-ended in-depth interview method, resembling an informal conversation' to investigate synergy between Western and Chinese business practices. To achieve this objective we used in-depth semi-structured interviews (Minichiello *et al.* 1995), with particular attention given to creating a non-threatening environment with a significant initial investment of time in the preliminaries of getting to know the respondent.

The sample frame was derived using a form of snowball sampling; which, according to Neuman (1994, p. 199), '. . . begins with one or two cases and spreads out on the basis of links'. While research in Chinese markets has grown in popularity in recent years, data collection in China is a notoriously difficult task (Stening and Zhang 2007). Yeung (1995, p. 317) called it the problem of 'getting in', and noted that opportunism and persistence were necessary if access were to be gained. The use of the snowballing process proved an effective way of gathering data, particularly for a non-Chinese outsider. However, a resulting challenge was to ensure that the referral and snowballing process gathered a cross-section of respondents, comprising a range of businesspeople and business styles in the various regions. In the case of this research, we used several initial factors (or *guanxi* bases) to identify a cross-section of potential informants. In particular, we considered the connectedness of potential respondents in terms of their family, friends and business colleagues (Tong and Yong 1998).

To keep the sample from being dominated by one person's *guanxi-wan* (or network) the research used nine access points. This reduced the possibility of bias, but also recognized that the presence of *guanxi* would help to identify respondents that would be more likely to participate. The nine original respondents (branches) were selected because they had an extensive *guanxi-wan* or network that was geographically different from other respondents (Yang 1994). Their networks provided further sub-branches in the target regions of China, and also provided sufficient data points to facilitate triangulation.

The final sample comprised of 32 respondents from Beijing, Hong Kong, Shanghai, Taipei and Xiamen. The inclusion of respondents from the special administration region of Hong Kong and the republic of Taiwan was intended to explore whether these regions had different perceptions of trust to mainland Chinese. This was considered important because a significant volume of the prior research exploring Chinese business relationships has been based in these regions (e.g. Yeung 1995, Buttery and Leung 1998, Leung *et al.* 2005). However, for the purpose of our research, we did not find any significant differences.

The respondents were given the choice of conducting the interviews in either English or Chinese, with the interview tape recorded for later reference. To ensure reliability and validity in the interpretations of the findings, two transcribers were used to review the tapes and cross-check the observations. In the case of the Chinese interviews, this process also included a verification of the accuracy of the translation.

Analysis of qualitative data

Pilot interviews

Because the research was conducted in a foreign environment, a 'pre-understanding' was important (Gummesson 1991). Similar to concerns that impact on traditional ethnographical methods, it is important that data collection is informed by 'an in-depth knowledge of its norms, practices and customs' (Neuman 1994, p. 393). This was certainly the case in the present study. Even though emic-based research relies on the observations of an outsider, the strong prior academic and industry experience of the research team in China and the findings of pilot research were used to ensure that relevant contextual issues were taken into consideration. Yet, Berry (1980) cautions that the emic approach always carries the risk of bias via an imposed etic. He adds that the best solution is to recognize the problem and to be open to counterintuitive data.

Detailed background discussions undertaken in Australia with expatriate Chinese businesspeople were used to understand the socio-cultural issues that might affect data collection. The pilot phase comprised 11 face-to-face semi-structured interviews in two regions of Australia. The findings of the pilot research suggested that use of cues and pictographs would be beneficial, and that aspects like *guanxi* needed to be eased into the discussion as this concept was not always viewed positively. In particular, several pilot interview respondents mentioned that Chinese business relationships also carried the risk of a darker side that had the potential to lead to unethical business practices (e.g. create a 'back door').

Overview of respondents

The final sample included a cross-section of Chinese businessmen and women at various levels of their organization (Hofstede 1997). All respondents had experience dealing with Western importers or exporters; were of Chinese ethnicity; were capable of explaining in detail the key elements involved; and had a willingness to provide sufficient details on the subject matter. Respondents represented a broad spectrum of Chinese firms including state-owned enterprises, joint ventures, foreign ventures, Chinese privately-owned ventures, and multinationals. The respondent profiles have been summarized in Table 1.

Of those interviewed, 36 advised that they held a graduate or postgraduate degree. Several had studied overseas. While extensive experience in dealing with Western firms was used as criterion for respondent selection, we did not capture data on the specific length or nature of this experience. The moderating impact of experience is something that

Table 1. Key characteristics of the respondents.

No	Gender	Interview length (hrs)	Interview location	Type of business	Origin of respondent(s)	Venue
1	Male	2.0	Brisbane	Engineering	Hong Kong	Office
2	Male	2.5	Brisbane	Trading	Beijing	Home
3	Male	3.0	Sydney	Trading	Xiamen	Office
4	Male	0.8	Sydney	Trading	Southern China	Office
5	Female	1.8	Sydney	Market research	Hubei	Office
6	Male	1.3	Sydney	Hotels	Southern China	Restaurant
7	Female	1.5	Sydney	Information	Fujian	Office
8	Female	1.8	Sydney	Insurance	North of Beijing	Café
9	Female	1.8	Sydney	Trading	Beijing	Office
10	Male	1.8	Brisbane	Trading	North of Beijing	Office
11	Female	3.0	Brisbane	Trading	Hong Kong	Home
12	Male	1.0	Hong Kong	Export advisor	Hong Kong	Office
13	Male	2.5	Hong Kong	IT	Hong Kong	Restaurant
14	Male	2.5	Hong Kong	Trading	Xiamen	Restaurant
15	Male	1.3	Hong Kong	Trading	Hong Kong	Office
16	Male	1.5	Taipei	Trading	Taipei	Office
17	Female	2.0	Taipei	Export advisor	Taipei	Office
18	Female	1.0	Taipei	Trading	Taipei	Office
19	Female	0.5	Taipei	Trading	Taipei	Office
20	Female	1.5	Taipei	PR	Taipei	Restaurant
21	Male	3.0	Taipei	Trading	Taipei/China	Café
22	Male	1.5	Taipei	Trading	Taipei	Office
23	Female	1.5	Taipei	Education	Taipei	Office
24	Both	2.5	Shanghai	Trading	Shanghai	Office
25	Male	1.3	Shanghai	Trade SOE	Shanghai	Office
26	Male	2.5	Shanghai	Trading	Shanghai	Restaurant
27	Female	2.0	Shanghai	Export advisor	Shanghai	Office
28	Female	1.0	Shanghai	Information	Shanghai	Office
29	Male	1.3	Shanghai	Export advisor	Shanghai	Office
30	Male	1.5	Shanghai	Trading	Shanghai	Office
31	Male	4.0	Beijing	Manuf SOE	Beijing	Café
32	Female	1.5	Beijing	Export advisor	Beijing	Office

Table 1 – *continued*

No	Gender	Interview length (hrs)	Interview location	Type of business	Origin of respondent(s)	Venue
33	Male	2.5	Beijing	Trading	Beijing	Café
34	Male	1.3	Beijing	Insurance	Beijing	Office
35	Male	1.5	Beijing	Information	Beijing	Café
36	Female	1.5	Beijing	R&D SOE	Beijing	Café
37	Male	1.0	Beijing	PR	Beijing	Office
38	Male	3.0	Xiamen	Education	Xiamen	Hotel room
39	Male	2.0	Xiamen	Trading	Xiamen	Café
40	Both	2.5	Xiamen	Trading	Xiamen	Hotel room
41	Male	3.0	Xiamen	Trading	Xiamen	Restaurant
42	Female	1.0	Hong Kong	Petrol MNC	Hong Kong	Office
43	Female	1.5	Hong Kong	Trading	Xiamen	Office

should be explored in future research. Interviews were undertaken in locations convenient to the respondents, including restaurants, coffee shops, business offices and occasionally the respondent's place of residence. Most had considerable fluency in English, which we acknowledge is very likely an artefact of education. In this regard, we recognize that while the level of education in our sample is not representative of the Chinese population, it is typical of the population of senior managers within Chinese state- and foreign-owned enterprises.

Toward a definition of trust

A discussion of relationships, in a generic sense, was used as an 'ice breaker' to gain confidence and empathy. When trust was introduced into the interview, an ideograph was used to confirm that the respondent and the interviewer were discussing an equivalent concept. Respondents then elaborated in sufficient depth on the nature of the ideograph known in pinyin as *xinren* and agreed that the characters represented what Westerners called trust. For example, respondent 21, on seeing the ideograph, reflected immediately on the constituent characters and stated, '... that's people, and that's words, that's trust'.

The term *xinren* is represented by the characters 信任, and this turned out to be the most agreed upon equivalent to what Chinese view as trust. As part of the emic study, Chinese respondents were asked to describe the ideograph representing *xinren*. Very often the response was 'people' and 'words'. The first part of the two characters for *xin* (信) and *ren* (任) pictorially shows a person: 亻. The general response was that you could believe in another's word. Results from this study suggest *xinyong*, which has also been used to describe trust, is more appropriately used as an ideograph representing trustworthiness: 信用.

When asked about the presence and depth of trust in Chinese business relationships, many respondents commented on the absence of deep trust (*xinren*). In particular, they suggested that it is difficult to develop a strong belief in business colleagues. This was because deep trust and strong emotional bonds were viewed as being limited to only the closest friends and family, and that such relationships require a degree of dependability that is usually absent from commercial relationships. The respondents identified that business is win–lose and mostly about money and profit.

Respondent 29 described *xinren* and building strong relationships: '... the first time they will forgive you, the second time they start to dislike, the third time they won't trust you. So it is important once you promise you must keep. If you say you will reply you must reply. Whatever the reason you must keep your word'.

For *xinren* to prosper, respondents generally believed mutuality is important. As one respondent suggests, he would be hurt if he made an emotional connection and it was not reciprocated. A number of respondents believed *xinren* contained honesty, and that this needs to be mutual. For instance, respondent 15 from Hong Kong suggested '... if I am saying that I have trust in somebody, I mean I have confidence that what he told me or what he is doing is reliable'. Notably, confidence (*xinxin*), belief (*xinnian*), and trust (*xinren*) share the same *xin* ideograph which emphasizes the need for sincerity.

Such observations coincide with respondent 8's more heartfelt view of *xinren*: '... when I look at these two characters there are warm feelings in my body ... it's not something in my mind, because I can't fit trust in my mind, because that's something in my heart'. Respondents also identified factors such as liking, sincerity, honesty and feeling as key drivers of *xinren*. Likewise, intuition, feelings and verbal dialogue emerged as ways of checking the credibility of trust. Respondent 26 from Shanghai, who was wary of the many swindlers coming to his firm, suggested, '... it's hard to express, you know, just to look at the person and feel how he is talking ... usually swindlers talk big, you know they say "wow" or whatever, and you become more and more suspicious'. Others suggested that one can learn a lot from looking at a person's eyes, while some suggested a common practice in China is to get a person drunk and then listen to their 'loose tongue'.

While the focus of interviews was on perceptions of trust, on 229 occasions respondents referred to another construct – help. Respondent 5 epitomized this: '... but as long as I know you are willing to ... you will offer me help. And I would do exactly the same and that's how you build up trust'. By help, the respondent was referring to both giving help (*bangzhu*) and receiving help (*huzhu*). The respondent also referred to *shuren* or a shallower form of relationship to *xinren*, indicating that reciprocation was a key differentiator between shallow and deep trust.

The interpretation of these themes provides the basis for a comprehensive definition of trust (*xinren*) in China. To this end, we define trust (*xinren*) as the heart-and-mind confidence and belief that the other person will perform, in a positive manner, what is expected of him or her, regardless of whether that expectation is stated or implied. The parts of this definition that refer to 'heart-and-mind' and to 'the other person' reinforce that, while business may desire to form relationships with other business, trust essentially occurs between people. Our definition underpins the importance in Chinese markets of inter-personal over inter-firm relationships, which has been increasingly understood through the significant volume of prior research into *guanxi* (e.g. Yeung and Tung 1996, Xin and Pearce 1996, Lovett *et al.* 1999, Tsui *et al.* 2000, Dunfee and Warren 2001, Fan 2002b). In Chinese markets, it became evident through the interviews that *guanxi* is good for opening doors, but it is *xinren* that determines the level of emotional commitment you receive once you are inside.

While we did not intend to gather the respondent's perceptions of trust in a Western setting, it was evident that level and depth of trust in Chinese business relationships was much more significant than that which they typically expected in their dealings with Western firms. A number of the respondents believed that trust goes deeper in Chinese business relationships and equates to deep emotional feelings.

Requirements for building deep trust

Respondent 41 discussed how business relationships are based on money, but friends or classmate relationships have strong feelings and emotion that run deep. Respondent 38 concurred, 'It's different, completely different. In some ways, business relationships are a money relationship, but friends or a classmate relationship has feelings'. A key aspect that emerged from the study in terms of emotional connections is the role of classmates, particularly in mainland China. After analysing the data, it became clear that the use of a web or network was an inappropriate metaphor for understanding *xinren* and *guanxi*. A better metaphor is that of a tree (*shu*) with roots, branches and stems. Using a *guanxishu* or *guanxi* tree metaphor, the classmate or *tongban-tongxue* contacts are considered a strong branch outside of familial roots. Personality and shared experiences seem to be a key, and few friends can achieve this deeper level of trust.

The respondents also questioned whether the trust that Westerners associate with Chinese firms qualifies as *xinren*. They described the absence of deep emotional bonds that characterize trust, and reaffirmed that they are limited to few people in their *guanxishu*, and that such notions of trust have limited applicability to a relationship between a person and an inanimate object (i.e. a firm). One of the respondents was emphatic that a firm is a legal entity – not a person – and referring to trust in such instances appears to trivialize the emotional depth of personal relationships. The Chinese, therefore, clearly see *xinren* as a function of social and emotional bonding. If the social relationship and bonding bring links to business, it is considered a bonus.

The respondents alluded to a Western misunderstanding relating to *guanxi*. As they suggested, *xinren* automatically implies you have *guanxi*, but *guanxi* is merely a connection and is not, therefore, deep trust. *Guanxi* is important because it allows for an extended branch (*shu*) of connectivity with a range of contacts, but it is *xinren* that guarantees that you will not be 'tricked'. Only a few thick branches can really be trusted. Concern with being tricked was something that appeared often. 'Tricky' was described using the characters for *guiji*, where *gui* refers to deceit and *ji* refers to stratagem and planning. Respondents knew immediately of the cues utilized to describe stratagem, suggesting that while it is sometimes taught, it is a critical part of their psyche and is encouraged from a young age through games such as *weiqi* (i.e. a Chinese board game based on stratagem). 'Tricky' business was consistently mentioned and was described by respondents as not being subject to discrimination, applying equally to the Chinese as well as Westerners.

The respondents noted that it is common for people to try to mimic trust to build ties, but that such ties only result in loose connections. Many respondents argued that if genuine trust is absent, it is impossible to do business. Yet other respondents suggested that they do not expect trust in business because business is a game – a kind of competition where cheating is acceptable. Interestingly, this viewpoint could explain why the Chinese were so bemused by the concept of win–win. Deciphering who is trustworthy is difficult and accounts for comments, such as those of respondent 12, who said that 'trust is a tricky thing. Everyone wants a slice of the profit, trust is a variable'. This variation comes back to the layering of connections that is an important concept of this research. Respondent 34 developed upon these aspects by discussing connections as opposed to deeper relationships ' ... sure you always have very close friends and so-so and very nominal friendships'. Notably, respondents also identified that it is possible for a third party to inherit a deeper level of relationship through a *xinren* referral.

Discussion

This study reveals that while lower forms of trust builds from initial connections and *guanxi*, deep trust does not occur until a threshold is achieved. Once this change occurs, the bond is very strong and is close to a deep relationship that is absolute. Prior research does not seem to appreciate that deep trust in China is not a dichotomy but, rather, requires a blend of both affective and cognitive aspects (Wong and Tam 2000, Leung and Wong 2001, Gu *et al.* 2008, Chua *et al.* 2009). This research tends to emphasize too much of the instrumental side and business art of *guanxi* without sufficient consideration to the value of *xinren*.

The respondents in our study were consistent in making a distinction between *guanxi* and *xinren*. It would be advantageous for future work on *guanxi* to clearly identify the nature and type of relationship they are referring to rather than leaving *guanxi* as a 'black box' shaped by expressive, mixed and instrumental ties. While some studies have sought to distinguish between the different types of *guanxi* (e.g. Fan 2002a, Su and Littlefield 2001), the vast majority have chosen to treat *guanxi* in a generic sense. Our findings highlight the importance of being clear when defining the type of *guanxi* being discussed, and in doing so, presents a more comprehensive understanding of the relationship between *xinren* and *guanxi*.

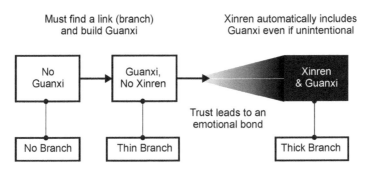

Figure 1.   Nexus between *guanxi* and *xinren*.

Figure 1 shows that to have trust (*xinren*) implies that you have a relationship (*guanxi*) whether the motives are intentional or unintentional; but *guanxi* does not have to include *xinren*. To have *xinren*, as the respondents highlighted, gives you more 'rights' with the person and will provide a stronger and more durable branch in your *guanxi* tree. Figure 1 illustrates through the shading that *guanxi* and *xinren* constitutes a thick branch or *cushuzhi*, whereas *guanxi* without the affective constitutes a thin branch, or *xishuzhi*, and remains open to stratagem. Therefore, to have *guanxi* alone means to have a thin branch in the *shu*. To this end, our findings concur with the work of Leung *et al.* (2005) who contend that what many refer to as trust is actually a lower form of reliance akin to systems-trust, rather than what we define here as deep trust.

In addressing the requirements for building deep trust in China, consideration was given to the factors that contribute to interpersonal relationships, as distinct from those factors that contribute to the willingness to form cooperative commercial relationships. Two key ingredients that build *xinren* emerged – honesty and sincerity. These ingredients can be interpreted as subjective assessments such as liking of words, tone, eyes, face and expression. These issues are central to the person-to-person feelings underpinning strong social bonds or emotional relationships. More objective assessments – such as rendering and reciprocating help and positive performance and actions – are also identified as contributing towards cooperation. The combination of honesty, sincerity and liking, together with positive cooperation, is believed to build *xinren*.

While our findings support the Western belief that trust is a function of liking (Nicholson *et al.* 2001) and confidence (Luhmann 1988), we identify other important terms representing the sincerity of belief (*xinnian*; *zhenxin* or *zhencheng*), being honest (*zhong*), and being loyal (*zhongxin*), that build deep trust or *xinren*. However, of particular significance was the emphasis by respondents on 'help'. Reciprocity is not a new concept in Chinese literature, but the emphasis on reciprocal help or *huzhu* is worth noting. Deep trust or *xinren* is not based on help alone, however, but also on affective feelings between the two parties. This finding is consistent with the work of Fan (2002a, 2002b), who highlights the importance of help in the formation of utility driven relationships.

Chinese literature refers to *renqing* (Chu 1995) and *li shang wang lai* (Fang 2001) in discussing favours, obligation, gift giving and the idea that courtesy demands reciprocity. This study reports that *xinren* also conforms to Triandis's (1995) view of in-groups, where in-groups do not demand equitable returns. This fits with the analysis in that help is no longer a game of 'tit-for-tat' when *xinren* is achieved but, rather, an obligation that must be met. The fable at the outset of this study identifies a token gesture from Deng in response to the grandfather's request. This highlights the difference between instrumental tokens and deeper long lasting relationships. Deng's old friend is representative of what respondents in our study referred to as 'old school ties'. These ties have a greater propensity for *xinren* because the friendships are not enamoured with the motives of business and financial exchange. Deng was a powerful figure and access to him had significant benefits. A referrer in this case (the grandfather) can gain the referee (grandson) significant access because of his own *xinren*. The quality of the tie is an important element here, as there are significant advantages afforded to those with deep trust as opposed to a shallow connection. This is the subtler lesson of the fable but it has profound importance for both Westerners and Chinese.

A model for deep trust

The findings of this study confirm the importance of trust (*xinren*) in Chinese business relationships, and emphasize that it is really an interpersonal construct that is built on emotional ties (Wank 1996, Kipnis 1997, Luo 2000). This builds on the assertion that trust is a function of liking (*yuan*) (Nicholson *et al.* 2001). However, the research has identified other elements important to the Chinese: sincerity (*zhenxin* or *zhencheng*) and honesty (*zhong*). The mainland Chinese believe they have a heightened ability to test *xinren* and insisted, without prompting, that 'You can't hide your eyes'. The subjective nature of *xinren* was encapsulated in the words of one respondent who suggested that it comes from the heart rather than from rational thought.

A conceptual model has been developed from the ensuing analysis and discussion (see Figure 2). The model has three key latent variables that consolidate the key themes identified in this study relating to *xinren*. The first variable, social bonds, focuses on the subjective nature of person-to-person relationships; the second variable, cooperation, looks at the more objective aspects of relationships within the business context; and the final variable, *xinren*, reflects trust with its associated characteristics of confidence and belief.

However, not all perceptions are emotional. Figure 2 provides an important tangible distinction influencing the Chinese understanding of *xinren*. The Chinese respondents reiterated the importance of the construct of 'help', referring to reciprocity (*renqing*) in terms of favours and the idea that courtesy demands reciprocity (Fang 2001). Reciprocity has also been acknowledged and incorporated in the BERT (bonding, empathy, reciprocity and trust) model of relationships (Yau *et al.* 2000). In this regard, while reciprocity is not a new concept, the emphasis on help (especially reciprocal help) seems to have escaped more detailed empirical scrutiny. Help with emotion has connotations that suggest more than simply a game of tit-for-tat.

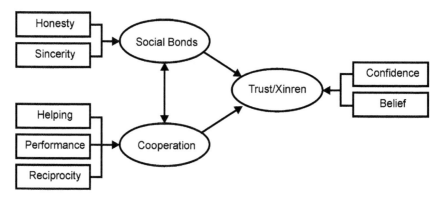

Figure 2. Conceptual model for trust in China.

Confidence (*xinxin*) and belief (*xinnian*) are also important in building *xinren*. The pictographs for confidence and belief reinforce the significance of the interpersonal heart and mind elements. While *xinren* can influence both social and business relationships, the notion of heart means that it is rarely achieved in business. This is because a deeper form of relationship carries the burden of reciprocation. Instead, the Chinese often choose to focus on more instrumental types of *guanxi* exchange where the aim is to obtain financial reward. For instance, one respondent indicated that, 'If I do business, I only believe I can trust money'. One way for the Chinese to extend *xinren* from the social into the business environment is to rely on classmates and close friends in addition to close family. Using the tree metaphor, the roots refer to family and thick branches refer to a person's *xinren*. As the branches and roots spread out the roots and branches become thinner; that is, relationships become simple connections. Twigs are easy to break and thin roots erode.

For Westerners, the challenge of developing *xinren* requires that they enact the process outlined in Figure 2. The reliance on legal structures and systems makes this difficult because Western business follows the rational and logical rather than the affective. Chua *et al.* (2009) are on the right track when they suggest that Chinese managers have a stronger reliance on affective trust than their American counterparts. However, their dissection of trust into two discrete components (i.e. cognitive and affective) may need redefining for the Chinese context. Chua *et al.* seem to overlook the interactive nature of these trust components, and by doing so can be criticized as focusing on a shallower form of relationship more akin to *shuren* than *xinren*.

Furthermore, *xinren* develops much more slowly than weaker relationship ties, and often precedes the formation of business relationships. This makes the task for foreigners who go to China purely for business purposes very difficult (Wank 1996). Fortunately, the basics of Western interpersonal relationships (in social settings) are probably not that far removed from what the Chinese, and this research, have described. The key for Westerners, as respondents suggested, is to build a *xinren* relationship through sincerity and a preparedness to acculturate. Affecting a friendly face for the sake of the exchange is not likely to be long-lasting because the Chinese are used to playing games like *weiqi* and perceive that they have a heightened ability to identify what Dunbar (1999) described as cheats and free-riders.

Implications for theory and practice

Few researchers have been successful in 'peeling the onion' in order to understand the intricacies of trust and associated affective values within the Chinese business context. This investigation of the Chinese perceptions of trust and its related themes provides an important contribution in this area. An empirically derived emic definition of *xinren* and its accompanying conceptual framework provides the foundation for future research in this area. For the Chinese, *xinren* remains a person-to-person construct and does not vary between social and business settings. Meanwhile, the notion of trust as affecting both the heart and mind seems to have diminished in importance over time in the Western business literature. It could be argued that the development of legal frameworks and transaction-based economics has ameliorated the businessperson's reliance on human socio-biological systems. This situation needs to change if Western firms are to be successful in China.

An important challenge for such Western firms is to enhance their social credit ratings and to identify who in China is trustworthy (*xinyong*). This is not simple and past mistakes have proven costly. Retribution through the courts has not provided an adequate solution in China, with many Chinese businesspeople hiding behind the complexity of the system and its limited and poorly enforced regulations (Tian 2007). Theory and practice will therefore benefit from a more detailed understanding of what constitutes trust for the Chinese business person. This research has identified that whoever is not within is an outsider, and this has similar implications for both Chinese and Westerners.

As this study has highlighted, *guanxi* is a connection. It can open doors, but a deep relationship built on *xinren* goes well beyond a connection. As some respondents emphasized, the Chinese often 'flatter' and give 'face', but this should not be perceived as *xinren*. Few Western firms have understood the importance of, or enjoyed the benefits of, *xinren*. Attaining *xinren* provides protection through a type of affective dissonance – where an individual can become respected as a 'Confucian Gentleman'. When a businessperson reaches the level of being 'within', the businessperson is not only protected but his or her positive gestures will be reciprocated ten-fold (Fang 1999).

However, while the identification of a Chinese-specific concept of trust is valuable, it does not guarantee that it would be easy to interpret this conceptualization in practice. For example, Ekman (1976) identified that Asian cultures exhibit different facial features to Western countries and that these features vary when 'off stage' (i.e. in informal friendly settings) as opposed to 'on stage' (i.e. formalized business settings). In such circumstances, trust is likely to be harder to detect, particularly if the person is not showing his or her full face (Herbig and Martin 1998). As such, Western firms will still need to use locals and develop connections in order to understand these other factors as they strive to achieve *xinren*. Alternatively, the process of acquiring and enhancing their social credit rating would obviously be improved by immersion in the Chinese environment, by building relationships, and by experiencing a form of cultural osmosis.

That said, this study has provided a substantial contribution to our understanding of *guanxi*, *xinren*, and the intricacies of doing business in China. It is important to further this understanding through more substantial empirical research. The conceptual model presented above provides an opportunity to further enhance the business and theoretical understanding of trust and its Chinese counterpart, *xinren*. These are not subtle differences for Western businesses to understand. *Xinren* and what it constitutes is a central tenet to success. This research, therefore, provides the Westerner with important native insights into an age-old construct: a construct that has for many generations determined Chinese business success or failure.

Limitations and future research

Like all studies, there are inherent limitations in our research design. The sample size (43) invariably limits generalizability. The interpretive method – however intrinsically well-suited it seems for the study's context – is still only one kind of data collection method. Using *guanxi* as a sampling tool is a useful methodological addition but it has potential bias. Bias also potentially pervades the study with many respondents schooled and exposed internationally to Western values. The study also includes an imposed etic (Berry 1980). An imposed etic is an acknowledgement that a person from another culture is doing the research. The richness of the data suggests that the techniques employed to manage the bias and ethnocentricity were effective. Notwithstanding, such limitations reinforce that this is an exploratory study and the findings need further testing.

This contribution focuses on an exploratory framework for understanding the Chinese perceptions of trust. The definition is a native interpretation of current perceptions and represents a snapshot of Chinese business people's perceptions of trust. Future research needs to test the conceptual framework for building trust and explore the boundaries of connections-relationships discussed in this study. The Chinese perceptions of trust need to be understood in this context. *Yin-yang* is not an either/or concept; it requires both components (Fang 2006). Achieving *xinren* is a leap of faith and it goes beyond a superficial friendship. It is deep and is built on strong emotions as well as on performance. The analysis and themes suggest a gestalt shift is necessary to achieve *xinren* and, therefore, it is only achieved by a few in the businessperson's tree (*shu*).

By linking trust to business, it may be that some of the traditional heart or affect has been eroded. It appears that Western marketing has deviated from psychologists' view that interpersonal trust is 'a generalised expectancy held by an individual or group that the word, promise, verbal or written statement of another individual or group can be trusted' (Rotter 1967, p. 651). Morgan and Hunt (1994) and Moorman *et al.* (1993), in adopting an 'exchange partner' (including firm) in their discussion of trust, might have inadvertently undervalued the interpersonal link. Accordingly, it is argued that trust, through such an adaptation, has become a loosely defined construct in Western business.

The proposed definition fills an important gap and offers Western business a detailed insight into what is reputedly the most important element of doing business in China. Researchers can now conduct empirical studies using a Chinese-derived definition based on a Chinese business person's emic values (Berry 1980). Ironically, this seems to be a feature that is lacking in our own Western business domain. Berry highlights that interpretations of culture need to be increasingly driven from within. Accordingly, it would also be appropriate to follow up this research with a similar emic appraisal of Western views of trust. This theory is in accordance with Berry's view that emic studies can be compared to other emic studies, but that universals should not be used to impose 'etics' on others. In addition, it would be interesting to understand whether the findings of this research are moderated by the experience of respondents. To this end, Chua *et al.* (2009) question whether the gradual adoption of Western management practices in China will change the way that personal ties are used in the business context.

Conclusion

This study has reviewed trust from a basal level. It has used rich, thick descriptions from Chinese markets to interpret the interpersonal nature of this important construct. Trust has been identified in Western and Chinese business literature as being a critical construct to be understood. The methodology has been adapted by the West to fit a difficult market, but a lack of success in China suggests retooling is appropriate. An emic qualitative approach is fit for the purpose when native business prescriptions are being sought. As described, the Western market needs to find its interpersonal edge, with affective notions prominent and performance built around help also critical. Firms (as separate entities) lack these interpersonal elements. Those chosen for such difficult markets need to be able to adapt and make a gestalt shift or they too will be the victims of stratagem. An indigenous definition and understanding of *xinren* is an important step in closing a gap in the literature. The next step for those involved in international business is to utilize the extant framework developed above to investigate this most important element of exchange. China is a global powerhouse, but it remains a country in a state of flux when it comes to institutional or systems trust. An in-depth understanding of social-cum-business constructs, like trust, appears pivotal to the future of Sino-Western interrelationships. Like the fable at the outset suggests, a little gesture can go a long way, and it may just be the start of a great and rewarding friendship.

References

Arnott, D., 2007. Research on trust: a bibliography and brief bibliometric analysis of the special issue submissions. *European journal of marketing*, 41 (9/10), 1203–1240.

Berry, J., 1980. Introduction to methodology. *In*: H. Triandis and J. Berry, eds. *Handbook of cross-cultural psychology: methodology – volume 2*. Boston, MA: Allyn and Bacon.

Bian, Y., 1997. Bringing strong ties back in: indirect ties, network bridges and job searches in China. *American sociological review*, 62 (3), 366–385.

Björkman, I. and Kock, S., 1995. Social relationships and business networks: the case of Western companies in China. *International business review*, 4 (4), 519–535.

Blackman, C., 2000. *China business: the rules of the game*. Crows Nest, NSW: Allen and Unwin.

Blois, K., 1999. Trust in business to business relationships: an evaluation of its status. *Journal of management studies*, 36 (2), 197–215.

Buttery, E. and Leung, T., 1998. The difference between Chinese and Western negotiations. *European journal of marketing*, 32 (3/4), 374–389.

Buttery, E. and Wong, Y., 1999. The development of a *guanxi* framework. *Marketing intelligence and planning*, 17 (3), 147–154.

Chan, H., 1995. Personal relations and relationship marketing in Chinese. *In*: *Proceedings of the seventh bi-annual world conference*, 6–10 July, Melbourne, Australia, 66–73.

Chen, M., 2001. *Inside Chinese business: a guide for managers worldwide*. Boston, MA: Harvard Business School Press.

Child, J. and Möllering, G., 2003. Contextual confidence and active trust development in the Chinese business environment. *Organizational science*, 14 (1), 69–80.

Chu, C., 1995. *The Asian mind game*. Sydney, Australia: Stealth Productions.

Chua, R., Morris, W., and Ingram, P., 2009. Guanxi vs networking: distinctive configurations of affect- and cognition-based trust in the networks of Chinese vs American managers. *Journal of international business studies*, 40 (3), 490–508.

Cleary, T., 1988. *Translation of Sun Tzu's The Art of War*. Boston, MA: Shambhala Publications.

Corbin, J. and Strauss, A., 1990. Grounded theory research: procedures, canons and evaluative criteria. *Qualitative sociology*, 13 (1), 3–21.

Cowles, D., 1997. The role of trust in customer relationships. *Asia–Australia marketing journal*, 4 (1), 31–41.

Curran, J., Rosen, D., and Surprenant, C., 1998. The development of trust: an alternative conceptualization. *In*: *Proceedings of the European Marketing Association Conference*, 20–23 May, Stockholm, Sweden, 111–130.

Doctoroff, T., 2005. *Billions: selling to the new Chinese consumer*. New York: Palgrave Macmillan.

Dunbar, R., 1999. Culture, honesty and the free rider problem. *In*: R. Dunbar, R. Knight and C. Power, eds. *The evolution of culture*. Piscataway, NJ: Rutgers University Press, 194–213.

Dunfee, T. and Warren, D., 2001. Is guanxi ethical? A normative analysis of doing business in China. *Journal of business ethics*, 32 (3), 191–204.

Ekman, P., 1976. Cross-cultural studies of facial expression. *In*: P. Ekman, ed. *Darwin and facial expression: a century of research in review*. New York: Academic Press.

Fan, Y., 2002a. Guanxi's consequences: personal gains at social cost. *Journal of business ethics*, 38 (4), 371–380.

Fan, Y., 2002b. Questioning guanxi: definition, classification and implications. *International business review*, 11 (5), 543–561.

Fang, T., 1999. *Chinese business negotiating style*. Thousand Oaks, CA: Sage.

Fang, T., 2001. Culture as a driving force for interfirm adaptation: a Chinese case. *Industrial marketing management*, 30 (1), 51–63.

Fang, T., 2004. The 'co-op-comp' Chinese negotiating strategy. *In*: J.B. Kidd and F.-J. Richter, eds. *Trust and antitrust in asian business alliances: historical roots and current practices*. New York: Palgrave MacMillan, 121–150.

Fang, T., 2006. From onion to ocean: paradox and change in national cultures. *International studies of management and organisation*, 35 (4), 71–90.

Fukuyama, F., 1995. *Trust: the social virtues and the creation of prosperity*. New York: Penguin Books.

Gioia, D. and Pitre, E., 1990. Multiparadigm perspective on theory building. *Academy of management review*, 15 (4), 584–602.

Glaser, G. and Straus, A., 1967. *The discovery of grounded theory: strategies for qualitative research*. New York: Aldine de Gruyter.

Graham, J. and Lam, M., 2003. The Chinese negotiation. *Harvard business review*, 81 (10), 82–91.

Gu, F., Hung, K., and Tse, D., 2008. When does guanxi matter? Issues of capitalization and its dark sides. *Journal of marketing*, 72 (July), 12–28.

Gummesson, E., 1991. *Qualitative methods in management research*. Newbury Park: Sage.

Herbig, P. and Martin, D., 1998. Negotiating with Chinese: A cultural perspective. *Cross cultural management*, 5 (3), 40–54.

Hofstede, G., 1997. *Culture and organisations: software of the mind*. London: McGraw-Hill.

International Monetary Fund, 2009. *World economic outlook: global economic slump challenges policies*. Washington, DC: International Monetary Fund.

Kipnis, A., 1997. *Producing guanxi: sentiment, self and subculture in a North China village*. London: Duke University Press.

Kriz, A. and Flint, J., 2003. Layers within layers within layers of Chinese business culture – a case for using etics, emics and emics within emics. *In*: R. Rugimbana and S. Nwankwo, eds. *Cross-cultural marketing*. London: International Thomson Business Press.

Leung, T. and Wong, Y., 2001. The ethics and positioning of *guanxi* in China. *Marketing intelligence and planning*, 19 (1), 55–64.

Leung, T., Lai, K., Chan, R., and Wong, Y., 2005. The roles of *xinyong* and *guanxi* in Chinese relationship marketing. *European journal of marketing*, 39 (5/6), 528–559.

Liang, S. and Whiteley, A., 2003. Australian business in China: searching for synergy. *Asia Pacific business review*, 9 (3), 41–60.

Lovett, S., Simmons, L., and Kali, R., 1999. Guanxi versus the market: ethics and efficiency. *Journal of international business studies*, 30 (2), 231–248.

Luhmann, N., 1988. Familiarity, confidence, trust: problems and alternatives. *In*: D. Gambetta, ed. *Trust: making and breaking cooperative relations*. New York: Basil Blackwell.

Lui, T., 1998. Trust and Chinese business behaviour. *Competition & change*, 3 (3), 335–357.

Luo, Y., 2000. *Guanxi and business*. Hackensack, NJ: World Scientific Publishing.

Luo, Y., 2002. Building trust in cross-cultural collaborations: toward a contingency perspective. *Journal of management*, 28 (5), 669–694.

Malhotra, N., Agarwal, J., and Peterson, M., 1996. Methodological issues in cross-cultural marketing research – a state of the art review. *International marketing review*, 13 (5), 7–43.

Minichiello, V., Aroni, R., Timewell, E., and Alexander, L., 1995. *In-depth interviewing: researching people*. Melbourne: Longman Cheshire.

Moorman, C., Deshpande, R., and Zaltman, G., 1993. Factors affecting trust in market research relationships. *Journal of marketing*, 57 (January), 81–101.

Morgan, R. and Hunt, S., 1994. The commitment–trust theory of relationship marketing. *Journal of marketing*, 58 (July), 20–38.

Morris, M., Leung, K., Ames, D., and Lickel, B., 1999. Views from inside and outside: integrating emic and etic insights about culture and justice judgement. *Academy of management review*, 24 (4), 781–796.

Neuman, W., 1994. *Social research methods*. Boston, MA: Allyn and Bacon.

Nicholson, C., Compeau, L., and Sethi, R., 2001. The role of interpersonal liking in building trust in long-term channel relationships. *Journal of the Academy of marketing science*, 29 (1), 3–15.

Patton, M., 2001. *Qualitative research and evaluation methods*. 3rd ed. Newbury Park: Sage.

Pearce, J. and Robinson, R., 2000. Cultivating *guanxi* as a foreign investor strategy. *Business horizons*, 43 (1), 31–38.

Perry, C. and Gummesson, E., 2004. Action research in marketing. *European journal of marketing*, 38 (3/4), 310–320.

Pye, L., 1992. *Chinese negotiating style: commercial approaches and cultural principles*. New York: Quorum Books.

Redding, G., 1990. *The spirit of Chinese capitalism*. Berlin: de Gruyter.

Redding, G. and Witt, M., 2007. *The future of Chinese capitalism: choices and chances*. New York: Oxford University Press.

Rotter, J., 1967. A new scale for the measurement of interpersonal trust. *Journal of personality*, 35, 651–665.

Sako, M., 1998. The information requirements of trust in supplier relations: evidence from Japan, Europe and the United States. *In*: N. Lazaric and E. Lorenz, eds. *Trust and economic learning*. Cheltenham, UK: Edward Elgar Publishing.

Stening, B. and Zhang, M., 2007. Methodological challenges confronted when conducting management research in China. *International journal of cross cultural management*, 7 (1), 121–142.

Su, C. and Littlefield, J., 2001. Entering guanxi: a business ethical dilemma in mainland China. *Journal of business ethics*, 33 (3), 199–210.

Svensson, G., 2001. Extending trust and mutual trust in business relationships towards a synchronised trust chain in marketing channels. *Management decision*, 39 (6), 431–440.

Tian, X., 2007. *Managing international business in China*. Cambridge, UK: Cambridge University Press.

Tong, C. and Yong, P., 1998. *Guanxi* bases, *xinyong* and Chinese business networks. *British journal of sociology*, 49 (1), 75–96.

Triandis, H., 1995. *Individualism and collectivism*. Boulder, CO: Westview Press.

Tsui, A., Farh, J., and Xin, K., 2000. Guanxi in the Chinese context. *In*: J. Li, A. Tsui and E. Weldon, eds. *Management and organizations in the Chinese context*. Houndsmills, UK: Macmillan Press.

Wank, D., 1996. The institutional process of market clientelism: *guanxi* and private business in a South China city. *China quarterly*, 147, 820–837.

Williamson, O., 1993. Calculativeness, trust and economic organization. *Journal of law and economics*, 36 (April), 453–486.

Wong, S., 1996. Chinese entrepreneurs and business trust. *In*: G. Hamilton, ed. *Asian business networks*. Berlin: Walter de Gruyter, 13–26.

Wong, Y., Maher, T., Evans, N., and Nicholson, J., 1998. Neo-confucianism: the bane of foreign firms in China. *Management research news*, 21 (1), 13–22.

Wong, Y. and Tam, J., 2000. Mapping relationships in China: *guanxi* dynamic approach. *Journal of business and industrial marketing*, 15 (1), 57–70.

Xin, K. and Pearce, J., 1996. Guanxi: connections as substitutes for formal institutional support. *Academy of management journal*, 39 (6), 1641–1658.

Yang, M., 1994. *Gifts, favors and banquets*. Ithaca, NY: Cornell University Press, Wilder House Series.

Yau, O., Lee, J., Chow, R., Leo, Y., and Tse, A., 2000. Relationship marketing the Chinese way. *Business horizons*, 43 (1), 16–23.

Yeung, H., 1995. Qualitative personal interviews in international business research: some lessons from a study of Hong Kong transnational corporations. *International business review*, 4 (3), 313–339.

Yeung, I. and Tung, R., 1996. Achieving business success in Confucian societies: the importance of 'guanxi' (connections). *Organizational dynamics*, 25 (2), 54–66.

Young, L. and Wilkinson, I., 1989. The role of trust and co-operation in marketing channels: a preliminary study. *European journal of marketing*, 23 (2), 109–122.

Small and medium-sized enterprises in China: a literature review, human resource management and suggestions for further research

Li Xue Cunningham and Chris Rowley

Centre for Research on Asian Management, Cass Business School, City University, London, UK

As the importance of small and medium-sized enterprises (SMEs) has increased, it has been accompanied by an increase in the amount of research attention paid to them. This has been the case in Asia, and also China. However, this work concentrates mainly on entrepreneurship, small business development and government support. Moreover, the fact is that in terms of issue focus, it is finance, marketing and ownership rather than people management that are the central themes of the discussion. However, there are some studies of human resource management (HRM) in SMEs in China. Our study here provides a broad review of prior work, and the results highlight some important issues for the study of HRM in SMEs and call for the development of more sophisticated theoretical models and more longitudinal research.

Introduction

China, a growing economic superpower, has achieved an annual gross domestic product (GDP) growth rate of 7 to 13% for nearly three decades from the 1980s, even through the Asian Financial Crisis of 1997 when some other high-growth economies in the region stagnated and declined (Hsiung 2003). Along with the quickening pace of the structural adjustment of Chinese state-owned enterprises (SOEs) in the past few years, small and medium-sized enterprises (SMEs) have played an important role in the economy, easing employment pressure, boosting non-governmental investment and helping in bringing about market prosperity (Anderson *et al.* 2003, Zhang 2005).

However, SMEs face enormous pressures as China integrates more into the world economy (Cunningham and Rowley 2008). Influences, such as globalization, technological innovation and demographic and social change (Yu *et al.* 2001), as well as the level of technology deployed, innovative ability, financial support and entrepreneurship that can be found in the business environment, all impact on SMEs as both external and internal factors. Consequently, the way SMEs develop in an increasingly competitive market has become one key issue. Part of this involves the use of human resources (HR).

Some non-Asian literature addresses the importance of human resource management (HRM) in SME development. A number of studies confirm the significance of a well-motivated, highly skilled workforce as being a key to the success of smaller firms (for example, Marlow 2000, Hornsby and Kuratko 2003, Gray and Mabey 2005). Although SMEs are criticized for their failure to use practices such as so-called high performance work practices (HPWP) (Kok and Uhlaner 2001, Cassell *et al.* 2002, Storey 2004), some research on SMEs demonstrates that not only is a HPWP utilized in some small businesses (Bacon *et al.* 1996, Baron and Kreps 1999), but also that the linkage between HRM and organizational outcomes exists in SMEs. By using structural equation modelling, for instance, Sels *et al.* (2006) conclude that the positive relation between an 'intensive' HRM system, which reflects a configuration of 'best practices' in six HRM areas (selection, training, careers, appraisal, compensation and participation), and profitability in Belgian small firms (<100 employees) matches prior empirical work on this topic in larger companies. The analysis of 371 small firms (<100 employees) in Australia also shows that the implementation of formal HRM structures and procedures necessary to support growth differs between successful and unsuccessful SMEs (Kotey and Slade 2005). Thus, it is evident that HRM is crucial in SMEs' development, as HRM may provide a useful vehicle for firms to obtain sustainable advantages in an increasingly competitive environment.

Although the potential of HRM to add value to the firm is recognized by a number of SMEs, little attention has been paid to the study of HRM in SMEs in China. As the importance of SMEs in China has increased, it is critical to review research on HRM in SMEs to identify the 'gaps' or areas that exist in current coverage. Therefore, the purpose of this present study is to provide an overall examination of research on HRM in SMEs in China. First, some literature addressing HRM in SMEs is discussed by looking at the nature of HRM in SMEs and the importance of contextual factors on HRM 'take-up' in enterprises. Then, research methods and data collection processes are described. The findings are then illustrated using data analysis. Finally, our study draws together some conclusions and offers useful possible future research perspectives for this increasingly important area.

HRM in SMEs

Of course, we need to note conceptual and definitional difficulties here. We will not become engrossed in debates about what HRM is and if and how it is different from earlier forms of people management, such as Personnel Management (PM) or that it is less likely to be found the smaller the organization. Rather, we simply note that as organizations grow in size and complexity, *a priori*, the likelihood of more systematic people management and PM, and finally HRM, do so too.

The nature of HRM in SMEs

Although the status of SMEs in the general management literature has been contested (for example, Torres and Julies 2005, Harney and Dundon 2006, Behrends 2007), many HRM researchers conclude that SMEs tend towards an informal HRM approach (see Table 1). They also argue that this approach reflects some key characteristics of SMEs themselves, such as flexibility, informality, external uncertainty and innovation. For example, Marlow's (2000) investigation of 64 SMEs (<210 employees) reveals that such firms rely largely on an informal and flexible approach to strategic HRM activities because of external uncertainty due to market volatility. Similarly, Hill and Stewart (2000) claim that the nature of HR development (HRD) in SMEs (<250 employees) mirrors the characteristics of SMEs themselves, such as being reactive, informal and short-term in outlook. Furthermore, the study in Hong Kong by Siu (2000) illustrates that SMEs (<500 employees) are highly sensitive to changing tendencies and environments, and that this sensitivity itself is deeply reflected in daily management practices.

Table 1. Overview of empirical research on HRM in SMEs.

Author(s)/ (year)	Country	Nature of sample	HRM characteristics in SMEs
Harney and Dundon (2006)	Ireland	6 SMEs (<250 employees)	*Informal* and emergent, heterogeneity and complexity.
Bacon and Hoque (2005)	UK	338 private sector workplaces (<250 employees)	*Informality* widespread and diverse range of 'enterprise characteristics' explains variation in employer strategies.
Kotey and Slade (2005)	Australia	371 small growing firms (<100 employees)	*Informal* in the majority.
Storey (2004)	OECD countries (6)	SMEs (<500 employees)	Most effective learning *not through formal training* but through experience.
Cassell et al. (2002)	UK	122 senior managers (<250 employees)	Fairly piecemeal and reactive, rather than proactive, holistic or systemic approach.
Marlow (2002)	UK	44 manufacturing firms (<200 employees)	*Informality* and flexibility are major characteristics of employee relations.
Kok and Uhlaner (2001)	The Netherlands	16 firms (<50 employees)	Heterogeneous and *informal*.
Marlow (2000)	UK	64 firms (<210 employees)	Activities far more *informal* and 'hands on' than previously suggested by design school advocates.
Hill and Stewart (2000)	UK	SMEs (<250 employees)	Nature of HRD is reactive, *informal* and short-term in outlook.
Carrol et al. (1999)	UK	40 service firms (7–207 employees)	*Little in way of formalized and systematic procedures* prescribed in textbooks.
Dundon et al. (1999)	UK	Service firm (65 employees)	Nature of labour management relations dynamic, contradictory and contingent.

While the literature suggests that informality is the basis of the nature of HRM in SMEs, the dynamic of informality has been highlighted by many researchers (for example, Ram *et al.* 2001, Harney and Dundon 2006). By analysing 338 workplaces in the private sector in the UK, Bacon and Hoque (2005) conclude that informality is widespread, but not universal. Kotey and Slade's (2005) study of 371 small firms (< 100 employees) in Australia also shows that HRM remains informal in the majority of firms, while a significant percentage of SMEs implement formal HRM practices with growth. Again, the findings by Harney and Dundon (2006) in six SMEs (< 250 employees) in Ireland confirm that there is a distinct mix of HRM policies and practices which are uneven and contradictory and imbued with varying levels of formality and informality amongst and within SMEs. Indeed, as Ram *et al.* (2001, p. 846) state, informality in SMEs is 'a matter of degree and not kind, and its nature may vary as much between firms of a given size as between large and small ones'. Thus, 'all firms combine formality and informality just as they combine control and consent. The balance differs as conditions vary' (Ram *et al.* 2001, p. 859).

Overall, the literature reinforces the view that informality, which is defined as 'a process of workforce engagement, collective and/or individual, based mainly on unwritten customs and the tacit understandings that arise out of the interaction of the parties at work' (Ram *et al.* 2001, p. 846), is the core concept upon which HRM in SMEs is based. Therefore, the following proposition is put forward:

1. The approach to HRM in SMEs in China will show informality, which is determined by the characteristics of a SME and the ever-changing market environment.

Contextual factors in HRM in SMEs

In SME studies, empirical evidence demonstrates that institutional influences have strong impacts on HRM practices (see Table 2). For instance, the evidence drawn from six SMEs operating in Ireland shows that a complex interplay of external structural factors and internal dynamics shaped HRM in the companies (Harney and Dundon 2006). Likewise, one of the greatest mistakes of much early research was its failing to link employee relations processes in small firms with external factors (tax, social insurance structures, product markets and inter-organizational relationships), or failing to place SMEs in a longer-term economic context (MacMahon 1996). Again, a number of researchers point out that one of the key characteristics of SMEs is that they are highly sensitive to changing tendencies and external environments (Siu 2000, Hill and Stewart 2000).

In the context of Asia, Whitley (1992) addresses the importance of national institutions in the development and continued effectiveness of particular business structures and practices. Related to HRM in particular, Rowley *et al.* (2004) argue that the area of HRM is probably the most context-sensitive aspect of management in the region since the history, culture and institutions of these countries have retained their power and influence even into the twenty-first century. In relation to HRM in China, a number of studies have verified that Chinese culture, national institutions and organizational factors all have strong impacts on the take-up of HRM practices (for example, Wright *et al.* 2002, Gamble 2003, Hassard *et al.* 2004, Wei and Lau 2005). Although the discussion is based mainly on large firms due to the lack of research into SMEs, it is believed that the factors affecting the transferability of HRM practices in larger firms will also influence SMEs because of the same national culture and institutions in which they are embedded (Chen 1995, Child and Warner 2003). In the view of the above, the following proposition is put forward:

Table 2.   Contextual factor findings of HRM in SME studies.

Author(s) (year/location)	Nature of sample (number/employees)	Context factors on HRM practices
Edwards and Ram (2006/UK)	123 (<50)	Survival relies on dynamic use of resources and context of changing economic and regulatory conditions.
Chandler and McEvoy (2000/US)	66 (median = 31)	Production strategy is key factor in determination of which practices adopted.
Hill and Stewart (2000/UK)	(<250)	More likely to evolve and change based on external environment than in larger firms.
Ram (2000/UK)	3 (<15)	Sectoral characteristics are key considerations in training practice.
Kinnie *et al.* (1999/UK)	3 (130–450)	Changing environment within which operating contributing to significant developments in way employee relations managed.
Wong *et al.* (1997/UK)	138 (25–500)	Factors shaping HR development: HR supply, industry sector, product–market structure, location, competition in product market, ownership and organizational character of firm.
Duberley and Walley (1995/UK)	(<500)	Key factor influencing adoption of practices – perceptions held by senior management about how best to deal with opportunities and threats posed by environment.
Stanworth and Curran (1981/UK)	8 (<200)	Small firm as a social grouping cannot be analysed as if isolated from trends in wider society.

2.   The development of HRM in SMEs in China has been affected by a set of wider influences, including social, cultural and institutional factors. Therefore, it is likely that this tendency will continue.

Methodology

Definition of SMEs

Table 3 shows that there is no general, legally binding definition for SMEs globally. SMEs are defined against various criteria, such as different sectors, the number of workers employed, the volume of output or sales, the value of assets employed and even the use of energy (ILO 2003). In addition, the definitions of SME differ from one country to another, as they can be based on a nation's history and economic situation. For example, Germany defines an SME as having fewer than 500 employees whereas South Korea classifies an SME as having fewer than 1000 employees (Zhou and Cheng 2003). Furthermore, within a country or region, definitions of SMEs vary at different stages of economic development. For example, in the US, the number of employees used to categorize SMEs in the manufacturing sector was less than 250 in 1953, but this figure was recently amended to no more than 1000 employees (Zhou and Cheng 2003). Another example is that in China the definitions and criteria of SME have been adjusted four times since 1949. In 2003, a new 'Standards on the Small and Medium-Sized Enterprises' document was published to relevant government agencies with the approval of the State Council in China (Cunningham and Rowley 2007). The standards apply to the government statistics for work and replace the old classification standards, which came into effect in 1988, and the supplementary standards published in 1992.

Table 3.   Definitions of SME in Asian countries.

Country	Sector category	Criteria/official definition
Hong Kong,	Manufacturing	<100 employees
China	Non-manufacturing	< 50 employees
Indonesia	SME	<100 employees
Japan	Manufacturing, mining and transportation, construction	<300 employees or invested capital <£0.42 million
	Wholesale trade	<100 employees or capitalization <£0.13 million
	Retail trade and services	<50 employees or capitalization <£41,920.843
Korea	Manufacturing	<300 employees, £10.89 – £43.57 million of capital (assets)
	Mining and transportation	<300 employees Construction; <200 employees Commerce and other service business; <20 employees
Malaysia	Small and medium	<150 full time workers or shareholder fund <£3.64 million
Philippines	SME	<200 employees, asset size <£0.63 million
Singapore	Manufacturing	fixed assets < S$ 15 million
	Services	<200 employees and fix assets <£4.98 million
Taiwan	Manufacturing, mining and construction	<200 employees and <£0.93 million
	Services industries and others	<50 employees and <£1.24 million sales volume
Thailand	SME	<= 200 employees or fixed assets <£1.49 million
Vietnam	SME	No fixed definition, generally <500 employees

Note: Local currency converted to GBP (£) based on exchange rate at www.xe.com.
Source: Adapted from Cunningham and Rowley (2007).

Sampling methods

Two online search engines, 'Business Premier Source' and 'Blackwell Encyclopaedia of Management Library', were used in this study. The reasons for using these two search engines are largely due to the fact of their leading roles in the world's scholarly business database. For example, the 'Blackwell Encyclopedia of Management Library' comprises 12 volumes, with over 4400 entries each covering major subject areas, while 'Business Source Complete' offers a comprehensive coverage for the most important scholarly business journals back as far as 1886, providing the leading collection of bibliographic and full text content. In order to reduce the stated weakness of the methodology, the search terms were also applied to some of the more general academic databases, such as 'ISI web of knowledge' and 'Google Scholar'.

From the perspective of managing people in China, the modern key reforms have occurred since 1986. Thus, the timeline for the current review was set up as between 1988 and 2008, assuming that most HRM studies would be carried out after 1986 and, given the normal research and publication lags, studies would not be completed and published until after 1988. The initial search was by using several search parameters ('China' or 'Chinese', 'human resource management' or 'human resource', 'small and medium sized enterprises' or 'SMEs' or 'small businesses', 'academic journal', '1988 to 2008'), but generated zero articles. After adjusting the parameters by removing 'small and medium sized enterprises' or 'SMEs' or 'small businesses', a total of 93 articles were derived from the databases. Those 93 articles were all China, HRM-related and published as academic articles between 1988 and 2008. Excluding studies with a focus on Hong Kong and/or Taiwan, introductions or conclusions from editors and book reviews, finally some 70 articles were selected. Then, the research process involved the printing of all the tables of contents and abstracts. After a thorough screening on these 70 articles, 16 articles were identified as paying special attention to HRM in SMEs in China (see Table 4).

Data analysis and results

Figure 1 exhibits the numbers of empirical HRM studies in China over the two decades from 1988 to 2008. It shows that there has been a significant rise of HRM studies since 1998. For instance, the total number of empirical studies in the last 10 years between 1998 and 2008 jumped to 6.6 times as many as those in the first 10 years from 1998. Moreover, the figure suggests that an impressive progress in HRM study in SMEs has been achieved. Thus, the number of SME-related HR articles has steadily increased to over one-third of the total numbers of HRM articles in the same period, going from 0% (1988–1997) to 28.5% (1998–2002) to 36% (2003–2008). Although large-sized enterprises are still the centre of the discussion, accounting for over two-thirds (36 studies, 68%), it is evident that the weight of HRM study in China has started to tilt more towards SME-related areas. Thus, the growth of HRM studies in SMEs implies that academics and researchers are recognizing the importance of SMEs in HRM studies.

Looking at the nature (organizational and sectoral types) of HRM studies in SMEs in China, Table 5 illustrates a focus on the importance of private enterprises (PEs) in SMEs' development in over one-half of the research (8 studies, 50%). Also, a sectoral bias continues, with manufacturing industry (7 studies, 44%) still the dominant sector to study. In addition, the geographical focus of HRM studies in SMEs is largely along the coastal regions of China. The two largest cities (Beijing and Shanghai) and the two main provinces (Guangdong and Jiangsu) of China were the most frequently chosen areas and/or cities for the research (13 studies, 81.25%). In contrast to a high involvement of coastal China, only 3 studies (18.75%) (Zheng 1999, 2006, Li et al. 2006) included central and/or Western China as part of their investigation.

In relation to the content of HRM studies in SMEs in China, three main themes can be concluded from looking at the previous research. These are, first, the relationship between HRM practices and organizational performance (5 studies, 31%); second, the impacts and importance of contextual factors in the adoption of HRM (7 studies, 44%); third, the differences between traditional Chinese personnel management (PM) and Western HRM practices (4 studies, 25%).

Whilst several key issues that are associated with HRM practices in SMEs in China are investigated from different perspectives (see Table 4), the results also show that a wide variety of HRM practices are examined in the studies (see Table 6). Those HRM practices can be categorized under the four major categories that capture much of HRM's content, namely, employee resourcing, development, rewards and relations. Among four key HRM categories, the findings illustrate that recruitment (7 studies, 43.75%) and selection practice (6 studies, 37.5%) are the most repeatedly studied areas in employee resourcing, while training practice (10 studies, 62.5%) is a central issue in employee development. Incentive pay (8 studies, 50%) and social benefits (6 studies, 37.5%) have drawn the most attention in HR research, whereas trade unions (4 studies, 25%) and workers' congress (2 studies, 12.5%) are two key aspects often covered in the discussion of employee relations.

The reasons that certain HRM practices are more frequently studied than others are several. For instance, effective recruitment and selection, high level training and high

Table 4. Review of HRM in SME studies, 1988–2008.

Authors (year)	Size by employees (no./%)	HRM examined/coverage
General HR practices		
Goodall, K. and Warner, M. (1998)	43–820 employees (20)	Practices in foreign-invested firms
Warner (1999)	<500 (8 out of 12)	Practices in small/large high-tech firms
Wang and Qiao (2007)	<150	Practices in small firms
Cunningham and Rowley (2008)	<500	Practices in small and medium sized firms
Link between HR practices and organizational performance		
Zheng, C (1999)	no definition	Practices in SMEs
Deng, Menguc, and Benson (2003)	<500 (96.9%)	Effects of HRM on export performance
Zheng, C. et al. (2006)	20–500	Performance effect of HRM practices in SMEs
Li, Y., Zhao, Y., and Liu, Y. (2006)	<500 (74.7%)	Effects of HRM on technological innovation and organizational performance
Staffing		
Chow, Fung, and Yue (1999)	<500 (76%)	Job turnover in large/small manufacturing enterprises
Training		
Ng, Y.C. and Siu, N.Y.M. (2004)	<500 (part)	Impact of training on firm performance in small and large firms
Compensation and Benefits		
Ding, Akhtar, and Ge (2006)	<500 (64%)	Impact of organizational factors on managers' compensation and benefits
Employee relations		
Cooke, F.L. (2002)	no definition	Employee relations in small manufacturing firms
Cooke, F.L. (2005)	<100	Employee relations in small commercial firms
Others		
Verburg et al. (1999)	Medium (no definition)	Comparison of HR practices in China and the Netherlands
Siu, N.Y.M. and Glover, L. (2001)	<500 (50 out of 129)	Culture and institutional factors in management practices
Ding, Ge, and Warner (2004)	<500 (14 out of 20)	HR practice changes related to shifts in corporate governance in small and large TVEs

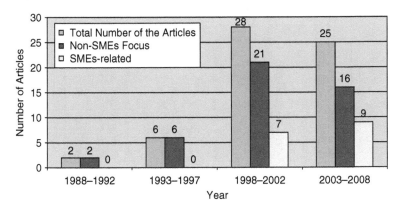

Figure 1. Empirical HRM studies, 1988 to 2008.

rewards at the core of HPWP have been highlighted by a number of HRM scholars and practitioners (for example, Huselid *et al.* 1997, Guest 1997, Guest *et al.* 2004, Michie and Sheehan 2005). Research confirms that the recruitment and selection process is of paramount importance in an organization, since such an effective procedure can attract and find the 'right' individuals who can contribute to organizational success. Training practice and rewards system are inevitable requirements for developing and retaining the competence of a workforce so that employees can work with new methods and technologies in the new environment. As China emerges more into the global economy, the increasingly high competition in both domestic and international markets encourages entrepreneurs to learn best experiences from the outside world. Thus, key HRM practices have become the focus of HRM study in China because of their important roles in the enhancement of competitiveness and organizational performance.

Not only does the external environment act as a key determinant in the centre of HRM study in China, but conflicts and problems occurring during any transfer process of Western management practices to China have also drawn increased interest from researchers. It is evident that the distinctive Chinese characteristics (political, economic, and cultural factors) have strong influences on HRM practices in Chinese firms, especially in areas such as recruitment and selection, training, rewards and employee relations (for example, Redding and Ng 1983, Easterby-Smith *et al.* 1995, Verburg *et al.* 1999, Child and Warner 2003, Cooke 2005, Cunningham and Rowley 2008). Thus, the focus on those HRM practices in HRM studies on China provides an interesting insight and deeper understandings on the transferability of management practices in a different cultural and societal context.

With regard to the different research methodological approaches applied by studies of HRM in SMEs in China, the findings show that 6 out of the 16 studies (37.5%) adopt case studies or interviews as their research methods, while the rest were carried out using mixed-methods (5 studies, 31%), surveys (4 studies, 25%), or secondary data analysis (1 study, 6%). This finding is in line with the research design employed in HRM studies in larger enterprises in China, and also confirms that qualitative approaches, such as case studies and/or interviews, are the preferred strategy in HRM studies in China (see Table 7).

In contrast to quantitative methods, qualitative approaches, such as case studies and interviews, are highlighted by many researchers as the preferred strategy when 'how' or 'why' questions are being posed, when the investigator has little control over events, and

Table 5. Nature of HRM in SME studies in China, 1988–2008.

Authors (year)	Location	Ownership	Industry	Research method
Goodall and Warner (1998)	E: Shanghai	FIEs (20)	Cross section	Interview and questionnaire
Zheng, C. (1999)	N, SE, E, SW: 10 cities	SOE, FIE, PE, JVE (74)	Cross section	Interview
Warner (1999)	N: Beijing	SOE, COE, PE, JVE (12)	Hi-tech	Cass study
Chow, Fung, and Yue (1999)	E: Shanghai	SOE, COE, JVE, FOE (5413)	Manufacturing	Firm-level panel data
Verburg et al. (1999)	E: Zhejiang	JVE, SOE (97)	Manufacturing	Survey and structured interview
Siu and Glover (2001)	N, S: Beijing, Guangzhou	SOE, COE, PE, JVE (129)	Service, manufac-turing	Questionnaire and case study
Cooke, F.L. (2002)	S: Guangdong	SOE (2)	Manufacturing	Case study
Deng, Menguc, and Benson (2003)	S: Shenzhen, Zhuhai, Shantou, Xiamen	SOE (96)	Manufacturing	Survey and questionnaire
Ding, Ge, and Warner (2004)	S: Guangdong	TVE (20)	Manufacturing	Interviews
Ng and Siu (2004)	E: Shanghai	SOE vs. non-SOE (485)	Manufacturing	Survey
Cooke (2005)	S: Guangdong	PE (24)	Commercial	Survey
Ding, Akhtar, and Ge (2006)	S, E: Shanghai, Nanjing, Guangzhou	SOE, PLF, FIE (465)	Cross section	Survey
Li, Zhao, and Liu (2006)	S, E, SE, W, N: 8 provinces	Various (194)	High-tech	Survey and interview
Zheng, C. et al. (2006)	N, SE, E, SW: 10 cities	DPEs, SOEs, FIEs, and COEs (74):	Cross section	Semi-structured interview
Wang and Qiao (2007)	N	PE (15)	Cross section	Semi-structured interview
Cunningham and Rowley (2008)	E: Jiangsu	PE, SOE, COE, FIE (114)	Cross section	Survey and semi-structured interview

Note: S = South; E = East; SE = South-east; W = West; N = North.

Table 6.   Key HR practices examined in HRM in SME studies in China, 1988–2008.

HRM practices	Total number of studies	Percentage of the sample
Employee resourcing:		
Recruitment	7	43.75
Selection	6	37.5
Job turnover	2	12.5
Employment contract	1	6.25
Employee development:		
Training and development	10	62.5
Performance appraisal	5	31.25
Employee rewards:		
Incentive pay	8	50
Reward system	7	43.75
Social benefit and welfare	6	37.5
Compensation	3	18.75
Career development and promotion	3	18.75
Employee relations:		
Trade union	4	25
Decision-making	4	25
Workers' congress	2	12.5
Party	1	6.25
Labour–management relations	1	6.25
Employee protection	1	6.25
Work time arrangement	1	6.25

Table 7.   Research methods applied in HRM studies in China.

Research method	HRM studies in SMEs		HRM studies in larger firms	
	No.	%	No.	%
Qualitative approach	6	37.5	20	44.4
Mixed-methods	5	31.3	14	31.1
Quantitative approach	5	31.3	11	24.4

Source: Cunningham (2007).

when the focus is on a contemporary phenomenon within some real-life context (Robson 1993, Yin 1993, Bryman 2001). For example, in a study of the adoption of HRM practices in 16 small and medium-sized manufacturing organizations (< 500 employees), Duberley and Walley (1995, p. 895) argue that 'the use of case studies should overcome the problem identified by Guest (1990), namely, that what companies tell the world they are doing can hide other practices that they may be less keen to publicize'. In a comparative study of small business management (< 500 employees) among 94 American firms and 37 Hong Kong firms, Siu (2000) also found that quantitative research methods (that is, a survey) might not be very useful when trying to determine how and why Chinese SMEs performed as they did. Instead of using a survey approach, Siu (2000) suggests that qualitative research methods, such as in-depth personal interviews or case studies, might be possible alternatives for advancing the knowledge of management of Chinese SMEs.

   Moreover, the lack of quantitative approach in studies of HRM in SMEs in China is largely due to the obstacles in gathering data in both SMEs and the developing market.

For example, in an in-depth qualitative assessment of three descriptive data sets, Heneman *et al.* (2000) found several major difficulties in conducting research in SMEs, such as the lack of information about HR, the impediments in gathering data and the reluctance to participate in academic studies. In addition, Wright and Hoa (2001) point out that asking questions in any form is viewed with suspicion in a developing market. Furthermore, Cooke (2002, p. 23) mentions that 'in general, academics in China do not have much bargaining power in negotiating research access with business organisations, which do not have a tradition of supporting social science research either in the form of surveys or case studies'. Again, various studies confirm that personal relationships are crucial in academic research in China, since little data is likely to be gathered without connections (for example, Ding *et al.* 2006, Zheng *et al.* 2006, Cunningham and Rowley 2008). As the investigator who is doing research in China has little control over events, and the emphasis of HRM study is mostly on a contemporary phenomenon within some real-life context, it is inevitable that a qualitative research design, such as case studies and/or interviews, is chosen in most studies of HRM in Chinese SMEs.

Discussion

In line with Proposition 1, the results of this review suggest that informality is the key concept of HRM in SMEs in China. For instance, Cunningham's (2007) research on HRM practices in 114 SMEs in China illustrates that informal approaches to the role of HR function (a belief in the importance of HR but lacking any formality), employee resourcing ('word-of-mouth'), training ('sitting by Nellie'), and employee relations (informal discussions, dismissal and termination procedures) are the most common methods applied.

The findings of previous research illustrates that two key factors contribute to the informal HRM approach in SMEs in China. One is the characteristics of SMEs (that is, external uncertainty and the 'dictatorship' of the owner manager), and the other is the market environment. For example, Ding *et al.* (2000) state that political fears of social instability limited the pace and depth of change in HRM. Siu and Glover (2001) claim that the turbulent political, economic and legal changes created barriers for Chinese managers to accurately forecast the market situation. Goodall and Warner (1998, p. 18) point out that 'much of what we … saw in China was to do with uncertainty and change'. Thus, it is clear that external uncertainty, which is led by the context of changing economic and regulatory conditions, encourages SMEs to adopt an informal and flexible approach in their HRM activities.

Not only external uncertainty, but ownership form reinforces the informal HRM approach in SMEs. Evidence shows that most SMEs in China are PEs (Cunningham and Rowley 2008). It is clear that the 'dictatorship' of the owner-manager remains as one of distinctive characteristics in most PEs in China, especially in SMEs (Schlevogt 2001, Cunningham 2007). For instance, in their study of HRM practices in 15 small private firms (< 150 employees), Wang and Qiao (2007) found that most HRM practices in SMEs were developed by the owners themselves, based on strong indigenous Chinese characteristics. Similarly, the owners' approach towards HRM is essential in deciding what kinds of HRM practices to apply and whether or not HRM is strategically important to the businesses' operation (Cunningham 2007).

Overall, this review confirms that HRM practices in SMEs in China are rather more informal than those formalized and systematic procedures prescribed in the concepts of Western HRM 'best practices'.

The findings of our analysis also shows that research has demonstrated that there is a positive link between enterprise performance and HRM practices in SMEs in China. For instance, Zheng (1999) researched 74 SMEs in 10 cities in China and argues that there is an underlying association among HRM practices, HRM outcomes and enterprise performance. By measuring export growth and the percentage of export sales of 96 SOEs in four special economic zones, Deng *et al.* (2003) also found that HRM had a substantial impact on enterprise performance. Again, Li *et al.*'s (2006) survey findings using 194 high-technology firms in eight provinces in China suggests that a firm's HRM practices (training, non-material incentives and process appraisal and control) can advance the firm's technological innovation, which in turn leads to that firm's superior performance. For instance, employee training helps high-tech firms to 'not only gain technological progress through increased knowledge, but also to find new market opportunities and to enhance their innovation ability through information exchange and skill improvement' (Li *et al.* 2006, p. 692). Therefore, current research on HRM in SMEs in China supports the arguments made by Sels *et al.* (2006) and Kotey and Slade (2005) by suggesting that HRM is crucial to SME development.

Although China provides a dynamic environment for SMEs to grow and evidence encourages a linkage between HRM and organizational performance, at the same time the research implies that it is clear that contextual influences restrain the pace and depth of HRM changes in SMEs. This result of this review supports our Proposition 2. It is evident that traditional Chinese culture limits the applicability of some HRM in non-Western countries, while institutional factors create barriers to effective management practices (for example, Verburg *et al.* 1999, Siu and Glover 2001, Cunningham 2007). For instance, Siu and Glover (2001) argue that harmony maintained within the hierarchy led to workers having less autonomy to make decisions, while too much interference from local government hindered economic development.

Not only do external factors have impacts on HRM take-up, but internal organizational factors also affect HRM evolution in SMEs. For example, firm size is a key determinant of the formalization of HRM practices (Ding *et al.* 2004), as commonly found in other countries. Additionally, type of ownership is another key factor in understanding job generation and reallocation (Chow *et al.* 1999). For example, the findings from Chow *et al.*'s (1999) study of manufacturing firms in Shanghai, China show that the rate of the net job growth of the smallest-sized firms is roughly three times that of the largest-sized firms. Again, location and industry strongly affect the variance in coverage of various workers' social welfare (Cunningham 2007), while the industrial sector has significant impacts on managerial compensation levels (Ding *et al.* 2006).

An important finding is that this review reveals that the research on HRM in SMEs in China is sparse, limited, geographically biased and concentrated, even though we have shown that the progress of SME-related HRM studies is promising. For example, only 16 out of 70 HR articles (22.85%) from 1988 to 2008 studied HRM in SMEs. In fact, if we delve a little deeper, this paucity becomes even more evident thus: only 7 articles (10%) focused on SMEs (<500 employees) entirely, while another 9 (12.85%) articles included SMEs as part of their studies.

Also, with regard to geographical focus, there is a lack of research in swathes of much of the country, such as central and Western China. One possible reason for the unevenness of HRM studies in China may relate to the difference between coastal and inland regions in terms of the market environment in which SMEs operate. It is obvious that economic growth is much more rapid in coastal areas (Cunningham and Rowley 2008). Therefore, on the one hand, studies in coastal China are popular as they will draw much more public attention, including that of policy-makers, Chinese managers and foreign-invested companies, academics and researchers, than those studies relating to inland and/or Western China. On the other hand, the attitudes of SMEs towards academic research are more positive, which is partly due to the higher competitive pressures from both local and foreign rivals. For instance, one of top issues that SMEs' senior management was concerned about was how to strengthen the firms' competitiveness to survive in the current market, so senior managers were keen to participate as one of the main purposes was hoping to find management 'best practices' that could be implemented to enhance the companies' performance (Cunningham 2007). Hence, public interests, active engagement from SMEs and personal connections lead to rich investigations along costal line regions of China (13 out of 16 studies, 81.25%).

Finally, this current review highlights that the political and socio-economic content and environment is one of the major determinants in the development of studies of HRM in SMEs in China. China's open door policy, economic reforms and WTO accession have stimulated SMEs' development as well as encouraging the proliferation of Western management theories and practices in China. As a result, studies of HRM in SMEs are increasing. The growing emergence of such studies not only underlines an important role of SMEs in HRM study, but also exemplifies that HRM has become a key factor in SME development.

Implications

Of course, the natures of the comparisons we are making also need noting. This is can be seen in Figure 2. This shows that we can have four broad comparisons. While we are looking at quadrant 4, and this should be in comparison to quadrant 3, too often it is actually comparing to quadrant 2 or even 1.

This overview and review indicates what may lie ahead for the development of HRM in SMEs in China. It implies that there is some tendency for people management in SMEs to move towards some convergence with HRM practices aimed at enhancing organizational performance. However, it is worth noting that convergence appears to be more on the macro level, pushed by competitive forces from the business environment in China and abroad, such as WTO accession and internal Chinese economic and social structural reforms. These institutional contingencies stimulate the development of SMEs and support the demands of Western management concepts, such as 'best practice'. At the enterprise level, indeed, evidence shows that current HRM practices in SMEs in China are quite different from the ones deployed in large enterprises in the West (Cooke 2005, Cunningham and Rowley 2008).

Moreover, the current review suggests that there are similarities between people management in SMEs in China and the early stages of HRM in the West. For instance, in the 1980s, some HRM scholars argued that the change from PM to HRM reflected wider changes in organizations and in society (Kochan et al. 1986, Guest 1987, 1991, Keenoy 1990). In a similar vein is the shift of people management in SMEs in China, which can be observed from the old Chinese personnel administration to a 'newer' PM model, and then

Focus	West	China
Large Firms	1	2
Small Firms	3	4

Figure 2. Comparison matrix.

a somewhat slow convergence towards HRM encouraged by external factors such as a new political ideology and the changed national and global environment. As some HRM researchers argue (Cooke 2002, Mok *et al.* 2002, Cunningham and Rowley 2008), additionally staff in SMEs in China are facing similar problems to those in Western countries (Cully *et al.* 1999, Hill *et al.* 2000), such as inequality of bargaining power between labour and management, job insecurity and employment contract issues. Therefore, although we cannot make conclusive predictions, since we are dealing with two very different systems, nevertheless the findings of this review seem to suggest that, if left to evolve, people management in SMEs in China will probably converge somewhat towards that in the West, while retaining unique Chinese characteristics. This reflects earlier views, such as Ng and Siu (2004), who found the training programme in SMEs incorporate a hybrid form combining Chinese management characteristics with an individualistic approach.

Limitations and future research

Some possible limitations of this study might remain despite the above implications. First, the current review only covers HRM studies in China from 1988 to 2008. In addition, the sample was chosen mainly from the two largest academic databases, although some of the more general academic databases were also applied. Other search engines, databases and years were not applied in this research. Thus, some relevant articles may not be included. However, despite these limitations, this study has offered an overview of recent studies of HRM in SMEs in China, its HRM development, and suggested the possible future direction of HRM in Chinese SMEs.

Another possible limitation is that the geographical focus of HRM studies in SMEs in China is constrained and the research methods applied in those studies are restrained by the difficulties relating to sampling SMEs in China. Thus, a longitudinal participating study would be the ideal way to offset the weaknesses of current HRM studies. Moreover, a more comprehensive analysis of HRM in SMEs in China is needed with the involvement of enterprises from different regions and perspectives. Furthermore, a systematic comparative study is encouraged across regions, sectors and countries, both inter and intra-Asian. By doing this, appropriate theories and theoretical models can be built which could act to guide HRM practices in SMEs in China.

Conclusion

SMEs have become recognized as being important to business development in many economies around the world. China is no exception to this. This review was conducted to enhance the understanding of HRM development in SMEs in China. The emphasis was to highlight the depth and breadth of research that has occurred and to identify the gaps that exist in the current studies. New directions are called for for the development of more longitudinal research, more rigorous empirical studies of HRM in SMEs in China.

Of course, this is a clarion call for more difficult and long-term but more meaningful research in an always difficult area dealing with employment matters. This is also against the grain and pressures and trends in academia to churn out salami-style publications to meet whatever the latest rankings are based on and their fetish of figures.

References

Anderson, A.R., Li, J., Harrison, R.T., and Robson, P.J.A., 2003. The increasing role of small business in the Chinese economy. *Journal of small business management*, 41 (3), 310–316.

Bacon, N., Ackers, P., Storey, J., and Coates, D., 1996. It's a small world: managing human resources in small businesses. *International journal of human resource management*, 7 (1), 82–100.

Bacon, N. and Hoque, K., 2005. HRM in the SME sector: valuable employees and coercive networks. *International journal of human resource management*, 16 (11), 1976–1999.

Baron, J.N. and Kreps, D.M., 1999. Consistent human resource practices. *California management review*, 41 (3), 29–53.

Behrends, T., 2007. Recruitment practices in small and medium size enterprises: an empirical study among knowledge-intensive professional service firms. *Management revue*, 18 (1), 55–74.

Bryman, A., 2001. *Social research methods*. New York: Oxford University Press.

Carrol, M., Marchington, M., Earnshaw, J., and Taylor, S., 1999. Recruitment in small firms – processes, methods and problems. *Employee relations*, 21 (3), 236–250.

Cassell, C., Nadin, S., Gray, M., and Clegg, C., 2002. Exploring human resource management practices in small and medium sized enterprises. *Personal review*, 31 (6), 671–692.

Chandler, G.N. and McEvoy, G.M., 2000. Human resource management, TQM, and firm performance in small and medium-size enterprises. *Entrepreneurship: theory and practice*, 25 (1), 43–58.

Chen, M., 1995. *Asian management systems*. London: Routledge.

Child, J. and Warner, M., 2003. Culture and management in China. *In*: M. Warner, ed. *Culture and management in Asia*. London: Routledge Curzon, 24–47.

Chow, C.K.W., Fung, M.K.Y., and Yue, N.H., 1999. Job turnover in China: a case study of Shanghai's manufacturing enterprises. *Industrial relations*, 38 (4), 482–503.

Cooke, F.L., 2002. Ownership change and reshaping of employee relations in China: a study of two manufacturing companies. *Journal of industrial relations*, 44 (1), 19–40.

Cooke, F.L., 2005. Employment relations in small commercial businesses in China. *Industrial relations*, 36 (1), 19–37.

Cully, M., Woodland, S., O'Reilly, A., and Dix, G., 1999. *Britain at work: as depicted by the 1998 workplace employee relations survey*. London: Routledge.

Cunningham, L., 2007. *People management in small and medium-sized enterprises in China*. Thesis (PhD). Cass Business School, City University, London.

Cunningham, L. and Rowley, C., 2007. Human resource management in Chinese small and medium enterprises: a review and research agenda. *Personnel review*, 36 (3), 415–439.

Cunningham, L. and Rowley, C., 2008. Human resource management in small and medium-sized enterprise in Jiangsu, China. *In*: R. Barrett and S. Mayson, eds. *International handbook of entrepreneurship and HRM*. Cheltenham, UK: Edward Elgar, 285–301.

Deng, J., Menguc, B., and Benson, J., 2003. The impact of human resource management on export performance of Chinese manufacturing enterprises. *Thunderbird international business review*, 45 (4), 409–429.

Ding, D.Z., Akhtar, S., and Ge, G.L., 2006. Organizational differences in managerial compensation and benefits in Chinese firms. *International journal of human resource management*, 17 (4), 693–715.

Ding, D.Z., Ge, G., and Warner, M., 2004. Evolution of organizational governance and human resource management in China's township and village enterprises. *International journal of human resource management*, 15 (4/5), 836–853.

Ding, D.Z., Goodall, K., and Warner, M., 2000. The end of the 'iron rice-bowl': whither Chinese human resource management? *International journal of human resource management*, 11 (2), 217–236.

Duberley, J.P. and Walley, P., 1995. Accessing the adoption of HRM by small and medium-sized manufacturing organisations. *International journal of human resource management*, 6 (4), 891–905.

Dundon, T., Grugulis, I., and Wilkinson, A., 1999. 'Looking out of the black-hole' – non-union relations in an SME. *Employee relations*, 21 (3), 251–266.

Easterby-Smith, M., Malina, D., and Lu, Y., 1995. How culture sensitive is HRM? A comparative analysis of practice in Chinese and UK companies. *International journal of human resource management*, 6 (1), 31–59.

Edwards, P. and Ram, M., 2006. Surviving on the margins of the economy: working relationships in small, low-wage firms. *Journal of management studies*, 43 (4), 895–916.

Gamble, J., 2003. Transferring human resource practices from the United Kingdom to China: the limits and potential for convergence. *International journal of human resource management*, 14 (3), 369–387.

Goodall, K. and Warner, M., 1998. HRM dilemmas in China: the case of foreign-invested enterprises in Shanghai. *Asia Pacific business review*, 4 (4), 1–21.

Gray, C. and Mabey, C., 2005. Management development: key differences between small and large businesses in Europe. *International small business journal*, 23 (5), 467–485.

Guest, D.E., 1987. Human resource management and industrial relations. *Journal of management studies*, 24 (5), 503–521.

Guest, D.E., 1990. Human resource management and the American dream. *Journal of management studies*, 27 (4), 378–397.

Guest, D.E., 1991. Personnel management: the end of orthodoxy? *British journal of industrial relations*, 29 (2), 149–176.

Guest, D.E., 1997. Human resource management and performance: a review and research agenda. *International journal of human resource management*, 8 (3), 263–276.

Guest, D.E., Neil, C., and Philip, D., 2004. Using sequential tree analysis to search for 'bundles' of HR practices. *Human resource management*, 14 (1), 79–96.

Harney, B. and Dundon, T., 2006. Capturing complexity: developing an integrated approach to analysing HRM in SMEs. *Human resource management*, 16 (1), 48–73.

Hassard, J., Morris, J., and Sheehan, J., 2004. The 'third way': the future of work and organization in a 'corporatized' Chinese economy. *International journal of human resource management*, 15 (2), 314–330.

Heneman, R.L., Tansky, J.W., and Camp, S.M., 2000. Human resource management practices in small and medium-sized enterprises: unanswered questions and future research perspectives. *Entrepreneurship: theory and practice*, Fall, 11–26.

Hill, R. and Stewart, J., 2000. Human resource development in small organizations. *Journal of European industrial*, 24 (2–4), 105–117.

Hill, S., McGovern, P., Mills, C., Smeaton, D., and White, M., 2000. Why study contracts? Employment contracts, psychological contracts and the changing nature of work. *Presented to the ESRC Conference: Future of Work III*, London School of Economics and Political Science, Policy Studies Institute.

Hornsby, J.S. and Kuratko, D.F., 2003. Human resource management in US small business: a replication and extension. *Journal of developmental entrepreneurship*, 8 (1), 73–92.

Hsiung, J.C., 2003. The aftermath of China's accession to the World Trade Organization. *Independent review summer*, 8 (1), 1086–1107.

Huselid, M., Jackson, S., and Schuler, R., 1997. Technical and strategic human resource management effectiveness as determinants of firm performance. *Academy of management journal*, 40 (1), 171–188.

ILO Report, 2003. Available from: www.ilo.org. [Accessed 6 June 2005].

Keenoy, T., 1990. HRM: rhetoric, reality and contradiction. *International journal of human resource management*, 3 (1), 363–384.

Kinnie, N., Purcell, J., Hutchinson, S., Terry, M., Collinson, M., and Scarbrough, H., 1999. Employment relations in SMEs – market-driven or customer-shaped. *Employee relations*, 21 (3), 218–235.

Kochan, T.A., Katz, H., and McKersie, R., 1986. *The transformation of American industrial relations*. New York: Basic Books.

Kok de, J. and Uhlaner, L.M., 2001. Organization context and human resource management in the small firm. *Small business economics*, 17, 273–291.

Kotey, B. and Slade, P., 2005. Formal human resource management practices in small growing firms. *Journal of small business management*, 43 (1), 16–40.

Li, Y., Zhao, Y., and Liu, Y., 2006. The relationship between HRM, technology innovation and performance in China. *International journal of manpower*, 27 (7), 679–697.

MacMahon, J., 1996. Employee relations in small firms in Ireland. *Employee relations*, 18 (5), 66–80.

Marlow, S., 2000. Investigating the use of emergent strategic human resource management activity in the small firm. *Journal of small business and enterprise development*, 7 (2), 135–148.

Marlow, S., 2002. Regulating labour management in small firms. *Human resource management*, 12 (3), 25–43.

Michie, J. and Sheehan, M., 2005. Business strategy, human resources, labour market flexibility and competitive advantage. *International journal of human resource management*, 16 (3), 445–464.

Mok, K., Wong, L., and Lee, G., 2002. The challenge of global capitalism: unemployment and state workers' reactions and responses in post-reform China. *International journal of human resource management*, 13 (3), 399–415.

Ng, Y.C. and Siu, N.Y.M., 2004. Training and enterprise performance in transition: evidence from China. *International journal of human resource management*, 15 (4), 878–894.

Ram, M., 2000. Investors in People in small firms – case study evidence from the business services sector. *Personnel review*, 29 (1), 69–91.

Ram, M., Edwards, P., Gilman, M., and Arrowsmith, J., 2001. The dynamics of informality: employment relations in small firms and the effects of regulatory change. *Work, employment and society*, 15 (4), 845–861.

Redding, S.G. and Ng, M., 1983. The role of 'face' in the organisational perceptions of Chinese managers. *International studies of management and organisation*, 13 (3), 92–123.

Robson, C., 1993. *Real world research*. Oxford: Blackwell Publisher Inc.

Rowley, C., Benson, J., and Warner, M., 2004. Towards an Asian model of human resource management? A comparative analysis of China, Japan and South Korea. *International journal of human resource management*, 15 (4), 917–933.

Schlevogt, K., 2001. The distinctive structure of Chinese private enterprises: state versus private sector. *Asia Pacific business review*, 7 (3), 1–33.

Sels, L., De Winne, S., Maes, J., Delmotte, J., Faems, D., and Forrier, A., 2006. Unravelling the HRM-performance link: value-creating and cost-increasing effects of small business HRM. *Journal of management studies*, 43 (2), 319–342.

Siu, W., 2000. Marketing philosophies and company performance of Chinese small firms in Hong Kong. *Journal of marketing theory and practice*, Winter, 25–37.

Siu, N. and Glover, L., 2001. Barriers to effective managerial practices in China. *Asia Pacific business review*, 7 (3), 57–74.

Stanworth, J. and Curran, J., 1981. The social dynamics of the small manufacturing enterprise. *Journal of management studies*, 18 (2), 141–158.

Storey, D.J., 2004. Exploring the link, among small firms, between management training and firm performance: a comparison between the UK and other OECD countries. *International journal of human resource management*, 15 (1), 112–130.

Torres, O. and Julies, P., 2005. Specificity and denaturing of small business. *International small business journal*, 23 (4), 355–375.

Verburg, R.M., Drenth, P.J.D., Koopman, P.L., Muijen, J.J., and Wang, Z.M., 1999. Managing human resources across cultures: a comparative analysis of practices in industrial enterprises in China and the Netherlands. *International journal of human resource management*, 10 (3), 391–410.

Wang, X. and Qiao, K., 2007. The human resource management practices in small private firms in China. *Academy of management proceeding*, 1–6.

Warner, M., 1999. Human resources and management in China's 'hi-tech' revolution: a study of selected computer hardware, software and related firms in the PRC. *International journal of human resource management*, 10 (1), 1–20.

Wei, L. and Lau, C., 2005. Market orientation, HRM importance and competency: determinants of strategic HRM in Chinese firms. *International journal of human resource management*, 16 (10), 1901–1918.

Whitley, R., 1992. *Business systems in east asia: firms, markets and societies*. London: Sage.

Wong, C., Marshall, J.N., Alderman, N., and Thwaites, A., 1997. Management training in small and medium-sized enterprises: methodological and conceptual issues. *International journal of human resource management*, 8 (1), 44–65.

Wright, P., Szeto, W.F., and Cheng, L.T.W., 2002. Guanxi and professional conduct in China: a management development perspective. *International journal of human resource management*, 13 (1), 15–1-82.

Wright, P.C. and Hoa, T.T.V., 2001. The role of personal relationships in the lending decisions of Vietnamese bankers. *International journal of management*, 18 (1), 41–49.

Yin, R.K., 1993. *Applications of case study research*. London: Sage.

Yu, J.G., Wang, Y.P., and Song, L., 2001. Zhongguo Xiaoqiye Fazhan Zhanlue Yanjiu (A strategic study on the development of small enterprises in China (In Chinese). *Management world*, (2), 157–166.

Zhang, W., 2005. Zhongguo Zhongxiao Qiye Fazhan Xianzhuang (In Chinese). Available from: www.ccw.com.cn. [Accessed 17 March 2006].

Zheng, C., 1999. The relationship between HRM and Chinese SME performance. *International journal of organizational behaviour*, 4 (4), 125–137.

Zheng, C., Morrison, M., and O'Neill, G., 2006. An empirical study of high performance HRM practices in Chinese SMEs. *International journal of human resource management*, 17 (10), 1772–1803.

Zhou, S.D. and Cheng, D.M., 2003. *A study on competitive capability of small and medium-sized chinese enterprises* (In Chinese). Nanjing, China: Nanjing University Press.

Employees' satisfaction with HRM in Chinese privately-owned enterprises

Jie Shen

School of Management, University of South Australia, Adelaide, Australia

This study investigated the levels of employees' satisfaction with human resource management (HRM) practices in Chinese privately-owned manufacturing enterprise, and differences in satisfaction between employee groups. It emerges that while the levels of employees' satisfaction with performance appraisals, staffing and pay were between high and moderate, levels of satisfaction regarding training and development were low. Employees' satisfaction levels with HRM varied according to personal characteristics including gender, age, education, position, working years and registration status. The implications of the research findings with regard to the avenue for further research and HRM improvement in the private sector have been discussed.

Introduction

People's behaviour is mainly determined by their perceptions of and cognitive responses to their environment, not actual environmental factors alone (Fiske and Taylor 1984). Similarly, employee commitment to organizations and employee in-role and extra-role performance are determined by employees' perceptions of and responses to enterprise policies that affect them, e.g. the human resource management (HRM) system (Bagraim and Sader 2007, Benkhoff 1997, Delaney and Huselid 1996, Guzzo and Noonan 1994, Pare and Tremblay 2007, Sanders *et al.* 2008). Consequently, understanding how employees perceive, and are satisfied with, HRM policies and practices is the key to improving employee job satisfaction, organizational commitment and employee in-role and extra-role performance.

HRM in China's transitional economy has been the subject of much research since the early 1990s. The research has generally concluded that HR is managed differently according to the type of economically-owned enterprises (Benson *et al.* 2000, Cooke 2005, Shen 2007, Warner 1996, Zhu 2005). In a broader context, HRM practices in small and medium-sized enterprises (SMEs) are generally characterized by informality, emergence, non-bureaucratic culture and absence of sophisticated management practices (Bacon and Hoque 2005, Harney and Dundon 2006, Kinnie *et al.* 1999, Kotey and Sheridan 2005, Mayson and Barrett 2006, Wilkinson 1999). This conclusion is proven to be applicable to the Chinese context. Most Chinese privately-owned enterprises (POEs), particularly those operate in rural areas so called 'township and village-owned enterprises (TVEs)', are SMEs. Chinese HRM researchers have agreed that privatization, as a key process of the economic reform, has exerted considerable impact on employment relations.

HRM systems in POEs tend to be pragmatic and marketized, leading to the problem that rapid economic change and unregulated industrial relations (IR) result in more acrimonious and labour disputes much faster than in other sectors (Cooke 2005, Li and Rozelle 2000, Shen 2007, 2008, Zhu and Warner 2005). However, although past studies, for example, Shen (2007, 2008) and Zhu and Warner (2005), have recognized that employees' expectation of and responses to the HRM reform in POEs are different from in other sectors, little research has examined this phenomenon. Consequently, little is known about to what extent Chinese employees are satisfied with specific HRM policies and practices. Given that over 80% of Chinese enterprises are privately-owned and that this number continues to grow (Shen 2008), understanding the levels of employees' satisfaction with specific HRM policies and practices would greatly help POEs optimize HRM and in turn improve employee and organizational performance in the sector.

This study hence sets out to investigate the extent to which employees are satisfied with recruitment and selection, training and development, performance appraisal and reward and compensation – the four major HRM functions in POEs. It also analyses the moderating effect of employee demographic factors on the levels of their satisfaction with HRM. The findings of this research are expected to contribute to the literature on Chinese employees' attitudes toward the on-going HRM reform and, broadly, the impact of privatization on employees, and have significant practical implications for: firstly, Chinese managers; and secondly, managers in other developing countries, which are experiencing similar economic transition. To achieve these research objectives the study first reviews the literature on the current HRM reform and employees' expectations of and responses to the HRM reform in China. It then reviews the literature on privatization and HRM in POEs and develops research hypotheses. Subsequently, it addresses the research methodology covering the profiles of the participating companies, data collection and measures and presents and analyses the empirical data. It concludes by revisiting the research objectives and discussing research and practical implications.

The HRM in transition

Human resource management (HRM), which is defined as 'productive use of people in achieving the organisation's strategic business objectives and the satisfaction of individual employee needs' (Stone 1998, p.4), is widely recognized as a potential source of competitive advantage (Becker and Huselid 1998). HRM researchers argue that a firm's decision on HRM is determined by a range of external and internal factors, such as political, legal, economic and social cultural factors, strategy, structure, industry, size, economic ownership and experience (Paauwe and Dewe 1995, Schuler et al. 1993). In order for the HRM system to be effective and contribute to the development and implementation of the corporate strategy a firm needs to ensure its HRM system to best fit its internal and external environment, the so-called the 'best-fit approach' (Shen 2005). HRM research shows that HRM with differentiated characteristics, e.g. high-involvement HRM, high-performance HRM, family-friendly HRM, affect differently employees' attitudes and behabiour (Bowen and Ostroff 2004, Nishii et al. 2008, Pare and Tremblay 2007). Next, we will examine how the Chinese economic reform has impacted HRM and how employees have responded to the changes to HRM in the private sector.

The past three decades have witnessed China's transition from a command economy to what has been termed as 'socialist market economy'. This transition has brought about drastic changes to China's social and economic context, and consequently, has resulted in new strategies and management systems in Chinese firms (Warner 2004). Following the establishment of the People's Republic of China (PRC) in 1949, the Chinese Communist Party (CCP) under Mao Zedong adopted a socialist employment relations system strategy, which included such concepts as the 'iron rice-bowl' (*tie fan wan*), 'iron wage' (*tie gong zi*) and 'iron chair', which ensured 'jobs for life', guaranteed salaries and a 'cradle to grave' welfare policy (Child 1994, Warner 1996, 2004). Under these three 'irons' all industries in China were owned and operated by the State, and throughout the country local government bureaucracies engaged in central planning and managed the labour force. Workers were allocated by labour bureaus and cadres were allocated by personnel bureaus respectively into enterprises that had no control over the numbers and quality of their workforce (Nolan 2001). This centralized administrative employment relations system did not allow enterprises to obtain organizational competitive advantages (i.e. make a profit), but instead created the conditions for economic inefficiency by mismatching the needs of the workforce with those of organizations and individuals (Shen 2007, Warner 1996, Zhu and Warner 2005).

Following the death of Mao Zedong in 1976, China in the late 1970s launched an unprecedented '*san xian gai ge*' (three reforms) policy, moving from central job allocation, lifetime employment, egalitarian pay and political control to a decentralized, marketized and performance-based labour contract HRM system (Child and Tse 2000, Goodall and Warner 1997, Warner 1996). The new HRM system that emerged enabled enterprises to recruit, allocate and reward people according to enterprise needs, employee skills and experience, such as education, expertise, training and performance, and the ability of the market to meet its financial responsibilities to workers (Benson *et al.* 2000, Shen 2007, Warner 2004). While the marketized and profit-oriented HRM reform has greatly improved the productivity and competitiveness of Chinese enterprises, it has also resulted in massive violations of workers' rights, such as unfair dismissal, non-payment of wages or social and unemployment insurance, poor work environment and inadequate investment in training, and inadequate social welfare (Chan 1998, Shen 2007, Zhu and Warner 2005). Workers have been disadvantaged due to the unequal power shared by employers and workers concerning employment relations (Cooke 2005, Shen 2007, Zhu and Warner 2005). Enterprises normally set wages, working hours, working conditions, as well as other terms of employment relations unilaterally without negotiating with workers' organizations (Shen 2007, Zhu 2005). Consequently, the new HRM system has contributed considerably to growing labour conflict. In order to redress the pro-employer bias of labour laws and regulations, China's government initiated a new labour contract law that became enforceable from 1 January 2008. However, it is not yet clear how the new labour contract law has affected employer and employee relations.

HRM in POEs

Prior to the Chinese economic reform, private firms were virtually non-existent in urban areas. Since the early 1990s privatization of state-owned enterprises (SOEs) and collectively-owned enterprises (COEs) has been an important agenda item regarding China's economic reform. The 1997 15th CCP Congress marked a watershed in the accelerating privatization process when then President Jiang Zemin endorsed the sale of China's largest loss-making SOEs and COEs (Lee 1999). Since then the proportion of SOEs and COEs that formerly dominated the Chinese economy has decreased sharply. The share of the output of SOEs and COEs dropped from 73.4% in 1983 to 11.1% in 2003 (*China Statistical Yearbook* 2004). The number of SOEs fell from 262,000 in 1997 to 159,000 in 2002. By 2006 about 90% of SOEs and COEs had been privatized (Shen 2007).

Table 1.   Number of employees in different ownership enterprises (2000–2004, unit 0,000).

Enterprise	2000	2001	2002	2003	2004
Enterprises in urban areas					
SOEs	8102	7640	7163	6876	6710
COEs	1499	1291	1122	1000	897
POEs	1268	1527	1999	2545	2994
FIEs	642	671	758	863	1033
Self-employed individuals	2136	2131	2269	2377	3521
Enterprises in rural areas					
TVEs	12,820	13,086	13,288	13,573	13,866
POEs	1139	1187	1411	1754	2024
Self-employed individuals	2934	2629	2474	2260	2066

Source: China Statistical Yearbook, 2005.

During the same period employees shifted significantly from SOEs and COEs to the private sector. Table 1 shows the number of employees working in different ownership enterprises from 2000 to 2004.

Scholars argue that privatization has a huge impact on employment relations, and has generated workplace dynamics that have equally important implications for workers' attitudes and behaviours regarding their jobs (Chiu 2002, Zheng et al. 2006, Zhu et al. 2005). Although all enterprises tend to be profit-oriented the private sector appears to manage its firms somewhat differently (Li and Rozelle 2000). In a recent empirical study, Shen (2008) examined HRM policies and practices in POEs, and argued that, increasingly, many POEs do not comply with the Labour Law regarding labour contracts. According to Shen, while POEs are flexible and responsive to the firm's short-term needs and market situation they tend not to make long-term HR planning for recruiting, utilizing and retaining qualified staff. Such managerial myopia undermines the quality of the workforce and may result in a shortage of qualified employees in the long-term. Selection criteria have shifted from the traditional political attitudes and moral behaviour to education, skills, experience and performance. There is a lack of commitment to training and management development and employee involvement and participation in POEs.

In seeking efficiency, POEs push employees to the limit in appraisals and pay, e.g. releasing appraisal results to all employees and linking labour contract renewal to performance. Performance-based bonuses have become the most important part of payment, resulting in significant discrepancies in people's incomes. Housing and medicare welfare and fringe benefits are gradually declining over time. The scenario of paying wages and social insurance (an organization's obligation to pay money into workers' superannuation funds) in the private sector is often worse than in other sectors. Unequal power relations between employees and employers do not allow much of workers' voices heard regarding labour terms. Chinese HRM researchers have argued that these HRM characteristics often result in low labour standards and exploitation of labour (Chan 1998, Cheng 2004, Shen 2007, 2008, Zhu and Warner 2005). These HRM characteristics are also likely to be associated with low level of employee satisfaction, resulting in tension between employees and enterprise management, increasing employee grievances and widespread labour disputes. Based upon these discussions one expects that the level of employee satisfaction with the all four major HRM functions HRM is low in POEs. Hypotheses 1, 2, 3 and 4 are hence developed as follows:

- Hypothesis 1: The level of employee satisfaction with recruitment and selection in POEs is low.
- Hypothesis 2: The level of employee satisfaction with training and development in POEs is low.
- Hypothesis 3: The level of employee satisfaction with performance management in POEs is low.
- Hypothesis 4: The level of employee satisfaction with reward and compensation in POEs is low.

This study also investigates the effect of demographic factors on employees' satisfaction with HRM in POEs. Different employees always have different views of the contract based on their own expectations and understandings (Rousseau 1990). From the individual perspective, factors shaping employee perceptions mainly include gender, age, education, position, employment experience and personal life (Anderson and Schalk 1998, Rousseau and Tijoriwala 1998). Men and women have different value priorities and varied orientations to work (Millward and Brewerton 2000). Women in particular embrace family-friendly human resources practices of the organization because of their concern for families, suggesting a demographic influence on time allocation, workload and work location. Changes in maturity of employees influence their perceptions of HRM. There is an indication that the more mobile employees seem to be younger and those with higher education, who expect to move positions many times in their careers (Guest and Conway 1997). Employee perceptions may change during the lifetime of an employment relationship; with relatively simple mutual obligations between the parties existing in the early days of employment, but becoming increasingly complex as the employment relationship develops (Shore and Tetrick 1994). The longer an employment relationship exists the higher the likely level of organizational commitment and employee satisfaction (Rousseau 2001). Position may be also a factor that differentiates employee satisfaction with HRM. Despite a lack of empirical evidence it is more likely that senior managers report higher levels of satisfaction due to their positions and responsibilities. Shen (2007) notices that there are more labour disputes resulting from labour contract termination in China's SOEs than in POEs, but more disputes regarding payment in POEs than in SOEs. Shen argues that this is likely because most employees in SOEs are urban citizens and the majority of employees in POEs are rural migrants, and they have different perceptions of employer obligations. Hence, household registration status may affect the level of employee satisfaction with HRM. Based on these discussions the following hypothesis is developed:

- Hypothesis 5: Demographic variables including gender, age, education, position, work experience and household registration status affect the level of employee satisfaction with HRM in POEs.

Methodology

This study uses the convenient sampling method consisting of four POEs in Jiangsu Province, including two state-owned enterprises (SOEs) that were privatized in 2001 and the others were established by private owners as TVEs. China's TVEs have been one of the major driving forces behind the country's rapid economic growth, and are viewed by Naughton (1994) as a natural response to a strategy of transition that first liberalized the

Table 2.   Summary of the case companies' profiles.

Company	Industry	TVE	Foundation year	Employees	Sales (0,000 RMB Yuan)	Ownership
JR	Luggage production	Y	1992	4500	2001: 13,290	POE
					2002: 20,808	
					2003: 26,825	
SS	Electrical wires and cables	N	1967	1508	2001: 85,937	1967–2000 COE
					2002: 127,753	2001– POE
					2003: 150,210	
YH	Liquor	Y	1984	350	2001: 254	POE
					2002: 265	
					2003: 340	
ZC	Cereal and feed machinery	N	1918	3500	2001: 42,988	1918–1949 POE
					2002: 45,506	1950–2000 COE
					2003: 55,261	2001– POE

Note: COE refers to collectively-owned enterprises.

product markets, without liberalizing factor markets. Privatization began in the TVE sector and this privatization has been even faster than that of SOEs and COEs (Shen 2007). The detailed companies' profiles are presented and summarized in Table 2.

The data for this study were obtained mainly through a survey in the four participating companies in June 2004. Although the new labour contract law has been effective since January 2008 it has not yet been fully implemented by many Chinese firms. Hence, the HRM practices reported in this study still reflect the current situation in China. The questionnaire was designed in English and translated into Chinese by the researcher. To ensure the accuracy of Chinese translation the Chinese version of the questionnaire was retranslated back into English by a bilingual Chinese colleague. Five hundred questionnaires were randomly distributed to employees by the researcher and his associates, and 305 were received with a response rate of 61%. Completed questionnaires were sealed and returned to designated survey boxes by respondents to ensure confidentiality. The first part of the survey questions focused on respondents' personal information, including gender, age, education, working years, position and registration status. The mean age of the survey participants was 40–50 (SD = 12 years) and 57.2% were male; 87.5% of the sample was married, with 67.6% having children. Fifty-four percent of the respondents had completed their high school education. Further statistics are as follows: 56.3% were urban citizens and others were off-farm migrants; 73% were workers; 18% were low level managers (supervisors); 7% were middle managers; and 2% were senior managers. The mean of working years that respondents had was 12.5 (SD = 7.5).

The second part of the survey questions asked how satisfied employees were with recruitment and selection, training and development, performance appraisal and reward and compensation, which consist of 16 variables (see Geringer et al. 2002). Recruitment and selection variables included equal job opportunity, selection process and criteria, labour contracts and dismissal (four items). Training and development consisted of training provisions and programmes, support for education and personal development, promotion opportunities and criteria, and support for promotion (six items). Performance

Table 3.   The interviewees' profiles.

Company	Age	Position	Sex	Qualification	Working years
ZC	35	HR Manager	Female	Diploma in Business	12
ZC	48	Deputy General Manager	Female	Diploma in Business	14
JR	34	Deputy General Manager	Male	High School Graduate	18
JR	38	Deputy General Manager	Male	High School Graduate	20
SS	40	Deputy General Manager	Female	Certificate in Business	20
SS	45	HR Manager	Male	High School Graduate	22
YH	36	General Manager	Male	High School Graduate	5
YH	63	Deputy General Manager	Male	High School Graduate	15

appraisal covered appraisal execution, appraisal criteria and the use of appraisal for personal development (three items). Reward and compensation included three items, namely pay competitiveness and equity, and welfare and benefits. Questions were answered on a seven-point Likert scale ranging from 'strongly dissatisfied' to 'strong satisfied'. A Cronbach alpha reliability of .94 for the 16 item scale was obtained.

The qualitative data derived from the respondents' comments on the survey, once available, will be also analysed. In addition to the survey the data for HRM policies and practices of the four firms were obtained through semi-structured interviews with HRM managers or the general managers who were in charge of HRM matters. The investigation of the HRM policies and practices would provide explanations for why employees were or were not satisfied with those policies and practices. The profiles of the interviewees are shown in Table 3.

Major findings

Employees' satisfaction with HRM

Out of all 16 variables the means of two performance appraisal-related items including appraisal execution and appraisal criteria were above five, indicating employees in POEs accepted rigorous performance appraisals that were irrelevant to the planned economy and regarded the execution and criteria of performance appraisals as basically being fair and objective. All interviewees considered performance appraisals to be the most important HRM activity in their firms because they were the key mechanism ensuring employees were performing effectively and paid on the basis of performance. As General Managers in YH stated, 'Appraisals are probably the most useful tool for quality control and productivity improvement'. The HR Manager in SS emphasised, 'My company has been very careful with performance appraisals; ensuring the procedures and criteria to be clear and fair to everyone. Poor appraisals affect both individuals and the enterprise'. All the four participating firms adopted a product unit or sales-based appraisal system for production workers and salespeople. The major appraisal criteria were quantity and quality of products, the number of sales and compliance with procedures. Production workers and salespeople were required to accomplish a certain number of products and sales in order to receive basic salaries. Goals for managers and office workers were preset monthly.

The appraisal processes were normally transparent; firms publicized preset goals and appraisal results to all employees. In addition to answering the survey questions some respondent employees made additional comments, like 'I feel great pressure due to rigorous appraisals, but our company's appraisal policy is fair and good for the company and for me'. However, the mean for the item 'the use of appraisal for personal development' scored less than four, indicating that employees believed performance appraisals were not used to improve employees' skills and career development. This finding lends support to Shen's (2007) study in which he points out that performance appraisals in Chinese industries are concerned mainly with short-term goals and used mainly to determine pay and renew contracts rather than to identify improvement areas for career development. Shen (2007) makes the point that Chinese companies normally do not provide feedback to employees, which is also evidenced in this study.

The means for five items including equitable pay, dismissal policy, equal job opportunity, fair selection process and criteria and competitive pay were greater than four but lower than five, indicating these practices, were also reasonably well received. In all the four participating firms basic salaries were limited and bonuses formed the major part of employees' incomes and were determined by employees' and their business's performance. Almost all interviewees reported that the principle of their pay system was 'you are paid for what you do' and this was generally regarded as one of the essences of the economic reform. This performance-based reward and compensation system was generally regarded as being pay equitable, and the ideology of Socialist egalitarianism had effectively become a thing of the past during the era of economic reform. A number of employees commented, 'I am fine if I am paid for what I deserve', or 'I am fine as long as am paid fairly compared to my colleagues'.

POEs have made faster moves in abolishing life employment and adopting the 'two-way selection' practice, i.e. free selection of occupation and employees. The data suggest that these strategies were reasonably tolerated, indicating that the abolition of the 'iron rice bowl' employment system was regarded as beneficial not only to employers but to employees as well. This finding supports the argument made in the studies of Li and Rozelle (2000) and Zhu and Warner (2005) that for many marketable workers, changing jobs has become an opportunity for career development. Furthermore, Shen (2008) found that employees in POEs have lower expectations of long-term employment, evidenced by the fact that some employees choose not to sign labour contracts as they do not want to be tied to their companies. While employees generally accepted the contract system they were only moderately satisfied with signing a labour contract, including whether and how contracts had been signed. The HR Manager in ZC reported, 'The labour terms stated in the labour contract have been set unilaterally, and are not negotiable. Employees do not have another choice if want to take the job'. This comment was generally supported by the other interviewees. The lack of negotiation over signing labour contracts upset many employees, as shown in the following comment, 'We are like commodities and our prices for sale are decided by buyers only'. This finding is consistent with past studies (e.g. Cooke 2005, Shen 2007, Zhu and Warner 2005) which argued that Chinese workers are generally nursing a grievance against their disadvantaged status in determining labour terms in terms of employment duration, working hours and working conditions.

The mean scores for promotion criteria, welfare and benefits, promotion opportunity, training and their link to career development, and organizational support for individual education and development were between 3.34 and 2.43, indicating the respondents had medium to low levels of satisfaction with these HRM practices. None of the four participating firms provided employees with medical, housing and children's education benefits, which had been the key components of the 'cradle-to-grave' welfarism of the planned economy. While YH, the liquor firm, did not make organizational contributions at all to employees' superannuation, the other three firms contributed to superannuation – yet only to those employees who signed the labour contracts. Moreover, the four firms

Table 4.   Means, standard deviation and reliability of 16 HRM variables.

	Minimum	Maximum	Mean	Std. deviation	Cronbach's Alpha if item deleted
Appraisals been executed fairly	3	7	5.65	0.80743	0.939
Appraisal criteria are objective	3	7	5.54	0.83540	0.937
Pay is equitable	2	6	5.28	0.80242	0.935
Dismissal policy is fair	1	7	5.04	0.89092	0.931
Job opportunity is open to everyone	1	7	4.72	1.247	0.923
Selection process and criteria are fair	2	7	4.64	1.312	0.931
Pay is competitive	2	6	4.61	0.82865	0.923
Signing labour contracts	1	7	3.65	1.71911	0.936
The use of appraisal for personal development	1	7	3.52	0.82577	0.931
Promotion criteria are objective	1	6	3.34	0.88956	0.934
Provision of welfare and benefits	2	6	3.19	0.87173	0.931
Promotion is open to everyone	1	6	3.05	0.82106	0.922
Training meets needs of development	1	6	3.01	1.345	0.941
Training is open to everyone	1	6	2.76	0.91362	0.935
Support for education and development	1	6	2.85	1.7543	0.928
Support for promotion	1	5	2.23	0.88448	0.931

provided only limited fringe benefits to employees. Most interviewees regarded fringe benefits as the product of the 'iron rice bowl' legacy and there was nothing wrong with their reduction. On the contrary, a number of employees commented that the diminishing fringe benefits made them feel as if they had lower status than those working in the state sector. Hence, it is not surprising that the welfare and benefit reductions had resulted in much dissatisfaction among employees.

The training and management development opportunities were regarded as inadequate in the four firms. Some employees commented that on-the-job training was provided only when new government regulations with regard to production or product safety were issued. When such training was provided training was of little help to personal and management development. This is in line with the findings of past studies, such as Cooke (2005) and Zhu (2005), who argued that training is normally not adequately provided in Chinese enterprises during this phase of economic transition. What employees were the least satisfied with was the lack of support from enterprises for personal and management or career development. The comments made on the survey included: 'Pursing a part-time study is regarded as employees' own business and is at employees' expenses and not supported by the company'; 'only those who know how to develop *guanxi* with managers would be given promotion'; and 'good performance does not result in promotion if the person does not have *guanxi* with important people'. These comments explained why the levels of employees' satisfaction with training and development policies and practices were generally low. The descriptive statistics and reliability of 16 HRM are shown in Table 4.

The means of relevant items were totalled and divided, and then computed into the four variables of recruitment and selection (RS), training and development (TD),

Table 5.   Means, standard deviation and reliability of four variables.

	Minimum	Maximum	Mean	Std. deviation	Cronbach's Alpha if item deleted
PA	2.33	7	4.9033	0.95520	0.875
RS	1.75	6.75	4.51	0.92847	0.874
RC	2.33	6	4.36	0.84773	0.799
TD	1.33	5.83	2.873	1.27416	0.835

performance appraisal (PA) and reward and compensation (RC). Table 5 illustrates the descriptive statistics and reliability of these four variables.

Overall, employees had a high to medium level of satisfaction with PA, medium level of satisfaction with RS and RC, and low level of satisfaction with TD. Hence, Hypotheses 1, 3 and 4 are not confirmed, but Hypothesis 2 is supported.

Differences in satisfaction between groups

A one-way between-group MANOVA was repeatedly performed to investigate how differently employees were satisfied with recruitment and selection, training and development, performance appraisal and reward and compensation according to age, gender, education, position, working years and registration status. The results are reported in Table 6, indicating Hypothesis 5 is partially supported. The differences in employees' satisfaction between males and females that did reach statistical significance were recruitment and selection and performance appraisal. An inspection of mean scores indicated that male employees were more satisfied than females with recruitment and selection (M 4.74/3.66) and performance appraisal (M 5.04/4.78). The differences in the levels of satisfaction with training and development and reward and compensation were not significant. The differences between urban citizens and off-farm migrants on all four variables appeared to be significant. Mean scores indicated that compared to urban citizens, migrants were less satisfied with recruitment and selection (M 3.54/4.47), training and development (M 1.76/3.28) and performance appraisal (4.15/5.41), but more satisfied with reward and compensation (M 4.73/3.96). Significant differences were found between workers and managers only in regard to their responses concerning training and development. Mean scores indicated that managers were more satisfied with training and development (M 2.98/2.52) and performance appraisal (M 5.62/4.23). Significant differences were found between married (including those with children) and unmarried employees regarding their responses to all four variables. An inspection of mean scores revealed that single employees were more satisfied with recruitment and selection (M 5.01/4.03), training and management (M 3.46/2.78), and performance appraisal (M 5.13/4.54), but less satisfied with reward and compensation (M 3.75/4.03).

Employees of varying ages and working years and different education levels had significant different responses to all four variables. An inspection of mean scores indicated that employees aged between 50 and 60 were most satisfied with all four variables. The levels of satisfaction decreased in workers below the age of 50 and higher than 60, with one exception that those aged 30–40 had a higher satisfaction level than those at 40–50 in regard to recruitment and selection and performance appraisal. Mean scores indicated that employees who had completed higher education tended to demonstrate higher levels of satisfaction with all four variables. Employees who had worked for 10–20 years had the highest level and employees who had worked for over 20 years had the lowest level of satisfaction with all four variables.

Table 6.   The results of tests concerning between-subjects effects.

Source	Dependent variable	df	F	Sig.	Partial Eta squared
Sex	RS	1	37.367*	0	0.131
	TD	1	2.321	0.133	0.010
	PA	1	23.347*	0	0.086
	RC	1	5.561	0.019	0.023
Registration	RS	1	26.152*	0	0.087
	TD	1	65.175*	0	0.246
	PA	1	22.135*	0	0.161
	RC	1	38.309*	0	0.137
Position	RS	1	7.053	0.046	0.019
	TD	1	8.437*	0.004	0.034
	PA	1	26.413*	0	0.098
	RC	1	1.568	0.230	0.006
Marriage	RS	1	22.474*	0	0.087
	TD	1	21.804*	0	0.075
	PA	1	7.457*	0.006	0.037
	RC	1	27.936*	0	0.178
Age	RS	4	97.265*	0	0.547
	TD	4	87.415*	0	0.624
	PA	4	86.096*	0	0.576
	RC	4	54.853*	0	0.527
Education	RS	3	172.118*	0	0.709
	TD	3	187.125*	0	0.724
	PA	3	36.271*	0	0.318
	RC	3	37.156*	0	0.413
Working years	RS	2	59.133*	0	0.327
	TD	2	43.725*	0	0.345
	PA	2	15.963*	0	0.219
	RC	2	47.317*	0	0.425

Note: * $p < .01$.

Discussion

Privatization has been an integral part of China's economic reform since the late 1970s, and privatization process has accelerated to the extent that over 80% of Chinese enterprises have become privately owned during the past decade. Privatization has also had a considerable impact on the reform and development of China's HRM system. As shown in this study and argued in the existing literature as well, HRM in POEs tends to be pragmatic and casual, and lacks long-term planning, strategic integration, commitment to employee development, and any consideration of what employees want; this is the so-called 'HRM with Chinese characteristics' (Warner 1996). While this kind of HRM is market and profit-oriented and contributes to the rapid development of the private economy, its myopic and profit-driven nature has become a source of tense employment relations and widespread labour disputes.

This study examines the levels of employees' satisfaction with HRM and the differences in satisfaction between employee groups in the private sector. The empirical evidence shows that the levels of employees of POEs were satisfied with HRM ranged from low to high. Employees were relatively more satisfied with performance appraisal, particularly appraisal criteria and appraisal execution, than other HRM policies and practices. Employees were moderately satisfied with contract-based employment relations, the two-way selection process and performance-based reward and compensation except for signing labour contracts and welfare and benefits. Employees were very dissatisfied with training provision and management development opportunities, and with the poor level of organizational support being offered for personal and management development.

These findings have revealed that during the past three decades the economic reforms have eroded Chinese employees' sense of having a truly socialist egalitarianism ideology. Chinese employees regard labour contracts and the two-way selection as giving them the freedom to choose jobs and employers. Rigorous performance appraisals, as long as they are fair and objective, are accepted because employees see performance appraisals and performance-based reward and compensation as important mechanisms that recognize their contribution and ability to receive equal and fair financial rewards. The Chinese marketization of the Chinese economy means that Chinese employees now realize that workers have become commodities and there is an urgent need to increase their marketability through training and development. This is particularly the case where enterprise bankruptcies take place on a regular basis resulting in massive lay-offs of employees who then rely on the vicissitudes of the labour market. Employees' low satisfaction with inadequate training and development reflects the progress of marketization of labour, as well as Chinese POEs' lack of commitment to corporate social responsibility, employee interests, in particular. Moreover, while workers have become accustomed to the abolition of life-long employment, they are upset about the demise of the 'cradle-to-grave' welfare system as evidenced by low satisfaction with declining welfare and benefits. However, this cannot be regarded as the lingering influence of socialist egalitarianism but the general concern that China's social security system remains underdeveloped and enterprises continue to provide inadequate superannuation contributions to their employees (Shen 2007).

Employees' satisfaction with the HRM reform varied significantly according to their own personal characteristics and experiences. A general conclusion can be drawn from this study that employees who were males, managers, middle-aged (between 40 and 50), had higher education and urban citizens scored the highest on satisfaction with the overall HRM system. One of the reasons for varied dissatisfaction is that some employees are more satisfied with HRM because they are treated better (e.g. given more training and promotion opportunities) than others. It is argued in the literature that managers often have privileges, while women and off-farmer migrants are often mistreated in any particular enterprise (Cooke 2005, Shen 2006, 2007, Zhu 2005). Another reason is that some employees sometimes do not realize that they are unfairly or unequally treated in employment relations due to their unprivileged status and lower expectations. This is evidenced by the fact revealed in this study that migrants were more satisfied than urban citizens with pay even though past studies, such as Shen (2007) reported that migrants are often underpaid.

Implications

The findings of this case study have significant implications for further research and practitioners. This research develops a better understanding of the effect of economic transition on HRM, and employees' responses to the changes to HRM systems in POEs. Its findings lend support to the past studies (e.g. Shen 2008, Warner 2005) arguing that HRM systems in POEs tend to be market-oriented and pragmatic, and employees with different demographic characteristics respond differently to the changes to HRM. An interesting finding this study has emerged that on one hand employees in POEs generally accepted the market-oriented HRM practices, such as labour contract, performance appraisal and market-based pay, indicating a strong support of the market-oriented economic reform in China, marketization on the other hand has mounted great pressure on employees. Such pressure was reflected in employees' strong desire to personal and management development in order to increase marketability. Employees became dissatisfied when they perceived a lack of training and development opportunities. However, Shen (2007) argues that a lack of training and development opportunity occasionally cause labour disputes, but is nowhere near a major cause of widespread labour disputes in comparison with pay and employment termination issues. The discrepant research findings indicate a lack of research into the effect of unsatisfied HRM practices on employee attitudes and behaviour in spite of extensive studies on the effect of 'good' HRM practices, such as ethical HRM, family-friendly HRM, high-performance HRM and high-involvement HRM. Hence, this research suggests an avenue for further research.

Developing a healthier private economy and preventing more labour disputes occurring in the private sector will depend to a great extent on better HR systems. This study identifies the improvement areas in HRM, specifically signing labour contracts, training and development and welfare and benefits. Given a lack of independent and strong employee organizations, enterprises should consider giving individual employees the right to negotiate labour terms, such as whether or not to sign a contract or at least discuss employment duration, working hours and pay. The new Labour Contract Law entitles workers and their organizations to have more bargaining power over labour terms. Chinese labour authorities should take measures to ensure that enterprises fully abide by this law.

More training and development opportunities should be provided to employees. Adequate provision of training and development opportunities are beneficial not only to employees for their increased marketability and their contribution being recognized but also to enterprises because employees will have more skills that can be used in qualified management teams. Employees have expressed the view that more support is needed with regard to promotion and career development, and performance appraisal should be used as a tool for such development, e.g. identifying improvement areas and training analysis. To make this possible feedback should be given and a mentoring programme ought to be put in place. Given the inadequacy of the state social welfare and social security system and the erosion of enterprise welfare and fringe benefits, enterprises should fulfill their obligation contribute to superannuation as this is crucial to maintaining the living standard of retired employees.

The improvement areas identified in this study resulted from a consideration of employee interests in employment relations, which are currently comparable with the significant progress made in efficiency-related practices such as rigorous performance appraisal and performance-based pay. It is argued that the poor management of employment relations has been the major cause of widespread labour disputes in China (Chan 1998, Shen 2007). If more socially responsible HRM policies and practices are adopted, Chinese POEs will then develop more harmonious employment relations, and consequently, achieve long-term sustainability. Moreover, enterprises should also consider different demands and needs of different employee groups in HRM policies and practices, for example, more work-life balance concerns for female employees with children, more attention paid to young employees' training and development needs. Furthermore, some vulnerable socio-economic groups like migrants, women and old workers, are currently experiencing disadvantages in employment relations. Therefore, equity in employment relations is an important and urgent issue that Chinese enterprise managers must resolve.

Conclusions

Although the existing literature recognizes that employees in different sectors expect and respond to the HRM reform differently and HRM in POEs in its current state is problematic, due to a lack of studies little is known about how employees in the private sector perceive the specific HRM policies and practices. As the private sector plays an increasingly more important role in the Chinese economy, it is important to understand employees' perceptions of HRM and how or whether it is being effectively managed and reformed. This study investigates the levels of employees' satisfaction with HRM and the differences in satisfaction between groups. It reveals new trend in Chinese employees' acceptance of and attitudes toward the HRM reform, indicating the diminishing influence of socialist egalitarianism ideology. This is evidenced by the general acceptance of modern HRM concepts, such as labour contracts and the two-way selection, need for training and development, performance appraisals, and performance-based reward and compensation. Currently, Chinese employees in POEs have a moderate to high level of satisfaction with all HRM policies and practices except for training and development. Also, the level of satisfaction with specific HRM policies and practices varies according to demographic variables. These findings have significant practical implications for developing more effective and harmonious employment relations in China's private economy.

References

Anderson, N. and Schalk, R., 1998. The psychological contract in retrospect and prospect. *Journal of organisational behaviour, special issue: the psychological contract at work,* 19, 649–664.

Bacon, N. and Hoque, K., 2005. HRM in the SME sector: valuable employees and coercive networks. *International journal of human resource management,* 16, 1976–1999.

Bagraim, J. and Sader, R., 2007. Family-friendly human resource practices and organizational commitment. *Management dynamics,* 16 (4), 2–10.

Becker, B.E. and Huselid, M.A., 1998. High performance work systems and firm performance: a synthesis of research and managerial implications. *In*: K.M. Rowland and G.R. Ferris, eds. *Research in personnel and human resources management,* 16. Greenwich, CT: JAI, 53–101.

Benkhoff, B., 1997. A test of the HRM model. Good for employers and employees. *Human resource management journal,* 7 (4), 44–60.

Benson, J., Debroux, P., Yuasa, M., and Zhu, Y., 2000. Flexibility and labour management: Chinese manufacturing enterprises in the 1990s. *International journal of human resource management,* 11 (2), 183–196.

Bonoma, T.V., 1985. Case research in marketing: opportunities, problems, and a process. *Journal of marketing,* 22 (2), 199–208.

Bowen, D.E. and Ostroff, C., 2004. Understanding HR-firm performance linkages – the role of the 'strength' of the HRM system. *Academy of management review,* 29 (2), 203–221.

Chan, A., 1998. Labor standards and human rights: the case of Chinese workers under market socialism. *Human rights quarterly,* 20 (4), 886–904.

Cheng, Y.Y., 2004. The development of labour disputes and the regulation of industrial relations in China. *The international journal of comparative labour law and industrial relations,* 20 (2), 277–295.

Child, J., 1994. *Management in China during the age of reform*. Cambridge: Cambridge University Press.

Child, J. and Tse, D.K., 2000. China's transition and its implications for international business. *Journal of international business studies*, 32 (1), 5–21.

China Statistical Yearbook, 2005. Beijing: China Statistics Press.

Chiu, W.C.K., 2002. Do types of economic ownership matter in getting employees to commit? An exploratory study in the People's Republic of China. *The international journal of human resource management*, 13 (6), 865–882.

Cooke, F.L., 2005. *HRM, work and employment in China*. London: Routledge.

De Cenzo, D.A. and Robbins, S.P., 2005. *Fundamentals of human resource management*. 8th ed. New York: John Wiley and Sons.

Delaney, J.T. and Huselid, M.A., 1996. The impact of human resource management practices on perceptions of organizational performance. *Academy of management journal*, 39 (4), 949–969.

Fiske, S.T. and Taylor, S.E., 1984. *Social cognition*. New York: McGraw-Hill.

Geringer, M.J., Frayne, C.A., and Milliman, J.F., 2002. In search of 'best practices' in international human resource management: research design and methodology. *Human resource management*, 41 (1), 5–30.

Goodall, K. and Warner, M., 1997. Human resources in sino-foreign joint ventures: selected case studies in Shanghai compared with Beijing. *The international journal of human resource management*, 8 (5), 569–593.

Guest, D. and Conway, N., 2000. *The psychological contract in the public sector*. London: CIPD.

Guzzo, R.A. and Noonan, K.A., 1994. Human resources practices as communications and the psychological contract. *Human resource management*, 33, 447–462.

Harney, B. and Dundon, T., 2006. Capturing complexity: developing an integrated approach to analysing HRM in SMEs. *Human resource management journal*, 16, 48–73.

Jiefeng Daily [Jiefeng Ribao], 2005. Private enterprises in Shanghai, 4 February. Available from: http://english.peopledaily.com.cn/200406/30/eng20040630_148056.html [Accessed 12 February 2009].

Kinnie, N., Purcell, J., Hutchinson, S., Terry, M., Collinson, M., and Scarbrough, H., 1999. Employment relations in SMEs: market-driven or customer-shaped? *Employee relations*, 21 (3), 218–235.

Kotey, B. and Slade, P., 2005. Formal human resource management practices in small growing firms. *Journal of small business management*, 43, 16–40.

Mayson, S. and Barrett, R., 2006. Human resource management in small firms: evidence from growing small firms in Australia. *In*: R. Heneman and J. Tansky, ed. *Human resource strategies for the high growth entrepreneurial firm, information age*. Greenwich, CT: Publishing Inc.

Millward, L. and Brewerton, P., 2000. Psychological contract: employment relations for the twenty-first century? *International review of industrial and organizational psychology*, 15, 1–62.

Mitsuhashi, H., Park, H.J., Wright, P.M., and Chua, R.S., 2000. 'Line and HR executives' perceptions of HR effectiveness in firms in the People's Republic of China. *International journal of human resource management*, 11 (2), 197–216.

Nolan, P., 2001. *China and the global business revolution*. Basingstoke: Palgrave.

Paauwe, J. and Dewe, P., 1995. Human resource management in multinational corporations: theories and models. *In*: A. Harzing and J. Ruysseveldt, eds. *International human resource management*. London: Sage Publication, 75–98.

Pan, P.P., 2003. China accelerates privatization, continuing shift from doctrine. *Washington Post*, 12 November, p. 713. Available from: http://globalpolicy.org/socecon/ffd/fdi/2003/1112china privatization.htm [Accessed 12 February 2009].

Pare, G. and Tremblay, M., 2007. The influence of high-involvement human resource management practices, procedural justice, organizational commitment, and citizen behaviour on information technology professionals' turnover intensions. *Group and organization management*, 32 (3), 326–357.

Nishii, L.H., Lepak, D., and Schneider, B., 2008. Employees' attributions of the 'why' of HR practices: their effects on employee attitudes and behaviours, and customer satisfaction. *Personnel psychology*, 61 (3), 503–545.

Rousseau, D.M., 1990. New hire perceptions of their own and their employer's obligations: a study of psychological contracts. *Journal of organisational behaviour*, 11 (5), 389–400.

Rousseau, D.M., 2001. Schema, promise and mutuality: the building blocks of the psychological contract. *Journal of occupational and organizational psychology*, 74, 511–541.

Rousseau, D.M. and Tijoriwala, S.A., 1998. Assessing psychological contracts: issues, alternatives and the types of measures. *Journal of organizational psychology*, 19, 675–679.

Sanders, K., Dorenbosch, L., and de Reuver, R., 2008. The impact of individual and shared employee perceptions of HRM on affective commitment – considering climate strength. *Personnel review*, 37 (4), 412–425.

Schuler, R.S., Dowling, P.J., and De Cieri, H., 1993. An integrative framework of strategic international human resource management. *Journal of management*, 19, 419–459.

Shen, J., 2005. Towards a generic IHRM model. *International journal of organisational transformation and social change*, 2 (2), 83–102.

Shen, J., 2007. *Labour disputes and their management in China*. Oxford: Chandos Publishing.

Shen, J., 2008. HRM in Chinese privatized enterprises. *Thunderbird international business review*, 50 (2), 91–104.

Shore, L.M. and Tetrick, L.E., 1994. The psychological contract as an explanatory framework in the employment relationship. *Trends in organizational behaviour*, 1, 91–109.

Stone, R.J., 1998. *Human resource management*. 5th ed. Auckland: John Wiley and Sons.

Warner, M., 1996. Economic reforms, industrial relations and human resources in the People's Republic of China: an overview. *Industrial relations journal*, 27 (3), 195–210.

Warner, M., 1997. Management–labour relations in the new Chinese economy. *Human resource management journal*, 7 (4), 30–43.

Warner, M., 2004. Human resource management in China revisited: introduction. *International journal of human resource management*, 15 (4/5), 617–634.

Wilkinson, A., 1999. Employment relations in SMEs. *Employee relations*, 21 (3), 206–217.

Zheng, C., Morrison, M., and O'Neill, G., 2006. An empirical study of high performance of HRM practices in Chinese SMEs. *International journal of human resource management*, 17 (10), 1772–1803.

Zhu, J.H., 2005. *Human resource management in China: past, current and future HR practices in the industrial sector*. London and New York: Routledge.

Zhu, J.H., Cooper, B., De Cieri, H., and Dowling, P., 2005. A problematic transition to a strategic role: human resource management in industrial enterprises in China. *International journal of human resource management*, 16 (4), 513–531.

Zhu, Y. and Warner, M., 2005. Changing Chinese employment relations since WTO accession. *Personnel review*, 34 (3), 354–369.

Corporate social responsibility and HRM in China: a study of textile and apparel enterprises

Fang Lee Cooke[a] and Qiaoling He[b]

[a]School of Management, RMIT University, 239 Bourke Street, Melbourne 3000, Australia;
[b]Manchester Business School, The University of Manchester, Manchester M15 6PB, UK

Issues related to corporate social responsibility (CSR) have been the subject of growing debate across an increasingly wide range of disciplines in social sciences and business and management studies. China has been facing mounting pressure to take CSR issues seriously especially vis a vis environmental issues and labour standards. However, issues related to CSR and human resource management (HRM) in China remain under-explored. This study investigates how managers of textile and apparel firms perceive CSR issues, what actions they are taking and what implications these may have for institutional bodies that seek to promote CSR in the country. The study concludes that firms tend to adopt a business case approach to CSR, focusing on the market rather than their employees.

Introduction

Issues related to corporate social responsibility (CSR) have been the subject of growing debate across an increasingly wide range of disciplines in social sciences and business and management studies. CSR has an expanding focus in both academic studies and business practices. China, a manufacturing-based economy that produces a large proportion of the world's products, has been facing mounting pressure to take CSR issues seriously, with particular reference to environmental issues and labour standards. However, issues related to CSR and human resource management (HRM) in China remain under-explored, and existing studies on the topic focus primarily on labour standards in the value chains (Chan 2001, Frenkel 2001, Chan and Ross 2003). While research interest on CSR has grown significantly in China (Wang 2005, Wang and Zhang 2005, Tang and Li 2008), few empirical studies have been undertaken to identify how companies, particularly those in the private sector, perceive CSR issues, what actions they are taking, if any, and what implications these may have for institutional bodies that seek to promote CSR in the country.

In order to address this research gap, this study investigates the current situation of CSR, of which HRM is an integral part, in China. We focus on the textile and apparel industry, which is highly export-oriented and cost-sensitive and where labour standards are often reported to be low. Through the survey and interviews with senior managers (all Chinese) in 31 textile and apparel enterprises, we explore the following issues: what is the level of understanding of CSR among managers in the Chinese textile and apparel enterprises? Who do they see as their important groups of stakeholders? What are the driving forces for them to engage in CSR? What do they think are the most important CSR issues for the firm and what practices do they adopt? To what extent does HRM feature as part of their CSR on the one hand and to what extent do they use HRM to achieve CSR outcomes on the other? What are the perceived barriers to adopting CSR practices in their companies? And what may help them improve and promote CSR practices?

Literature review

Theoretical perspectives of CSR

The study of CSR dates back to the 1950s and initially it focused primarily on philanthropy (see Carroll 1979, Garriga and Melé 2004 for more detailed reviews). Despite more than four decades of debate, there is still no consensus on what the concept of CSR really means (Carroll 1979, Bhattacharya and Sen 2004, Crowther and Capaldi 2008). Corporate responsibility, corporate citizenship, responsible business and corporate social opportunity are some of its variant terms. Carroll (1991, p. 42) argued that CSR is a multi-dimensional construct embracing four sets of responsibilities: economic, legal, ethical, and philanthropic. Through representing the four components of total CSR in a pyramid, Carroll (1991) proposed that each of these responsibilities should be fulfilled together and in parallel rather than within a sequence. According to Blowfield and Murray (2008), the different definitions of CSR share a common feature: the belief that companies have a responsibility for the public good – but they emphasize different elements of this.

Two schools of thoughts have been influential in the debate on corporate ethical and social responsibility: the efficiency theory and the social responsibility theory. The efficiency perspective, as represented by Milton Friedman, has a utilitarian and narrow focus on the shareholder value. According to Friedman,

> There is one and only one social responsibility of business – to use its resources and engage in activities designed to increase its profits so long as it stays within the rules of the game, which is to say, engages in open and free competition, without deception or fraud. (Friedman 1962, p. 133)

By contrast, the social responsibility theory, or the integrated-strategy perspective (Baron 2001), adopts a much broader focus that stresses the stakeholder value (Freeman 1984). It argues that corporations should take into account the interests of different stakeholders, such as employees, customers, suppliers, and communities when making business decisions. It follows that,

> Socially responsible companies not only try to be economically sustainable and profitable, but also endeavour to work with their employees, families, local communities and nation states to improve the quality of life in ways that are both ethical and sustainable in relation to society and the environment. (Cacioppe *et al.* 2008, p. 684)

Driving forces for CSR and business benefits

Firms' CSR efforts may be influenced by several driving forces in general, some of which are related. One is the rising awareness of ethical consumerism, particularly related to environmental issues, health concern, and human and animal rights. Another driving force comes from international and domestic pressure groups. As business competition intensifies globally and MNCs are under increasing pressure to reduce their costs on the one hand, they are, on the other hand, under growing demand to review their labour standards, sourcing strategy, environment policy and their wider role in the economic and social development in developing countries (Frenkel 2001, Chan and Ross 2003).

The business benefit of CSR is subject to much debate and controversy (Hillman and Keim 2001, Sen and Bhattacharya 2001, Zinkin 2004). Proponents argue that there is a strong business case for CSR in that adopting a proactive approach to CSR can help companies to avoid business risks, gain access to capital, attract and retain talented employees, develop new customer base, enhance customer loyalty and gain acceptance by the local communities. Indeed, a number of empirical studies have provided evidence to support these benefits claims, though sometimes conditioned by other factors (Hillman and Keim 2001, Roozen et al. 2001, Sen and Bhattacharya 2001, also see below for further discussion of CSR and HRM). For example, Baron (2001, p. 7) argued, based on his economic modeling, that CSR not only has 'a direct effect on the costs of the firm', but also has 'a strategic effect by altering the competitive positions of firms in an industry'.

It should be noted, however, that existing studies on the payoffs of improved social responsibility remain inconclusive. Sen and Bhattacharya's (2001) study, for example, found that CSR does not always influence consumers' purchasing behaviour in a positive way. Similarly, Hillman and Keim's (2001, p. 135) study showed that strategic stakeholder management will contribute to the financial performance of the firm whereas social issue participation does not. In addition, good corporate social performance only has a positive impact on job seekers with high levels of job choice and awareness of CSR issues, but no impact on those who have a limited job choice and are unaware or less concerned with CSR issues (Albinger and Freeman 2000).

A number of concerns have been raised by critics of CSR. Some see CSR as a distraction from the fundamental purpose of the business (Friedman 1962). Others question firms' motives for engaging in CSR, seeing it as a public relations exercise and an attempt to pre-empt interventions from governments and pressure groups (Rodriguez et al. 2006). Those who are concerned with companies sincerity in CSR argue that better regulation and enforcement at the national and international level, instead of voluntary measures, are necessary to ensure that MNCs behave in an ethical and socially responsible manner (Chan and Ross 2003).

The inter-relationship between CSR and HRM

The stakeholder approach to CSR is highly relevant to HRM. There are two aspects of CSR that are linked to the employees (see Figure 1). One is through HRM practices, the other is through the participation of employees in CSR activities. As employers, firms need to adopt socially responsible HR practices to fulfill a firm's social responsibility (fundamental obligation) and to attract and retain talent (competitive advantage). At the minimum level, firms need to observe labour standards and equal opportunity legislation to ensure demonstrable legal compliance. Beyond that, firms have the moral obligation (the social justice argument) to ensure the quality of their employees' working life, which includes job quality, work-life quality and personal wellbeing associated with work. This has a direct impact on the economic and social development of the country, particularly the less developed ones (Stiglitz 2002). Adopting socially responsible HRM practices not only fulfills firms' legal and social justice obligations, but also creates business benefits through ethical behaviour and enhanced HRM outcome.

The other aspect relates to CSR activities that firms adopt to demonstrate their commitment to, for example, environmental protection and the development of local

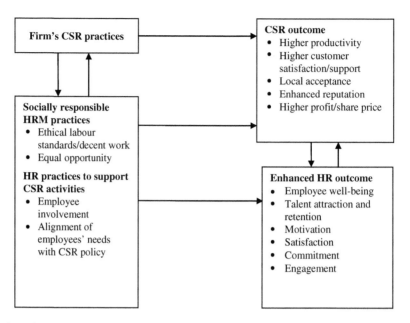

Figure 1.   The two-way relationship between CSR and HRM.

communities. These activities are not part of the HR policy but may have strong impact on HR outcomes, on the one hand, and may yield better result through employee involvement on the other (Cooke forthcoming). It is believed that CSR activities may help to attract, develop, retain and motivate employees who share similar values projected in these activities. This positive HR outcome will lead to enhanced organizational performance. Cacioppe *et al.*'s (2008, p. 681) study, for example, found that well-educated managers and professionals are likely to take into account 'the ethical and social responsibility reputations of companies when deciding whether to work for them, use their services or buy shares in their companies'. Roozen *et al.*'s (2001) study found that employees who work for firms that behave in an ethical way by taking into account the welfare of their stakeholders are more likely to accept and be committed to ethical behaviour and suppress their self-interest for the greater organizational and communal good.

Other studies have shown that socially responsible corporations may have a competitive advantage because they are more attractive to potential employees and therefore benefit from a larger talent pool of job candidates (Turban and Greening 1997, Albinger and Freeman 2000). They are also more likely to have a more committed workforce because employees will be proud to work for companies with favourable reputations through acting in socially and environmentally responsible ways (see Brammer *et al.* 2007). Similarly, CSR activities are found to be positively associated with job satisfaction (Brammer *et al.* 2007, Valentine and Fleischman 2008). Furthermore, CSR programmes introduced by firms may lead to 'the development of leadership skills and a high level of motivation among employees who are inspired to become involved in CSR programmes' (Cacioppe *et al.* 2008, p. 689).

However, despite the growing awareness of and commitment to CSR by firms, research evidence suggests that they are not engaging their employees sufficiently to get the full benefit of their investment. Bhattacharya *et al.*'s (2008) study, for instance, revealed that most companies in their study take a top-down approach to designing, implementing and managing CSR programmes. Few firms communicate systematically with their employees on the firm's CSR efforts. They rarely consider the needs and values of employees and how these can be fulfilled by developing CSR programmes to align the values of employees with the firm. Most firms do not have a clear understanding of the positive impact that CSR activities may have on employee productivity through enhanced organizational identification and commitment. It follows that better understanding of employees' needs and greater involvement of employees in CSR initiatives will help to improve the return on investment of CSR.

Indeed, tension may arise between CSR efforts and employees' perception, where the interests of the two are seen to diverge. For example, corporate donations of large sums of money to charity work may not be appreciated by employees who are low paid and work in harsh conditions. This altruistic act may be seen as hypocritical and may create the impression that the firm is treating outsiders better than its own employees, therefore de-motivating its staff. This calls for an approach that promotes employee involvement and participation in organizational decision-making. It also requires firms to take into consideration employees' interests when engaging in CSR activities (Cooke forthcoming).

CSR activities and standards

Building on a base of compliance with legislation and regulations, CSR typically includes commitments and activities beyond what are required by laws. A wide range of CSR activities are being practiced by companies, which vary considerably across countries and industries (European Commission 2005). These activities can be clustered into five main groups: workforce activities; environmental activities; marketplace activities (relations with suppliers and customers); community activities; and company leadership, vision and values; which are integrated with business operations in interaction with the stakeholders (European Commission 2005). More specifically, workplace CSR activities can affect many different areas of a company's human resources policy such as workplace health and safety, work-life balance, staff diversity, and career development (European Commission 2005). These five categories will be used to develop the conceptual framework for this study.

In addition, a number of CSR standards and guidelines exist to provide normative guidance for business. These can be divided into two main categories. The first category relates to the meaning of socially responsible by referring to governmental and inter-governmental standards. At the national level, this includes national and sub-national laws and regulations governing businesses. At the inter-governmental level, this includes an instrument such as the OECD Guidelines for Multinational Enterprises (ISO Advisory Group on Social Responsibility 2004, HKTDC 2005). The second category relates to private standards developed by non-governmental organizations (NGOs), such as SA8000 (Social Accountability 8000), ISO 9000 Quality Management Standard and ISO 14000 Environmental Management Standard (HKTDC 2005). ISO 9000 and ISO 14000 standards are two of the most widely recognized 'generic management systems standards', which were developed by the International Organisation for Standardization (ISO) (Gawel 2006, p. 15). In addition, MNCs have developed their own codes of conduct concerning their social and environmental activities around the world. At the same time, consumers and other NGOs have been promoting the development of standards and certification programmes (HKTDC 2005).

CSR in China

The implementation of CSR in China has been influenced by economic globalization and China' accession to WTO (Wang 2005). Despite the fact that the growing significance of China in the global economy is now widely acknowledged, the country has been heavily criticised on its environmental protection and labour rights fronts, as well as other political and social issues (Economy 2004, Ho and Vermeer 2006, Towers and Peng 2006, Lee 2007). Chinese manufacturers, as the main suppliers for MNCs around the world, are facing mounting pressure from global CSR campaigns (Wang 2005). China's poor reputation in labour standards creates risks for corporate brands and sales to ethically concerned markets (Buhrmann 2008). In addition, there is rising, albeit still moderate, internal pressure for Chinese enterprises to address CSR issues. Under international and domestic pressure, the Chinese government has a growing interest in engaging companies in social and environmental activities to contribute to China's sustainable development. It places greater emphasis, at least in principle, on safeguarding the legal rights and interests of citizens. A number of labour laws and regulations, including the Labour Contract Law, Trade Union Law, Production Safety Law and Regulations on Enterprise Minimum Wage, for example, all contain CSR elements and requirements (CNTAC 2006). However, China is still in the initial stage of developing a standardized, systematic and widely participated CSR social movement (Wang 2005, Zhou 2006).

China's reception of CSR has so far been an incremental process. The CSR movement was introduced into China in the mid 1990s, when MNCs started to impose supplier codes of conduct on the Chinese textiles and garment factories and began auditing them under pressure from anti-sweatshop activities abroad (Chan and Ross 2003). Accordingly, Chinese enterprises reluctantly accepted some of these foreign CSR requirements. CSR was still a new concept then to many Chinese and public debates on CSR were limited (Zhou 2006).

Since the 2000s, the CSR concept has attracted growing attention and debate. Government departments began to take an interest in the development of CSR among companies. The Ministry of Labour, the Ministry of Commerce and the Chinese Enterprise Confederation (CEC) have all set up CSR investigation committees to study the development of CSR in China (Zhou 2006). Two influential forums were held – the China-EU Conference on CSR held in Beijing in September 2005 and the 'Global Compact China Summit' held in Shanghai in November 2005 (CNTAC 2006, p. 7). Developing CSR is promoted by the Chinese government as an effective tool to build a harmonious society and to achieve sustainable development. Meanwhile, Chinese academic institutions, international organizations and NGOs are making more efforts to explore and promote the concept of CSR.

Existing studies show that the conceptualization and configuration of CSR in Chinese firms may be diverse and externally focused. The analysis of 30 of the Top-50 Chinese Private Enterprises of 2004 by Cooke (2008a), for example, revealed that only 11 of the top 30 firms reported having adopted CSR activities, although this does not necessarily mean that those who have not reported these activities do not demonstrate CSR. CSR activities reported by the 11 firms include: sponsoring social events, organising employees to take part in charity work, donations to education, environmental protection actions, providing jobs to disabled workers and laid-off workers, and supporting the development of the Western Region of China. These CSR activities were often described by these firms as gestures 'to reciprocate the society', although other intentions might include corporate image and reputation building.

Hill and Knowlton's (2004) survey study shows that western CEOs adopt a broader and more complex approach to CSR than the Chinese CEOs. Human rights and environmental issues, employer branding, identification of national and local culture, and community projects may all be part of western firms' CSR concerns. By contrast, firms in developing countries, including China, tend to focus on employment creation, charitable actions, and the influence in local communities as the key indicators of their CSR achievements.

CSR standards for the Chinese textile and apparel industry

As one of the most traditional industries in China and the largest supplier to the world market (Towers and Peng 2006), the Chinese textile and apparel industry is experiencing substantial pressure to address their CSR problems, especially how to incorporate labour-related and environmental standards into its core business operations (ILO-Beijing 2008). A number of guidelines have been promoted by the government and associations of the industry. These include, for example, the 'Development Guidelines for the Textile Industry in the 11th Five-year Plan Period (2006–2010)' by the government, and the CSC9000T (China Social Compliance 9000 for Textile and Apparel Industry) management system introduced by the China National Textile and Apparel Council (CNTAC) in 2005. The CSC9000T is the first local socially responsible auditing standard for the textile industry in China (Ho 2005). It is an adaptation of ISO 9000 and SA8000, and draws on Chinese laws and regulations, international conventions, as well as taking into account Chinese characteristics (CNTAC 2006, Buhrmann 2008). CSC9000T consists of 10 elements, including 'the management system, employment contracts, child labour, forced or compulsory labour, working hours, wages and welfare, discrimination, trade unions and collective bargaining, harassment and abuse, and health and safety concerns' (CNTAC 2006). The focus of CSC9000T is labour standards, which is an important part of CSR.

The effective adoption of CSR requires a good regulatory institutional environment and a strong moral and ethical commitment from the business community. The ineffective enforcement of laws and regulations in China has been widely observed (Warner 1996, Potter 1999, Taylor *et al.* 2003, Cooney 2007). The business model of textile and apparel industry in China is typically based on the short-term relationship between buyers and suppliers. Short-term gains are often the focus of firms due to fierce competition and increasing pressure on price and quality (Lai 2006). It is reported that a large proportion of CSR practices in China are implemented under the pressure of MNCs which impose supplier codes of conduct to their Chinese partners and audit them (Lai 2006, Towers and Peng 2006). Firms that implement CSR to satisfy their MNC customers may risk losing out to their counterparts who do not implement CSR with the resultant cost advantage (Lai 2006). In addition, as manufacturing suppliers, Chinese companies are said to be confused and discouraged by the diverse codes of conduct among MNCs and the absence of a universal set of CSR standards (Lai 2006). They are sceptical about the business benefits of CSR and see CSR-related accreditation (such as SA8000) as a financial burden and a trade barrier (Lai 2006). Apart from regulations and industrial policy guidelines, there is little economic incentive to encourage domestic companies to implement CSR (Lai 2006).

Research methods

Primary data for this study were collected by both quantitative (survey) and qualitative (semi-structured interviews) methods. Survey data came from 20 companies and interview data came from managers from 11 companies in the textile and apparel industry, all based in Guangdong province in southern China. This empirical data is complemented by secondary data such as company reports and websites of government and professional bodies. The focus was to investigate CSR practices in Chinese textile and apparel enterprises in order to address the research questions identified in the Introduction. A questionnaire on CSR was designed in English and then translated into Chinese. The questionnaire was designed to have the majority of questions in closed questions and scale questions format, in addition to a small number of open-ended questions. Based on the above literature review and the conceptual framework, a questionnaire was developed which consisted of five parts, including personal information of respondent, company profile, company's perception of CSR, company's CSR practices and implications of CSR. Five-point Likert scales were used for some of the questions (1 = 'strongly disagree'; 5 = 'strongly agree') or (1 = 'least important'; 5 = 'most important'). In designing the questionnaire, we included the company's philosophical position of CSR (using the four categories developed by Carroll 1991), driving forces/perceived business benefits for adopting CSR, contents of CSR practices (using the five categories developed by the EC 2005 and other CSR-related standards such as ISO 9000), perceived barriers to implementing CSR, and measures that may facilitate the adoption of CSR.

The questionnaire and a covering letter introducing the research objectives and a statement of guaranteed anonymity were then sent to a list of selected companies by email to invite one manager to fill in. Only one manager, such as owner, CEO, general manager, public relations, marketing or human resources manager, was targeted in each firm. Managers were targeted because they were more likely to be more informed than ordinary workers on the issues we are investigating.

In order to target sample companies, some of the well-known web pages of organisations relating to Chinese textile and apparel industry and enterprises were visited by one of the authors. These include, for example, The Responsible Supply Chain Association (http://www.csc9000.org.cn/en/), China National Garment Association (http://www.cnga.org.cn/index.asp), Sonhoo Fashion (http://fashion.sonhoo.com/), and hljfz (http://www.hljfz.cn). About 60 Chinese textile and apparel enterprises were identified. The web pages of these 60 companies were studied carefully for CSR information and corresponding CSR reports. Since the objective of this study was to investigate CSR in Chinese textile and apparel enterprises, 50 companies with this kind of information and documents were selected and contacted. After two rounds of emailing (initial contact and a reminder email), 20 responses (all valid) were received, giving a response rate of 40%. These sample companies represent those that have publicised CSR policies and claim to have CSR practices in place. They tend to be larger firms and therefore perhaps have more formal policies and resources. Due to resource constraints and difficulty in gaining access, we were not able to conduct interviews with the managers surveyed or other managers in the sample companies in order to obtain more indepth information. However, the quantitative data does provide a snapshot on the perception and configuration of CSR practices in these sample firms.

In addition, the CEO or deputy general manager (referred to hereafter as managers, for brevity) of 11 privately owned textile and apparel enterprises were interviewed in 2008 by the first author. These managers are all owners/co-owners of the enterprise they are managing. The educational background of these owner managers were relatively low, none of them have attended university. The youngest firm was four years old and the oldest one had 16 years of history at the time of the interview. They are relatively small firms, employing between 130–600 employees. Only six firms have a company website which contains only basic company and product information. Access to these firms was gained through personal contact. This personal relationship enhanced the willingness of the informants to disclose company information and share their honest opinions with the interviewer.

We targeted small private firms because they make up a relatively large proportion of economy in China, particularly in the manufacturing sector in southern China (Garnaut and Huang 2001, China Statistical Yearbook 2007, Cooke 2008b). These interviews provide more indepth information than that found in the survey of larger firms. They reveal some of the practices adopted and problems encountered, by smaller firms, which may or may not be shared by larger firms. This qualitative method is highly relevant to the study of the textile and apparel industry. As Towers and Chen (2008, p. 628) observed, interest in gaining a better understanding of the global fashion textiles sector has led to 'the use of inductive qualitative methodologies to broaden the knowledge base'.

Questions asked in the interviews covered similar issues to those in the survey. However, an attempt to carry out the same survey on the owner managers interviewed for methodological triangulation had to be abandoned because the majority of them preferred to talk about what they do rather than having to fill in forms, and they failed to see the need to do both. Since the interviews were conducted after the survey and its subsequent analysis, as far as possible issues identified in the survey were explored in the interviews. An important limitation of these two small sets of data collected with different methods is that we are not able to establish the extent to which information found in one sample is generalizable to the other. Nevertheless, this exploratory study may serve as a useful pilot study on which future research of a larger scale can build.

Table 1. Demographic details of respondents (N = 20).

Demographic variable	Number	Percentage (%)
Level of job position		
Upper management	10	50
Middle management	6	30
Lower management	4	20
Number of years in current position		
Less than 3 years	2	10
3–6 years	4	20
6–10 years	8	40
10 years or more	6	30
Gender		
Male	16	80
Female	4	20
Age		
20–29	3	15
30–39	9	45
40–49	6	30
50 and above	2	10

Table 2. Respondent company demographics (N = 20).

Demographic variable	Number	Percentage (%)
Age of the company		
Less than 10 years	3	15
10–20 years	11	55
20–30 years	3	15
More than 30 years	3	15
Number of employees		
100–499	3	15
500–999	10	50
1000 or more	7	35
Company ownership		
State-owned enterprises	3	15
Private enterprises	9	45
Sino-foreign joint ventures	3	15
Collectively-owned enterprises	5	25

Findings and analysis

Respondent demographics

The majority of respondents hold upper (50%) or middle (30%) management positions (see Table 1). Most of the respondents have been in their current position for six years or more. Most of the respondents are male. Respondents are relatively young, with 60% of them below 40 years of age.

Surveyed company demographics

Some 85% of the companies have been established for at least 10 years, some much longer (see Table 2). The majority of the companies are medium to large enterprises by the industry's standard. More specifically, 85% of the firms employ 500 employees or more. The ownership forms of the surveyed firms spread across four types: state-owned enterprises (SOEs), privately owned enterprises (POEs), Sino-foreign joint ventures (JVs), collectively owned enterprises (COEs) and others. POEs form the largest category amongst the surveyed firms.

Perception of CSR

Table 3 shows that the majority of respondents have some knowledge about what CSR is, although half of them understand only a little and 10% have heard of but do not understand the term. These results indicate that there is an awareness of CSR in the majority of the surveyed firms, although it must be noted that only those firms that have CSR statements on the company websites were targeted for the survey. Thus, this level of CSR awareness may not be representative of that of the whole industry and, more broadly, the whole country.

Relatedly, 70% of respondents believed that their company has a CSR policy, even though all the companies' websites contained CSR statements. Nearly two-thirds of the companies are 'quite concerned' or 'extremely concerned' with CSR issues. Respondents were asked how they would define CSR in their companies by choosing three of the most applicable factors: ethical conduct in activities, complying with existing regulations,

Table 3.   Descriptive analysis of perception of CSR (part 1) (N = 20).

Questions and answers	Number	Percentage (%)
Have you heard about CSR?		
No, never heard of	0	0
Yes, I heard of but don't understand	2	10
Yes, I heard of and understand a little	10	50
Yes, I heard of and understand fairly clearly	8	40
Does your company have a CSR policy?		
Yes	14	70
No	6	30
How much is your company concerned about CSR?		
Extremely concerned	5	25
Quite concerned	8	40
Neutral	6	30
Not very concerned	1	5
Extremely unconcerned	0	0
How do you define CSR in your company? (choose three most important answers)		
Ethical conduct in activities	12	60
Complying with existing regulations	15	75
Transparency in operations	6	30
Making profits	9	45
Environmentally friendly activities	6	30
Commitment to employees	9	45
Commitment to the public, communities, and overall society	3	15
Does your company have a specific department devoted to CSR issues?		
Yes	8	40
No	12	60
Which of the following standards have been passed by your company? (multiple-choice)		
SA8000	5	25
ISO 14000	4	20
ISO 9000	9	45
CSC9000T	5	25
None	2	10

making profits, transparency in operations, environmentally friendly activities, commitment to employees, commitment to the public, communities and overall society, and others. Compliance with regulations (75%) and carrying out an ethical conduct in activities (60%) appear to be the top two concerns. Making profits and commitment to employees appear to share the same level of attention by the companies (45%). In comparison, transparency in operations and environmentally friendly activities are lower down the company's priorities (30%). Commitment to the public, communities and overall society features the lowest (15%).

The majority (60%) of the respondent companies have not established a specific department responsible for CSR issues. However, these respondents explained that their companies have designated specialist personnel or departments for managing CSR affairs, such as the Public Relations Department, Marketing Department, Human Resource Department and Administrative Department. This implies that CSR issues are often seen as public relations, marketing or administrative functions by the sample companies.

Only a small number of firms have obtained standards that contain CSR requirements, such as ISO 9000, ISO 14000, CSC9000T or SA8000. While these standards are not mutually exclusive, few firms obtained two or more of these accreditations. Among those that have accreditations, quality assurance seems to be the major concern instead of labour standards. This is indicated by the small number of accreditations on CSC9000T and SA8000, which focus on labour standards, in contrast to the number of accreditations obtained on ISO 9000, a quality kite mark that has been popular among Chinese firms in the last two decades (see Cooke 2008b). This finding suggests that the uptake of CSR standards by Chinese textile and apparel enterprises are still limited. It is also important to note that the larger sample companies are more likely to have obtained CSR standards than the smaller ones.

With regard to the important aspect of social responsibility of business, the majority of respondents believed that legal responsibility and economic responsibility are more important than ethical responsibility and philanthropic responsibility (see Table 4). Shareholders and owners (mean = 4.15; SD = 1.13) and employees (mean = 3.90;

Table 4.   Descriptive analysis of perception of CSR (part 2) (N = 20).

Variables	Mean	SD
Important aspect of social responsibility of business		
a) Economic responsibility	4.15	1.14
b) Legal responsibility	4.25	1.16
c) Ethical responsibility	3.75	1.41
d) Philanthropic responsibility	3.40	1.43
The company's stakeholder groups		
a) Shareholders and owners	4.15	1.13
b) Employees	3.90	1.21
c) Marketplace stakeholders (customers, suppliers, etc.)	3.15	1.27
d) Governmental and other pressure groups (trade unions, local communities, the press and media)	2.80	1.24
Factors motivate your company to engage in CSR		
a) Personal interest of CEO/Managing Director	2.80	1.54
b) Giving back to society	3.25	1.52
c) For reputation purposes	4.15	1.14
d) Part of business strategy	3.45	1.32
e) Gain competitive advantage	3.90	1.12
f) Help to recruit and retain employees	3.45	1.36
g) Important to customer satisfaction	4.10	1.12
h) Expected by community	2.85	1.39
i) Help to manage regulatory pressures	3.05	1.57
Factors determine decisions on the CSR activities that a company can incorporate		
a) Type of industry	3.70	1.30
b) Company size	3.85	1.23
c) Financial performance of company	4.05	1.15
d) Products	3.40	1.47
e) Suppliers	2.95	1.47
f) Location	3.00	1.49

SD = 1.21) are seen as the two most important groups of stakeholders, compared with the other two groups of stakeholders: marketplace stakeholders (mean = 3.15; SD = 1.27) and governmental and other pressure groups such as trade unions, local communities, the press and media (mean = 2.8; SD = 1.24). This suggests that external bodies, official and unofficial, may have little influence on firms' CSR agenda in China. It is interesting to note that all SOEs strongly agree or agree that the government is the most important stakeholder, which is essentially the shareholder of the SOEs.

Nevertheless, firms' engagement in CSR activities is primarily motivated by the desire to have a better reputation (mean = 4.15; SD = 1.14), improve customer satisfaction (mean = 4.10; SD = 1.11), gain competitive advantage (mean = 3.90; SD = 1.11), and help recruit and retain employees (mean = 3.45; SD = 1.36). It is interesting to note that all large companies strongly agree or agree that they engage in CSR because of the personal interest of CEO/Managing Director and the desire to reciprocate the society, and as part of their business strategy. By contrast, the majority of small- and medium-sized companies implement CSR in response to regulatory pressures and to gain a better reputation. Consistent with the findings on the importance of stakeholders above, reciprocating the society (philanthropic) appears to be less of a concern of the firms in their CSR decisions. It also indicates that large firms may be more strategic in their CSR than smaller ones and that the CEO's attitude and support is a strong source of influence on firms' CSR agenda.

In addition, the data indicates that financial performance of the firm, company size and type of industry are the most important factors that determine the kind of CSR activities to be implemented (see Table 4). Revealingly, suppliers do not appear to have influence on firms' CSR activities.

CSR practices – employee activities

In terms of the HRM aspect of the CSR practices (see Table 5), the majority of respondent companies reported that they 'have a process to ensure adequate steps are taken against all forms of discrimination, both in the workplace and at the time of recruitment' (mean = 3.80; SD = 1.28), and 'provide constant training to employees' (mean = 3.55; SD = 1.36). However, companies appear to be doing less well on 'consulting with employees on important issues' (mean = 3.20; SD = 1.44) and on 'actively offering a good work-life balance to employees' (mean = 3.05; SD = 1.36). Perhaps the most revealing finding is that firms surveyed do poorly, in general, on the HR

Table 5. Descriptive analysis of employee activities (N = 20).

Variables	Mean	SD
Employee activities		
Have a process to ensure adequate steps are taken against all forms of discrimination, both in the workplace and at the time of recruitment	3.80	1.28
Consult with employees on important issues	3.20	1.44
Actively offer a good work-life balance to employees	3.05	1.36
Provide constant trainings to employees	3.55	1.36
Provide procedures that help to ensure the health and safety of employees	2.80	1.24
Pay staff salaries properly and timely	2.75	1.45
Never use child labour	2.60	1.47
Employees are not forced to work overtime	2.65	1.53

Table 6. Descriptive analysis of environmental activities (N = 20).

Variables	Mean	SD
Environmental activities		
Minimize the environmental impact of all your company's activities in terms of:		
a) energy conservation	3.75	1.29
b) waste minimization and recycling	3.40	1.47
c) pollution prevention	3.55	1.36
d) protection of the natural environment	3.05	1.57
Consider the potential environmental impacts when developing new products and services	3.10	1.37
Supply clear and accurate environmental information on its products, services and activities to customers, suppliers, local community, etc.	4.00	1.12
Incorporate environmental concerns in your business decisions	2.85	1.46
Financially support environmental initiatives	3.20	1.40
Measure your company's environmental performance	3.10	1.37

aspects that are most relevant to the labour standards, notably health and safety, wage payment, use of child labour and overtime work. This finding is ironic in view of the fact that managers surveyed claimed that employees are one of the two most important groups of stakeholders.

CSR practices – environmental activities

The majority of companies seem to make efforts on environmental protection, such as energy conservation and pollution and waste control (see Table 6). However, they are much less concerned with the potential environmental impacts when developing new products and services. In addition, it is worth noting that SOEs engage in environmental activities and projects more than private companies. Smaller companies seem to be less active than larger ones in these activities.

CSR practices – marketplace activities

According to Table 7, the companies surveyed appear to take into account the interests of customers and suppliers in their business activities. However, they are relatively poor in

Table 7. Descriptive analysis of marketplace activities (N = 20).

Variables	Mean	SD
Marketplace activities		
Have a policy to ensure honesty and quality in all company's contracts, dealings and advertizing	3.65	1.31
Provide all customers with clear and accurate information needed to make sound purchasing decisions	3.80	1.28
Satisfy the complaints of customers about products and services	3.40	1.47
Treat suppliers, regardless of their size and location, fairly and respectfully	3.90	1.21
Have a process to ensure effective feedback, consultation and/or dialogue with customers, suppliers and the other people you do business with	3.00	1.49
Work together with other companies or other organizations to implement CSR	2.75	1.48

Table 8.   Descriptive analysis of community activities (N = 20).

Variables	Mean	SD
Community activities		
Offer training opportunities to people from the local community	2.80	1.24
Try to purchase locally	4.00	1.12
Employees are encouraged to participate in local community activities	2.90	1.48
Give financial support to local community activities and projects in the aspect of:		
a) Education	3.40	1.47
b) Disaster relief	3.65	1.31
c) Charity	3.00	1.49
d) Sports, art, culture	2.80	1.51
e) Healthcare support and sponsorship	2.70	1.49
Stimulate the economic development in the communities where the company operate	3.80	1.28

establishing a communication and consultation relationship with their external stakeholders and working with them to share experience and information related to CSR.

CSR practices – community activities

Companies surveyed demonstrate their commitment to the local community mainly through three aspects: purchasing locally, stimulating the economic development in the communities where the company operate, and donations for education and disaster relief (see Table 8). However, purchasing locally and stimulating the economic development in the local communities may be strongly associated with the company's business interest (financial cost and development of new customer bases), whereas donations for education and disaster relief are two of the most conventional philanthropic gestures in China (Cooke 2008a). These charitable acts are largely *ad hoc* and are sometimes carried out due to peer pressure or implicit requirements from the local government (also see interview findings below).

What the surveyed companies fall short of doing is to demonstrate a clear longer-term financial commitment to supporting the local communities by providing training opportunities to people from the local community, encouraging employees to participate in local community activities, or sponsoring healthcare and sports, arts and cultural activities.

Table 9.   Descriptive analysis of company values and rules of conduct (N = 20).

Variables	Mean	SD
Company values and rules of conduct		
Have clearly defined values and rules of conduct	3.50	1.40
Communicate your company's values to customers, business partners, suppliers and other interested parties (in sales presentations, marketing material or informal communication)	3.35	1.42
Your customers are aware of your company's values and rules of conduct	2.80	1.24
Your company trains employees on the importance of its values and rules of conduct	3.75	1.29
Your company has written standards of CSR	2.85	1.46
Your company produces quarterly or annual reports including social responsibility contents	2.75	1.48

Table 10. Descriptive analysis of each type of CSR practices (N = 20).

Variables	Mean	SD
Employee activities	3.05	1.39
Environmental activities	3.33	1.38
Marketplace activities	3.42	1.37
Community activities	3.23	1.38
Company values and rules of conduct	3.17	1.38

CSR practices – company values and rules of conduct

The majority of companies surveyed reported that they have clearly defined values and rules of conduct, and educate their employees on the importance of them (see Table 9). However, written standards of CSR and inclusion of CSR information in company reports are still not universal practices. This finding is perhaps not surprising, given the fact that corporate social reporting remains a patchy and inconsistent practice worldwide (Vuontisjärvi 2006) and in the lack of a tradition of Chinese businesses revealing company information (Luo 2006).

Comparison of performances of each type of CSR practices

Drawing the five CSR activity areas together, we can see that companies are not passionately active in their engagement of CSR activities (see Table 10). In comparison, they are more active in marketplace activities and environmental activities but are the least oriented in employee activities. This finding is in line with that by Bhattacharya et al. (2008) that firms are not engaging their employees sufficiently in their CSR activities. It also shows that HRM is not seen as an important part of their CSR in comparison with other aspects of the CSR activities.

Barriers to adopting CSR practices

According to the respondents, the biggest barrier to the broader adoption of CSR practices appears to be associated with costs and the lack of tangible results, particularly financial return (see Table 11). The absence of CSR regulation and government involvement further serve as disincentives for firms to take CSR issues seriously.

Table 11. Descriptive analysis of barriers to adopting CSR practices (N = 20).

Barriers to adopting CSR practices	Mean	SD
No appropriate regulation	4.20	1.11
Lack of government involvement	3.80	1.28
Lack of visible results	4.00	1.12
No appropriate institutions	3.65	1.31
Overall cost	4.30	1.13
Focus on short-term gains	3.90	1.21
Lack of link to financial success	4.05	1.10
Lack of staff incentives	3.40	1.47
Employees resistance	3.00	1.49
Management resistance	3.50	1.40

Table 12.   Descriptive analysis of actions that improve CSR practices (N = 20).

Actions that can improve CSR practices	Mean	SD
Establish and enforce a suitable social responsibility system	4.00	1.12
Issue appropriate laws and regulations related to CSR	4.30	1.13
Strengthen institutions related to detecting, reporting and auditing CSR	4.20	1.11
Offer incentives and rewards for implementing CSR	4.50	1.15
Government involvement and interventions	4.35	1.13
Recognition by stakeholders	3.80	1.18
Increase involvement of the public	3.30	1.45
Effective dialogue with all stakeholder groups	3.65	1.31
Incorporate CSR into corporate culture and business strategy	3.90	1.21
Get employees involved	3.75	1.30
Encourage firms to participate in CSR forums, workshops, etc.	3.10	1.56
Government and NGOs provide CSR training and consulting services	3.50	1.40

Driving forces for improving CSR practices

Respondents were asked what kind of actions would assist them in improving their CSR practices. The majority of them believe that the most effective incentives and actions for the improvement and growth of CSR practices would be the positive attitude of the government towards socially responsible companies, displayed through a system of incentives and rewards for firms' implementation of CSR initiatives (see Table 12). In addition, government involvement and institutional interventions, as well as appropriate laws and regulations are seen as important driving forces. Public involvement, CSR forums and workshops, and training and consultancy services provided by government bodies and NGOs are seen as the least effective actions to stimulate firms' enthusiasm in CSR. The role of government intervention in achieving CSR performance is also identified in the interviews. We will now turn to this set of data.

Interview findings

None of the 11 firms has a stated CSR policy. In fact, many of them do not even have a written HR policy. Whilst all managers interviewed have heard of the term CSR, most of them have only a basic understanding of what it means to the firm – in their words, 'to be responsible to the society'. How this responsibility is translated into company practices is much less well articulated. Environmental protection and charitable actions are the two main manifestations named by the informants as CSR actions. Five of the 11 firms have donated money to the local schools and nine have donated money or materials as relief for the Sichuan earthquake victims (the earthquake occurred in May 2008).

Interview information appears to be in line with that from the survey in general but more so with that from the smaller private firms (Cooke 2008c). In addition, interesting information was revealed which was not captured in the survey. For example, four of the five firms that have donated money to the local schools admitted doing so because their children or grandchildren were studying there and they were 'invited' by the school to give financial support. In most cases, a moderate amount was donated on an irregular basis 'in order to keep the school happy'. Managers also revealed that they were contacted by local government officials to give donations to support earthquake victims.

No firms reported having any formal discussion on CSR issues with their suppliers, customers or employees. Few of them reported receiving pressure from their supplier or customer firms on CSR issues as a condition for awarding business contracts. When asked if they would be more engaged in CSR issues in the near future, 'probably not' was the common answer because of 'no time', 'no financial resource' and 'no clear benefit'. Three of the managers even claimed that 'CSR matter is for large companies and does not apply to small businesses like ours'. However, managers generally agreed that they would do more on CSR if the government were to make specific requirements for them to do so.

Most managers admitted that the health and safety environment of the factory 'could be improved' and that overtime working is quite common when they have to rush the orders through. Seven companies did not sign employment contracts with their production workers and only two firms had bought partial social security benefits for their workers, as stipulated in the employment laws. No firms have engaged their employees consciously on CSR activities because 'we are all too busy with production work'. However, one owner CEO of a textile dye works (the largest firm amongst the 11 companies) did reveal how he used efficiency gain-sharing with his workers to reduce energy consumption and waste discharge. Here is his story:

> The company employs about 600 people who are mainly migrant workers from rural China. Education level is generally low among these workers and earning a reasonable wage to support the family is their main concern. Due to the nature of the business, the cost of energy and waste (waste water and exhaust) discharge has been high each month. In recent years, environmental protection has ascended in the government's agenda. We were being fined by the local government for excessive waste discharge. The company had initially taken different measures in an attempt to reduce the cost. These included educating the workers and imposing energy consumption quotas on production departments. But the result had been negligible. In 2006, the company decided to introduce the 'efficiency gains-sharing scheme'. Each month, a certain percentage of the company's financial gain from energy saving and reduced waste discharge is shared by its employees as bonus. A small amount of additional fund is allocated to the subsidized staff canteen to improve the menu. In addition, a small amount of capital fund will also be allocated from the efficiency gain to improve the working environment in the factory. This scheme was well received by employees and considerable saving has been made by the company through reduced cost of energy and waste treatment. We are not fined by the local government any more.

Discussion and conclusions

This study has revealed views of senior managers in 31 Chinese textile and apparel enterprises in southern China on issues related to CSR and CSR practices adopted by their company. Our findings suggest that the Chinese textile and apparel firms are beginning to realize the importance of adopting CSR. This is in spite of the fact that many of the enterprises do not have a written CSR policy and that the majority of enterprises have not obtained CSR standards. The main reasons for firms to implement CSR practices are to enhance their reputation, improve customer satisfaction and reduce operating cost. In other words, a business case approach is adopted. In addition, companies believe that legal and economic responsibilities are more important than ethical and voluntary responsibilities. This implies that legal compliance remains the main source of pressure for adopting CSR activities and that a firm's public statement of their commitment to CSR may be little more than lip service. Firms are also more likely to respond to pressure from the government. For example, firms' philanthropic gestures may be responses to pressure covertly exerted by local government officials.

In deciding the types of CSR activities to adopt, the firms studied revealed an external focus on marketplace activities. While firms recognize employees as being one of the stakeholders, they pay less attention to labour standards issues, especially health and safety provisions, social security contribution, anti-child labour, wage payment and overtime work, than on other aspects of the CSR. They also score badly on other HR issues such as employee involvement in decision-making and work-life balance. There is little evidence of strategic involvement of employees in delivering the firm's CSR activities. In the few cases where employee involvement takes place, financial incentive, rather than moral education, appears to be a more effective motivator for employees to help the company achieve its environment protection target. Nevertheless, it provides evidence that effective employee involvement schemes do have a positive impact on CSR outcomes.

The findings of this study suggest that external bodies and value chains are not the main drivers for firms' CSR activities in China. The majority of companies have not yet developed a working relationship with other companies to share experience and information related to CSR. They have not received sufficient pressure in the value chain to engage in CSR activities. Nor have they become a source of pressure for other firms in the value chain to do the same. This is in line with that of other studies (Frenkel 2001), which highlight the difficulty of international pressure groups and MNCs to exert pressure on Chinese sub-contracting/supplier firms to adopt labour standards as part of their CSR. This is perhaps partly due to the fact that there are few influential CSR organizations in China (Peng *et al.* 2005).

Based on this evidence, we suggest that pressure, both internal and external, for Chinese firms to assume CSR is limited. Without tangible benefits, as well as effective punitive measure for non-compliance, firms are unlikely to demonstrate a high level of interest in engagement with CSR. This has serious implications for the mechanisms to be deployed in promoting CSR in China. Currently, a voluntary approach is adopted, with forums and training workshops provided by government-related bodies and NGOs being the main methods of educating firms and managers. These prove to have limited impact on managers. By contrast, legal mechanism, when effectively enforced, may be a more effective approach to ensure firms become more conscientious in their social responsibility. This can be coupled with an effective system for monitoring and auditing companies CSR behaviour and activities. Incentives, such as subsidized interest rates, and sustainable tax exemptions for a period may also be introduced (Peng *et al.* 2005).

Studies of CSR in Chinese firms remain limited, many focused on the labour standards in export-oriented manufacturing firms (Chan 2001, Frenkel 2001, Pun and Smith 2007). This study contributes to our existing understanding on CSR and HRM in the textile and apparel industry in China. It covers a relatively wide range of aspects of CSR at firm level, including motives, practices and, importantly, the level of involvement of employees. In other words, it not only investigated HRM as part of the CSR activities, but also explored the role of HRM in achieving CSR results. This two-way relationship has received little research attention so far (Cooke forthcoming). Whilst many of our findings reflect those found in other studies outside China (Vuontisjärvi 2006, Bhattacharya *et al.* 2008), suggesting some universal patterns in the adoption of CSR activities, our findings also reveal a number of unique characteristics and institutional weaknesses specific in the Chinese context. These include, for example, the role of the government and the types of incentives that may prove effective to motivate firms and their employees to engage in CSR activities. The limited power of non-government led pressure groups is evident and a voluntary approach to CSR is unlikely to have much effect in the current business environment in China.

There are a number of limitations in this study. The sample size is small and only one senior manager in each firm was surveyed or interviewed. Informants may be biased in their response for various reasons and portray their company in a better light than is warranted. They may also have incomplete and/or inaccurate knowledge of the CSR practices adopted by the firm. The study also draws mainly from western-developed concepts and framework for CSR studies, which may not be universally applicable. Future studies should include a much larger sample, involving different stakeholders of each organization studied, and across different industries. Future studies also need to investigate how, and in what areas, firms can develop a strategic approach to CSR for the benefits of the firm, including the alignment of company strategy and practices with employees' needs.

References

Albinger, H. and Freeman, S., 2000. Corporate social performance and attractiveness as an employer to different job seeking populations. *Journal of business ethics*, 28 (3), 243–253.

Baron, D., 2001. Private politics, corporate social responsibility, and integrated strategy. *Journal of economics and management strategy*, 10 (1), 7–45.

Bhattacharya, C. and Sen, S., 2004. Doing better at doing good: when, why, and how consumers respond to corporate social initiatives. *California management review*, 47 (1), 9–24.

Bhattacharya, C., Sen, S., and Korschun, D., 2008. Using corporate social responsibility to win the war for talent. *MIT Sloan management review*, 49 (2), 37–44.

Blowfield, M. and Murray, A., 2008. *Corporate responsibility: a critical introduction*. New York: Oxford University Press.

Brammer, S., Millington, A., and Rayton, B., 2007. The contribution of corporate social responsibility to organizational commitment. *International journal of human resource management*, 18 (10), 1701–1719.

Buhrmann, K., 2008. *Corporate social responsibility: a China approach* [online]. Asia Portal. Available from: http://www.asiaportal.info/infocusblog/?p=39 [Accessed 20 April 2009].

Cacioppe, R., Forster, N., and Fox, M., 2008. A survey of managers' perceptions of corporate ethics and social responsibility and actions that may affect companies' success. *Journal of business ethics*, 82 (3), 681–700.

Carroll, A., 1979. A three-dimensional conceptual model of corporate performance. *Academy of management review*, 4 (4), 497–505.

Carroll, A., 1991. The pyramid of corporate social responsibility: toward the moral management of organizational stakeholders. *Business horizons*, 34 (4), 39–48.

Chan, A., 2001. *China's workers under assault: the exploitation of labour in a globalizing economy*. New York: M.E. Sharpe.

Chan, A. and Ross, R., 2003. Racing to the bottom: international trade without a social clause. *Third world quarterly*, 24 (6), 1011–1028.

China Statistical Yearbook, 2007. Beijing: China Statistics Press.

CNTAC, 2006. Pilot enterprises of implementing CSC9000T [online]. Available from: http://www. csc9000.org.cn/cn/NewsDetail.asp?AID=13211 [Accessed on 14 June 2008].

Cooke, F.L., 2008a. Competition and strategy of Chinese firms: an analysis of top performing Chinese private enterprises. *Competitiveness review*, 18 (1/2), 29–56.

Cooke, F.L., 2008b. Enterprise culture management in China: an 'insiders' perspective. *Management and organization review*, 4 (2), 291–314.

Cooke, F.L., 2008c. *Competition, strategy and management in China.* Basingstoke: Palgrave Macmillan.

Cooke, F.L., forthcoming. Social responsibility, sustainability and diversity of human resources. *In*: A. Harzing and A. Pinnington, eds. *International human resource management.* 3rd ed. London: Sage.

Cooney, S., 2007. China's labour law, compliance and flaws in implementing institutions. *Journal of industrial relations*, 49 (5), 673–686.

Crowther, D. and Capaldi, N., eds, 2008. *The Ashgate research companion to corporate social responsibility.* Aldershot: Ashgate.

Economy, E.C., 2004. *The river runs black: the environmental challenge to China's future.* Ithaca: Cornell University Press.

European Commission, 2005. *Awareness-raising questionnaire* [online]. Available from: http://ec. europa.eu/enterprise/csr/campaign/documentation/download/questionaire_en.pdf [Accessed on 5 July 2008].

Freeman, E., 1984. *Strategic management: a stakeholder approach.* Boston MA: Pitman.

Frenkel, S., 2001. Globalization, athletic footwear commodity chains and employment relations in China. *Organization studies*, 22 (4), 531–562.

Friedman, M., 1962. *Capitalism and freedom.* Chicago: The University of Chicago Press.

Garnaut, R. and Huang, Y.P., 2001. *Growth without miracles – readings on the Chinese economy in the era of reform.* Oxford: Oxford University Press.

Garriga, E. and Melé, D., 2004. Corporate social responsibility theories: mapping the territory. *Journal of business ethics*, 53 (1–2), 51–71.

Gawel, A., 2006. *Corporate social responsibility: standards and objectives driving corporate initiatives.* Available from: www.pollutionprobe.org/Reports/csr_january06.pdf [Accessed 14 December 2008].

Hill and Knowlton, 2004. *China corporate reputation watch survey* [online]. Available from: http:// hillandknowlton.com/crw [Accessed on 2 August 2005].

Hillman, A. and Keim, G., 2001. Shareholder value, stakeholder management, and social issues: what's the bottom line? *Strategic management journal*, 22 (2), 125–139.

HKTDC, 2005. *Corporate social responsibility and implications for Hong Kong's manufacturers and exporters* [online]. Available from: http://www.hktdc.com/econforum/tdc/tdc050202.htm [Accessed on 18 March 2008].

Ho, B., 2005. *China social responsibility standard for textile industry launched* [online]. CSR-Asia. Available from: http://www.csr-asia.com/index.php?id=2224 [Accessed on 6 March 2008].

Ho, P. and Vermeer, E., eds, 2006. *China's limits to growth: greening state and society.* Oxford: Blackwell Publishing.

ILO-Beijing, 2008. *Corporate social responsibility (CSR) in the Chinese textile industry* [online]. Available from: http://www.ilo.org/public/english/region/asro/beijing/whatwedo/csr.htm [Accessed on 12 March 2008].

ISO Advisory Group on Social Responsibility, 2004. *Working report on social responsibility* [online]. Available from: http://www.jsa.or.jp/stdz/sr/pdf/sagreport_eng.pdf [Accessed on 6 August 2008].

Lai, Q., 2006. *Corporate social responsibility of SMEs in China: challenges and outlooks.* Bremen: University of Bremen.

Lee, C.K., ed., 2007. *Working in China: ethnographies of labour and workplace transformation.* London: Routledge.

Luo, Y.D., 2006. Political behaviour, social responsibility, and perceived corruption: a structuration perspective. *Journal of international business studies*, 37 (6), 747–766.

Peng, L., Long, B.J., and Pamlin, D., 2005. Chinese companies in the 21st century: helping or destroying the planet? Corporate social responsibility and beyond. Switzerland: WWF's Trade and Investment Programme.

Potter, P., 1999. The Chinese legal system: continuing commitment to the primacy of state power. *China quarterly*, 159, 673–683.

Pun, N. and Smith, C., 2007. Putting transnational labour process in its place: the dormitory labour regime in post-socialist China. *Work, employment and society*, 21 (1), 47–65.

Rodriguez, P., Siegel, D., Hillman, A., and Eden, L., 2006. Three lenses on the multinational enterprise: politics, corruption, and corporate social responsibility. *Journal of international business studies*, 37 (6), 733–746.

Roozen, I., Pelsmacker, P., and Bostyn, F., 2001. The ethical dimensions of decision processes of employees. *Journal of business ethics*, 33 (2), 87–100.

Sen, S. and Bhattacharya, C., 2001. Does doing good always lead to doing better? Consumer reactions to corporate social responsibility. *Journal of marketing research*, 38 (2), 225–243.

Stiglitz, J., 2002. *Globalization and its discontent*. London: Penguin Books.

Tang, Z. and Li, W.C., 2008. An empirical analysis of influential factors of social responsibility of privately owned enterprises in Zhejiang Province. *Journal of Zhejiang Gongshang university*, 90 (3), 75–79.

Taylor, B., Chang, K., and Li, Q., 2003. *Industrial relations in China*. Cheltenham: Edward Elgar.

Towers, N. and Chen, R., 2008. Employing the participative paradigm as a valid empirical approach to gaining a greater understanding of contemporary supply chain and distribution management issues. *International journal of retail and distribution management*, 36 (8), 627–637.

Towers, N. and Peng, X., 2006. An assessment of international strategic merchandising from China, post-quota elimination in January 2005 for the UK apparel market. *Journal of the textile institute*, 97 (6), 541–548.

Turban, D. and Greening, D., 1997. Corporate social performance and organizational attractiveness to prospective employees. *Academy of management journal*, 40 (3), 658–672.

Valentine, S. and Fleischman, G., 2008. Ethics programs, perceived corporate social responsibility and job satisfaction. *Journal of business ethics*, 77 (2), 159–172.

Vuontisjärvi, T., 2006. Corporate social reporting in the European context and human resource disclosures: an analysis of Finnish companies. *Journal of business ethics*, 69 (4), 331–354.

Wang, C., 2005. The current situation and countermeasures of Chinese enterprises' social responsibilities. *Journal of Yanan university* (social science), 27 (5), 72–73.

Wang, D. and Zhang, L., 2005. Chinese enterprises' social responsibility condition and promotion measures. *The northern forum*, 2, 142–144.

Warner, M., 1996. Chinese enterprise reform, human resources and the 1994 Labour Law. *International journal of human resource management*, 7 (4), 779–796.

Zhou, W.D., 2006. *Will CSR work in China?* [online]. China-CSR. Available from: http://www. chinacsr.com/en/2006/08/10/653-will-csr-work-in-china/ [Accessed on 10 March 2008].

Zinkin, J., 2004. Maximizing the 'licence to operate': CSR from an Asian perspective. *Journal of corporate citizenship*, 14, 67–80.

Hukou-based HRM in contemporary China: the case of Jiangsu and Shanghai

Mingqiong Zhang, Chris Nyland and Cherrie Jiuhua Zhu

Department of Management, Monash University, Australia

Based on case studies of 12 firms, this research documents how the hukou-based human resource management (HRM) system in contemporary China informs six human resource management functions. It is shown that the system has generated a division between urbanites as core employees and rural migrants as peripheral workers. Rural workers tend to suffer from job and wage discrimination and have less access to training, welfare benefits, social insurance, and promotion than urban-hukou holders. The hierarchical nature of this division reflects the fact that human resource management policy and practice in China is a product of the larger institutional environment and lends support to the theoretical notion of 'socially embedded HRM'.

Introduction

In recent decades, China has been at the forefront of scholarly attention in the field of human resource management (HRM) (Benson and Zhu 1999, Ding *et al.* 2000, Warner 2000, Zhu 2005). It is the consensus that there remain significant differences between the styles of managing employees in China and in Western countries because of the different cultural and political systems (Björkman and Lu 2000). Chinese culture, which is characterized by respect for age and authority, emphasis on harmonious interpersonal relations, the importance of personal connections (*guanxi*), a group orientation and the avoidance of loss of 'face' (*mianzi*), has endowed HRM in China with many Chinese characteristics (Lockett 1988, Child and Markoczy 1993, Warner 2008). This development has also been shaped by China's experiment with state socialism which until the 1990s made job allocation, lifetime employment, egalitarian pay and cradle-to-grave welfare benefits the norm and which remains a tradition that continues to influence the practices of many enterprises (Goodall and Warner 1997). Though Chinese managers are utilizing more western HRM practices such as merit-based staffing and performance-based reward systems (Farley *et al.* 2004), vestiges of the state socialist regime remain (Ahlstrom *et al.* 2005). Consequently, a Chinese hybrid HRM model has emerged which combines practices that reflect Chinese culture, politics and history and the influence of Western and East Asian practices (Warner 1996, 2002, Ahlstrom *et al.* 2005, Ng and Siu 2005).

A feature of this hybrid, examined in this study, is the tendency for the household registration (*hukou*) system to influence how managers treat workers. The *hukou* system was established in the late 1950s and categorizes Chinese citizens into two groups: urban-*hukou* and non-urban-*hukou* holders and provides the two groups with different rights and entitlements (Cheng and Selden 1994, Chan and Zhang 1999). This development is important not least because, since the early 1980s, millions of farmers (non-urban-*hukou* holders – 'rural migrant workers') have flooded into China's cities and towns for work (Solinger 1999, Liang 2001, Roberts 2002). China's Fifth Census in 2000 showed that rural migrants made up to 52.6%, 68.2% and 79.8% of the labour force of restaurant and food services, manufacture and construction, respectively (National Bureau of Statistics of China 2002). By the end of 2006, the number of rural workers had increased to 134 million (Hu *et al.* 2007). Although rural migrants have grown to be a very large part of the urban workforce their registration status means they are not eligible to enjoy urban services such as social welfare, subsidized housing, and reemployment assistance. Rural workers, moreover, do not have the right to vote and stand for election in urban areas and though they have a range of employment rights they are often relegated to 'three D' jobs (difficult, dirty and dangerous) that are shunned by urban residents. To be brief, the *hukou* system has created a dual society divided between urban-*hukou* and non-urban-*hukou* holders. As Chan and Zhang note, the *hukou* system divides the population into 'two "castes", one [urban-*hukou* holders] economically and socially superior to the other [non-urban-*hukou* holders], with vastly different opportunities, obligations and socio-economic statuses' (Chan and Zhang 1999, p. 830, see also Chan and Buckingham 2008).

Although the impact of the *hukou*-based division has significantly diminished in recent years, because of government reform, it remains a social identity which finds expression both within and outside the workplace. Few urban residents are willing to socialize with rural migrants, let alone make friends with them. Rural-urban intermarriages are rare because marrying a rural-*hukou holder* is regarded as unwise due to the large rural-urban social and economic gap (Xu 2000). The *hukou*-based social division also finds expression in the HRM policy and practice of firms. Rural workers tend to suffer from job and wage discrimination (Knight and Song 1999) and have less access to training, social insurances, welfare benefits, and promotion than urban-*hukou* holders (Solinger 1999, Xu 2000, Research Office of State Council 2006). Consequently, job-, wage-, training-, social insurance-, welfare- and promotion-hierarchies based on *hukou* status have emerged in firms and rural migrants are usually at the low end of every hierarchy (Xu 2000). Chinese scholars describe this *hukou*-based division of labour as 'one factory, two systems' (Lu 2006).

Despite the significance of the *hukou* system, it has received little attention in the HRM literature. In order to confront this omission, this study explores *hukou*-based HRM practices by discussing key aspects of the employment relationship based on empirical data drawn from twelve firms. In so doing we add weight to Chan and Buckingham's (2008) claim that reports of the demise of the *hukou* system are greatly exaggerated. The remainder of this study proceeds as follows. Following a section discussing the theoretical perspective and research method, the case study evidence on *hukou*-based HRM is presented and the study concludes with implications, limitations of the study and suggestions for future research.

Theoretical perspective

HRM research falls largely into two categories: 'managerialist determined HRM' and 'socially embedded HRM' (Morishima 1995). The former assumes that the pattern of HRM a firm may adopt is determined by managers primarily based on their business strategies. Managers enjoy enormous freedom in designing and implementing HRM policy and practice. Therefore, scholars who believe in the notion of managerial determination of HRM tend to concentrate on examining specific HRM policies and practices, what constitutes the best-fit HRM, and the convergence and divergence of HRM patterns but ignore the impact of institutional context upon HRM system (Morishima 1995, Rosenthal 1995). Advocates of 'socially embedded HRM', by contrast, believe firms are 'institutionally deeply enrooted and socially embedded into their respective national [institutional] contexts' (Matten and Geppert 2004, p. 179). In short, HRM policy and practice are reflections of, or responses to, organizations larger institutional environment, and can be understood only in relation to the institutional contexts in which they are embedded. HRM research has been dominated by the 'managerialist determined HRM' tradition and little explicit attention has been accorded the institutional context in HRM research (Morishima 1995, Rosenthal 1995, Paauwe 2004). However, 'managerialist-determined-HRM without institutional context' is problematic because empirical findings show that HRM policy and practice are primarily based on local labour regulations (Rosenzweig and Nohria 1994, Godard 2002, Stahl and Björkman 2006, Björkman *et al.* 2007, Schroder *et al.* 2009).

Chinese HRM research has also been dominated by the 'managerialist determined HRM' perspective, although a few scholars have tried to link Chinese HRM to China's unique culture and political system. By contrast, this study explores how the institutional environment influences HRM by examining the association between the institution of *hukou* and Chinese HRM. Drawing on the 'socially embedded HRM' perspective, we hypothesize that Chinese HRM should be *hukou*-based given the long-lasting *hukou*-based rural-urban separation. *Based on this assumption, we examine three research questions in order to generate insights on how the hukou system impacts on HRM practices. First, are rural workers managed in ways different from their urban co-workers? Second, are perceived HRM differences clearly hukou-based? Third, how do regulative, normative and cognitive influences shape hukou-based HRM?*

Methodology

The study was conducted in Jiangsu province and Shanghai from November 2006 to March 2007. These regions were chosen because they are situated in the fastest industrializing coastal provinces in China and are primary destinations for rural to urban migrants. By the end of 2006, there were 9.03 million rural migrants working in cities of Jiangsu province, amounting to 66% of total urban employment (Jiangsu Statistics Bureau 2007); and 3.80 million in Shanghai, amounting to half of all urban employees (Shanghai Statistics Bureau 2007). Therefore, there are many firms that employ both urban workers and rural migrants. This made it possible to compare firms' HRM policy and practice toward employees with and without urban-*hukou*.

According to Yin (1984, 2003), the main strength of the case study approach is that it can employ many different data collection strategies to validate and cross-check findings. In this study, the researchers selected 12 cases from a set of enterprises and adopted interviewing and documentation analysis as major strategies of data collection. The rationale for selecting these cases included location, ownership, size and age (Table 1). Accessibility was also a criterion for case selection. The reason was that discrimination has been a sensitive topic in China in recent years and many managers are wary of allowing researchers to examine situations where discrimination is manifest. In the fieldwork, interviews were conducted with HR managers and/or general managers and with rural workers in order to avoid 'elite bias' (Drenth *et al.* 1998). Company documents were collected for background information.

Table 1. Profile of the 12 case firms in 2005.

Case firm/ ownership	Year started	Location	Country of origin	Main products	Size (No. of employees) (Persons)		Probability to be cadres (%)		Average annual salary (yuan/ per person)		Average annual training expenditure (yuan/ per person)		Unionization rate (%)	
					Urban employees	Rural workers	Urban employees	Rural workers	Urban employees	Rural workers	Urban employees	Rural workers	Urban employees	Rural workers
SOE1	1958	Wuxi	N/A	Auto spare parts	2923	600	14	0	24,000	16,700	332	117	100	100
SOE2	1949	Shanghai	N/A	Electric motor	2860	413	7.7	0	22,000	15,000	266	N/A	100	0
POE1	1992	Nanjing	N/A	Real estate	592	126	25	4	28,000	15,000	507	238	80	0
POE2	1998	Shanghai	N/A	House decoration	30	48	47	4	21,000	18,000	5000	833	100	0
JV1	2002	Nanjing	Taiwan	Photo-electric displays	200	210	28	0	28,000	18,000	175	71	80	0
JV2	1993	Shanghai	Canada	Photo-electric displays	100	80	25	25.7	36,000	19,200	600	500	0	0
JV3	1994	Suzhou	Germany	Yarn	1100	600	12.7	1	16,200	10,800	136	83	0	0
WFOE1	2001	Shanghai	USA	Electronic devices	297	328	61	4	27,000	9000	438	213	0	0
WFOE2	2001	Nantong	Japan	Aluminium pigment	180	50	10	0	33,408	20,824	578	720	100	100
WFOE3	1990	Wuxi	Hong Kong	Cocoa products	93	185	15	19	21,000	18,000	108	162	0	0
WFOE4	2003	Taizhou	Korea, South	Fittings of home appliance	55	105	87	17	10,900	10,900	N/A	N/A	5	7
WFOE5	2003	Taizhou	Taiwan	Gifts	31	230	100	3	17,000	12,000	129	22	0	3

Notes: SOE = state-owned enterprise; POE = private-owned enterprises; JV = Joint venture; WFOE = Wholly-foreign-owned enterprise. Probability for urban employees to be cadres = number of urban cadres / number of urban employees in the firm; Probability for rural workers to be cadres = number of rural cadres / number of rural migrant workers in the firm. Wuxi, Nanjing, Nantong, Suzhou and Taizhou are cities of Jiangsu Province.

In the end, 33 executives and 37 rural migrant workers were interviewed (see Table 2), including 50 from the 12 case firms and 20 from other firms. In order to triangulate the case findings, the study also interviewed managers of three staffing agencies in Jiangsu province.

The findings

In order to address the three research questions, this study examined and analysed the practices associated with the six HRM functions identified by Ding *et al.* (2005), that is, recruitment, training, reward system, performance evaluation, social security and unionization.

Recruitment

In 1992, the Chinese central government issued the *Regulations on Remodelling the Operation Mechanisms of State-owned Enterprises* and granted SOEs the freedom to recruit employees independently. Consequently, two broad recruitment arrangements have emerged: direct and indirect employment (Figure 1). Under direct employment, employers hire employees and utilize their capacity to labour. Under indirect employment arrangements, employers utilize workers' labour capacity but do not hire them directly. Instead, workers are employed by staffing agencies and sign contracts with these agencies which then allocate them to firms. This is an important distinction because indirect employees are protected by the PRC Civil Law, while direct employees are covered by the PRC Labour Law.

Direct employees include contract workers and non-contract workers and the former can be grouped into three categories. Permanent contract workers entered SOEs or SOE-turned private firms before the firms were restructured in the late 1990s. Long-term contract employees are usually college graduates with professional skills and have been recruited from the time of the restructure. Fixed and long-term employees usually occupy central positions in firms. The third category are short-term contract employees who were employed after the restructure and who normally undertake less skilled jobs.

The *hukou* system has exerted significant influence on the recruitment practice of firms. Very few rural migrants have been employed as permanent employees. It is also difficult for them to be employed on long-term contracts and, hence, are confined to short-term contract, non-contract or rented employment. In short, recruitment practices are sharply divided along *hukou*-based lines.

Although not all short-term, non-contract and rented workers are rural-*hukou* holders, the latter are greatly overrepresented in these categories. Wuxi, for example, a major city in Jiangsu, had 100,000 rented workers in 2005, of whom around 80,000 were rural migrant workers. Although the influence of *hukou*-status on the recruitment practice of firms has decreased in recent years, it remains significant. In the labour market of *Zhouzhuang* town of *Jiangsu*, the researcher found that among the 24 job wanted advertisements, 16 of them had clear requirement of *hukou* status such as 'local-*hukou* holders only', 'local-*hukou* holders have priority' or 'non-local-*hukou* holders should have native warrantors'. Among the 33 executives interviewed by the researcher, 21 said that some positions such as accountant and warehouse keeper would not be filled by rural migrants.

Among the 12 case firms, the HR managers of eight firms stated that they would take into account the *hukou*-status when they recruited regular staff (SOE1, SOE2, POE1, JV1,

Table 2. Interviewees.

Interviewees	SOE1	SOE2	POE1	POE2	JV1	JV2	JV3	WFOE1	WFOE2	WFOE3	WFOE4	WFOE5	Other 19 firms	Other institutions	Total
General and/or HR managers	1	1	1	1	1	1	1	1	2	1	1	1	20		33
Rural workers	4	3	3	2	3	4	3	4	3	3	2	3			37
Managers of staffing agencies														3	3
Total	5	4	4	3	4	5	4	5	5	4	3	3	20	3	73

Notes: Cases are coded according to the confidential rule; MSA = Manager of staffing agencies.

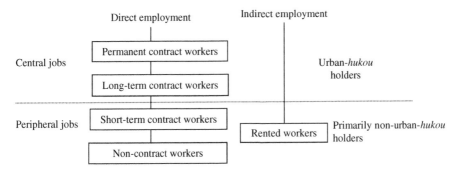

Figure 1.   Employment categories in Jiangsu and Shanghai.
Source: Based on the researcher's interview and documents reviewed during the field study.

JV2, WFOE1, WFOE2 and WFOE3). The HR manager in SOE1 described the firm's recruitment policy as follows:

> Our company has recruited 'Alternate Rural Workers' since the mid 1980s. 'Alternate Rural Workers' implies that they cannot be employed as permanent staff and have to return to the countryside after five to eight years according to the state policy. Some of them, about 150 or so, still work here since then, they are still short-term contract workers although they have worked well and become indispensable. Since 2003, we have stopped recruiting new rural workers directly as short-term contract workers. Rather, we rent them from staffing agencies for the unimportant jobs. To rent, not to recruit workers can reduce labour costs because government has levied many kinds of fees on firms, about 158 yuan per employee per year, for garbage, tree planting, and the like, based on employee numbers. The rented workers were not our regular employees, so we do not need to pay such fees to government. Currently, [SOE1] has three kinds of employees: fixed, long- and short-term contract workers and rented workers. The fixed employees, less than 1500, are urban workers who were recruited before 1994 when our company restructured as a shareholding company. These people enjoy de facto lifetime employment. The contract staffs are mainly college graduates who occupy the key managerial and technical positions. Their contracts range from three to five years and can be renewed based on their performance. The rented workers, including only a few urban-*hukou* holders who have difficulty in finding desirable jobs, are generally rural migrants who work in the auxiliary positions.

SOE2, JV1, and JV2 also grouped their employees into permanent, long-term contract employees, short-term and rented workers. Newly-recruited contract workers of SOE2 and JV2 were only offered three-month-contracts. When they had successfully renewed their contract eight times (for two years), urban-*hukou* holders were eligible for a two-year-contract while rural migrants were only eligible for a one-year-contract. The privately owned enterprises (POEs) and wholly foreign owned enterprises (WFOEs) had no permanent staff and employed only contract employees and rented workers, with the majority of contract workers being urban-*hukou* holders and rented workers being primarily rural migrants.

The *hukou*-based recruitment practice has regulative and cognitive roots. From a regulative perspective, *hukou*-based recruitment is grounded in policy-enabled or policy driven regulations that discriminate against rural migrants. In 1984, the central government issued three documents and conditionally granted SOEs in mining, construction and transportation industries the right to recruit rural migrants. According to these documents, SOEs should utilize rural migrants for hard, dangerous and temporary jobs, as temporary contract workers and no rural-urban *hukou* transfers were permitted for such employees. Since 1992, although government no longer accepted responsibility for

SOEs' recruitment, urban governments have checked the recruitment of rural migrants through a certificate-card system, occupation reservation and the imposition of fees. Rural migrants have to bring many certificates (such as *hukou* certificate) and obtain many permits from urban governments (such as the temporary residence permit, work permit, and the like), in order to be employed in a city. Firms have to pay extra fees to urban governments in order to employ rural migrants. Regulations also require that decent jobs be reserved for local residents and though such restrictions on recruitment have been gradually abolished, these policies have ossified into the belief that rural workers are different from urban workers and should be treated differently.

From a cognitive perspective, rural-*hukou* has also impacted negatively on the recruitment of rural workers. It has become a shared belief amongst HR managers that important jobs such as accountant, warehouse keeper, customs declarer and shop walker cannot be undertaken effectively by rural migrants. Accountants and warehouse keepers should be reliable, custom declarers should have social resources such as *guanxi*, and shop walkers should have a good image and be canvassers. It was accepted by HR managers that rural migrants cannot meet these requirements. Self-interested calculation of firms has certainly played an important role in the *hukou*-based recruitment practices. Interestingly, rural migrants who worked with POEs and WFOEs (such as POE1, WFOE1, WFOE2) tended to believe they were employed as casual workers to undertake auxiliary jobs because they 'cannot do anything else', while migrants who worked with SOEs and SOE-turned JVs (SOE1, SOE2, JV1, JV3) tended to attribute their plight to their rural-*hukou* status. A rural worker in JV1 complained, 'Even if we are more qualified than some urbanites, we will not be employed as fixed or long-term contract employees as urban dwellers. Who tells us farmers to be? This is our fate'.

Training

A *hukou*-based training-hierarchy was found in all the case firms. It seemed cognitive beliefs were the most important element influencing *hukou*-based training decisions. According to most human resource (HR) managers, rural migrants were characterized by a high turnover rate and low occupational and organizational commitment. Therefore, it was held that there was little incentive for firms to invest in the training of such workers. As the HR manager of POE1 observed, 'as they [rural migrants] are too ready to transfer to other companies offering higher pay it is impossible for employers to provide them the same training as regular employees'. His perspective was shared by another HR manager in a privately owned firm who observed that access to training was intimately linked to recruitment practices, 'rural workers kept on looking for better jobs. Moreover, since we hired them only for the auxiliary non-skilled jobs, there is not much need to train them'. Consequently, as the HR manager of SOE1 concluded,

> We provide basic internal training for all employees, including contract and rented rural workers. However, for further training such as degree and certificate education which are helpful for career development, we only consider the regular employees, not including short-term contract workers and rented workers.

Accordingly, the resources allocated for the training of rural workers was limited, with training confined to teaching basic operational skills. Table 1 showed that the annual training expenditure for rural workers was much less than is allocated to urban employees in most firms. For example, the annual average training expenditure of rural migrant workers in SOE1 was only 117 *yuan*, 62% lower than that of urban employees. Although HR managers of the case firms claimed their companies had spent a lot of money on the training of rural migrants, no case firm could provide a training plan for rural workers. Rural workers interviewed tended to report they had few training opportunities or their training was much less than that of urban staff. A rural migrant in WFOE4 told the researcher his HR manager asked him not to complain that there was no training, 'Work is de facto the best way of training'.

Reward system

In 1992, the central government granted SOEs the right to design their own reward system including compensation and benefits, and subsequently the salary system of firms became increasingly diversified. Many salary types emerged such as basic salary plus bonus, efficiency salary, position plus skill salary. Through this period, welfare benefits such as unit-based housing and medical protection were commercialized or changed into contribution-based social insurances. Although the reward system of firms has been increasingly performance-based, the influence of *hukou*-identity was manifest. According to a sample survey conducted by the Guangdong provincial government in 2005, among the 10,000 rural worker respondents, 57% believed the *hukou* system had a negative influence on their employment because it caused them to be paid less than urban workers even when they were in similar positions (Research Team of Guangdong Provincial Government 2006).

It was a common practice for domestic firms to pay rural migrants on piece rates when performance could be precisely measured or in the form of fixed daily, monthly or even annual salary when performance could not be precisely measured, whereas urban staff were usually paid on position, skill and efficiency because the majority of these employees were managerial or technical staff. However, piece-wage, 'the form of wages most in harmony with the capitalist mode of production' (Marx 1967, p. 556), 'is not a system of reward for increased productivity – it is a way of pushing wages down' (Coyle 1982, p. 19). Consequently, the salary of rural workers was usually much lower than that of their urban counterparts, even if they shared similar job positions. In the 12 case firms, the annual average wage of rural migrants was 33–85.7% of that of urban employees. The HR manager of POE1 described their reward system as follows:

> Our company has four types of salary systems: position plus skill salary for the managerial and technical jobs, piece-wage for the jobs which can be measured, and fixed wage for the jobs which cannot be measured. For the rented workers, we negotiate with staffing agencies for a lump sum payment, of which about 10 percent is the agency commission. It is true that rural workers tend to be paid on piece-rate or time-rate, and their salary is much lower than that of urban workers. It is the common practice for firms to pay the auxiliary jobs according to the local minimum salary level. We take care not to pay them less than this level in order to avoid labour disputes. Rural migrants as rented workers can earn even less than as short-term contract workers because they can be paid based on the minimum salary level of their underdeveloped hometown. As rented workers, they usually enjoy half the benefits because they are not the regular employees. If the year-end bonus is 2000 yuan for regular employees, they can obtain 1000 yuan at best. These bonuses are de facto their overtime pay sometimes.

It seems that the salaries of urban regular workers and rural workers are based on different criteria. Figart and Mutari (2004, p. 182–183) identify three wage criteria: wages as a living, wages as a price, and wages as a social practice. Wages as a cost of living are determined by 'socially defined appropriate living standards'. Wages as a price are determined by market mechanisms such as job evaluation, labour supply, and demand. Wages as a social practice are determined by gender, class, and race-ethnicity and reflect social norms. In contemporary China, market mechanisms such as the oversupply of rural workers negatively impacts upon the wages of all workers but the wages of urban employees primarily reflect the cost of living, while the wages of rural migrant workers are more closely attuned to normative and cognitive social beliefs about rural migrant workers. This point was highlighted by the HR manager of POE2 though interestingly he also felt it was necessary to justify the urban-rural wage differential by referencing the cost of living:

> Scholars tend to believe rural migrants are suffering from wage discrimination based on the fact that their wages are much lower than urban employees and have little increased in the last decade. I do not think so given rural workers have land at hometown as another income source and they have earned much more in city than in countryside as farmers. They are farmers and have different life style. Their expenditures are also much lower than that of urban residents because most of their families are in rural area. The labour costs for firms are too high nowadays. At this stage of economic development, to offer rural migrant workers jobs and pay them on time are enough, equal employment rights should be future social goals.

Unfortunately, it appears that some rural migrants have also accepted the notion of wages as a social practice. A rural migrant interviewed in WFOE2 argued: 'In the land of the blind the one-eyed man is king. I am satisfied with my wage. I am a farmer. If I stay at home to grow crops, how much can I earn?'

Performance evaluation and promotion

The influence of the *hukou* system on performance evaluation and promotion was also identified in the case firms. Before 2005, evaluation of rural and urban employees was usually conducted separately because non-contract or rented workers could not be recognized as Model Workers. From 2005 when the All-China Federation of Trade Unions (ACFTU) permitted rural migrants to receive this recognition, many firms began evaluating the performance of urban and rural employees together. The HR manager of SOE2 described their performance evaluation system as follows:

> The performance of all employees is evaluated monthly, semi-yearly and annually through self-assessment, peer assessment, and vertical assessment based on labour discipline, accomplishment of tasks, quality and production safety. The results are related to monthly salary and annual bonus. Before 2005, rented workers were evaluated separately by the staffing agencies. Because rural workers lived in the dormitories of our company, the criteria of performance appraisal also included their behaviour in dormitory. The Model Rural Workers would be awarded by the staffing agencies. In this year [2006], we evaluated rented workers together with regular employees. If they are elected as model workers or technical experts, we will employ them as long-term contract workers. Currently, five rented workers have been admitted as regular employees through performance evaluation and skill competition, their income has also increased consequently.

Even though in principle rural workers currently enjoy the same honour rights as urban workers, they have less opportunity to be promoted than their urban counterparts. Around 60% of rural workers interviewed reported they had no opportunity for promotion or fewer opportunities than urban workers. In the case firms, the proportion of rural workers who were cadres ranged from 0–25.7%, whereas the proportion of urban employees who enjoyed this status ranged from 7.7–100%. Although rural migrants in JV2 and WFOE3 had a greater percentage of rural workers as cadres (25.7% and 19%, respectively), the primary reason was that the two firms were located in rural areas which were far from a city centre and qualified urban managerial staffs were reluctant to work there. As the HR manager of POE3 explained:

> We are a privately owned company and do not pay much attention to the *hukou*-status of employees as SOEs do. We choose some team leaders from rural workers for their retention and management. We usually hire about the same number of rural workers from different

areas for easy management. Migrants coming from the same area need at least two team leaders to help us to manage their fellow-villagers. The criteria to choose a team leader from migrants include many factors such as education level, performance records, authority over workers, and managerial ability, etc. Unlike the promotion of urban workers, we have to take into account their birthplaces. It is impossible for rural workers to be promoted to senior managerial staffs since they have no college degrees.

Social security

Social security in China has three elements: social insurance, social relief and social welfare. *Rural migrants* are not eligible for urban social relief and social welfare. They are only eligible for urban social insurance programmes, including pension, medical, unemployment, work-related injury and maternity insurance. Although all the social insurance programmes are contribution-based, they are *hukou*-based given rural migrants have much less access to these benefits than their urban co-workers. Among the case firms, SOE1 extended coverage of the five main insurance programmes to core rural workers; POE1 and WFOE 3 covered urban employees with the five main insurances, while their rural workers were covered only by pension and injury insurances. POE2 let its rural workers join the comprehensive insurance designed specifically for rural migrants by the Shanghai government, whereas the migrants in SOE2, JV1, JV2, WFOE4 and WFOE5 did not have any social insurance coverage.

As with other aspects of the *hukou*-based regime, social insurance programmes have institutional roots. From a regulative perspective, the urban social insurance programmes are not designed for all Chinese citizens, but for urban residents. They are not suitable for the low-income floating rural migrants who consequently are reluctant to join them. A rural migrant interviewed in WFOE5 told one of the researchers most of his rural co-workers did not trust the non-transferable social insurance programmes. They preferred to convert social insurance into cash to increase their current income. Normatively, many urban governments believe it is not necessary for rural migrants to join the urban social insurance given they are likely to return to the countryside. Moreover, to cover rural migrants with social insurance would increase labour costs and discourage investment. Cognitively, discriminating against rural workers has become a socially shared patterned HRM practice. It is a common practice for firms to exclude rural workers from social insurance programmes. The attitude of the HR manager in JV1 toward the extension of social insurance coverage to rural workers is typical:

> It is not necessary for rural migrants to join social insurances. They have land in their hometown as their social security and most of them will return to the countryside in future. Who could guarantee that they will enjoy the benefits of social insurances when they have returned to their hometown? What's more, social insurance is a heavy burden for both firms and rural migrants. The current total contribution rate for the five insurances and housing fund is 43.3 percent of wages for firms (pension: 18 percent, medical: 9.2 percent, unemployment: 2 percent, work-related injury and maternity: 2.1 percent, and housing fund: 12 percent), 10 percent for rural migrants (pension: 8 percent, medical: 2 percent). The contribution base reached 1048 yuan in 2006 in Jiangsu. Therefore, firms have to pay at least 5000 yuan for each rural worker per year. Even if firms do not contribute to the housing fund, they still should pay about 4000 yuan annual premium for each rural migrant. And each rural worker has to pay about 1200 yuan each year. In order to avoid the contribution, it is a common practice for firms not to sign a labour contract with rural migrants, or recruit them as regular employees but to rent them from staffing agencies. According to the current policy, it is not compulsory for rented workers to join all the social insurance programs. They can join some of the insurance programs and pay the premium in line with the much lower contribution rate and base in their hometown.

Unionization

The different treatment of urban and rural workers can also be identified in the labour relations of firms, especially in SOEs and POEs. SOEs have the heritage that all regular employees are members of the official union (ACFTU). POEs are usually not against unionism because the official union is actually dependent on employers and primarily plays a welfare role in firms (Clarke *et al.* 2004). Therefore, all the domestic case firms, no matter what the ownership form, were unionized. Nevertheless, firms limited their recognition of union membership to urban workers and did so even though the state wished all workers to become union members. Among the four domestic firms, only SOE1 and POE2 had allowed rural migrant workers to unionize. Such a difference was not evident in the case JVs and WFOEs because they either had no trade union (JV2, JV3, WFOE1, and WFOE2) or the trade union was only window dressing, with a very low unionization rate (WFOE 4 and WFOE5). The HR manager in JV1 argued that 'it is understandable for the lower unionization rate of rural migrant workers. Anyway, it is only in recent years that government permits rural migrants to join the trade union'. The HR manager of WFOE3 concluded it had been an urban norm to not take rural migrants into account in public resource distribution. 'They [rural migrants] have been forgotten by the urban society for decades. It is appropriate not to cover them with the official trade union because they were farmers who worked temporarily in the city and were not formal members of urban society'. Another reason for the low unionization rate of rural workers was that rural migrants were reluctant to join the official trade union. A rural migrant interviewed in JV2 asked the researcher, 'even if we joined a trade union and paid 2 percent of our salary to it [as membership fee], do you believe it can protect us and help us enjoy the same rights as urban residents?'

In summary, although the impact of the *hukou* system upon the HRM in China has been greatly reduced in recent years, this multiple case study has found rural migrant workers are managed in ways different from urban employees due to *hukou*-based HRM practices. There is a clear division within firms between urbanites who tend overwhelmingly to be core employees and rural migrants who remain a peripheral work force. Rural migrant workers tend to suffer from job and wage discrimination and have less access to training, benefits, social insurance, and promotion than urban employees. In other words, current HRM in China is still shaped by the *hukou* system as indicated in Table 3.

Implications

This study is among the first to examine the influence of the *hukou* system on Chinese HRM. Our research provides rich first-hand information that can assist the development of a deeper understanding of Chinese HRM and management. The findings of our research have important implications for researchers, managers and government. The study has implications for researchers in three respects. First, our findings show the close linkage between HRM and institutional context and lend support both to the argument of Chan and Buckingham (2008) that the *hukou* system is still a powerful institution controlling Chinese society, and to the 'socially embedded HRM' perspective advocated by Morishima (1995), Rosenthal (1995) and Paauwe (2004). The study is designed to evoke discussion and to stimulate further HRM studies that embrace the perspective of 'socially embedded HRM'. We suggest Chinese HRM studies should pay more attention to the institutional environment. Second, our research has implications for workforce diversity management. Traditional workforce diversity studies have focused on race and

Table 3. A comparison of HRM practices for urban employees and rural migrant workers.

HRM activities		Urban workers	Rural migrant workers
Recruitment	Position	Mainly technical and managerial	Mainly auxiliary
	Employment type	Mainly contracted	Mainly casual or rented workers
Training	Contents	Basic operational and technical skills, safety, discipline and law knowledge	Mainly basic operation skills, safety, discipline and law knowledge
	Amount	Further study for skill certificate or college degree	Limited
		Extensive	
Reward system	Salary	Mainly performance- and efficiency-based	Mainly piece-rate, time-rate or fixed
	Benefits	Full benefits	Partial benefits, no paid leave, less bonus
	Honour rights	Full honour rights	Some firms still evaluate the performance of urban and rural workers separately
Performance evaluation	Promotion	More opportunity, can be managers of all levels	Less opportunity, usually are confined to team leaders
Social security		The majority has been covered	The majority has not been covered
Unionization		Most are union members	Most are not union members

Source: Based on the researcher's interview and documents reviewed during the field study.

gender. However, our research shows that managing rural migrants has become a challenging issue in contemporary China as rural workers become the main body of the Chinese workforce. Chinese urban and rural employees are different in many aspects including work value, motivation, and labour discipline. How to manage rural employees is critical not only for economic performance, for improving the quality of the Chinese workforce but also for industrial development, social inclusion and harmony. However, rural migrant management has been ignored by studies of Chinese management and workforce diversity management. Third, our research has implications for the ongoing debate regarding the dual pressures of localization and standardization faced by subsidiaries of multinational enterprises (MNEs). Our research shows that the forces of local isomorphism tend to be more powerful than the forces of standardization and, consequently, MNE subsidiaries tend to share similar behaviour characteristics with local firms in response to institutional environments.

Our research also has implications for managers of MNE subsidiaries. Since the *hukou*-based HRM system has been established in contemporary China for decades, it may have become so taken for granted as to be invisible to managers of both domestic firms and MNE subsidiaries. However, given the 'liability of foreignness' (Zaheer 1995), MNE subsidiaries usually have more visibility and the public usually have more social expectations of MNEs than of local firms (Tsai and Child 1997). Therefore, MNEs are more likely than local firms to experience crises of social legitimacy if they engage in unethical employment practice associated with the *hukou*-based HRM regime, whereas social legitimacy is critical for the success and survival of MNEs (Zaheer 1995).

Finally our findings that HRM policies and practices are often reflections of, or responses to, the larger institutional environment have profound implications for government. That is, in order to encourage companies to employ policies that emphasize the human aspect of HRM and that limit the influence of the *hukou* system, government needs to address its reform efforts to all three dimensions of the *hukou* system or the institution of *hukou*. In short, promoting reform merely by changing laws and regulations is unlikely to be effective. What is needed is a unified approach to reform that recognizes this institution has multiple dimensions all of which needs to be addressed concurrently if reforms are to be advanced effectively.

Conclusion

The purpose of this study was to test our hypothesis that Chinese HRM is *hukou*-based due to the *hukou*-based rural-urban separation in contemporary China. Our findings show the *hukou* system has ossified into socially shared normative and cognitive templates and, consequently, continues to have a major impact on Chinese HRM even though the national government has diluted many of the regulations that previously ensured the *hukou* system severely discriminated against off-farm workers. This situation has ensured that rural migrant workers have been and continue to be managed in ways different from their urban counterparts. Our case study findings indicate Chinese HRM is clearly *hukou*-based even though Chinese HRM has been moving toward the western HRM model. Therefore, even if firms in China are increasingly utilizing western HRM practices, these practices might be *hukou*-based as they are primarily used for urban employees only. Our findings show that the *hukou* system has shaped not only the HRM of domestic firms but also that of foreign-funded firms. Therefore, the empirical support of our hypothesis indicates that ignoring the influence of the *hukou* system and assuming that the HRM policy and practice of Chinese firms cover all employees is problematic when studying HRM in China.

The present study is based on interviews and archival data. Although the indepth investigation provides first-hand information and deeper insight into the *hukou*-based HRM at firm-level, it cannot detail the extent to which rural migrants are discriminated against. Larger systematic surveys are needed in future research to quantify the *hukou*-based HRM for accuracy and generalization, to measure the extent to which rural migrants are discriminated against in workplace, and to capture the influence of factors such as firm size, ownership, sector, region and history of firms on the *hukou*-based HRM practices. Given the heterogeneity of Chinese society, case study and large-sample survey also should be conducted in other areas such as in the Pearl River Delta Region, another major destination for rural migrants, to enhance the generalizability of the findings.

Acknowledgements

The authors gratefully acknowledge the cooperation of the participants in the study, the helpful editors' and reviewers' comments, and the Monash University Postgraduate Publications Award.

References

Ahlstrom, D., Foley, S., Young, M.N., and Chan, E.S., 2005. Human resource strategies in post-WTO China. *Thunderbird international business review*, 47 (3), 263–285.

Benson, J. and Zhu, Y., 1999. Market, firms and workers: the transformation of human resource management in Chinese manufacturing enterprises. *Human resource management journal*, 9 (4), 58–74.

Björkman, I., Fey, C.F., and Park, H.J., 2007. Institutional theory and MNC subsidiary HRM practices: evidence from a three-country study. *Journal of international business studies*, 38 (3), 430–446.

Björkman, I. and Lu, Y., 2000. Local or global? Human resource management in international joint venture. *In*: M. Warner, ed. *Changing workplace relations in the Chinese economy*. London: Macmillan Press, 117–138.

Chan, K.W. and Buckingham, W., 2008. Is China abolishing the *Hukou* system? *The China quarterly*, 195, 582–606.

Chan, K.W. and Zhang, L., 1999. The *hukou* system and rural-urban migration in China: processes and changes. *The China quarterly*, 160, 818–855.

Cheng, T. and Selden, M., 1994. The origins and social consequences of China's *Hukou* system. *The China quarterly*, 139, 644–668.

Child, J. and Markoczy, L., 1993. Host-country managerial behaviour and learning in Chinese and Hungarian joint ventures. *Journal of management studies*, 30 (4), 611–631.

Clarke, S., Lee, C.H., and Li, Q., 2004. Collective consultation and industrial relations in China. *British journal of industrial relations*, 42 (2), 235–254.

Coyle, A., 1982. Sex and skill in the organization of the clothing industry. *In*: J. West, ed. *Work, women, and the labour market*. London: Routledge and Kegan Paul, 10–26.

Ding, D.Z., Ge, G., and Warner, M., 2005. Evolution of organizational governance and human resource management in China's township and village enterprises. *In*: M. Warner, ed. *Human resource management in China revisited*. London: Routledge, 220–236.

Ding, D.Z., Goodall, K., and Warner, M., 2000. The end of the 'Iron Rice-Bowl'. *The international journal of human resource management*, 11 (2), 217–236.

Drenth, P.J.D., Thierry, H., and de Wolff, C.J., 1998. *Handbook of work and organizational psychology*. Vol. 4. Hove: Psychology Press.

Farley, J.U., Hoenig, S., and Yang, J.Z., 2004. Key factors influencing HRM practices of overseas subsidiaries in China's transition economy. *The international journal of human resource management*, 15 (4–5), 688–704.

Figart, D.M. and Mutari, E., 2004. Wage discrimination in context: enlarging the field of view. *In*: D.P. Champlin and J.T. Knoedler, eds. *The institutionalist tradition in labour economics*. New York: M.E. Sharpe, 179–189.

Godard, J., 2002. Institutional environments, employer practices, and states in liberal market economies. *Industrial relations*, 41 (2), 249–286.

Goodall, K. and Warner, M., 1997. Human resources in sino-foreign joint ventures: selected case studies in Shanghai, compared with Beijing. *The international journal of human resource management*, 8 (5), 569–594.

Hu, W.Q., Zhang, Z.Y., and Zhang, G.J., 2007. How much of the difference of the contribution and returns of rural migrant workers? [online]. Chinese Scientific Papers Online. Available from: http://www.paper.edu.cn [Accessed 18 February 2007].

Jiangsu Statistics Bureau, 2007. *Jiangsu statistical yearbook*. Beijing: China Statistical Press.

Knight, J. and Song, L., 1999. Employment constraints and sub-optimality in Chinese enterprises. *Oxford economic papers*, 51 (2), 284–298.

Lockett, M., 1988. Culture and the problems of Chinese management. *Organization studies*, 9 (4), 475–496.

Liang, Z., 2001. The age of migration in China. *Population and development review*, 27 (3), 499–524.

Lu, X.Y., 2006. Paying attention to research and resolve the problems related to mingong. *In*: Research Office of China State Council, ed. *Survey report on the problems of rural migrant workers in China*. Beijing: China Yanshi Press, 487–492.

Marx, K., 1967. *Capital*. New York: International Publishers.

Matten, D. and Geppert, M., 2004. Work systems in heavy engineering: the role of national culture and national institutions in multinational corporations. *Journal of international management*, 10 (2), 177–198.

Morishima, M., 1995. Embedding HRM in a social context. *British journal of industrial relations*, 33 (4), 617–640.

National Bureau of Statistics of China, 2002. *China statistical yearbook*. Beijing: China Statistics Press.

Ng, Y.C. and Siu, N.Y.M., 2005. Training and enterprise performance in transition: evidence from China. *In*: M. Warner, ed. *Human resource management in China revisited*. London: Routledge, 262–278.

Paauwe, J., 2004. HRM in its context: an institutional perspective. *In*: J. Paauwe, ed. *HRM and performance: achieving long-term viability*. New York: Oxford University Press, 35–50.

Research Office of State Council, 2006. *Survey report on the problems of rural migrant workers in China*. Beijing: China Yanshi Press.

Research Team of Guangdong Provincial Government, 2006. Report of the sample survey on 10,000 rural migrant workers and 1,000 firms in Guangdong province. *In*: Research Office of China State Council, ed. *Survey report on the problems of rural migrant workers in China*. Beijing: China *Yanshi* Press, 447–454.

Roberts, K.D., 2002. Rural migrants in urban China: willing workers, invisible residents. *In*: Y.A. Debrah, ed. *Migrant workers in pacific Asia*. London: Frank Cass Publishers, 141–158.

Rosenthal, P., 1995. Balancing the organizational and institutional perspectives in research on HRM change. *British journal of industrial relations*, 33 (4), 651–656.

Rosenzweig, P.M. and Nohria, N., 1994. Influences on human resource management practices in multinational corporations. *Journal of international business studies*, 25 (2), 229–251.

Schroder, H., Hofacker, D., and Muller-Camen, M., 2009. HRM and the employment of older workers: Germany and Britain compared. *International journal of human resources development and management*, 9 (2/3), 162–179.

Shanghai Statistics Bureau, 2007. *Shanghai statistical yearbook*. Beijing: China Statistical Press.

Solinger, D.J., 1999. Citizenship issues in China's internal migration: comparisons with Germany and Japan. *Political science quarterly*, 114 (3), 455–478.

Stahl, G. and Björkman, I., 2006. *Handbook of research in international human resource management*. London: Edward Elgar Publishing.

Tsai, S.-H.T. and Child, J., 1997. Strategic responses of multinational corporations to environmental demands. *Journal of general management*, 23 (1), 1–22.

Warner, M., 1996. Beyond the iron rice-bowl: comprehensive labour reform in state owned enterprises in north-east China. *In*: D.H. Brown and P. Porter, eds. *Management issues in China*. London: Routledge, 214–236.

Warner, M., 2000. Introduction: the Asia-Pacific HRM model revisited. *The international journal of human resource management*, 11 (2), 171–182.

Warner, M., 2002. Globalization, labour markets and human resources in Asia-Pacific economies: an overview. *International journal of human resource management*, 13, 384–398.

Warner, M., 2008. Reassessing human resource management 'with Chinese characteristics': an overview. *The international journal of human resource management*, 19 (5), 771–801.

Xu, F., 2000. *Women migrant workers in China's economic reform*. London: Macmillan.

Yin, R.K., 1984. *Case study research: design and methods*. Beverly Hills, CA: SAGE.

Yin, R.K., 2003. *Case study research: design and methods*. 3rd ed. Thousand Oaks: Sage.

Zaheer, S., 1995. Overcoming the liability of foreignness. *Academy of management journal*, 38 (2), 341–363.

Zhu, C.J., 2005. *Human resource management in China: past, current and future HR practices in the industrial sector*. London: Routledge.

The antecedents and consequences of commitment in bank–corporate relationships: evidence from the Chinese banking market

Xin Guo[a], Angus Duff[a] and Mario Hair[b]

[a]Paisley Business School, Univeristy of the West of Scotland, Paisley, UK; [b]School of Engineering and Science, University of the West of Scotland, Paisley, UK

This study draws on the exchange relationships literature to create a model of what motivates corporate customers to continue their relationships with their primary banking services providers. The study reports the results of a questionnaire survey administered to financial managers ($N = 259$) in China. Results provide evidence for the existence of a number of antecedents and consequences of commitment in bank–corporate relationships. Notably, service quality is found to be a significant antecedent of affective commitment, which in turn leads to cooperation and continuance intentions. Implications for bank management are discussed along with avenues for future research.

Introduction

Markets for corporate banking services are now facing intensified competition in the new deregulated environment. Traditional banks have lost a substantial proportion of their business to non-bank financial intermediaries (Zineldin 2005), and this has led many banks to incorporate relationship banking issues into their strategic planning in order to achieve sustainable competitive advantage (Proenca and de Castro 2005). The change in the marketplace is reflected in a paradigm shift in academic literature, with recent research highlighting the role customer relationships play in terms of future earnings, profitability, market share and customer satisfaction (Seybold 2001).

A review of the extant literature identified that empirical studies in financial services marketing generally focus on the conceptualization of relationship banking and its associated costs and benefits (for example, Boot 2000). However, little is known of what motivates corporate customers to continue their relationships with their banking service providers. Particularly, few researchers offer empirical data in the Chinese banking sector. The dearth of research is unexpected given the rapid economic development of China. For example, China's 1.3 billion people hold nearly 2.3 trillion US dollars in personal savings, and its banking sector has proved to be one of the most attractive prospects in the world for international banks and investment institutions (KPMG 2007). More importantly, the opening of the Chinese banking market in accordance with the World Trade Organization (WTO) requirements provides both Chinese domestic and foreign banks with huge challenges and opportunities (Deloitte 2007). Therefore, investigating bank–corporate relations in the Chinese banking sector is significant to practitioner audiences, allowing both Chinese domestic and foreign banks to incorporate service provision and relationship banking issues into their strategic planning.

This study attempts to draw on the exchange relationships literature to create a model of what motivates corporate customers to continue their relationships with a bank. A number of hypotheses relating to the relationship between the financial manager (as customer) and the bank (as service provider) are developed and empirically tested.

The remainder of this study is structured as follows. The next section reviews the literature concerning the Chinese banking sector, relationship banking and develops hypotheses relating to the antecedents and consequences of commitment. Section three describes the conduct of questionnaire survey, the development of the questionnaire and the data analysis techniques used. Section four reports the results of hypothesis testing using structural equation modelling (SEM). The final section summarizes and concludes the study.

Literature review

Research context: the Chinese banking sector

Established in 1948, the People's Bank of China (PBC) dominated the entire banking sector in China, reflecting its centrally planned economy. Since 1978, China has begun reform towards a market-based economy, with the PBC monopoly removed and a series of changes to the Chinese banking industry. Government-led banking activities were separated from commercial banking activities and four specialized state-owned banks[1] were established in the early 1990s. Competition then started to intensify in 1994, when China set up three policy-related banks[2] to promote specific financial activities under government direction and support. National commercial banks, shareholding commercial banks and non-bank financial organizations have grown rapidly owing to the government's release policy to develop all types of financial institutions. However, the four specialized state-owned banks still dominate the domestic banking market, with 1.4 million employees and 116,000 branches holding over 65% of deposits of Chinese citizens (Deloitte 2007). Additionally, to strengthen corporate governance, the Chinese Banking Regulation Commission (CBRC) was formed in 2003 to oversee the commercial banking and trust business. Although significant change has occurred within the Chinese banking sector, change has been made problematic by a number of structural issues (for example, increasing non-performing loans and inadequate corporate governance). More importantly, the banking sector has been facing global competition after China completely opened the gates to foreign banks in 2006.[3] It is anticipated the Chinese banking market will be attractive to foreign banks and create significant competitive pressures for domestic banks (Deloitte 2007).

Relationship banking

The acceptance and application of relationship marketing has grown in the financial services sector over the past two decades (Howcroft and Durkin 2000, Dibb and Meadows 2001). Berry (1983) first introduced the relationship marketing paradigm into service industries by viewing it as attracting, maintaining and enhancing customer relationships in multi-service organizations. A well-accepted definition of relationship marketing is provided by Grönroos (1997, p. 410):

> Relationship marketing is to identify and establish, maintain and enhance and when necessary also to terminate relationship with customer and other stakeholders, at a profit, so that the objectives of all parties involved are met, and that this is done by a mutual exchange and fulfillment of promises.

Within the context of the banking sector, relationship marketing has been termed as *relationship banking* where it is in the interest of banks to establish and maintain a long-term bond with customers (Ritter 1993). Moriarty *et al.* (1983, p. 13) describe relationship banking as 'a recognition that the bank can increase earnings by maximizing the profitability of the total customer relationship over time, rather than by seeking to extract the most profit from many individual products or transactions'. Extending this view, Boot (2000, p. 10) defines relationship banking as the provision of financial services by a financial intermediary that: '(i) invests in obtaining customer-specific information, often proprietary in nature' and '(ii) evaluates the profitability of these investments through multiple interactions with the same customer over time and/or across products'. Holland (1993) differentiates relationship banking from transaction banking (that is, arms-length banking) by characterizing relationship banking as possessing: rich flows of information between both parties; a regular level of business with low margins; privileged access by the bank to large deals; strong loyalty and commitment between both parties; and expectations for a fair long-term relationship. In contrast, transaction banking focuses on a single transaction with a customer or multiple identical transactions with various customers rather than an information-intensive relationship with a customer (Boot 2000, Boot and Thakor 2000).

The bank–corporate relationships have been recognized as critical in the financial services marketing literature (Boot 2000). The relationships are said to be vital to maintain future earnings, maximize profits for both banks, reduce cost and safeguard against uncertainty for the buyer of financial services (Holland 1993, Ndubisi 2003, Seybold 2001). Other benefits of relationship banking are said to include commitment (Kassim *et al.* 2006), cooperation (Zineldin 1995), exchange of information (Boot 2000) and social benefits (Henning-Thurau *et al.* 2002).

Similar to relationship banking in the West, the importance of business relationships has been well-acknowledged in the context for our research (that is, China), where the relationship is termed as *guanxi* (Leung and Wong 2001). *Guanxi* literally means 'passing the gate and getting connected' and refers to relationships or social connections based on mutual interests and benefits of exchange partners (Don and Dawes 2005). *Guanxi* brings the exchange partners together through reciprocal exchange of preferential treatment for example, easy access to limited resources, increased accessibility to controlled information, and protection from external competitors (Lee *et al.* 2001). *Guanxi* is said to possess some unique features distinguishable from relationship banking in the West; for example, direct personal relationships among individuals and more implicit role expectations beyond the existing role expectations (Lee *et al.* 2001). However, some commentators (for example, Bjorkman and Kock 1995) have suggested that *guanxi* is another form of relationship marketing in China.

The conceptualization of commitment

Dwyer *et al.* (1987) describe the behavioural dimensions of a relationship development process with a five-phase model. First, the awareness phase is the recognition of a potential cooperative partnership based on self-analysis, chemistry and compatibility. In a banking context this would reflect simply an awareness in both parties that each other existed, without any formal contact taking place. Following awareness, in the exploratory phase, the ability and willingness to deliver satisfaction is tested. In bank–corporate relationships, this would be characterized by some contact, a meeting or lunch, where each party made the other aware of their organizational needs and ability to deliver.

This stage remains tenuous, as neither has made any significant investment in financial terms or management time. The third phase, expansion, is an official endorsement or approval of the relationship by key stakeholders within each partner's environment. The expansion phase is differentiated from exploratory by the level of trust that exists between the parties. In corporate banking relationships, each would have to share some proprietary information at this stage to make this work. For example, the financial manager might reveal future financial plans, and the banker might disseminate pricing and credit information. Fourth, in the commitment phase, the partners achieve a level of satisfaction from the exchange process and exclude other substitute primary exchanges partners. For commitment to occur, there needs to be a relatively high degree of input from both parties and an expectation that the relationship will continue. For example, the bank might agree to provide a committed line of credit, in return for the company to purchase other services (for example, foreign exchange, interest-rate swaps) from the banking service portfolio. The fifth and final phase, dissolution, is the outcome of unresolved problems such as operational and cultural differences.

Among the five phases of relationship exchange, commitment is recognized as the most desirable phase in relationship development between business partners (Dwyer *et al.* 1987, Ndubisi 2007). Commitment is defined as 'an implicit or explicit pledge of relational continuity between exchange partners' (Dwyer *et al.* 1987, p. 19) and is central to the foundation of successful relationship marketing (Sweeney and Webb 2007). Morgan and Hunt (1994, p. 23) argue that commitment is 'an exchange partner believing that an ongoing relationship with another is so important as to warrant maximum efforts at maintaining it'. These definitions, along with others in the exchange relationships literature (for example, Fullerton 2003), draw on the organizational behaviour literature's conceptualization of employee commitment, to inform understanding of customer commitment.

A review of current literature identified that commitment is conceptualized as a central element in the development and maintenance of long-term customer relationships. In the social exchange literature, Cook and Emerson (1978, p. 728) characterized commitment as 'a variable we believe to be central elements distinguishing social from economic exchange'. In the organizational and buyer behaviour literature, it is viewed as central as it leads to important outcomes such as decreased turnover, higher motivation, recruiting and training practice, job equity and organizational support (Porter *et al.* 1974, Caldwell *et al.* 1990, Eisenberger *et al.* 1990). In the services marketing literature, mutual commitment is said to be the foundation of the development of relationships and brand loyalty (Assael 1987, Berry and Parasuraman 1991). Therefore, commitment should be a central feature in any model that introduces relationship exchanges to the bank–corporate relationships (De Ruyter and Wetzels 1999).

Two different types of commitment are identified in the literature: (1) Affective Commitment; and (2) Calculative Commitment. Affective Commitment is an approach to viewing commitment as an affective state of mind that one partner has toward a relationship with the other (Rhoades *et al.* 2001, Fullerton 2003). Meyer and Allen (1991) regard affective commitment as the desire to continue a relationship because of positive affective feeling towards the partner. These relationships where an affective commitment plays a role are likely to be more enduring than those based solely on the material merits of the exchange (De Ruyter and Wetzels 1999).

Calculative Commitment, in contrast to Affective Commitment, is characterized by being more behavioural rather than affective (Meyer and Allen 1991, Gilliland and Bello 2002). Geyskens *et al.* (1996) defined calculative commitment as the extent to which exchange partners perceive the need to maintain a relationship, given the anticipated termination or switching costs associated with leaving. This definition implies an explicit evaluation of the costs and benefits involved in developing and maintaining the relationship, as Morgan and Hunt (1994) noted that all gains and losses, pluses and minuses, rewards and punishments are calculated.

Antecedents of commitment

De Ruyter and Wetzels (1999) identified six antecedents of commitment drawing on the prior research in the field of exchange relationships. We adopt these antecedents in this study with minor change of wording namely: (1) Shared Values; (2) Service Quality; (3) Trust; (4) Interdependence; (5) Service Portfolio; and (6) Customer Orientation.

Shared Values is a variable of significant interest in the organizational commitment literature (Chatman 1991). Morgan and Hunt (1994, p. 25) posited shared values as a direct precursor of relationship commitment, defining it as 'the extent to which partners have beliefs in common about what behaviours, goals and policies are important or unimportant, appropriate or inappropriate, and right or wrong'. Dwyer *et al.* (1987) proposed that shared values contribute to the development of commitment and trust. It was also empirically demonstrated that shared values contribute positively to the development of affective commitment (Morgan and Hunt 1994). Therefore, we hypothesize that:

H_1:   There will be a positive relationship between Shared Values and Affective Commitment.

Service Quality is 'one of the most investigated constructs in the service sector' (Fullerton 2005, p. 1375) and has long been recognized as a key issue for service organizations (Ndubisi 2003). Grönroos (1984, p. 37) defined service quality as 'the outcome of an evaluation process, where consumer compares his expectations with the service he has received' and argued that customers' overall evaluations of service quality are a result of their assessment of two dimensions: (1) functional quality; and (2) technical quality. Extending this view, Parasuraman *et al.* (1988, p. 16) conceptualized service quality as 'a global judgment, or attitude, relating to superiority of the service, whereas satisfaction is related to a specific transaction'. Prior research on financial services has shown that favourable perceptions of service quality lead to positive word-of-mouth referrals, customer satisfaction, increased future usage intentions and continuity in customer relationships (Angur *et al.* 1999, Caruana 2002). It was also suggested that service quality is a significant determinant and predictor of commitment (Gruen *et al.* 2000). Therefore, we hypothesize that:

H_2:   There will be a positive relationship between Service Quality and Affective Commitment.

Trust is said to be a 'cornerstone of the strategic partnership' (Spekman 1988, p. 79) and leads to a strong desire to maintain a relationship between exchange partners (Ndubisi 2006). Moorman *et al.* (1993) conceptualized trust as a willingness to rely on an exchange partner in whom one has confidence. Anderson and Weitz (1989) defined it as one party's belief that its needs will be fulfilled in the future by actions undertaken by the other party. Trust is said to exist only when one party has confidence in the reliability and integrity of the exchange partner (Morgan and Hunt 1994). Adamson *et al.* (2003) and Armstrong and Seng (2000) view trust as an antecedent of commitment. Empirically, trust has a positive influence on affective commitment (Lin *et al.* 2003, Martin *et al.* 2004) and a negative influence on calculative commitment (Geyskens and Steenkamp 1995). Therefore, we hypothesize that:

H_3:   There will be a positive relationship between Trust and Affective Commitment.
H_4:   There will be a negative relationship between Trust and Calculative Commitment.

Interdependence is another antecedent of commitment, as Terawatanavong *et al.* (2007, p. 918) suggest it 'represents a level of cohesion in terms of roles, tasks and resources between buyers and suppliers'. High magnitude interdependence produces an environment in which trust and commitment can be cultivated because of the convergence of the partners' interests (Kumar *et al.* 1995, Izquierdo and Cillan 2004). In a state of relatively high interdependence, both partners in a relationship benefit from valued contribution from each other and create their own switching barriers (Anderson and Weitz 1989). Empirically, Kumar *et al.* (1995) provided evidence for a positive relationship between interdependence and affective commitment. Geyskens and Steenkamp (1995) reported that there is a positive relationship between interdependence and calculative commitment. Therefore, we hypothesize that:

H_5:   There will be a positive relationship between Interdependence and Affective Commitment.
H_6:   There will be a positive relationship between Interdependence and Calculative Commitment.

The Service Portfolio of an organization is a collection of services offered by the organization. In the corporate banking sector, banks are always willing to enrich their service portfolio in order to gain competitive advantage over their competitors. An extended service portfolio goes beyond traditional lending or funding (Boot 2000), and contains a full range of corporate banking services such as letter of credit, cash management services, currency management services and risk management services. As the service portfolio is primarily a cost–benefit issue (MacKenzie 1992), we posit a positive relationship between service portfolio and calculative commitment:

H_7:   There will be a positive relationship between Service Portfolio and Calculative Commitment.

Customer Orientation is viewed as the practice of the marketing concept, which holds that, 'the key to achieving organizational goals consists in determining the needs and wants of target markets and delivering the desired satisfactions more effectively and efficiently than competitors' (Kotler 1998, p. 17). Coulter and Coulter (2002) view it as the service provider's ability to vary the services offered in terms of specific service attributes in order to suit the customer needs. By incorporating customer orientation into their strategic planning, an organization can be sensitive to customer needs and outperform their competitors (Kulp *et al.* 2004, Cross *et al.* 2007). In the financial services industry, Adamson *et al.* (2003) suggest that banks must adapt a customer-oriented approach in order to be successful in the corporate sector. Empirically, customer orientation has been viewed as mainly affectively oriented as it involves interaction between service provider and customers (Saxe and Weitz 1982). This is particularly evident in relationship banking that normally involves a high degree of interaction between bankers and financial managers. Therefore, we hypothesize that:

H_8:   There will be a positive relationship between Customer Orientation and Affective Commitment.

Consequences of commitment

An ultimate objective of any organization engaged in relationships is an interest in the continuance of those relationships (Gundlach *et al.* 1995). Two dimensions key to the continuance of relationships are identified in the extant relationship literature: (1) Cooperation; and (2) Opportunistic Behaviour.

Cooperation refers to the situation in which exchange partners work together to achieve mutual objectives with expected reciprocity over time (Anderson and Narus 1990). Pesämaa and Hair (2007) view cooperation as an essential strategy to improve an organization's competitiveness. However, both parties may experience a reduction of their expected profit as cooperation requires them to invest in their relationships. Empirically, Morgan and Hunt (1994) demonstrated the presence of a positive relationship between affective commitment and cooperation. Kumar *et al.* (1994) reported that calculative commitment has a negative impact on an intermediary's desire to stay and invest in the relationship. Therefore, we hypothesize that:

H_9:   There will be a positive relationship between Affective Commitment and Cooperation.

H_{10}:   There will be a negative relationship between Calculative Commitment and Cooperation.

In the organizational behaviour literature, opportunistic behaviour has been described as the behaviour of a party that endangers a relationship for the purpose of taking advantage of a new opportunity, which may cause the relationship to become unstable (Gundlach *et al.* 1995). Grzeskowiak and Al-Khatib (2009) argue that opportunistic behaviour results from a multidimensional set of moral convictions held by an exchange partner. Many commentators (Klein *et al.* 1978, Provan and Skinner 1989) have suggested that an organization is likely to behave opportunistically when its exchange partner is heavily dependent on it. Empirically, Kumar *et al.* (1994) reported that business parties with higher levels of affective commitment are less inclined to engage in opportunistic behaviour, whist business parties with higher levels of calculative commitment are more likely to seek to develop alternatives to their counterparts. Therefore, we hypothesize that:

H_{11}:   There will be a negative relationship between Affective Commitment and Opportunistic Behaviour.

H_{12}:   There will be a positive relationship between Calculative Commitment and Opportunistic Behaviour.

Finally, commitment only becomes meaningful when it develops consistently over time and results in Continuance Intentions (Moorman *et al.* 1993). High levels of commitment and cooperation are said to lead to a strong intention to stay in a relationship (Kumar *et al.* 1994). In the corporate banking sector, continuance intentions reflect a company's intention to keep a bank as its primary financial services provider and to maintain the relationship with the bank. We therefore posit that a positive relationship will exist between cooperation and continuance intentions. We also hypothesize that opportunistic behaviour will negatively influence continuance intentions, as this type of behaviour is likely to result in the dissolution of relationships (Heide and John 1992). These hypotheses are framed as:

H_{13}:   There will be a positive relationship between Cooperation and Continuance Intentions.

H_{14}:   There will be a negative relationship between Opportunistic Behaviour and Continuance Intentions.

To summarize, we have developed 14 positive or negative hypothesized relationships relating to the antecedents and consequences of commitment. We further introduce them into a hypothesized conceptual model (see Figure 1). The next section describes the conduct of questionnaire survey and the development of research instruments.

Method

Inventory administration procedure

Financial managers were chosen as respondents for our survey as these individuals manage their company's relationship with its corporate bankers (that is, primary financial services providers). The company sample was drawn from the *'Directory of Chinese Companies (Beijing Area)'*. Using stratified random sampling,[4] a sample of 800 was selected. Each questionnaire was accompanied by a personalized covering letter describing the purpose of the study and a prepaid, self-addressed envelope. The covering letter was addressed to financial managers. To increase response rate, a reminder letter was sent out two weeks later. A second reminder letter was sent out along with another copy of questionnaire.

Participants

In total, 259 usable responses were received, representing a response rate of 32.4%. Among the respondents, 54.8% were from companies within the urban area; 45.2% were from suburb area. Small, medium and large companies accounted for 64.5%, 19.7% and 15.8%, respectively. The respondents also represented companies which were engaged in the first industry (10.8%), the second industry (33.2%), and the third industry (56.0%).[5] An analysis of response by company size, location and industry classification is provided in Table 1.

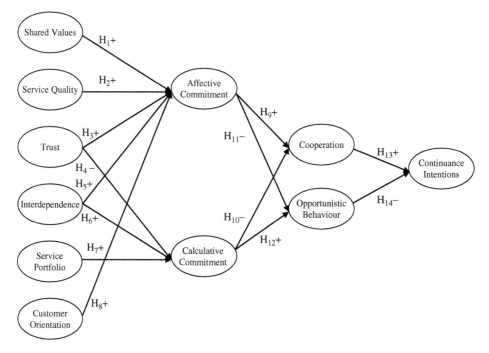

Figure 1.   Hypothesized conceptual model.

Table 1. Analysis of respondents by company size, location and industry classification ($N = 259$).

Company size	No.	%	Location	No.	%	Industry classification	No.	%
Small	167	64.5	Urban	142	54.8	First	28	10.8
Medium	51	19.7	Suburb	117	45.2	Second	86	33.2
Large	41	15.8				Third	145	56
Total	259	100	Total	259	100	Total	259	100

Questionnaire development

A 34-item questionnaire was developed to measure Chinese financial managers' attitudes towards bank–corporate relationships using closed-form questions only.[6] All of the items were presented in seven-point Likert response format with the anchors 'strongly disagree' and 'strongly agree'. The questionnaire contained four sections and each of the items pertained to the constructs presented in our conceptual model. Table 2 provides examples of items used. The contents of the four sections are described as follows.

(1) Commitment. This section covers affective commitment and calculative commitment. Affective commitment is measured by three items based on the scales from organizational research (Kumar *et al.* 1995). Calculative commitment is measured by three items derived from the previous commitment research (Geyskens *et al.* 1996, De Ruyter and Wetzels 1999).

(2) Antecedents of commitment. This section covers the six antecedents of commitment aforementioned. Shared values are measured using two items derived from the scale developed by Morgan and Hunt (1994). Service quality is measured by two items derived from the scale of Zeithaml *et al.* (1990). Trust is measured by three items based on the scale of Kumar *et al.* (1995). Interdependence is measured

Table 2. Examples of items used in the questionnaire.

Construct	Number of items	Item
1. Affective commitment	3	'You want to remain a member of this bank's network because you genuinely enjoy your relationship with it'
2. Calculative commitment	3	'You want to maintain your relationship with this bank given the anticipated termination or switching costs'
3. Shared values	2	'To succeed in this business, it is often necessary to compromise one's ethics'
4. Service quality	2	'You feel that this bank's service quality is excellent'
5. Trust	3	'You can count on this bank to be sincere'
6. Interdependence	3	'There are no other banks which could provide you with the comparable services'
7. Service portfolio	2	'The service portfolio of this bank meets your expectations'
8. Customer orientation	3	'This bank tries to understand what services you really need'
9. Cooperation	4	'This bank and your company actively work together as partners'
10. Opportunistic behaviour	3	'If there is a good alternative to this bank, your will terminate your relationship with the bank'
11. Continuance intentions	3	'You expect that your relationship with this bank will continue for a long time'

by three items derived from the scale of Kumar *et al.* (1995). Service portfolio is measured by two items derived from the scale of Van der Walt *et al.* (1994) and De Ruyter and Wetzels (1999). To measure customer orientation, three items are modified from the *SOCO* scale of Saxe and Weitz (1982).

(3) Consequences of commitment. This section covers the three hypothesized consequences of commitment. Cooperation is measured by three items based on the scale developed by MacKenzie (1992). Opportunistic behaviour uses three items derived from the scales of Morgan and Hunt (1994) and De Ruyter and Wetzels (1999). Continuance intentions are measured by three items adopted from the scale developed by Shemwell *et al.* (1994).

(4) Demographic items. This section contains three demographic questions relating to company size, location and industry classification.

The questionnaire was translated into Chinese following Brislin's (1970) back-translation procedure. They were then piloted by bilinguals to avoid misinterpretation and pre-tested by financial managers to detect biases. This was deemed necessary, since the concern was not so much with a literal translation but with generating meaning which was as similar as possible to the English version.

Statistical analysis

The statistical analysis proceeds in three parts. First, alpha coefficients are calculated for scores yielded by the questionnaire in terms of each hypothesized constructs to estimate internal consistency reliability. Second, correlation coefficients are used to primarily assess the relationships between the hypothesized constructs. Third, the hypothesized conceptual model is tested by SEM.

Confirmatory factor analysis (CFA) using AMOS[7] (Arbuckle 2003) was undertaken to assess the fit of the conceptual model. Maximum likelihood estimation via AMOS was used to conduct CFA using the covariance matrices of the scaled scores. To evaluate the fit of the hypothesized model, Tucker-Lewis index (TLI), comparative fit index (CFI), and the standardized root mean square residual (SRMSR) were used in tandem with the root mean square error of approximation (RMSEA). To perform the hypothesis testing, standardized path coefficients were calculated and statistical significance testing was undertaken ($\alpha = 0.05$).

Results

Response bias

A number of tests for response bias were performed on the sample of 259 financial managers. Statistical significance testing was undertaken ($\alpha = 0.05$). First, the timing of response was analysed as a test of non-response bias (Armstrong and Overton 1977). Scores of the hypothesized constructs were compared between early respondents (first 50) and late respondents (last 50) in the sample, using independent samples t-test. This assumes late respondents are similar to non-respondents (Dillman 1978). No statistically significant differences ($\alpha = 0.05$) were found across the 11 hypothesized constructs and 31 questionnaire items between the early respondent group and the late respondent group. Second, companies were formed into three groups based on their company size (small, medium and large companies). A chi-squared test indicated no significant association between company size and early/late responders ($\chi^2(2, N = 100) = 0.069$, $p = 0.966$).

Third, this comparison was also applied to groups divided by geographic location (urban and suburb area). A chi-squared test indicated no significant association between geographic location and early/late responders ($\chi^2(1, N = 100) = 0.119, p = 0.942$). Finally, early and late responding companies were compared on the basis of industry classification (that is, first, second and third industry). A chi-squared test indicated no significant association between industry classification and early/late responders (χ^2 (2, $N = 100) = 0.364, p = 0.833$).

Considering the results of response bias tests and the response rate (32.4%), response bias is not a serious threat to the validity of this research. In addition, all respondents were financial managers who are the individuals who manage the company's relationship with its corporate bankers. The covering letters of the research instrument were also addressed to these financial managers. Consequently, the risk of uninformed response bias is considered to be minimal.

Internal consistency reliability

The internal consistency reliability of scores yielded by the constructs of the hypothesized conceptual model is assessed – see Table 3. Alpha coefficients of the constructs ranged from 0.81 to 0.94, whilst the overall reliability reached a level of 0.85. These values exceed the cut-off value of 0.70 suggested by Nunnally (1978) for instruments suitable for applied research in a variety of settings. The correlation coefficients between all the constructs in the conceptual model are shown in Table 4.

Hypothesis testing using SEM

Structural equation modeling (SEM) is used to test the hypothesized conceptual model. CFA was conducted and the hypothesized model demonstrated a satisfactory fit to the data. All model fit measures exceeded the recommended cut-off values.[8,9] The standardized path coefficients and corresponding p–values are reported in Table 5.

First, the hypothesized relationships between the two types of commitment and their antecedents are tested (hypotheses 1–8). H_1 is supported on the basis of a significant positive relationship between shared values and affective commitment (standardized path coefficient $= 0.17, p < 0.01$). With regard to service quality as the antecedent to affective commitment, a statistically significant positive relationship is found between service quality and affective commitment (standardized path coefficient $= 0.79, p < 0.01$), which supports

Table 3. Internal reliability estimates, means and standard deviations of constructs in commitment, antecedents and consequences of commitment ($N = 259$).

Construct	Alpha coefficient	Mean	Std dev
Affective commitment	0.88	4.98	1.85
Calculative commitment	0.86	4.22	1.37
Shared ethical values	0.81	5.18	1.39
Perceived service quality	0.94	5.06	1.43
Trust	0.89	4.83	1.32
Perceived interdependence	0.89	2.93	1.33
Service portfolio	0.90	4.57	1.45
Customer orientation	0.90	3.26	1.80
Cooperation	0.88	3.78	1.46
Opportunistic behaviour	0.93	3.76	1.37
Continuance intentions	0.87	5.39	1.25

Table 4. Correlations between constructs in commitment, antecedents and consequences of commitment ($N = 259$).

	AC	CC	SV	SQ	TR	ID	SP	CO	COOP	OPB
AC										
CC	0.30**									
SV	0.13*	−0.24**								
SQ	0.80**	0.15*	0.04							
TR	0.50**	−0.15*	−0.01	0.71**						
ID	−0.12*	0.29**	−0.39**	0.13*	0.31**					
SP	0.41**	0.37**	−0.01	0.35**	0.36**	0.18**				
CO	0.57**	0.36**	−0.06	0.48**	0.41**	0.23**	0.39**			
COOP	0.28**	−0.12**	0.18**	0.32**	0.21**	−0.30**	0.11	0.54**		
OPB	−0.11	0.39**	−0.36**	−0.04	−0.10	0.30**	−0.14*	0.25**	0.05	
CON	0.41**	−0.03	0.22**	0.57**	0.44**	−0.11	0.15*	0.10	0.23**	−0.27**

Notes: AC = Affective commitment; CC = Calculative commitment; SV = Shared values; SQ = Service quality; TR = Trust; ID = Interdependence; SP = Service portfolio; CO = Customer orientation; COOP = Cooperation; OPB = Opportunistic behaviour; CON = Continuance intentions. ** Correlation coefficient is statistically significant at $p < 0.01$. * Correlation coefficient is statistically significant at $p < 0.05$.

Table 5. Result of hypothesis testing by SEM.

Hypothesis	Relationships	Hypothesized relationships	Standardized path coefficient	p-value
H_1	SV → AC	Positive	0.17	**
H_2	SQ → AC	Positive	0.79	**
H_3	TR → AC	Positive	0.16	**
H_4	TR → CC	Negative	− 0.15	0.14
H_5	ID → AC	Positive	− 0.06	0.06
H_6	ID → CC	Positive	0.27	**
H_7	SP → CC	Positive	0.31	**
H_8	CO → AC	Positive	0.24	**
H_9	AC → COOP	Positive	0.34	**
H_{10}	CC → COOP	Negative	− 0.22	**
H_{11}	AC → OPB	Negative	− 0.01	0.82
H_{12}	CC → OPB	Positive	0.39	**
H_{13}	COOP → CON	Positive	0.24	**
H_{14}	OPB → CON	Negative	− 0.28	**
CFA				
Goodness-of-fit statistics	$\chi^2 = 79.43$; df $= 41$; $\chi^2/df = 1.94$; RMSEA $= 0.057$; SRMR $= 0.076$			

Note: SV = Shared values; SQ = Service quality; AC = Affective commitment; CC = Calculative commitment; TR = Trust; ID = Interdependence; SP = Service portfolio; CO = Customer orientation; COOP = Cooperation; OPB = Opportunistic behaviour; CON = Continuance intentions.
** Standardized path coefficient is statistically significant ($p < 0.01$).

H_2. A positive relationship between trust and affective commitment is identified, supporting H_3 (standardized path coefficient $= 0.16$, $p < 0.01$). A negative relationship between trust and calculative commitment is found as hypothesized; however, the result is not statistically significant (standardized path coefficient $= -0.15$, $p = 0.14$), so that H_4 cannot be supported. A non-statistically significant relationship is also found between interdependence and affective commitment (standardized path coefficient $= -0.06$, $p = 0.06$). Moreover, in this case the relationship found is negative where a positive relationship was hypothesized, so that H_5 is also not supported. A positive relationship is found between interdependence and calculative commitment (standardized path coefficient $= 0.27$, $p < 0.01$), which supports H_6. H_7 is supported, as a positive relationship between service portfolio and calculative commitment is identified (standardized path coefficient $= 0.31$, $p < 0.01$). Finally, customer orientation is positively related to affective commitment (standardized path coefficient $= 0.24$, $p < 0.01$), a result that supports H_8.

Second, the relationships between two types of commitment and their consequences are tested (hypotheses H_{9-14}). A positive relationship is identified between affective commitment and cooperation (standardized path coefficient $= 0.34$, $p < 0.01$), and a negative relationship between calculative commitment and cooperation (standardized path coefficient $= -0.22$, $p < 0.01$). These findings are similar to previous research of Morgan and Hunt (1994) and Kumar et al. (1994); therefore both H_9 and H_{10} are supported. There is a negative relationship between affective commitment and opportunistic behaviour as hypothesized; however the result is not statistically significant (standardized path coefficient $= -0.01$, $p = 0.82$), so H_{11} is not supported. A positive association between calculative commitment and opportunistic behaviour is identified (standardized path coefficient $= 0.39$, $p < 0.01$), therefore H_{12} is supported. A positive relationship between cooperation and continuance intentions is identified (standardized path coefficient $= 0.24$, $p < 0.01$), therefore H_{13} is supported. Finally, a negative relationship between

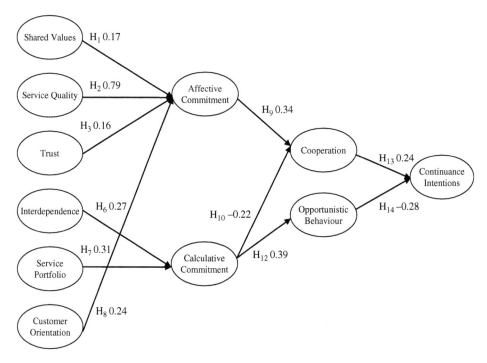

Figure 2.   SEM results.

opportunistic behaviour and continuance intentions is found (standardized path coefficient $= -0.28$, $p < 0.01$), which supports H_{14}. The results of the SEM, that is, the final model, are shown in Figure 2.

Discussion and implications

Discussion

This study aims to create a model of what motivates corporate customers to continue their relationships with their primary banks. By reference to the exchange relationships literature in the West, we proposed a conceptual model by hypothesizing positive or negative relationships between the constructs relating to commitment. The model was tested using a research instrument specifically designed for the purpose, and data collected from 259 financial managers in China.

Our results show that sufficient evidence exists to support the hypothesized positive relationships between the antecedents of commitment and the two types of commitment (Affective Commitment and Calculative Commitment). Shared Values is positively associated with Affective Commitment. Service Quality is an important indicator of Affective Commitment, with a high standardized path coefficient value (0.79). This result is in line with the prior research in the field of financial services (Angur *et al.* 1999, Caruana 2002). Trust is positively associated with Affective Commitment, which reflects prior work by and Morgan and Hunt (1994). Finally, Customer Orientation is positively related to Affective Commitment, supporting the findings of Saxe and Weitz (1982).

Considering Calculative Commitment, the results suggest a positive relationship between Interdependence and Calculative Commitment, which provides strong support to Geyskens and Steenkamp (1995). It is also demonstrated that Service Portfolio is positively associated with Calculative Commitment.

Considering the consequences of commitment, a positive relationship is found between Affective Commitment and Cooperation, supporting the findings of Morgan and Hunt (1994). Corporate customers and their banker become more dedicated to cooperate together to achieve the mutual goals when they have affective feelings towards each other. Moreover, our results extend existing findings in that high levels of cooperation are found to lead to a strong intention for corporate customers to keep the bank as its major financial service provider. Consequently, Affective Commitment leads to affirmative Continuance Intentions.

Calculative Commitment is negatively related to Cooperation which is consistent with the previous research of Kumar *et al.* (1994). Corporate customers are subject to a reduction of profit, as staying in a relationship enforces them to invest in the relationship. This exposes the existing relationship to insecurity that stimulates corporate customers to switch to other banks for lower cost. Consequently, corporate customers with higher levels of Calculative Commitment are more inclined to exhibit opportunism and hence discontinue the relationship. This is an important finding, as it demonstrates that commitment can both enhance and undermine continuance intentions. While affective commitment reduces switching intentions, calculative commitment without an affective dimension increases the likelihood of the dissolution of the relationship.

Collectively, the final model is found to be more parsimonious than the hypothesized conceptual model. Considering the antecedents of commitment, shared values, service quality, trust and customer orientation are the four precursors of affective commitment; interdependence and service portfolio are the two precursors of calculative commitment. Considering the consequences of commitment, affective commitment leads to cooperation and results in continuance intentions; calculative commitment leads to opportunistic behaviour and failure to cooperate, and hence pushes a relationship into a state of discontinuance or dissolution.

The data collected from 259 financial managers in China provided an excellent fit to our hypothesized model. Psychometric support was found for a majority of 11 (of 14) hypotheses, despite the fact that the hypothesized relationships were proposed on the basis of the exchange relationships literature in the West. This is another important finding, as although a large cohort of commentators (for example, Davies *et al.* 1995, Lee *et al.* 2001) have suggested that business relationships in China possess some unique cultural features (for example, *guanxi*), our hypothesis-testing results indicate that many concepts in the exchange relationships literature in the West can be adopted into the Chinese corporate banking sector.

Implications

The policy implications arising from this investigation for bank management and treasury practitioners are many and varied. The positive relationships between the antecedents of commitment and two types of commitments suggest that bank management should cautiously consider which kind of shared values corporate customers expect from their banks (Wetzel *et al.* 1998). The creation of trust in the relationship could also be a focus for both bankers and financial managers. Trust arises if the service provider is honest and benevolent with the customer; therefore, fair treatment, open communication and cooperative orientation should be considered to build up the blocks of trust (Geyskens *et al.* 1996). Bank management should also carefully target the market and gain access to those customers who genuinely wish to engage in relationships with their bankers.

In particular, our results suggest affective commitment is significantly influenced by service quality. We conclude that service quality is a significant precursor of affective commitment, which in turn leads to cooperation and continuance intentions. Given intense competition within the corporate banking market, bank management should be aware of the importance of service quality in contributing to the development of good bank–corporate relationships (Turnbull and Moustakatos 1996). Banks will benefit economically from focusing their efforts on improving service quality, for example, regularly visiting corporate customers, providing adequate training for bank staff, and recruiting staff with social skills that assist the development of long-standing customer relationships.

To foster calculative commitment, bank management should concentrate more on service portfolio and other technical quality matters, that is, *what* is provided, rather than the functional quality issue, *how* the service is provided (Grönroos 1984). However, bank management should also try to avoid those relationships where corporate customers only demonstrate calculative commitment, as our results identify calculative commitment as positively associated with opportunistic behaviour and negatively correlated with cooperation, reducing expectations of relationship continuation. Without a genuine attempt to develop affective commitment, banks' efforts to develop their relationships with corporate customers will be ineffective.

Finally, this study has four limitations that are suggestive of future research. First, concerns may arise with regard to the lack of complexity of the constructs used in the hypothesized conceptual model. Actually, only the major constructs in the exchange relationships literature were adopted in the conceptual model. Other possible constructs in the commitment literature may be added into the model, for example moral commitment, that is, the feeling of obligation to stay with an organization or partner (Kumar *et al.* 1994). Other potential constructs that have been identified from the relationship banking literature may also be included, for example exchange of information (Boot 2000), communication (Adamson *et al.* 2003) and word-of-mouth (Henning-Thurau *et al.* 2002, Wong and Zhou 2006). Second, several relationships remain uncertain, as three hypothesized relationships were found to be statistically unsupported: the relationship between Trust and Calculative Commitment; the relationship between Interdependence and Affective Commitment; and the relationship between Affective Commitment and Opportunistic Behaviour. This could be due to the specific nature of the Chinese banking market we investigated, and hence further research is deemed necessary to illuminate these unclear relationships. Third, this study has hypothesized and empirically tested many relationships between the constructs relating to affective and calculative commitment. However, it would be both interesting and necessary to examine other direct relationships that may exist between the hypothesized constructs in our conceptual model. For example, further research could usefully test the relationship between trust and cooperation and the relationship between trust and continuance intentions. Finally, the data were collected from corporate customers in China and hence the finding of this study should be cautiously translated to other contexts. A direction for further research would be to replicate this study in other cultures (for example, Korea and Thailand) to assess the structure of committed bank–corporate relationships.

Notes

1. The four specialized state-owned banks include Agricultural Bank of China, providing banking services for agricultural and rural industrial projects, Bank of China, conducting foreign exchange operation, China Construction Bank, providing loans for fixed assets investment, and Industrial and Commercial Bank of China, majoring in industrial and commercial business.

2. The three policy banks include State Development Bank for infrastructure financing, Export–Import Bank for trade financing, and Agricultural Development Bank for agricultural financing.
3. China accessed the World Trade Organization (WTO) in December 2001. According to the WTO timetable, the entrance impediments of the Chinese banking market were fully removed in December 2006, and foreign and domestic banks should be able to provide the same products to all customers throughout the country.
4. The stratified sampling was based on both company size (that is, small company, medium company and large company) and geographic location (urban area and suburban area).
5. The classification criterion of company location, size and industry was enacted by the Statistics Bureau of Beijing in 2002.

Urban area:	Within the 4th Ring Road (Beijing)
Suburb area:	Beyond the 4th Ring Road (Beijing)
Small company:	Less than 50 people
Medium company:	Between 51–100 people
Large company:	More than 101 people
The first industry:	Agriculture, forestry, stock raising and fishery
The second industry:	Mining, manufacturing, construction, production and distribution of electricity, gas and water
The third industry:	All the rest industries apart from first and second industries, including transport, communication, wholesale and retail, eating and drinking, finance and insurance, real estate, services and government, etc.

6. The questionnaire is attached in the Appendix.
7. AMOS is a statistical program to perform structural equation modelling, a form of multivariate analysis.
8. The combinational rule of $RMSEA < 0.06$ and $SRMR < 0.08$ for samples ($N < 500$) was used, as it is 'extremely sensitive in detecting models with mispecified factor covariances' (Hu and Bentler 1999, p. 26).
9. Many authors (Marsh *et al.* 1998, Hu and Bentler 1999) warn against use of more common goodness-of-fit indices such as the goodness-of-fit index (GFI) and adjusted goodness-of-fit index (AGFI) which are widely used in the structural equation modelling literature.

Notes on contributors

Xin Guo is a Lecturer in Accounting and Finance at the Business School of the University of the West of Scotland. His main research interests include banking relations, service quality measurement, accounting education, structural equation modelling, and accounting and finance in China.

Angus Duff is a Professor of Accounting and Finance at the University of the West of Scotland and Research Advisor to the Institute of Chartered Accountants of Scotland. He has published extensively in academic and professional journals. His current interests lie in accounting education, the accounting profession, credit rating agencies and credit markets.

Mario Hair is a statistics Lecturer at the University of West of Scotland and is also an active researcher and consultant within the Statistics Consultancy Unit based at the university.

References

Adamson, I., Chan, K.M., and Handford, D., 2003. Relationship marketing: customer commitment and trust as a strategy for the smaller Hong Kong corporate banking sector. *International journal of bank marketing*, 21 (6/7), 347–358.
Anderson, E. and Weitz, B., 1989. Determinants of continuity in conventional industrial channel dyads. *Marketing science*, 4, 310–323.
Anderson, J.C. and Narus, J.A., 1990. A model of distributor firm and manufacturer firm working partnerships. *Journal of marketing research*, 54, 42–58.

Angur, M.G., Nataraajan, R., and Jahera, J.S. Jr., 1999. Service quality in the banking industry: an assessment in a developing economy. *International journal of bank marketing*, 17, 116–123.

Arbuckle, J.L., 2003. *Amos 5.0 update to the user's guide*. Chicago, IL: SmallWaters Corporation.

Armstrong, J.S. and Overton, T.S., 1977. Estimating non-response bias in mail surveys. *Journal of marketing research*, 14, 396–402.

Armstrong, R.W. and Seng, T.B., 2000. Corporate-customer satisfaction in the banking industry of Singapore. *International journal of bank marketing*, 18 (3), 97–111.

Assael, H., 1987. *Consumer behaviour and marketing action*. Boston: Kent Publishing Company.

Berry, L.L., 1983. Relationship marketing. *In*: L.L. Berry, G.L. Shostack and G.D. Upah, eds. *Emerging perspectives on service marketing*. Chicago, IL: AMA, 25–28.

Berry, L.L. and Parasuraman, A., 1991. *Marketing services: competing through quality*. New York: The Free Press.

Bjorkman, I. and Kock, S., 1995. Social relationships and business networks: the case of western companies in China. *International business review*, 4, 519–535.

Boot, A.W.A. and Thakor, A.V., 2000. Can relationship banking survive competition? *Journal of finance*, 55, 679–713.

Boot, W.A., 2000. Relationship banking: what do we know? *Journal of financial intermediation*, 9, 7–25.

Brislin, R.W., 1970. Back-translation for cross-cultural research. *Journal of cross-cultural psychology*, 1, 185–216.

Caldwell, D.F., Chatman, J.A., and O'Reilly, C.A., 1990. Building organizational commitment: a multiform study. *Journal of occupational psychology*, 63, 245–261.

Caruana, A., 2002. Service loyalty: the effect of service quality and the mediating role of customer satisfaction. *European journal of marketing*, 36, 811–828.

Chatman, J., 1991. Matching people and organizations: selection and socialization in public accounting firms. *Administrative science quarterly*, 36, 459–484.

Cook, K.S. and Emerson, R.M., 1978. Power, equity, and commitment in exchange networks. *American sociological review*, 43, 721–739.

Coulter, K.S. and Coulter, R.A., 2002. Determinants of trust in service providers: the moderating role of length of relationship. *Journal of service marketing*, 16 (1), 35–50.

Cross, M.E., Brashear, T.G., Rigdon, E.E., and Bellenger, D.N., 2007. Customer orientation and salesperson performance. *European journal of marketing*, 41 (7/8), 821–835.

Davies, H., Leung, T.K.P., Luk, S.T.K., and Wong, Y.H., 1995. The benefits of guanxi: the value of relationships in developing the Chinese market. *Industrial marketing management*, 24, 207–214.

Deloitte, 2007. *China's banking sector: growing towards diversification*. Deloitte: Touche Tohmatsu.

De Ruyter, K. and Wetzels, M., 1999. Commitment in auditor-client relationships: antecedents and consequences. *Accounting, organization and society*, 24, 57–75.

Dibb, S. and Meadows, M., 2001. The application of a relationship marketing perspective in retail banking. *Services industries journal*, 21 (1), 169–194.

Dillman, D.A., 1978. *Mail and telephone surveys: the total design method*. New York: John Wiley & Sons.

Don, Y. and Dawes, P.L., 2005. Guanxi, trust, and long-term orientation in Chinese business markets. *Journal of international marketing*, 13 (2), 28–56.

Dwyer, F.R., Schurr, P.H., and Oh, S., 1987. Developing buyer-seller relationships. *Journal of marketing*, 51, 11–27.

Eisenberger, R., Fasolo, P., and Davis-LaMastro, V., 1990. Perceived organizational support and employee diligence, commitment and innovation. *Journal of applied psychology*, 75, 51–59.

Fullerton, G., 2003. When does commitment lead to loyalty? *Journal of service research*, 5, 333–344.

Fullerton, G., 2005. How commitment both enables and undermines marketing relationships. *European journal of marketing*, 39, 1372–1388.

Geyskens, I. and Steenkamp, J.B., 1995. An investigation into the joint effects of trust and interdependence on relationship commitment. *In: EMAC proceedings*. Paris, 351–371.

Geyskens, I., Steenkamp, J.B., Scheer, L.K., and Kumar, N., 1996. The effects of trust and interdependence on relationship commitment: a transatlantic study. *International journal of research in marketing*, 13, 303–317.

Gilliland, D.I. and Bello, D.C., 2002. Two sides to attitudinal commitment: the effect of calculative and loyalty commitment on enforcement mechanisms in distribution channels. *Journal of the academy of marketing science*, 30 (1), 24–43.

Grönroos, C., 1984. A service quality model and its marketing implications. *European journal of marketing*, 18, 36–44.

Grönroos, C., 1997. Value-driven relational marketing: from products to resources and competences. *Journal of marketing management*, 13, 407–439.

Gruen, T., Summers, J., and Acito, F., 2000. Relationship marketing activities commitment, and membership behaviours in professional associations. *Journal of marketing*, 64, 34–39.

Grzeskowiak, S. and Al-Khatib, J.A., 2009. Does morality explain opportunism in marketing channel negotiations? The moderating role of trust. *International journal of retail and distribution management*, 37 (2), 142–160.

Gundlach, G.T., Achrol, R.S., and Mentzer, J.T., 1995. The structure of commitment in exchange. *Journal of marketing*, 59, 78–92.

Heide, J.B. and John, G., 1992. Do norms really matter? *Journal of marketing*, 56, 32–44.

Hennig-Thurau, T., Gwinner, K.P., and Gremler, D.D., 2002. Understanding relationship marketing outcomes: an integration of relational benefits and relationship quality. *Journal of service research*, 4 (February), 230–247.

Holland, J.B., 1993. Bank-corporate relations: change issues in the international enterprise. *Accounting and business research*, 23, 273–283.

Howcroft, B. and Durkin, M., 2000. Reflections on bank–customer interactions in the new millennium. *Journal of financial services marketing*, 5 (1), 9–20.

Hu, L. and Bentler, P.M., 1999. Cut-off criteria for fit indices in covariance structure analysis: conventional versus new alternatives. *Structural equation modeling*, 6, 1–55.

Izquierdo, C.C. and Cillan, J.G., 2004. The interaction of dependence and trust in long-term industrial relationships. *European journal of marketing*, 38 (8), 974–994.

Kassim, N.M., Mohammed, A.K., and Abdulla, A., 2006. The influence of attraction on internet banking: an extension to the trust-relationship commitment model. *International journal of bank marketing*, 24 (6), 424–442.

Klein, B., Crawford, R.G., and Alchian, A.A., 1978. Vertical integration, appropriable rents and the competitive contracting process. *Journal of marketing research*, 13, 382–390.

Kotler, P., 1998. *Marketing management: analysis, planning, implementation, and control.* Englewood Cliffs, NJ: Prentice Hall.

KPMG, 2007. *Retail banking in China: new frontiers.* Hong Kong: KPMG.

Kulp, S.C., Lee, H.L., and Ofek, E., 2004. Manufacturer benefits from information integration with retail customers. *Management science*, 50 (4), 431–444.

Kumar, N., Hibbard, J.D., and Stern, L.W., 1994. *The nature and consequences of marketing channel intermediary commitment.* Cambridge: Marketing Science Institute.

Kumar, N., Scheer, L.K., and Steenkamp, J.E.M., 1995. The effects of perceived interdependence on dealer attitudes. *Journal of marketing research*, 32, 348–356.

Lee, D., Pae, J.H., and Wong, Y.H., 2001. A model of close business relationships in China: guanxi. *European journal of marketing*, 35, 51–69.

Leung, T.K.P. and Wong, Y.H., 2001. The ethics and positioning of Guanxi in China. *Marketing intelligence and planning*, 19, 55–64.

Lin, N., Weng, J.C.M., and Hsiem, Y., 2003. Relational bond and customer's trust and commitment: a study on the moderating effects of web site usage. *The service industries journal*, 23 (3), 103–124.

MacKenzie, H.F., 1992. *Partnering attractiveness in buyer–seller relationships.* Thesis (PhD). University of Western Ontario.

Marsh, H.W., Balla, T.R., and Hau, K.T., 1998. Goodness-of-fit indexes in confirmatory factor analysis: the effect of sample size. *Psychological bulletin*, 103 (3), 391–441.

Martin, S.S., Gutierrez, J., and Camarero, C., 2004. Trust as the key to relational commitment. *Journal of relationship marketing*, 3 (1), 53–77.

Meyer, J.P. and Allen, N.J., 1991. A three-component conceptualization of organizational commitment. *Human resource management review*, 1, 61–89.

Moorman, C., Deshpande, R., and Zaltman, G., 1993. Factors affecting trust in market research relationships. *Journal of marketing*, 57, 81–101.

Morgan, R.M. and Hunt, S.D., 1994. The commitment–trust theory of relationship marketing. *Journal of marketing*, 58, 20–38.

Moriarty, R.T., Kimball, R.C., and Gay, J.H., 1983. The management of corporate banking relationships. *Sloan management review*, 1, 3–15.

Ndubisi, N.O., 2003. Service quality: understanding customer perception and reaction, and its impact on business. *International journal of business*, 5 (2), 207–219.

Ndubisi, N.O., 2006. Effect of gender on customer loyalty: a relationship marketing approach. *Marketing intelligence and planning*, 24 (1), 48–61.

Ndubisi, N.O., 2007. Relationship quality antecedents: the Malaysian retail banking perspective. *International journal of quality and reliability management*, 24 (8), 829–845.

Nunnally, C.J., 1978. *Psychometric methods*. New York: Harper and Row.

Parasuraman, A., Zeithaml, V.A., and Berry, L.L., 1988. SERVQUAL: a multiple-item scale for measuring consumer perceptions of service quality. *Journal of retailing*, 64, 2–40.

Pesämaa, O. and Hair, J.F. Jr., 2007. More than friendship is required: an empirical test of cooperative firm strategies. *Management decision*, 45 (3), 602–615.

Porter, L.W., Richard, M.S., Richard, T.M., and Baulian, P.V., 1974. Organizational commitment, job satisfaction, and turnover among psychiatric technicians. *Journal of applied psychology*, 59, 603–609.

Proenca, J.F. and de Castro, L.M., 2005. 'Stress' in business relationships: a study on corporate bank services. *International journal of bank marketing*, 23 (7), 527–541.

Provan, K.G. and Skinner, S.J., 1989. Inter-organizational dependence and control as predictors of opportunism in dealer–supplier relations. *Academy of management journal*, 32, 202–212.

Rhoades, L., Eisenberger, S., and Armeli, S., 2001. Affective commitment to the organization: the contribution of perceived organizational support. *Journal of applied psychology*, 86 (5), 825–836.

Ritter, D.S., 1993. *Relationship banking: cross-selling the banks products and services to meet your customers every financial need*. Chicago, IL: Bankers Pub. Co.

Saxe, R. and Weitz, B., 1982. SOCO scale: a measurement of the customer orientation of salespeople. *Journal of marketing research*, 20, 343–359.

Seybold, P., 2001. *The customer revolution: how to thrive when your customers are in control*. New York: Random House Business Books.

Shemwell, D.J., Cronin, J.J., and Bullard, W., 1994. Relational exchange in services: an empirical investigation of ongoing customer service-provider relationship. *International journal of service industry management*, 5, 57–68.

Spekman, R.E., 1988. Strategic supplier selection: understanding long-term buyer relationships. *Business horizons*, 31, 75–81.

Sweeney, J.C. and Webb, A., 2007. How functional, psychological, and social relationship benefits influence individual and firm commitment to the relationship. *Journal of business and industrial marketing*, 22 (7), 474–488.

Terawatanavong, C., Whitwell, G.J., and Widing, R.E., 2007. Buyer satisfaction with relational exchange across the relationship lifecycle. *European journal of marketing*, 41 (7/8), 915–938.

Turnbull, P.W. and Moustakatos, T., 1996. Marketing and investment banking: relationships and competitive advantage. *International journal of bank marketing*, 14, 38–49.

Van der Walt, S.D, Scott, D., and Woodside, A.G., 1994. CPA service providers: a profile of client types and their assessment of performance. *Journal of business research*, 31, 225–233.

Wetzels, M., De Ruyter, K., and Van Birgelen, M., 1998. Marketing service relationships: the role of commitment. *Journal of business and industrial marketing*, 13, 406–423.

Wong, A. and Zhou, L., 2006. Determinants and outcomes of relationship quality: a conceptual model and empirical evidence. *Journal of international consumer marketing*, 18 (3), 81–105.

Zeithaml, V.A., Parasuraman, A., and Berry, L.L., 1990. *Delivering quality service: balancing customer perceptions and expectation*. New York: The Free Press.

Zineldin, M., 1995. Bank–company interactions and relationships: some empirical evidence. *International journal of bank marketing*, 13, 30–40.

Zineldin, M., 2005. Quality and customer relationship management (CRM) as competitive strategy in the Swedish banking industry. *The TQM magazine*, 17, 329–344.

Appendix: The questionnaire

The following set of statements relate to the relationship between your company and its *primary* Chinese bank. Please indicate the degree to which you would agree with the following statements. (Circling a 1 means that you strongly disagree; circling a 7 means that you strongly agree. You may circle any of the numbers in the middle that show how strong your feelings are.)

	Strongly disagree		Strongly agree
1. Even if you could, you would not drop this bank because you like being associated with it.	1	2 3 4 5 6	7
2. You want to remain a member of this bank's network because you genuinely enjoy your relationship with it.	1	2 3 4 5 6	7
3. Your positive feelings towards this bank are a major reason you continue working with it.	1	2 3 4 5 6	7
4. There is just too much time, energy and expense involved in terminating your relationship with this bank.	1	2 3 4 5 6	7
5. You want to maintain your relationship with this bank given the anticipated termination or switching costs.	1	2 3 4 5 6	7
6. This bank benefits your company (e.g. profit) more than any other banks.	1	2 3 4 5 6	7
7. To succeed in this business, it is often necessary to compromise one's ethics.	1	2 3 4 5 6	7
8. If an employee is discovered to have engaged in unethical behaviour that results primarily in personal gain (rather than corporate gain), he or she should be promptly reprimanded.	1	2 3 4 5 6	7
9. You feel that this bank's service quality is excellent.	1	2 3 4 5 6	7
10. You are satisfied with the services provided by this bank.	1	2 3 4 5 6	7
11. You can count on this bank to be sincere.	1	2 3 4 5 6	7
12. Though circumstances change, you believe that this bank will be ready and willing to offer you assistance and support.	1	2 3 4 5 6	7
13. When it comes to things that are important to you, you can depend on this bank's support.	1	2 3 4 5 6	7
14. There are no other banks which could provide you with the comparable services.	1	2 3 4 5 6	7
15. It would be difficult for your company to switch to another bank.	1	2 3 4 5 6	7
16. The cost of switching to another competing bank would be prohibitive.	1	2 3 4 5 6	7
17. You make use of a large portion of the range of services offered by this bank.	1	2 3 4 5 6	7
18. The service portfolio of this bank meets your expectations.	1	2 3 4 5 6	7
19. This bank tries to understand what services you really need.	1	2 3 4 5 6	7
20. This bank tries to provide an accurate expectation of what the product/service will do for your company.	1	2 3 4 5 6	7
21. This bank tries to help your company achieve its goals.	1	2 3 4 5 6	7
22. This bank and your company actively work together as partners.	1	2 3 4 5 6	7
23. The working relationship between your company and this bank can be characterized as one where there is a lot of mutual cooperation.	1	2 3 4 5 6	7
24. This bank helps out your company in whatever ways you ask.	1	2 3 4 5 6	7
25. Your company helps out this bank in whatever ways it asks.	1	2 3 4 5 6	7

26. If there is a good alternative to this bank, you will terminate your relationship with the bank.   1   2 3 4 5 6   7

27. To accomplish its own objectives, sometimes this bank alters the facts slightly.   1   2 3 4 5 6   7

28. To accomplish its own objectives, sometimes this bank promises to do things without actually doing them later.   1   2 3 4 5 6   7

29. You expect that your relationship with this bank will continue for a long time.   1   2 3 4 5 6   7

30. You plan to continue your relationship with this bank.   1   2 3 4 5 6   7

31. The renewal of your relationship with this bank is virtually automatic.   1   2 3 4 5 6   7

Demographic items:

1. How many people does your company employ?
☐ Under 50   ☐ 51–100   ☐ Over 101

2. Where is your company based?
☐ Inside the 4th Ring Road   ☐ Outside the 4th Ring Road   ☐ Other

3. In which industry is your company?

☐ Agriculture, forestry, stock raising and fishery   ☐ Mining, manufacturing, construction and production

☐ Distribution of electricity, gas and water   ☐ Transport, communication, wholesale and retail, eating and drinking

☐ Finance and insurance, real estate, services and government   ☐ Other, please specify_____

The influence of western banks on corporate governance in China

Jane Nolan

Nuffield Foundation New Career Fellow, Department of Sociology, University of Cambridge, Free School Lane, Cambridge, United Kingdom, CB2 3RQ

This study draws on in-depth qualitative interviews to investigate the variety of institutional forces which influence the adoption of western corporate governance mechanisms in Chinese banks. Following path dependency models of institutional change it was shown that cognitive and normative institutions, including a 'who you know' or guanxi credit culture, mean that the practical influence of western banks on corporate governance reforms was perceived to be ineffectual in most cases. Given the failure of western credit-rating systems in the sub-prime crisis, it is likely that this perception will increase in the future. The majority of western actors believed that the main reason Chinese banks seek to co-operate with western institutions was to enhance the legitimacy of the Chinese bank in the global financial environment, rather than to actively change existing governance mechanisms.

Introduction

The development of China's economy has, to date, been driven by its considerable supply of cheap labour and its many and varied production opportunities. Whether or not capital was allocated efficiently has been of little consequence and, until fairly recently, the financial sector has been characterized by state-owned banks lending to state-owned enterprises (SOEs) on the basis of social policy principles rather than profitability and managerial competence (Branstetter 2007, Cousin 2007). Yet as China's economy advances the development of the financial sector is set to become ever more important. Banks cannot indefinitely continue to make huge loans to inefficient enterprises which will never be repaid and many financial institutions remain compromised by the corporate governance problems associated with having the state as both official regulator and principal shareholder (IFC 2005, Li *et al.* 2008)

That said, the reform of China's banks is now well underway and the basic methods employed for restructuring have been large capital injections, the setting up of 'bad-banks' and asset management companies, initial public offerings, partnerships with foreign banks (with the aim of improving management and IT development) and the inclusion of overseas board members to help improve corporate governance (Hu 2005, Cousin 2007). Some see these moves as part of a broader interest by Chinese officials in developing an economic institutional environment which is more reflective of the international business community (Guthrie 1998, Wang 2007). And, at a theoretical level, these adjustments raise some important questions about the nature of institutional change in China's economic transition, such as whether China will develop its own unique form of corporate governance, or whether it will converge towards the more market-based models commonly found in the west.

While the opening of the market to western banks has been seen as a key plank of the reform programme (Huan 2005, Liu *et al.* 2005), at the time of writing, many economies in the western world are struggling to cope with the fall-out from the sub-prime mortgage debacle, and the credibility of western banks is under severe strain (Bloomberg 2009). Some have argued that recent events could see economic power shift from west to east and much attention is now focused on the nature of China's position in the global economic order (Brown 2008, Time 2009). China's banks are now very large, with three in the world's top 10 by market capitalization.[1] However, such large assets should not detract from the problems which remain in the Chinese banking system including a shallow talent pool, a shortage of managerial and technical expertise, a local currency that is not convertible and weak corporate governance mechanisms (Brown and Skully 2005, Calomiris 2007, Cousin 2007).

This study aims to investigate the institutional forces which affect the adoption of western corporate governance mechanisms in Chinese banks. The data comes from a series of in-depth qualitative interviews with senior managers who were either employed in western banks with stockholdings in Chinese institutions, held non-executive directorships of Chinese banks, or had participated in other financial advisory roles. The following sections will enlarge on the corporate governance literature in relation to both western and Chinese banks and discuss the theoretical frameworks which can help explain how goals, beliefs and organizations are structured by institutions. Next, the research methodology will be outlined and the findings will be introduced structured around the institutional forces which influence both internal and external governance mechanisms as well as related technical assistance projects. The study concludes with a discussion of the importance of legitimacy-seeking in motivating Chinese banks to seek collaboration with western institutions and will underscore the importance of local informal institutions in ensuring path dependent change. Finally, some of the key assumptions of western models of governance will be challenged, particularly the belief that market forces alone can ensure the efficient allocation of credit.

Literature review

The Chinese banking sector is extremely large and highly complex. According to the most recently available data at the end of 2007, the total assets of the banking sector amounted to RMB 52.6 trillion (over 7.5 trillion dollars) while liabilities reached RMB 49.6 trillion (around 7.1 trillion dollars) (CBRC 2008). As of June 2007 the banking system consisted of over 8877 institutions, with 189,921 outlets and 2,696,760 employees. The top three types of institution, assessed by asset scale were:

- the 5 state-owned commercial banks with 53% of total banking assets (including such recognizable names as the Bank of China and the Industrial and Commercial Bank of China).
- the 12 joint-stock commercial banks with 14% of total banking assets (for example the Bank of Communications, China Minsheng Banking Corporation and China Everbright Bank).
- the 8348 rural co-operative financial institutions with 11% of total assets.

Other important banking institutions are the 3 remaining policy banks, the 124 city commercial banks and the 29 locally incorporated foreign bank subsidiaries (such as HSBC and Citibank).

Couple this enormous size and diversity of form with an organizational history driven by the goals of socialist planning, where the key purpose of the bank was to act as a conduit for the implementation of the state's objectives, and it comes as no surprise to find that transforming the financial system has been, and continues to be, a difficult and complicated process. As well as reducing staggeringly large non-performing loans, the bank reforms involved moving from lending practices based on government policy aims to those based on commercial and market principles. This required fundamental shifts in regulation and accounting standards, which, in turn, required building new skills in risk management and creating new forms of management incentives, both of which required a radical and extremely challenging shift in organizational culture (Cousin 2007, Hamid and Tenev 2008, Stiglitz 1999).

However, in an extensive report for the OECD, Thompson (2005) notes that a number of steps have been taken by the Chinese authorities in recent years with the aim of improving the corporate governance of Chinese banks. These include capacity building and specialization amongst the regulators, such as the creation of the China Banking Regulatory Commission (CBRC), improvements in the legal regulatory environment and methods for enforcement, increased information disclosure and market discipline mechanisms, ownership structure reform (such as the diversification of shareholders and the inclusion of foreign strategic investors), and increased competition through direct foreign market entry at the end of WTO transition period. On the other hand, Ewing (2005) argues that despite these reforms, the fact remains that in most cases the state is still the controlling shareholder and continues to allocate to enterprises social and welfare goals such as generating employment and encouraging economic growth in certain industries. Working with traditional agency and transaction cost models, Ewing argues that as the state is both outsider and insider at the same time, the principal does not become the control entity and conflicts of interest inevitably arise between the state and the bank, or in theoretical terms, between the principal and the agent. In the Chinese context, much analysis of the principal-agent relationship has pointed out that state ownership means that there is never an effective ultimate principal because, technically speaking, state ownership equates to ownership by the citizenry of China, a group which is generally considered too powerless and dispersed to play an effective monitoring role at the level of the firm (Clarke 2003). The lack of a visible and present human principal who can both pressurize managers and monitor their actions so as to increase asset value, leads to significant agency costs, including losses associated with corruption (Li *et al.* 2008, Peng 2001). Moreover, principal-agent relationships are complex in China because profit maximization for the principal is not the only incentive for managers. As Ling and Guo (2006) note, the chairman of the Board of Directors is usually also the firms' secretary of the Party Committee. Consequently managers' incentives are also partly driven by party loyalty which can be in conflict with other, more market-orientated, governance mechanisms. Moreover, there are often a number of different types of government agencies, (central, local or regional) which control the equity stake of companies and they may have different (and possibly conflicting) objectives and management incentives which further complicate the nature of the principal-agent relationship (Li *et al.* 2008).

Against this background, the introduction of western corporate governance structures are viewed as particularly important (OECD 2005) because it is believed that they can reduce the inefficiencies associated with confused principal-agent relationships and can also improve internal controls and risk management. To expand on this it is helpful to distinguish between corporate governance mechanisms which are internal and those which are external (Denis and McConnell 2003, Wei 2005). The Board of Directors (in conjunction with a supervisory board in China) and the nature of the ownership structure of a company are the two most important internal control mechanisms. In theory, the board's responsibility is to hire, monitor and fire senior management, in practice, however, the separation between the roles and responsibilities of the board and management is not always clear cut (Cousin 2007, Clarke 2003, Xu *et al.* 2002). Interestingly, a number of studies have shown that foreign ownership can help to align management and shareholders interests and has a positive effect on market valuation, largely through the generation of investor confidence (Bai *et al.* 2003). The threat of take-over or bankruptcy and the legal and enforceable protection of investor rights are the key external mechanisms which encourage managers to perform in the interests of shareholders (Ewing 2005). However, it should be noted that in the Chinese case the threat of bankruptcy is a rather weak mechanism as banks are likely to be restructured, merged or 'saved' in some way by the state (Cousin 2007, Liu *et al.* 2005).

Although many of these governance mechanisms are being introduced and developed in China they remain somewhat fragile. While corporate governance is considered to be a high priority by Chinese banking regulators and authorities (CBRC 2008), it is still problematic to assess how much power the authorities, who are also acting as shareholders, are willing to defer in the process of improving governance standards. On the face of it, Chinese banks use a Board of Directors consisting of, among others, independent directors supervising senior management and a Supervisory Board which supervises the Board of Directors. However, in a review of international investors' perspectives on this structure, the Institute of International Finance notes that in China the power of the Board of Directors is often very restricted and in practice it has little more than a 'rubber stamp' function (IIF 2006).

From the perspective of Chinese banks, it is thought that part foreign ownership is particularly helpful in improving internal governance structures such as risk management and performance incentives, and helping with the development of new technology and products (Cousin 2007, CBRC 2008). Moreover, the inclusion of a well-known foreign brand name can be attractive to some customers and can also help increase opportunities for international funding (Liu *et al.* 2005). There is certainly some evidence that so-called 'technical assistance' projects between Chinese and western banks have worked reasonably well (Hamid and Tenev 2008). One of the most quotable examples are the investments made by the International Finance Corporation's (IFC) in several city commercial banks, the China Minsheng Banking Corporation, and a number of rural credit cooperatives. In addition to their equity investments, the IFC engaged in technical assistance to facilitate the transfer of internal corporate governance practices, credit analysis, risk management practices and the development of internal lending controls, see Table 1.

Noting that Chinese banks continue to offer a very restricted range of products and poor quality service, IFC emphasizes that foreign banks have had, and will continue to have, a positive influence on product development and corporate governance in the mainland and they remain optimistic about the future of co-operation between Chinese and western banks (Hamid and Tenev 2008). The data and its analyses is provided by the IFC itself and although they are generally positive about progress to date they continue to note that corporate governance remains weak and credit risk management skills low.

Theory

In the west it is possible to distinguish at least two forms of corporate governance: i) the Anglo-Saxon model based on prioritizing shareholder interests and a belief that

Table 1. International Finance Corporation's (IFC) technical assistance to Chinese banks.

Bank	Pre-investment	At investment	Post-investment
Bank of Shanghai	Since 1995 IFC supported, with funding form Japan and EU, human resources management review, credit analysis, credit policies and procedures	Arranged for the adoption of IAS* audits	Review of credit procedures, stress test to monitor portfolio risks, SME business diagnostics and SME banking strategy.
Bank of Beijing	Credit risk management, business strategy development	Arranged for the adoption of IAS audits	Training for board members, portfolio stress test.
China Minsheng Banking Corporation	$700,000 in technical assistance at time of establishment; advice on strategic issues and business development, training of staff on credit analysis	Arranged for the adoption of IAS audits	At the request of Minsheng identified independent director, supported diagnostic review of SME lending and SME strategy development; supported energy efficiency loan program; introduced methodology for portfolio stress test.
Nanjing City Commercial Bank	Supported risk management training through Price Waterhouse and Coopers	Arranged for the adoption of IAS audits	With funding from Italy offered series of training programs on risk control; supported board members training; introduced portfolio stress test methodology.
United Rural Cooperative Bank		Arranged for the adoption of IAS audits	Upgraded credit policy and loan recovery manuals, introduced new credit scoring system; set up a Risk and Compliance Department, and a Credit Review Centre; conducted training on credit management; started branch management and benchmark models.
Xian City Bank	Training for bank staff on credit analysis	Arranged for the adoption of IAS audits	Supported credit training program in 2005; advised on acquisition of credit cooperative.
China Industrial Bank		Arranged for the adoption of IAS audits	Provided corporate governance technical assistance in 2004; portfolio stress test in 2005; technical assistance on IT framework; SME lending diagnostics and strategy; supported energy efficiency lending.

Note: *IAS – International Accounting Standards.
Source: IFC cited in Hamid and Tenev (2008).

self-interest and decentralized markets are capable of functioning efficiently and fairly; and ii) the continental European model based on a stakeholder theory of the firm, where the interests of not just shareholders, but of other groups, such as trade unions and work councils, are also considered (Luo 2007). In East Asia there are also a number of distinctive models including the Keiretsu model in Japan (sets of companies with interlocking relationships and shareholdings) (Witt 2006) and the Chaebol model in South Korea (Government-supported global conglomerates such as Samsung) (Sung 2003). Liu (2006) has argued that the corporate governance system in China is one which is 'control-based', rather than market orientated because China's unique institutional setting means that the regulators and authorities still make extensive use of administrative measures to control developments in the economy.

Cousin (2007) argues that corporate governance in Chinese banks poses a distinctive set of problems which are somewhat different to those encountered by other Chinese firms. First, the principal-agent relations are even more complex because they must take account of a wider range of stakeholders including depositors, lenders, supervisors and regulators (Cao and Zhao 2004). Second because of the importance of the financial system to economic growth and social stability bank failures will not be allowed and in the event of potential collapse they are likely to be saved (Wang and Huang 2004). Of course, recent events in the global economy have shown that this behaviour is not unique to the Chinese system, however the implications of a government guarantee to maintain 'financial security' means that internal controls should, in theory, be much stronger than in industries where the threat of collapse is far more real (Cao and Zhao 2004, Wang and Huang 2004). Finally, information asymmetry is deeper in banks than in other companies because quality in financial intermediation cannot be assessed immediately. For example, non-performing loans tend to be discovered in the future not at the time of issuance (Wei 2005). It is clear that, in the Chinese case, the state has allocated to itself the main role in the banking system and, historically speaking at least, this differentiates Chinese corporate governance models from those found in Anglo-Saxon countries. Officials argue for the merits of this system on the basis that, at China's current stage of development, markets would not fairly allocate resources and the government has a responsibility for managing the financial system so that development occurs rapidly, but with stability (Zhou 2004).

That there are differences between the Anglo-Saxon and the Chinese models of corporate governance is hardly surprising. The 'varieties of capitalism' research tradition has produced numerous case studies demonstrating that there has been little convergence in terms of governance structures or economic policy making over the last 20 years despite extensive financial globalization (Clarke 2003, Nee 2005, Streek and Thelen 2005). Comparative organizational scholars have also produced many studies which show that firms adopt various modes of economic action and organizational forms which are largely based on the institutional structures embedded in their nation-state base (Boisot and Child 1998, Guillen 2001, Redding and Witt 2007). Moreover, Chinese thinking about international norms has been shown to vary across time, sector and issue (Wang 2007). In a study of policy documents and media commentary, Wang suggests that Chinese officials remain open to international norms in the economic and technical realms but less so to those governing other issues, especially political and military matters. Wang argues that it seems likely that China will abide by prevailing international economic and technical norms and will become an increasingly congruent and co-operative economic partner in the global arena. It is probably fair to say that, at the official level, the reform of China's banking system was partly influenced by the policy discourse 'link up with the international track' (yu guoji jieguei) whereby China's banks were encouraged to move towards international standards both in terms of product innovation, accounting procedures and corporate governance mechanisms (Cousin 2007, Calomiris 2007, Wang 2007).

This publicly-stated objective, does, however, raise interesting questions as to the practicalities of transferring corporate governance practices across culture, and, following Aguiler and Jackson (2003), this study will argue that multiple institutions will interact to influence the perceived legitimacy and utility of western corporate governance practices in the Chinese context. Although there is some discussion over just quite what an 'institution' is, it is probably fair to say that most would agree that an institution encompasses both the informal beliefs and behaviours of a given society and the formal organizations of the state that govern those beliefs and behaviours (Nee 2005). Within this general framework, it is possible to differentiate further between functionalist or 'rational choice' theories and path dependency or 'varieties of capitalism' approaches to institutional change (with the latter sometimes referred to as 'neo-institutionalism'). Each approach rests on different behavioural assumptions (principally the degree to which rational action is limited and shaped by context), and foregrounds different explanatory mechanisms (social networks and ties, state regulations, collective action, transaction-cost economising, and so on) (Nee 2005, Campbell 2004).

The fundamental premise of the functional approach is that, in a global arena, institutions tend to converge, or become similar in form, because markets create incentives for actors to replace poor institutions with more efficient ones and actors learn from the behaviour of institutions who survive in the face of competition (North 1990, Weingast 2002). In other words, efficient institutions in some way or another promote *rational* behaviour and reduce transactions costs (Williamson 1981).

There are, however, problems in accounting for the pace of institutional change within the functional framework, which, some argue, has been somewhat slower in certain countries than would be expected given efficiency and rational-choice assumptions (Furubotn and Richter 1997). For example, China's adoption of a gradualist approach to reform, focusing on selective economic development in specific regions, and avoiding radical political change altogether seem to raise doubts over the degree to which functionalist theories are relevant in the Chinese case (Nee and Yang 1999). Indeed, what the Chinese example highlights is the way in which pre-existing social and institutional arrangements, which are embedded in interpersonal ties, networks, and cultural beliefs, have enduring influence and thus contribute to a process of 'path dependence' (Nee 2005, Wilson 2008, Redding and Witt 2007). In this framework, institutional change is not viewed as a product of rationalization and market forces, but, rather, is theorized as a gradually emerging outcome based on local ideological preferences (Campbell 2004, DiMaggio and Powell 1983).

Building on both DiMaggio and Powell (1983, 1991) and North (1990), Scott's (2001) highly influential account of institutional theory categorizes formal and informal institutions into regulatory, normative and cognitive groupings. The regulatory level is the most formal and includes such things as legal rules and other forms of codified sanctions. Normative institutions are somewhat less formal and can be identified as the authority systems or principles that guide behavioural goals and legitimate ways to achieve them. Finally cultural-cognitive institutions are the most informal and represent the most taken for granted assumptions about reality and the way in which it is perceived, and are established and developed through social interactions. While it is probably fair to say that these dimensions must be intertwined and mutually reinforcing, it is reasonable to assume that there may be inconsistencies between the dimensions and the logics which guide them, particularly during a period of transition (Campbell 2004). A key theoretical assumption within institutional theory, however, is that social and organizational actors are, essentially, seeking legitimacy, as well as material advancement. Subsequently, they are constantly re-inventing legitimacy norms within an evolving institutional environment (Scott 2001). It is this fundamental principle which will guide the research aims of this study.

Research questions

Based on the theoretical and empirical literature outlined above, the following questions will direct the empirical and theoretical focus of the study:

(i) *What are the different kinds of institutional influences which structure the role of foreign banks in developing external and internal corporate governance mechanisms in China?*

(ii) *Why do constraints and enablers on governance vary at different institutional levels (such as the regulatory, normative or cognitive)?*

(iii) *How pertinent is legitimacy-seeking in understanding the attitudes and behaviour of key actors in the banking sector?*

Methodology

Method of data collection

Theorizing on corporate governance in China's banks is still in its infancy due to the rapid changes which have occurred in the sector since the end of the WTO transition period in 2006. New topic areas such as this are often studied using qualitative techniques because it is believed that these approaches allow for maximum exploration of the subject matter (Campbell 2004, Eisenhardt 1989, Meyer *et al.* 1987, Strauss and Corbin 2008). By interviewing influential actors face-to-face it is possible to elicit their views in an open-ended format which allows for the discovery of new concepts, relationships and perceptions. For these reasons, the method adopted in this study was the in-depth semi-structured interview.

Sample characteristics

The informants in this study were regional chief executive officers (CEOs), chief representative officers and general managers who were either employed in western banks with shareholdings in Chinese banks, or had been involved in an advisory role or non-executive directorship with a Chinese bank. All of the participants were men and were aged between 37 and 63. The total population of western banks in China is, in fact, relatively small. According to the China Financial Services Directory in September 2007 there were 69 banks in total, with 53 from Europe, 13 from North America and three from Australia (Guo 2007). The banks selected for the sample were either locally incorporated (offering retail and commercial banking services to Chinese customers) or banks with representative offices in China (who principally provide support to home-based customers but may also be involved in technical assistance projects or other advisory roles with Chinese banks). Initially fifty of the bank managers were approached on the basis that their bank was either Tier 1 or Tier 2 capitally-rated and that they had been established in China for more than 12 months[2]. Of the 50 that were approached 26 agreed to be interviewed; one from Australia, six from North America (three of whom were Chinese-American) and 19 from Europe. Compared to the population the sample contains a good geographical spread, but has more banks from the Tier 1 range. Nevertheless, as the aim is not to make a statistically generalizable statement about corporate governance at a macro level but to examine the specific attitudes and experiences of senior managers in a given context, the sample is certainly heterogeneous enough to serve this purpose.

Procedure

Access was obtained through personal introductions and through direct approach by email and letter. The interviews were conducted under conditions of anonymity and confidentiality. It is not possible to reveal the identity of the banks because, given the seniority of some of the individuals interviewed, this could lead to the identification of the participant. The interviews took place in Hong Kong, Shanghai and Beijing between October 2007 and May 2008. Managers in Hong Kong were interviewed about their experiences of banking in mainland China. The interview schedule contained questions relating to the work history of the participant and the performance of the company and also examined the following themes: i) perceptions of the regulatory environment in China; ii) perceptions and views of the importance of governance mechanisms; and iii) the practical steps and specific behaviours used in order to develop governance procedures. The interviews were recorded in 19 of the 26 interviews, however seven participants requested not to be recorded and notes were taken during these interviews which were typed up immediately following the meeting.

Data analysis method

The data was analysed using a grounded theory approach (Strauss and Corbin 2008) where the emphasis is placed on concept and thematic development and an examination of the conditions and consequences which influence perceptions. It was possible to divide the participants into groups based on emerging themes. However, these should not be taken as an indicator of generalizability but, rather, of heterogeneity in the specific sample under investigation.

Data analysis

External governance mechanisms

Legal environment

As Ewing (2005) notes, perhaps the most important external governance control mechanism is the existence of a robust legal environment. In the case of banking, this would mean that a detailed and comprehensive set of legislation, which is impartially enforced so as to protect investor rights, should be in place. Certainly, some scholars believe that China has made good progress towards establishing a sound rational-legal framework which has reduced the influence of personal connections (or *guanxi*) on business decision making (Guthrie 1998). In the banking sector it is notable that the CBRC, working with high profile foreign advisors such as Howard Davis (former Chairman of the UK Financial Services Authority) Gerald Corrigan (Managing Director of Goldman Sachs) and Jamie Caruna (Director of the IMF Monetary and Capital Markets Department) has been heavily involved in developing national legislation in the financial sector. Some of the key areas of development have been the introduction of the Anti-Money Laundering Law, the Anti-Monopoly Law and the Banking Supervision Law (CBRC 2008). At the regulatory level, therefore, it is certainly true that there have been some significant institutional changes in recent years.

A small number of participants (seven) noted with optimism their belief that sufficient regulations were now in place to protect shareholders. An American institutional investor noted:

> I do believe that in spite of everything that's happening, the next 5 years will be extremely exciting, particularly given that the legal framework has changed. For example, the bankruptcy law, and enterprise law, partnership law. We can be much more confident that what we buy will give us a return. There is more certainty, so that part is better.

It is interesting that this participant felt reassured by the development of the legal framework despite the widely reported difficulties in enforcing certain laws, such as the bankruptcy law (Cousin 2007). Bankruptcy is a two-sided issue for banks in relation both to the failure of an enterprise which the bank has lent to, and to the failure of the bank itself. In the first case, the failure of enterprises, Chinese bank behaviour is most likely to be that of a 'passive creditor' (Goodhart and Zeng 2005) who avoids pushing for bankruptcy, which is expensive and time consuming in China (World Bank 2000, Wormuth 2004). As for the case of the bankruptcy of the bank itself, it is widely acknowledged that, as an external sanctioning tool, it is somewhat ineffective as the large state owned banks frequently fall into the 'too big to fail' category (Cousin 2007). Moreover, in the case of smaller failing banks, the usual process is an order by the regulator to merge, a take-over or some other form of restructuring (Zhang and Cheng 2003). As such, despite the introduction of new laws, developed with the assistance of foreign experts, banks often have few external governance incentives to improve their practices.

Enduring influence of guanxi

Indeed, the majority of informants were not optimistic about the effectiveness of new regulations and were concerned with the practical implications of working within a constantly changing legal framework. This, in fact, contributed to a sense of uncertainty which the managers sought to alleviate through their local Chinese networks, what they defined as '*guanxi*'. One of the main reasons why *guanxi* networks were seen as essential was because the quality of information available through the local financial press was viewed as in some way biased and overly-influenced by the state. Indeed, as Roe (2002) argues, if corporate governance is to be effective, it is not enough just to introduce formal regulations, other, robust, intermediate institutions must also be in place, not least of which is a dynamic, well-informed and accurate financial press. It is no secret that the financial services industry in China faces significant drawbacks because of the state's enduring control over information (Clarke 2003, Cousin 2007). As one general manager noted:

> We don't have the Wall Street Journal or the Dow Jones to tell us what's going on. The way this economy works it's been developed by the government in a way to obfuscate. The way I stay on top of what's happening with regulation is through my network, through my guanxi.

However, in contrast to the theoretical assumption that information asymmetry occurs in these situations because one party has greater knowledge than the other (Guthrie 2002), managers here felt that one of the key difficulties was that the regulatory system wasn't clearly understood by those on the Chinese side either. In other words, the information deficit related to a perception that officials themselves are uncertain of the rules and of where internal power bases lie. The chief representative officer of a European bank noted:

> I think one problem is that you don't really know who sits on the power. There are different layers, different ministries, different persons, and they themselves have not decided who has got the power. So we don't have a clear picture of who is in charge, and, I think, neither do they.

In brief, for the majority of managers, the cultural-cognitive institution of informal relationships was of much more importance to them than the establishment of external governance mechanisms such as formal laws and enforcement procedures.

Internal governance mechanisms

Board of Directors

Internal control mechanisms such as the structure of the Board of Directors are thought to be essential for the establishment of sound corporate governance because they ensure clarification of lines of responsibility and help prevent conflicts of interest between agents and principals. Three of the participants were positive about the role foreign board members play in contributing to the development of this aspect of governance in Chinese banks. As one consultant who was closely involved with some of the IFC reforms noted:

> ... it is very clear that the foreign appointed non-executive director in a Chinese bank make a contribution of genuine value ... and this includes such things as the establishment and monitoring of credit committees and supervisory committees and they absolutely do help to maintain standards of corporate governance that simply would not be otherwise maintained.

While acknowledging that the changes in board composition were an evolving 'process' rather than a completed transition, these informants remained optimistic in their assessment of the influence of foreign non-executive directors in improving governance structures, pointing out the now almost ubiquitous adoption of separate credit and supervisory committees in Chinese banks. Those who were confident about the role of non-executive foreign directors on boards were, however, in the distinct minority. The overwhelming majority of participants were deeply sceptical about their role. A senior executive at a locally-incorporated foreign bank noted:

> They have no influence, the board doesn't feel any real obligation to take on their advice, the overall direction of the Bank is determined by the majority shareholder, i.e. the Communist party, the appointment of any influential board member is made by them and that person may be technically and managerially quite competent, but ultimately they're motivated by factors which are not commercial and they think about their career in terms of political progression as much as anything.

Clearly those informants who were at the cynical end of the spectrum (the majority) were unconvinced that the inclusion of foreign non-executive directors was resolving the principal-agent problem. When the state is the principal shareholder then the power of the minority shareholder is extremely weak and blurred boundaries in roles and responsibilities remain embedded in the management structure.

Ownership structure

In a similar way to adopting a Board of Directors management structure, diversified ownership was thought to be important for improving governance because it can help align management and shareholder interests. In the Chinese context, foreign ownership has been shown to improve the market valuation of a company through an increase in investor confidence by the association with a well-known international brand name. However, in a similar vein to the discussion of the role of the Board of Directors, participants were somewhat sceptical about the ability of foreign investment to actually improve governance. As one director involved in a co-operation agreement with a Chinese bank notes:

> I'm cautious about over-stating the influence of foreign investment in reforming the banks. Our experience hasn't been good. Obviously we remain minority shareholders and have no rights ... the way they see it, is that they are in control and they're going to do what they like.

They want us to help them develop their consumer credit cards and that's it, they really have no interest in us as far as corporate governance issues are concerned.

This is an interesting example of the difficulties in assuming that the inclusion of foreign investment will align managers' and shareholders' interests. Given that the limits on outside share-ownership remains capped at 20%, banks, like other large SOEs, are not, in fact, exposed to the market rigours and ownership pressures which are presumed in the Anglo-Saxon model to create sound governance systems. Indeed, a number of other participants noted that the belief that a foreign investor had any significant influence over governance issues was naive. Most emphasized that it was the *belief* by those outside the region that foreign investment could offer good governance which was important. A management consultant who had been involved in the IPO listing of a major Chinese bank noted:

When you're looking at a 'big name' deal with one of the State-Owned Commercial Banks, it's done mainly because of the branding. Really the Chinese bank isn't that interested in advice about governance, what they want is to get listed on the Hong Kong market, and for that a foreign brand name really helps. These guys aren't comfortable with strict rules. So everyone just pretends that everyone needs governance advice but actually they [Chinese banks] don't really pay any attention to this.

This observation highlights the importance of legitimacy-seeking in the motivation of Chinese banks to seek foreign investment. The sociological approach to the analysis of institutions makes much of the importance of perceived legitimacy in shaping institutions (Suchman 1995). To the extent that China wishes to develop an international profile for its major companies, including banks, then it must seek legitimacy with its international business peers. As such, the perception that it is trying to develop corporate governance practices is clearly important. Life within the organizational context itself, however, appears to be lagging behind publicly stated aims. This becomes more apparent in the following sections when we begin to examine some of the technical assistance projects linked to corporate governance issues, such as credit risk management and related product development.

Technical assistance

Credit rating and risk management

Perhaps one of the major hurdles which China faces in relation to the development of the banking sector is its lack of reliable credit rating systems which would allow for consumer credit checks. This matter looks set to remain a problem in the near future because, as Caijing (2008) reports, China still has no clear regulations in this area and the central bank is plagued by difficulties in establishing a rating system. Difficulties include gaining the cooperation of other government departments in the sharing of credit-related information, and difficulties in finding a way of consolidating diverse and complex data systems.

As was shown in the discussion of the IFC technical assistance projects, the co-operation between foreign and Chinese banks is viewed as an important means of improving credit checking systems and risk management, systems which are particularly important for the establishment of good governance. The participants interviewed in this study noted, however, that there are major organizational difficulties in actualising knowledge transfer. One executive directly involved in a technical assistance project noted:

The practicality of it is that we don't have any way to do the technology transfer. We don't have anybody really of consequence to go in and train the people. And the Chinese can't get access to the people that they need to access to because they are not in Asia, they're in America. And so what do we do, we say, put your hand up everybody who speaks Chinese.

We find some relatively low-level people in America, we find some people here and there. ... And then you hear great things in the newspaper [about technical assistance]. *But then you go and talk to the rank and file and its like: "Get me out of here, this is awful, it doesn't work". They feel they are going into a situation that's completely contrived.*

Such accounts alert us to the difficulties of initiating organizational change when skills deficits run high on both sides. On top of this, however, was a widely-held perception that in the majority of cases 'technical assistance' was no longer really required. The main object of collaboration was to boost investor confidence. A regional CEO noted:

But your typical guy who is working at a relatively senior level at a bank in China has more exposure to state of the art credit scoring, credit analysis than anybody in a US bank, and then these American guys are sitting there trying to sell it to them. The Chinese know what they're doing now; it has nothing to do with that anymore, they know how to do all that. This is nothing to do with learning from [US Bank][3] *– that's all nonsense. It's a show for everybody outside the region. That's what it's for.*

The majority of participants in this study believed that it was not lack of 'know how' that was impeding the development of effective credit rating, but, rather, enduring organizational and cultural factors. Given the history of Chinese banks as policy lenders facing few commercial pressures, there has traditionally been little culture of credit checking and risk management. Moreover, the reform process in this area is generally hindered by the lack of cooperation by bank managers (Caijing 2008). In particular, the problem of so-called *guanxi* loans is still a major difficulty, where loans are based on subjective considerations such as connections of influence rather than on objective credit criteria such as assets and repayment history. As one Regional Chief Executive Officer noted:

Typically the problem with the Chinese banks I've worked with is that, well, the provincial governor, his brother is running the bank and the customers are working on building up those links. Then those people in the top positions approve the credits then those people start falling behind and don't pay back. That's the biggest problem in the Chinese banking system today – those guanxi credits.

Further illustration for this problem is abundant. Liu Jiayi, auditor general of the National Audit Office, reported that financial investigations in 2008 uncovered that six billion yuan (878 million dollars) was misused in 20 major cases. About half of the cases involved three of China's biggest state-owned banks: Industrial and Commercial Bank of China, Bank of China and Construction Bank of China (AFP, February 18, 2009). That the loans were examples of 'serious illegality and economic crime' was largely attributed to the fact that the loans were granted, not on the basis of risk management principles, but on the 'who you know' basis, or as *guanxi* loans (Reuters, February 19, 2009). All of this indicates that there is much work to be done on implementing a valid and reliable credit rating system in China which has little to do with influence of foreign investment and technical assistance. A much more fundamental shift in the local cognitive institutions of *guanxi* would be required to achieve that goal.

Securitization

A final related point is the link between credit rating, risk management and the development of new financial products. Prior to the sub-prime crisis a widely held assumption was that western credit rating systems were sound enough to act as a safety net for the development of more sophisticated forms of finance. While it is too early to assess the implications of the significant failings of western credit-rating agencies in this regard, it is interesting to note here that the vast majority of participants felt that the technical expertise, credibility and legitimacy of western banks in China had been severely damaged by the problem relating to securitization. One senior Chinese-American banker noted:

> ...*look at Northern Rock, look at the entire sub-prime issue in the US, these global banks have been out here preaching about how to do banking and they are now all in dire straits and coming here to ask for capital ... So of course we're wondering, should we really listen to these guys? The western rating agencies that say they know everything, they have totally messed up.*

It should come as no surprise that the general view was that western financial systems now face credibility issues. One investment banker working for an American bank with shares in a State-Owned Commercial Bank noted:

> ...*before 2007, securitization was a big buzz word in China – everyone was excited about it. "You can diversify etc". Now all this has come to a halt because we don't understand securitization. And I think we've also come to the shock realization that the western experts actually didn't understand securitization either.*

As the global financial environment is currently in a state of rapid flux, the influence of recent events on the relationships between western and Chinese banks remains to be seen. However, Howard Davis (former Chairman of the UK Financial Services Authority) noted that in a meeting with the vice-Premier Wang Qisheng he had been pointedly asked 'Whether we should continue to take our Wall Street teachers' lessons seriously' (Davis 2008). It is certainly questionable as to what extent either 'legitimacy-seeking' or 'technical expertise' will continue to be important influences in the future.

Discussion

This study has investigated the variety of institutional forces which influence the adoption of western corporate governance mechanisms in Chinese banks. A summary of the findings is shown in Table 2. External governance mechanisms, such as the development of a robust legal environment are certainly developing a-pace. However, most participants felt that lack of transparency and significant information asymmetry would ensure that informal cognitive institutions such as *guanxi* would continue to be of influence for some time to come. Internal governance mechanisms, such as the Board of Directors and diversified ownership structures have been widely adopted. The perception of the informants, however, was that as the majority shareholder in most banks is still the state, then the inclusion of foreign shareholders and non-executive directors is not a solution to the principal-agent problem. In fact, the main advantage of having foreign co-operation was, to use the words of one participant 'a show for those outside the region'. It was the view of participants that the main reason for including foreign directors on the board or of pursuing foreign ownership was to enhance the perceived legitimacy of Chinese banks in the international financial community. Similar themes were found in the examination of technical assistance projects related to credit rating and risk management. Here, however, the managers were also coping with the implications of the sub-prime crisis which was seen as a severe blow to the credibility of western rating systems. The study shows, then, that although regulatory, normative and cognitive institutional forces impact government mechanisms to varying degrees, western managers perceive that the over-riding concern of Chinese banks is with establishing legitimacy rather than practically changing existing forms of governance.

However, it is important to re-iterate that the publicly-stated aim of allowing foreign banks entry into the Chinese market was that they could assist local banks with the introduction of new technologies and products, and enhance corporate governance of local

Table 2. Summary of institutional forces influencing corporate governance mechanisms between Chinese and western banks.

Governance Mechanism	Institutional Influences	Explanation and examples
External		
Legal environment	Regulatory and normative institutions	High level international advisory board at CBRC. Introduction of a range of new legislation aimed at improving governance in the banking system including bankruptcy law, enterprise law and partnership law. Few participants optimistic about the reform of legal environment.
Informal relationship	Cognitive institutions	Enduring influence of *guanxi* in an environment where information is limited. Information asymmetry amongst Chinese regulators and managers as well as between western and Chinese managers.
Internal		
Board of Directors	Normative institutions	Widespread adoption of governance structures such as separate credit and supervisory committees and the appointment of non-executive directors. Majority of participants pessimistic about the ability of foreign directors to reduce conflict of interest associated with principal-agent problem in the Chinese context.
Ownership structure	Regulatory and normative	Foreign ownership largely perceived as a means of improving investor confidence. Satisfies legitimacy-seeking goals of Chinese institution. Majority shareholder, the state, continues to guide strategy.
Technical Assistance		
Credit rating and risk management	Normative and cognitive	Organizational constraints impede knowledge transfer: language skills of foreign bankers, enduring influence of *guanxi* loan practices. Partnerships perceived to be driven by legitimacy-seeking associated with having a foreign partner.
Securitization	Normative	Failure in western credit rating systems in the sub-prime crises indicates a shift in the perception of the importance foreign expertise of in certain corporate governance mechanisms.

banks, both directly (through joint ventures and shareholdings in Chinese banks) and indirectly (through creating competitive pressures) (Cousins 2007). Some theorists have argued that these moves are indicators that Chinese officials wish to develop an economic institutional environment which broadly converges with the international business community (Guthrie 1998, Wang 2007). As would be predicted by the path dependency approach to institutional change, however, this study has shown that cognitive and normative institutions remain powerful influences on the inclination and capacity of Chinese banks to engage in changing corporate governance mechanisms. While regulators may still aim for international standardization, the experience of the participants in this study is that, at the level of the organization, there is little will, and few incentives, to change current practices.

Of course it is important to remember that change occurs at different rates in different dimensions of an institution and so there is a need to be sensitive to the time-frames used in interpreting the data. While it was possible to observe relatively rapid change in the formal legislative environment in which the banks operated, the informal normative and cultural-cognitive realms were clearly lagging behind. As a cross-sectional study, this study can only offer a snapshot of the range of perceptions at a given point in time. What cannot be discussed is how these will change in the mid to long term, particularly as the impact of the sub-prime crises becomes more apparent. Furthermore, it is important to emphasize that the perceptions analysed here are mainly those of foreign managers and senior employees. It is highly likely that a somewhat different set of narratives would have been presented if the views of senior Chinese managers who have worked with foreign board members had been analysed. Indeed, one would expect that other cognitive institutions, besides *guanxi,* may be more pertinent to this group, such as, for example, low-trust relationships, face (*mianzi*) and fatalism. Ongoing research by the author is addressing this issue and it is hoped that future publications will offer an even more detailed analysis of the similarities and differences between western and Chinese perceptions of the influence of foreign banks on corporate governance in China. Moreover, there is a need to recognize that this study, because it is focusing on individuals responding to their social and institutional situations, is following a weak version of methodological individualism and does not consider in great detail the structural frameworks, particularly the role of the state as the sovereign actor, which can form ideas (including norms like 'legitimacy') in the first place (North 1981, Yee 1996). The study is not, however, an attempt to argue that micro-level analysis will account for all the complexity of institutional change (Arrow 1994). The point here has been to track the perceptions of key western actors involved in transforming governance mechanisms in Chinese banks. By doing so, it has been possible to offer a more nuanced account of the variety of institutional influences which have been in play in this particular sector.

Theory and policy implications

A key plank of neo-institutional theory is that social and organizational actors are seeking legitimacy in a constantly changing environment. In other words legitimacy-seeking is not static and, as Scott (2001) argues, actors are constantly re-inventing legitimacy norms within an evolving institutional context. It is certainly true that the institutional environment in the Chinese financial sector is rapidly changing both internally and externally. Internally, actors encounter an uncertain and uncoordinated financial system in China where there is a low level of compliance with evolving rules, a scenario which encourages continuing reliance on informal cognitive institutions such as *guanxi*. However, we have also seen that, externally, the international environment is also in a state of flux and uncertainty and western credit-rating systems and related forms of governance have taken a severe blow to their credibility. Indeed, there are early indicators that they may well be unable to maintain their legitimacy as the 'standard' form. Wang (2007) has argued that, in relation to economic norms, China will become increasingly congruent with international standards. However, while this argument may yet prove to be valid, environmental pressures both in the global and the Chinese environment mean that a more specifically Chinese form of corporate governance in relation to banking may develop.

The assumption that convergence on western, particularly Anglo-Saxon, models of corporate governance was likely to occur was, to a large extent, informed by neo-classical economic assumptions that market forces have the power to efficiently allocate credit unaided by state 'interference' (Cernat 2004, Luo 2007). However, as participants' discussion of securitization has illustrated, this model is under question. There is now a growing realization that the rapid expansion of securitization was linked to the expansion of government guarantees, both explicit and implicit, of large western financial institutions (White 2009). Certainly, in light of recent events in the global financial arena, strong state intervention in some western countries is also proving necessary in order to encourage the primary goal of banking: that the people and institutions who should borrow money get to borrow money in a safe and secure way. The rather rigid view that when the principal is the state, then inefficiencies must inevitably follow, overlooks not only examples of non-profit organizations which operate effectively, but also the numerous instances of profit-based organizations with distant human 'owners' (such as pension funds) who have been shown to be able to increase value in efficient ways (Clarke 2003). There is no doubt that the assumption that market forces and managerial incentives alone can ensure the most efficient allocation of money throughout society has been severely tested in the last two years. In this regard, it is interesting to note that the 'control-based' model of governance which is common in China, where the state takes a guiding role in ensuring that financial intermediation does not upset social stability, has now been adopted as a policy (at least in the short-term) by the UK and US. Of course, the fact that the Chinese state has access to abundant funds to recapitalize any inefficient banks or to replenish the numerous large scale thefts which still regularly occur, should not detract from the fact that such moves are rather pointless if, in the long term, more fundamental changes in governance structures do not occur. But as the sub-prime crisis has shown, this can no longer be said to be a particularly Chinese 'problem'.

Conclusion

This study has shown that while there has been relatively rapid change in the formal legislative environment in which banks operated, the informal normative and cultural-cognitive realms are changing at a much slower pace. Components of western models of corporate governance such as the Board of Directors, diversified ownership structures, and technical assistance in areas such as credit rating and risk management have certainly been widely adopted. However, the over-riding perception was that the motivation for this was legitimacy-seeking by Chinese banks in the global financial environment. Enduring cognitive and normative institutions including a 'who you know' credit culture and the importance of informal institutions such as *guanxi* mean that the influence of foreign banks on corporate governance reforms in China is perceived by informants as usually ineffective. Given the serious failures of western credit rating systems in the sub-prime crisis, it is likely that this perception will increase in the future. At the time of writing, the Chinese 'control-based' model of corporate governance, where the state intervenes in the banking sector to ensure financial stability and the achievement of social objectives such as employment and enterprise support, is showing itself to be a workable policy model for some western economies too.

Acknowledgements

I am grateful to the Nuffield Foundation for supporting the fellowship and fieldwork associated with this research project. I would also like to thank Professor Malcolm Warner of the Judge Business Institute of Management at the University of Cambridge for invaluable academic support, friendship and advice.

Notes

1. Though this is partly due to the fall in market value of some western banks as opposed to the rise in Chinese banks per se.
2. Tier rating indicates the size of capital adequacy in the bank as assessed by regulators. Tier 1 represents a bank with more resources than a Tier 2 institution.
3. Names of banks are anonymized to protect confidentiality.

References

AFP, 2009. China's banks misuse millions of dollars: Auditor. *AFP News Agency*, 18 February. Available at: http://www.google.com/hostednews/afp/article/ALeqM5gF2FaLybid_meit4T dwsu_2GjA.

Aguilera, R. and Jackson, G., 2003. The cross-national diversity of corporate governance: dimensions and determinants. *The Academy of management review*, 28 (3), 447–465.

Arrow, K., 1994. Methodological individualism and social knowledge. *American economic review*, 84 (2), 1–9.

Bai, G., Liu, Q., Lu, J., Song, F., and Zhang, J., 2003. *Corporate Governance and Market Valuation in China*, William Davidson Institute Working Paper 564.

Bloomberg, 2009. Goldman dumps China as U.S. seeks damage control. *Bloomberg.com*, 3 June. Available at: http://www.bloomberg.com/apps/news?sid=aPOsPudBhblk&pid=20601039.

Boisot, M. and Child, J., 1998. The iron law of fiefs: bureaucratic failure and the problem of governance in China's economic reforms. *Administrative science quarterly*, 33, 507–527.

Branstetter, L., 2007. China's financial markets: an overview. *In*: C. Calomiris, ed. *China's financial transition at a crossroads*. New York: Columbia University Press, 23–79.

Brown, K. and Skully, M., 2005. Regional comparative analysis of China's banking system. *In*: R. Smyth, O.K. Tam, M. Warner and C. Zhu, eds. *China's business reforms: institutional challenges in a globalised economy*. London: Routledge, 27–45.

Brown, K., 2008. *The rise of the dragon: Inward and outward investment in china in the reform period 1978-2007*. Oxford: Chandos Publishing.

Caijing, 2008. Billions in loans unlawfully invested in stock market. *Caijing Magazine*, 28 August.

Calomiris, C., 2007. Introduction. *In*: C. Calomiris, ed. *China's financial transition at a crossroads*. New York: Columbia University Press, 23–79.

Campbell, J., 2004. *Institutional Change and Globalization*. Princetown: Princetown University Press.

Cao, X. and Zhao, X., 2004. Research into issues of corporate governance in SOCBs. *Finance Forum*, 1, 3–8 Beijing, cited in Cousin, V. (2007).

Cernat, L., 2004. The emerging European corporate governance model: Anglo-Saxon, Continental, or still the century of diversity? *Journal of european public policy*, 11 (1), 147–166.

China Banking Regulatory Commission, 2008. *Annual report*. Beijing: CBRC.

Clarke, D., 2003. Corporate governance in China: an overview. *China economic review*, 14 (4), 494–507.

Cousin, V., 2007. *Banking in China*. Basingstoke: Palgrave Macmillan.

Davis, H., 2008. *China and Financial Reform*, LSE Public Lecture, London, October. Available at: http://www.lse.ac.uk/collections/CCPN/resources/HowardDavies.htm.

Dennis, D. and McConnell, J., 2003. *International corporate governance*, European Corporate Governance Institute Working Paper No. 05.

DiMaggio, P. and Powell, W., 1983. The iron cage revisited: institutional isomorphism and collective rationality in organizational fields. *American sociological review*, 48, 147–160.

DiMaggio, P. and Powell, W., 1991. *The new institutionalism in organizational analysis*. Chicago: University of Chicago Press.

Eisenhardt, K., 1989. Building theories from case study research. *The Academy of management review*, 14 (4), 532–550.

Ewing, R., 2005. Chinese corporate governance and prospects for reform. *Journal of contemporary China*, 14 (43), 317–338.

Furubotn, E. and Richter, R., 1997. *Institutions and economic theory. The contribution of the new institutional economics*. Ann Arbor: University of Michigan Press.

Goodhart, C. and Zeng, X., 2005. *China's banking reform: problems and potential solutions*, Financial Markets Group Special Paper, sp 163. Cited in Cousin (2007).

Guillen, M., 2001. *The limits of convergence: globalization and organizational change in Argentina, South Korea and Spain*. Princeton NJ: Princeton University Press.

Guo, A., ed., 2007. *China financial service directory*. Hong Kong: China Economic Review Publishing.

Guthrie, D., 1998. The seclining aignificance of Guanxi in China's economic transition. *The China quarterly*, 154, 254–282.

Guthrie, D., 2002. Information asymmetries and the problems of perception: the significance of structural position in assessing the importance of guanxi in China. *In*: T. Gold and D. Guthrie, D. Wank, eds. *Social connections in China: institutions, culture and the changing nature of guanxi*. Cambridge: Cambridge University Press, 37–56.

Hamid, J. and Tenev, S., 2008. Transforming China's banks: the IFC's experience. *Journal of contemporary China*, 17 (5), 449–468.

Hu, Z., 2005. Does the Chinese bank reform require international strategic investors? *Economic observer*, 12 December. Cited in Cousin (2007).

Huan, G., 2005. Three questions on the drawing of foreign strategic investors in SOCBs. *Caijing magazine*, 12 December 2005.

Institute of International Finance (IIF), 2006. *Corporate governance in China: an investor perspective*. Washington DC: IIF, IIF Task Force Report.

International Finance Corporation (IFC), 2005. *Step by step: corporate governance models in China*. Washington, DC: International Finance Corporation.

Judge, W., Douglas, T., and Kutan, A., 2008. Institutional antecedents of corporate governance legitimacy. *Journal of management*, 34 (4), 765–785.

Li, L., Naughton, T., and Hovey, M., 2008. *A review of corporate governance in China*, 18 August. Available at: SSRN: http://ssrn.com/abstract=1233070.

Ling, H. and Guo, Q., 2006. Banking: compared with the reform of incentives systems, the reform of human resources system is more crucial. *Caijing magazine*, 6 February.

Liu, L., Yu, N., and Ling, H., 2005. Big game: analysis of the model for attracting investments in China's banking industry. *Caijing magazine*, 19 September.

Liu, Q., 2006. Corporate governance in China: current practices, economic effects and institutional determinants. *Working Paper CESifo Economic Studies*, doi:10,1093/cesifo/ifl001.

Luo, Y., 2007. *Global dimensions of corporate governance*. Oxford: Blackwell.

Meyer, J., Boli, J., and Thomas, G., 1987. Ontology and rationalization in the western cultural account. *In*: G. Thomas, J. Meyer, F. Ramirez, and J. Boli, eds. *Institutional structure: constituting state, society and the individual*. Beverly Hills: Sage, 12–37.

Nee, V., 2005. The new institutionalisms in economics and sociology. *In*: N. Smelser and R. Swedberg, eds. *The handbook of economic sociology*. 2nd ed. Princeton: Princeton University Press.

Nee, V. and Yang, C., 1999. Path dependent societal transformations. *Theory and society*, 28, 799–834.

North, D., 1990. *Institutions, institutional change and economic performance*. Cambridge: Cambridge University Press.

Organisation for Economic Cooperation and Development (OECD), 2005. *China OECD economic survey*. Paris: OECD Publishing.

Peng, Y., 2001. Chinese villages and townships as industrial corporations: ownership, governance, and market discipline. *American journal of sociology*, 106 (5), 1338–1370.

Redding, G. and Witt, M., 2007. *The future of chinese capitalism*. Oxford: Oxford University Press.

Reuters, 2009. China bank audit finds loan procedures still weak, Reuters News Agency, 19 February. Available at: http://www.reuters.com/article/rbssFinancialServicesAndRealEstate New/idSPEK20263520090219.

Roe, M., 2002. Corporate law's limits. *Journal of legal studies*, 31, 233–271.

Scott, W.R., 1995. *Institutions and organizations*. 1st ed. California: Sage.

Scott, W.R., 2001. *Institutions and organizations*. 2nd ed. California: Sage.

Sherer, A. and Palazzo, G., 2008. Globalization and corporate social responsibility. *In*: A. Crane, A. McWilliams, D. Matten, J. Moon, and D. Siegel, eds. *The Oxford handbook of corporate social responsibility*. Oxford: Oxford University, 656.

Stearns, L. and Mizruchi, M., 2005. Banking and financial markets. *In*: N. Smelser and R. Swedberg, eds. *The handbook of economic sociology*. 2nd ed. Princeton: Princeton University Press, 49–73.

Stiglitz, J., 1999. *Second-generation strategies for reforms for China*. (The World Banks, speech in Beijing, 20 July 1999), cited in Hamid, J. and Tenev, S. (2008).

Strauss, A. and Corbin, J., 2008. *Basics of qualitative research: techniques and procedure for developing Grounded Theory*. 3rd ed. London: Sage.

Streeck, W. and Thelen, K., 2005. Introduction: institutional change in advanced political economies. *In*: W. Streek and K. Thelen, eds. *Beyond continuity: institutional change in advanced political economies*. Oxford: 1–39.

Suchman, M., 1995. Managing legitimacy: strategic and institutional approaches. *Academy of management review*, 20 (3), 571–610.

Sung, W.J., 2003. Corporate governance and firm profitability: evidence from Korea before the economic crisis. *Journal of financial economics*, 68, 287–322.

Thompson, J., 2005. Governance of banks in China. *Financial market trends, OECD*, 89 (2), 67–105.

Time, 2009. Why Chinese banks are stronger than America's. *Time.com*, June. Available at: http://www.time.com/time/business/article/0,8599,1902404,00.html.

Wang, H., 2007. Linking up with the international track: what's in a slogan? *The China quarterly*, 189 (March), 1–23.

Wang, X. and Huang, Y., 2004. Reform of Chinese commercial banks: ownership structure, corporate governance and market competition. *Ji'nan finance*, 7, 10–13 in Cousin, V. (2007).

Wei, W., 2005. *The banking law system in transitional China – a comparative review in the light of EU banking rules*. Zurich: Schulthess Juristische Medien.

Weingast, B., 2002. Rational-choice individualism. *In*: I. Katznelson and H. Milner, eds. *Political science: state of the discipline*. New York: W.W. Norton & Company, 670–692.

White, L., 2009. *Statement of Lawrence White, Professor of economics, Stern School of Business, New York University, for the hearing on: "the present condition and future status of Fannie Mae and Freddie Mac", before the Subcommittee on Capital Markets*, Insurance, U.S. House of Representatives, 3 June. Available at: http://w4.stern.nyu.edu/news/docs/prof_white_testimony_6-3-09.pdf.

Williamson, O., 1981. The economics of organization: the transaction cost approach. *American journal of sociology*, 87, 548–577.

Wilson, S., 2008. Law Guanxi: MNCs, state actors, and legal reform in China. *Journal of contemporary China*, 17, 25–51.

Witt, M., 2006. *Changing Japanese capitalism*. Cambridge: Cambridge University Press.

World Bank (WB), 2000. *Bankruptcy of state enterprises in China – a case and agenda for reforming the insolvency system*. Washington: World Bank.

Wormuth, M., 2004. *The bankruptcy law of the PRC – continuity and change*. Hamburg: Institut fur Asienkunde.

Xu, L., Zhu, T., and Lin, Y., 2002. *Politician control, agency problems and ownership reform: evidence from China*, SSRN Working Paper.

Yee, A., 1996. The causal effects of ideas on policies. *International Organizatin*, 50, 69–108.

Zhang, H. and Cheng, M., 2003. 100 billions for paying the bills of the SOCBs, how long can we sustain the transfusion? *Economic Observer*, 6 December, Beijing.

Zhang, J., 2005. Ten main development characteristics of Chinese City Banks. *Digital fortune*, 10 January, pp. 65–71.

Zhou, X., 2004. *Improve corporate governance and develop capital market*, Speech by Mr Zhou Xiaochuan, Govesrnor of the PBOC at the 'China Forum: Capital Market and Corporate Governance, 1 December, cited in Cousin, V. (2007).

Intangible management and enterprise success in the Chinese transitional economy

Ying Zhu[a], Michael Webber[b] and John Benson[c]

[a]Department of Management and Marketing, University of Melbourne, Parkville, Australia; [b]School of Resource Management and Geography, University of Melbourne, Parkville, Victoria, Australia [c]School of Management, University of South Australia, Australia

China has undergone extensive reform of its business system in its rapid transition to a market economy. In this process, the success of enterprises has depended heavily on changing structural conditions, such as the transformation of ownership and market competition, on the ability of management to adapt to new labour and product markets, and on new ways of getting workers to commit to the enterprises' goals. This study explores enterprise success by modelling organizational performance as a function of intangible management practices, either directly or through their effects on employee satisfaction, all within the context of transition. The findings of the research demonstrate that employee satisfaction is influenced by some forms of intangible management; that enterprise success is conditioned by employee satisfaction, by some measures of transition and by a range of intangible management practices.

Introduction

China has undergone a remarkable economic transformation since the decision to adopt market principles and open its economy was implemented in the late 1970s. Considerable research has now been undertaken on various aspects of this transition (see, for example, Warner [1987], Child [1994], Benson and Zhu [1999], Zhang [2000], Zhu and Warner [2000b], Warner et al. [2005], Tan and Tan [2005], Ralston et al. [2006]). Over much the same period, there has emerged within the management literature a broad understanding of the role of business management and employee satisfaction in underpinning the success of Western corporations (see Pfeffer [1998] for a summary of much of this literature).

These facts generate three questions about the role of management within a transitional economy like China. First, to what degree in China do intangible aspects of management such as organizational culture, management structures and management systems, affect enterprise output and productivity? This is the 'transitional question': have enterprises in China fully cast off the legacy of the old command and control economy so that their success now responds to managerial behaviour in the same manner as Western enterprises? Since the reform of urban enterprises in China has a history of less than 30 years, it would be surprising if the traces of the past have been completely eliminated. Secondly, do the various elements making up intangible management directly affect enterprise success, or do they work indirectly through other critical factors such as employee satisfaction? This is a question of theoretical significance, largely not addressed in the literature about intangible management, that offers insight into the mechanisms through which intangible management influences enterprise success and that permits us to link two literatures – about intangible management and enterprise success and about employee satisfaction and enterprise success. Thirdly, what is the relative role of intangible management and other contextual conditions (such as market competition, ownership form, age of the enterprise and location) in determining the success of enterprises? Again, this question has theoretical importance, for it offers an understanding of the significance of contextual conditions (that reflect China's transition and that are outside the control of management) in influencing the adoption of new forms of intangible management, the levels of employee satisfaction and the performance of enterprises.

This study addresses these questions concerning whether and through what means intangible management practices affect the success of Chinese organizations. Put simply, we examine the interrelationships between three important factors that determine enterprise success: management actions; employees' responses; and contextual conditions. In contrast to the research based on the high commitment/performance of HRM, we believe that the intangible management approach would provide a more comprehensive understanding of both organizational and individual action and responses towards changes both within the organization and in external social and economic environments. Therefore, the study is organized as follows. First, we review the theoretical underpinnings of the Western management literature on the role of intangible elements and related empirical research on the adoption of 'modern management systems' in China. The research framework and hypotheses will be defined in this section. The next section identifies our research methods, sample selection and analytical procedures. This is followed by a results section that links intangible management practices, various dimensions of employee satisfaction, and a range of structural contextual variables with enterprise performance. Based on the results of the data analysis, the penultimate section interprets the findings in terms of the central hypotheses of this research. The theoretical and practical implications of the results are considered in the conclusion.

Theoretical and empirical framework

The Resource-Based View of the firm postulates that enterprise resources are the main determinants of competitive advantage and firm profitability (Wernerfelt 1984, Mahoney and Pandian 1992). According to this view, if such resources are unique or possess attributes superior to those of the enterprise's competitors, they become strategic assets. The way these assets are managed and used to their best advantage thus becomes a key task of management (Michalisin et al. 1997). Despite these claims, it is only in recent years that evidence has emerged that lends support to such contentions (see, for example, Carmeli and Tishler [2004]). In general, these strategic assets are made up of what may be termed tangible elements such as the management of facilities, raw materials, equipment and capital (Itami and Roehl 1987), and intangible elements such as organizational culture, communication and knowledge (Michalisin et al. 1997). Intangible assets can be further broken down into several elements including (intangible) management, which is the central interest of this study.

Intangible management

The literature refers to 'intangible management' as those aspects of management that incorporate organizational culture, management structures, management mechanisms and management systems (Chatterjee and Wernerfelt 1991, Canals 2000, Teece 2000, Hitt *et al.* 2001, Carmeli and Tishler 2004). Organizational culture refers to the perceptions held about an enterprise and how managers attempt to rally employees around common projects, values or symbols through interactions among the various members of the organization (Dupuis 2008). The concept brings out the importance of certain non visible management elements of organizational life (Dupuis 2008). Management structure, mechanisms and systems refer to the way people are integrated into the organization to achieve its objectives. More specifically, management structure is the levels and means of communication, the degree of decentralization and the forms of problem-solving within an organization. Structure sets the parameters by which the enterprise formalizes the temporary and ephemeral occurrence of social interactions in organizational settings, which in turn are closely connected to interrelations among organizational actors (Strati 2008). Management mechanisms involve financial rewards and forms of participation, including employee commitment schemes. These mechanisms allow employees to exert influence over the decisions that affect their work and work environment (Cabrera 2008). Some of the many forms that these mechanisms can take include participative management, information sharing, profit sharing and employee stock ownership programmes (Cabrera 2008). Management systems include the forms of corporate ownership (including privatization), the adoption of innovative management practices and formalized quality control. The adoption of new management systems is associated with organizational changes in the areas of production process and the establishment of new management/work practices (Marceau 2008).

It is these aspects of intangible management that are the concern of this study. The literature concerning intangible management includes both the management of intangible assets and intangible management as we have defined it above. Intangible assets, such as the embodied knowledge and skills that exist within an organization (Carmeli and Tishler 2004), will not be considered in this study, as we are interested in the implications of (intangible forms of) management actions rather than the management of intangibles. The elements making up intangible management can affect multiple uses at the same time, serve simultaneously as inputs and outputs of corporate activities and are not consumed when in use. For some (Teece 2000, Hitt *et al.* 2001), an organization's superior performance depends on its ability to defend and use the intangible assets it creates, such as culture and unique management systems. In contrast, the distinction we make is between assets, whether tangible or intangible, and (intangible forms of) management – the culture, structures, mechanisms and systems that are deployed by managers to create value and to encourage employees to create value.

The existing research on intangible management, however, has significant limitations. Most quantitative research has focused on a single element such as a particular mechanism or system (e.g. Hitt *et al.* 2001, Waldman *et al.* 2001), and seeks to identify its role in performance. In addition, most studies have ignored the interplay between the intangible elements and other influential variables, such as ownership, size, location, history and market orientation (see the research of Desarbo *et al.* [2005] on enterprises in China, Japan and the US). Furthermore, most research has examined each relationship separately, without a comprehensive understanding of the combined effects of management initiatives, their impact on employees, and the influence of both on enterprise performance. Finally, previous studies of the topic are largely limited to developed economies with relatively stable and established institutional environments (see Wright *et al.* [2005] for one exception).

The role of intangible elements

A number of empirical studies have demonstrated that intangible management contributes to enterprise success. Koys (2001) found that in 28 stores in a restaurant chain, organizational citizen behaviour in year one was related to profitability in year two, although no attempt was made to control for a range of contextual and management factors. Tzafrir (2005), using a survey of 104 leading industrial, service and trade companies in Israel, found that enterprises exhibited higher organizational performance when trust and commitment among employees were high. However, more comprehensive research was undertaken by Carmeli and Tishler (2004). They investigated local government authorities in Israel through a set of intangible management elements (including managerial capabilities, organizational reputation, organizational culture) and identified their effect on the performance of the enterprise. They found that intangible management, together with environmental uncertainty and geographical location, strongly affected the performance of local authorities. The contribution of this research was not only that a set of intangible management elements was analysed in relation to enterprise performance, but that perceived environmental uncertainty was employed as a control variable in order to improve the conceptualization and measurement of organizational task environments (Dess and Beard 1984). Pfeffer (1998) reviews a number of other studies that confirm this evidence.

The studies referred to above, with the exception of Koys (2001), ignored other possible key intervening variables such as employee satisfaction. While there is an extensive literature on job satisfaction and job performance, these tend to link job satisfaction with employee job performance and not overall enterprise success (Iaffaldano and Muchinsky 1985, Judge *et al.* 2001). There are, however, some recent relevant studies for our research based on the idea of the psychological contract. For instance, Guest's (2004) research on the impact of the psychological contract on employment relations provided both a theoretical underpinning as well as an empirical illustration about organizational performance and well being on the one hand, and employees' commitment to the organization, job satisfaction and intention to stay on the other hand (also see Shore and Tetrick [1994] and Rousseau [1995] on the notion of psychological contracts, as well as the case analysis of a large Norwegian sample by Kalleberg and Rogues [2000]). Nevertheless, these studies only illustrated the relationship between enterprise performance and employees' responses, and not their links to intangible management. In addition, these studies did not measure the impact of employees' responses on organizational performance. Our central aim in this study is to develop a more holistic approach by bringing all of these elements together to understand enterprise success more completely. In order to achieve such an aim, we examine four key intangible management elements, namely organizational culture, management structure, management mechanisms and management systems. These four elements represent the major dimensions of intangible management identified in the literature.

Therefore, we propose the following hypotheses:

Hypothesis 1: intangible management variables (organizational culture, management structure, management mechanisms and management systems) influence enterprise success;

Hypothesis 2: intangible management variables directly influence enterprise success and indirectly influence enterprise success through their effect on measures of employee satisfaction.

The general form of hypothesis 1 is broadly confirmed in the literature; however, we are mostly interested in what is less well known – the specific forms of intangible management that most influence enterprise success. Likewise, it is accepted that forms of intangible management influence employee satisfaction and that satisfaction has an influence on enterprise success; what is less clear is which forms of management influence employee satisfaction and whether intangible management influences enterprise success principally through its effect on satisfaction or more directly. Our modelling strategy to reflect the underlying theory and to test these hypotheses is summarized in Figure 1.

The impact of 'new' management systems in China

China has a different kind of economic system than that examined in most research on intangible management. The transformation of Chinese management structure and systems (Huang 1996) is closely related to wider market forces and reflects both greater globalization and increased market orientation (Warner *et al.* 2005). In such a transition, the new management system will have both *general* and *particular* characteristics that mark its evolution (Warner *et al.* 2005, Zhu and Warner 2000a). A key question is, therefore, whether a Western-derived model such as that encapsulated by the hypotheses can capture significant elements of the performance of Chinese enterprises.

This question is quite different from that which has driven most empirical research on the performance of Chinese enterprises. Much of this has been devoted to describing and analysing changes in the structure of state-owned enterprises (SOEs) (Benson and Zhu 1999, Zhang 2000) and the introduction of modern management systems (Zhu and Warner 2000b). Others have begun to investigate the strategies and management behaviour in the new SOEs (Tan and Litschert 1994, Tan and Tan 2005) or compared the behaviour of SOEs, domestic private enterprises (DPEs) and foreign-invested enterprises (FIEs) within a framework of internal changes and external challenges (Ralston *et al.* 2006).

From this and other research it is clear that the modern SOEs in China are no longer the cumbersome, bureaucratic and inefficient organizations of the pre-reform period. This research reaffirms Warner's (1987) claims that learning Western-style management theories and practices has been a priority in the country's reform strategy. Ralston *et al.*'s (2006) research is an important contribution to understanding Chinese management in transition, as it not only identifies SOEs' organizational culture and the elements of their transformation, but also makes a comparison with other forms of organizational

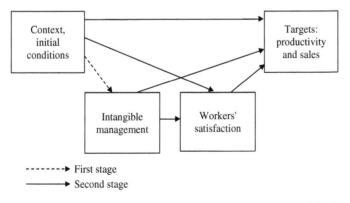

Figure 1. Model of enterprise success as a function of workers' satisfaction, intangible management factors and external variables.

ownership. However, Ralston's research is based on only one element of intangible management, namely organizational culture, and a more comprehensive approach with multiple elements of intangible management is now required.

This literature leads to the conclusion that the performance of Chinese enterprises reflects not only variables that are generally important (such as intangible management and employee satisfaction), but also the condition of transition. Therefore, we use measures of such contextual conditions as level of competition, form of ownership, age of enterprise and location to reflect the transitional character of the Chinese economy. These variables all measure traces of the past: non-market linkages between enterprises and government protections against competition (level of competition); continuing bureaucratic interference in some elements of the operation of SOEs and collective enterprises (ownership); inherited structures of employee relations and compensation systems (age of enterprise); and inter-provincial differences in rates of economic reform (location). Our hypothesis is that:

Hypothesis 3: intangible management practices, employee satisfaction and enterprise success also depend on a range of contextual factors (notably level of competition, form of ownership, age of enterprise and location) that reflect the transitional character of the Chinese economy.

Data, research method and analysis

Research sites and data collection

This research forms part of a larger study intended to map out the way in which Chinese management has restructured as a consequence of the economic reforms and to explore the impact of the restructuring on employees and enterprises. As the development of reform has been uneven, we selected six locations in China that reflect this diversity. The first two locations, Beijing and Hangzhou, represent regions with the highest levels of economic development and up-to-date management systems. The next two locations, Wuhan and Haerbin, represent older industrial regions that are now undergoing substantial transformation, while the last two locations, Kunming and Lanzhou, represent less developed regions.

Within each location we chose two industries: textiles, clothing and footwear (TCF) and electronics. These two industries are reasonably representative of Chinese industry, employ a large number of employees in China and have experienced systematic change since the beginning of the economic reform and, in particular, after China joined the World Trade Organization (WTO) in 2001. Within each location, we selected six enterprises (eight in Kunming) drawn from a cross section of ownership forms (SOEs, DPEs, FIEs and collective-owned enterprises (COEs)) and size (small-medium and large enterprises). In each enterprise, we interviewed one manager and five employees in order to gauge and represent the perceptions of both employers and employees. In each enterprise, three women and three men were interviewed in order to maintain a gender balance. (We address below the issue of representing enterprises by information from six employees.) In total, 228 interviews were conducted in 38 enterprises. It is these 38 enterprises that are the units of analysis: information from individual interviews is averaged to provide a characterization of each of the 38 enterprises.

To allow us to investigate a wide range of issues that have been raised by the existing literature and to represent the variety of Chinese enterprises, we created separate interview questionnaires for managers and for workers. The questions were developed to measure the variables specified in the hypotheses and finalized only after we field tested them. In conducting the field research, we worked with the China Industrial Relations Institute in Beijing (the Institute). In particular, we assigned the Institute the tasks of selecting appropriate enterprises within the guidelines specified above and conducting the interviews with managers and employees. The employees' questionnaire contained 95 questions, often with multiple sub-questions; the managers' questionnaire contained 84 questions. The questionnaires were administered in person, in the enterprise, in interviews that each took between one and one-and-a-half hours to complete. To allow for cross-checking of responses from employees and managers, the two questionnaires contained some common questions. All completed questionnaires, from managers and workers, were coded by one of the authors.

Reduction of variables

The large number of questions contained in the questionnaires allowed us to measure many elements of enterprise success, employee satisfaction and management practices, as well as a variety of contextual conditions. Our central aim in this study is to model enterprise success as a function of the contextual conditions, intangible management and employee satisfaction. However, the number of variables is far larger than the number of cases – a not-uncommon problem in the social sciences. There are three general approaches to this problem: canonical correlation (Cliff 1987); robust canonical analysis (Tishler and Lipovetsky 2000); and data reduction through principal components analysis (Rao 1993). Since our model is inherently three-stage (the contextual conditions influence management; management influences satisfaction and success; and satisfaction influences success), we used principal components factor analyses to reduce the large number of indicators to a much smaller number (on the theoretical underpinnings of this approach, see Zeller and Carmines [1980]). The factor analyses were conducted using the Statistical Package for the Social Sciences (SPSS); all extracted factors are after Varimax rotation with Kaiser normalization.

Enterprise success

The outcome variables, reflecting the success of the enterprise, sought to measure the well being of the organization. In this study, the four target measures of success are 2003 sales, log transformed; percentage increase in sales, 1998–2003; 2003 labour productivity, log transformed; percentage increase in productivity, 1998–2003; all for the 38 firms. Levels of sales and of productivity in 1998 (log transformed) are deployed as predictor variables.

Variables were identified from the managers' interviews: the level of total sales and number of employees in 1998 and 2003. From these figures we calculated labour productivity (total sales divided by number of employees). Log transformations were needed to remove the skew in the 1998 and 2003 levels of sales, employment and productivity. As some of the sample enterprises were only established after 1998, their five-year rates of growth were calculated from the annual average rates observed during the actual period of operation of the enterprise, and the 1998 values of sales, employees and productivity were extrapolated from the 2003 data and these growth rates.

Employee satisfaction

One aspect of the well-being of employees is their satisfaction with their working environment. Employees were asked, on a three point scale (dissatisfied; it's all right;

satisfied), how satisfied they were with ten aspects of their work: tasks; accountability; responsibility; participation; promotion opportunities; pay; overtime pay rates; workload; job security; and management. For each enterprise, we thus have five employees' reports on 10 measures of satisfaction in 2003. For each enterprise, an average satisfaction score on each of the 10 aspects in 2003 was calculated by averaging the five employees' responses (scored as 0; 0.5; 1).

The matrix of 38 enterprises' scores on the 10 aspects of current satisfaction was subject to a principal components analysis. Two components accounted for 73% of the variance in the 10 variables. The first component primarily reflected satisfaction with promotion opportunities, pay, overtime pay rates, workload and job security. This component was labelled satisfaction with benefits. The second component reflected satisfaction with responsibilities and accountabilities and was labelled satisfaction with responsibilities. Thus, two variables reflect employee satisfaction at work: satisfaction with benefits and satisfaction with responsibilities. The factor scores for satisfaction with responsibilities were first made positive (by adding the minimum score to all scores) and then squared to remove skew.

Intangible management

Four aspects of intangible management – organizational culture, management structure, management mechanisms and management systems – were considered. These aspects of management were measured by a variety of indicators and all except management structure were obtained from the manager interviews.

The key aspects of organizational culture were selected after a consideration of both Chinese tradition as well as the influence of Western practices. The measure of organizational culture was derived by asking managers to rank the three most important elements of their organizational culture. The options were: 'organization is family'; 'harmony'; 'efficiency'; 'productivity'; 'quality'; 'employee satisfaction'; 'customer satisfaction'; 'individual value'; 'internal competition'; and 'external competition'. Each of the 10 measures was scored 1, if ranked in the top three by the managers, and 0 otherwise. Although the measures appear to overlap, only six of the 45 pairs of measures are significantly correlated (at $p < 0.05$) and the factor structure is quite weak: principal components factor analysis extracts five components to account for 74% of the total variance in these measures:

(1) Cultures that emphasize productivity and external competition as opposed to customer satisfaction ('productivity culture');
(2) Cultures that refer to organization as family rather than quality ('family culture');
(3) Cultures that emphasize efficiency ('efficiency culture');
(4) Cultures that refer to harmony ('harmony culture'); and
(5) Cultures that focused on employee satisfaction ('employee culture').

The second variable developed to reflect intangible management was management structure. Employees were asked whether their organization's structure could be characterized as 'open communication', 'centralized', 'many management levels', 'democratic', 'whether it works well', 'whether it enables managers and employees to communicate well' and 'whether it is easy to resolve problems'. Responses were scored 0 (for no), 0.5 (for partly) or 1 (for yes) and averaged for each enterprise. These averages are thus the proportion of employees who regard the structure as open, or centralized, and so on. The enterprise averages were subjected to principal components factor analysis. Two components were found to account for 62% of the total variance in the seven variables:

(1) Decentralization, well-functioning, effective communication and problem resolution (a component that reflects the usefulness of the structure: 'effective structure');
(2) Open communication and democratic (a component that reflects the character of the structure: 'open structure').

The two components reflect different ways of characterizing a management structure – by its effects or by its character – and not significantly uncorrelated (at $p < 0.05$).

Measures of management mechanisms are derived from managers' responses to questions about whether their enterprise had an involvement/participation scheme, information sharing mechanisms, individual grievance/complaint system, employee stock ownership, profit sharing, some form of employee empowerment, or employee commitment schemes. Thus there are seven measures for each enterprise, scored 1 if the enterprise had this practice or 0 if the enterprise did not have this practice. These practices are weakly correlated with each other, and so the mechanisms variable is derived as the simple sum of each enterprise's score on these measures. Thus, this variable measures the total number of management mechanisms implemented by the enterprise.

Measures of management systems are based on the concept of 'modern management systems' adapted from Western business. Managers were asked which of the following had been adopted in their enterprise: private or corporate ownership; reform of management system; professional business management; incentive-based pay system; comprehensive shareholding system; quality control through ISO 9000; and quality control through ISO 14000. Responses are coded 1 (for adopted) or 0 (not adopted). Again, these measures are only weakly correlated with each other and so the management systems variable is simply the sum of each enterprise's score on these measures and thus represents the number of management systems implemented by the enterprise.

Contextual variables

A number of key contextual variables may influence success and the responses of management and employees. These include enterprise age, industry sector, ownership, location, market competition and market-orientation – the traditional drivers of firm success (Zhu and Warner 2004). All reflect to some degree the stage of transition within the sphere of operation of the enterprise: for example, the extent of history in the enterprise and industry; the speed of reform in the province; the extent of protections from competition. This information was collected in the managers' interviews. Age is the year of formation of the enterprise. Industry sector is 1 (textiles, clothing and footwear) or 0 (electronics). Ownership is measured by four dummy variables: SOEs; FIEs; DPEs; and others (principally COEs). Location was also measured by dummy variables that reflected the city of location of each enterprise. Market competition was scored as 1 (high), 2 (medium) or 3 (low). Market orientation was measured by three dummy variables, namely whether the main market is within the province or nearby, within China as a whole or focused on exports.

Many of these control variables were found to be correlated with each other, as would be expected given their relationship to transition. Both age and market competition were significantly correlated with three other variables; ownership variables were correlated with two or more other variables. In order to reduce the number of these variables, principal component factor analysis was used to identify, four components that together account for 78% of the total variance of the contextual variables. These components identify different elements of the transition:

(1) Enterprises that are young and DPEs rather than old and SOEs (the new private economy);
(2) Enterprises that are in China-wide markets with low competition rather than provincial or export markets with higher levels of competition (the old, protected economy);
(3) Enterprises that are DPEs serving provincial markets rather than FIEs serving export markets (the local private economy);
(4) Enterprises that are in older industrial cities (Haerbin) rather than more modern cities (Hangzhou) (the regions in which reform is lagging).

Summary of data

The data thus has the following structure.

(A) The measures of success are:
(1) Sales: logarithm of 2003 level, in RMB;
(2) Sales: percentage growth 1998–2003;
(3) Productivity: logarithm of sales (RMB) per employee, 2003;
(4) Productivity: percentage growth 1998–2003.

Two other measures of performance are used as control variables:

(1) Sales: logarithm of 1998 level, in RMB;
(2) Productivity: logarithm of sales (RMB) per employee, 1998.

(B) There are four contextual (transition-related) variables:
(1) Enterprises in the new private economy;
(2) Enterprises in the old, protected economy;
(3) Enterprises in the local private economy;
(4) Enterprises in the regions in which reform is lagging.

(C) There are two variables related to employee satisfaction:
(1) Satisfaction with benefits;
(2) Satisfaction with responsibilities.

(D) There are nine intangible management variables in four groups:
(1) Organizational culture: productivity culture; family culture; efficiency culture; harmony culture; employee culture;
(2) Management structure: effective structure; open structure;
(3) (Number of) management mechanisms;
(4) (Number of) management systems.

As indicated earlier, the predictor variables (satisfaction, management and contextual conditions) are all measured in 2003. This means that the variables are measured as the sales are occurring rather than historically before the growth in sales between 1998 and 2003. We have adopted this approach because we did not conduct the survey in 1998 and we presume that managers' and employees' responses to questions about management or satisfaction now are more accurate than responses to questions about management or satisfaction as they were in 1998. This means that, although we are hypothesizing a direction of causality, the data about causes and effects are in fact, concurrent rather than sequential.

Sample size

Finally, we address the question of the size of our sample. There are two issues: the first concerns the power of statistical tests that rely on a sample of 38 enterprises; the second is the validity of relying on information from only six persons in each enterprise.

Formally, power is the probability of correctly accepting a correct hypothesis – that is, of identifying an effect, given that the effect actually exists. If the sample size (here, the number of enterprises) is small, it may be incapable of detecting 'really' significant variables. As a rule of thumb, it is recommended that the statistical power of any design should exceed 0.8. Soper (2008) provides a calculator for computing the power of multiple regression models, depending on R^2, sample size, number of predictors and the conventional significance probability. Some of our analyses have 15 predictors; if significance is taken as $p \leq 0.05$, then $R^2 > 0.45$ implies that power exceeds 0.81; if significance is taken as $p \leq 0.10$, then $R^2 > 0.39$ implies that power exceeds 0.81. Two of the six models in Table 1 fail the less stringent test, but both full models with all predictors present pass it. Other analyses have 17 predictors; if significance is taken as $p \leq 0.05$, then $R^2 > 0.48$ implies that power exceeds 0.81; if significance is taken as $p \leq 0.10$, then $R^2 > 0.42$ implies that power exceeds 0.81. The less stringent test is passed by all the models in Tables 2–5; the more stringent test is passed by all the full models with all predictors present. In other words, although the number of enterprises is relatively small, the power of the individual regression models is sufficient to identify effects that actually exist.

Most of the data required to measure the variables deployed in the analyses come from managers. Certainly, the best information about the characteristics of the enterprises and their success would combine data from managers with data from 'the books' (see, for example, Koys [2001]). But we were not given access to firms' records and have to rely on managers for this information.

Information about management structure, satisfaction with benefits and satisfaction with responsibilities was obtained from five workers in each enterprise. This is clearly a small sample from which to estimate these characteristics of the enterprise, and as a result the standard errors of estimate of these three variables are high, which means that their measurement is subject to random error. This error attenuates (biases towards zero) the regression coefficients. It is possible to correct for attenuation, but the procedure is controversial and the resultant R^2 values are not appropriate for inferential statistics and hypothesis testing (Muchinsky 1996). As a consequence, our results need to be understood as conservative, likely to understate rather than overstate the effects that we are examining.

Results

The key questions that directed this research can be expressed in terms of the model presented in Figure 1. The model is estimated in three stages. In the first stage, the measures of intangible management are estimated as a function of the contextual variables and the initial conditions (1998 measures of sales and productivity). Only one of the nine measures of intangible management (effective structure) showed any sign of a relationship with the contextual variables (Adjusted $R^2 = 0.272$, df = 14, 23, F = 1.988, p = 0.070). In general, intangible management variables are independent of the contextual variables and the initial conditions. This means that the adoption of various forms of intangible management is independent of the progress of transition within firms of different ages and degree of protection from competition, in different industries and in different localities.

Subsequent analyses employ the original measures of management rather than the measures estimated in the first stage. The second stage involved estimating the two measures of workers' satisfaction as a function of the contextual variables and initial conditions and of the intangible management variables. In the third stage, the measures of success (log transformed sales and productivity 2003 and growth of sales and productivity 1998–2003) are estimated as a function of the contextual variables and initial conditions, of the intangible management variables and of the two measures of workers' satisfaction (predicted values from stage 2). For reasons of brevity, the study reports only the analyses of employee satisfaction (from the second stage) and measures of success (from the third stage); other results are available on request from the authors.

Employee satisfaction

A variety of models of employee satisfaction is reported in Table 1. The predictor variable for Models 1–3 is satisfaction with benefits. All three forms of the model are statistically significant ($p < 0.05$) and explain a substantial proportion of variance in employee satisfaction with benefits (Adjusted $R^2 = 0.34$–0.46). Satisfaction with benefits is associated with several of the intangible management variables: management structures (effective structures and open structures) and management mechanisms. In one model (2), there is weak evidence of an initial condition (logarithm of 1998 productivity per worker) negatively affecting satisfaction with benefits. There is no evidence of a statistically significant relationship between either the contextual variables or other measures of management and satisfaction with benefits.

The predictor variable for Models 4–6 is satisfaction with responsibilities. These models are less successful than those estimating satisfaction with benefits. Values of Adjusted R^2 range from 0.03 to 0.23, and only the two backwards stepwise models are significant at $p < 0.05$. Two management variables, culture (productivity culture) and management mechanisms, have a significant effect on satisfaction with benefits. Neither the initial conditions nor the contextual variables are associated with satisfaction with responsibilities.

The levels of satisfaction predicted by Models 1 and 4 are used in the third stage of the analysis.

Enterprise success

Tables 2–5 present the estimates of the effects of the initial conditions, contextual variables, intangible management and (predicted) employees' satisfaction on the four measures of enterprise success. In the analyses, when all variables were entered, it was found that two variables (management systems and management structures represented by effective structures) were eliminated because of low tolerance. Therefore, two separate models were estimated: Models 1 and 3, in which management systems and effective structures were not included; and Models 4 and 6, in which the five enterprise culture variables were omitted. Models 1 and 4 contain the full set of variables; Models 3 and 6 are estimated by a backwards stepwise procedure (with probability to remove = 0.10).

The four models estimating the logarithm of 2003 sales are presented in Table 2. All models were statistically significant, and all explained a substantial proportion of variance with the Adjusted R^2 values ranging between 0.95 and 0.97. The coefficient estimates are

Table 1. Models of average employee satisfaction in 38 enterprises.

	Satisfaction: benefits			Satisfaction: responsibilities		
	1	2	3	1	2	3
(Constant)	3.369	3.058	0.000	−5.587	3.566	3.780*
	1.512	1.817	0.000	−0.468	2.050	2.194
Initial conditions						
Log sales 1998	0.002			0.203		
	0.021			0.325		
Log productivity 1998	−0.268	−0.269		0.559		
	−1.304	−1.820		0.507		
Contextual variables						
Young, DEPs	0.178	0.187		−0.050		
	0.797	1.320		−0.042		
China market, low comp	0.232	0.190		−0.874		
	1.355	1.270		−0.952		
Provincial, DPEs	−0.052			0.350		
	−0.322			0.402		
Old industrial cities	−0.123			1.231	1.189	
	−0.665			1.243	1.700	
Intangible management						
Productivity culture	−0.166	−0.166		1.81*	1.495	1.791*
	−1.018	−1.266		2.077	2.076	2.530
Family culture	−0.053			0.135		
	−0.324			0.155		
Efficiency structure	−0.226	−0.216		−0.808	−0.854	
	−1.474	−1.646		−0.984	−1.277	
Harmony structure	−0.217	−0.197		−0.763	−0.781	
	−1.481	−1.581		−0.972	−1.213	
Employee culture	−0.085			0.675		
	−0.538			0.796		
Effective structure	0.665**	0.670**	0.633**	1.186	0.855	
	3.340	4.329	5.090	1.111	1.227	
Open structure	0.239	0.247	0.241	−0.131		
	1.595	1.918	1.940	−0.164		
Mechanisms	−0.032		1.216*	1.111	1.054*	
	−0.312		2.224	2.569	2.481	
Systems	−0.113		−0.508			
	−0.698		−0.587			
Rsq	0.605	0.574	0.459	0.420	0.353	0.210
Adjusted Rsq	0.336	0.457	0.428	0.025	0.228	0.165
F (df)	2.248	4.890	14.836	1.063	2.817	4.661
df	15,22	8,29	2,35	15,22	6,31	2,35
p	0.041	0.001	<0.001	0.438	0.026	0.016

$0.05 < p < = 0.10$; *$0.01 < p < = 0.05$; **$p < = 0.01$.
Note: For each variable, the data reported are the un-standardized coefficients (first row) and t values (second row). Models 1 and 4 contain all the predictor variables; Models 2 and 5 are estimated as backward stepwise to the highest value of Adjusted R^2; Models 3 and 6 are the final backward stepwise estimated model (with probability to remove = 0.10).

Table 2. Models of sales in 38 enterprises, 2003.

	Logarithm of 2003 sales (RMB)			
	1	3	4	6
(Constant)	0.713	1.057	−1.020	−0.681
	0.500	1.051	−0.727	−0.590
Initial conditions				
Log sales 1998	1.194**	1.183**	1.198**	1.217**
	16.927	18.818	15.519	18.486
Log productivity 1998	−0.316*	−0.349**	−0.169	−0.248*
	−2.130	−3.387	−1.291	−2.106
Contextual variables				
Young, DPEs	0.447**	0.446**	0.322*	0.338**
	2.926	3.524	2.178	2.797
China market, low comp	0.422**	0.405**	0.287*	0.237*
	3.088	3.975	2.411	2.415
Provincial, DPEs	0.067		0.177	0.184
	0.677		1.836	1.970
Old industrial cities	−0.215	−0.170	−0.154	
	−1.590	−1.856	−1.094	
Predicted satisfaction				
with benefits	−0.291	−0.278	0.163	
	−1.459	−1.868	0.571	
With responsibilities	−0.004		−0.008	−0.210*
	−0.077		−0.171	−2.305
Intangible management				
Productivity culture	0.011		F	F
	0.095			
Family culture	−0.182	−0.229**	F	F
	−1.809	−2.810		
Efficiency culture	−0.162	−0.149	F	F
	−1.713	−1.728		
Harmony culture	−0.045		F	F
	−0.476			
Employee culture	−0.236*	' −0.235**	F	F
	−2.293	−2.940		
Effective structure	E	E	−0.224	
			−0.962	
Open structure	−0.207*	−0.214*	−0.237	
	−2.169	−2.456	−1.912	
Mechanisms	−0.092		−0.068	
	−1.006		−0.086	
Systems	E	E	−0.006	
			−0.675	
Rsq	0.971	0.969	0.959	0.950
Adjusted Rsq	0.951	0.957	0.939	0.941
F	49.161	83.757	48.240	98.619
df	15,22	10,27	12,25	6,31
p	<0.001	<0.001	<0.001	<0.001

$0.05 < p < = 0.10$; *$0.01 < p < = 0.05$; **$p < = 0.01$; E: Variable omitted, lack of tolerance; F: Variable omitted.

Note: For each variable, the data reported are the un-standardized coefficients (first row) and t values (second row). Models 1 and 4 contain all of the predictor variables; Models 3 and 6 are the final backward stepwise estimated model (with probability to remove = 0.10). Models 1 and 3 start with all variables, but management systems and effective structures are eliminated because of low tolerance; Models 4 and 6 omit the five enterprise culture variables.

Table 3. Models of percentage growth in sales in 38 enterprises, 1998–2003.

	Percentage increase in sales, 1998–2003			
	1	3	4	6
(Constant)	0.232	0.283	−0.187	−0.115
	0.724	1.245	−0.597	−0.442
Initial conditions				
Log sales 1998	0.039*	0.037*	0.040*	0.046**
	2.483	2.632	2.350	3.080
Log productivity 1998	−0.072*	−0.076**	−0.036	−0.054
	−2.148	−3.277	−1.240	−2.033
Contextual variables				
Young, DPEs	0.099**	0.097**	0.069*	0.073*
	2.873	3.393	2.109	2.687
China market, low comp	0.095**	0.088**	0.062*	0.050
	3.095	3.837	2.344	2.254
Provincial, DPEs	0.015		0.040	0.041
	0.675		1.838	1.962
Old industrial cities	−0.054	−0.041	−0.039	
	−1.787	−1.986	−1.246	
Predicted satisfaction				
with benefits	−0.069	−0.062	0.041	
	−1.544	−1.855	0.645	
With responsibilities	0.001		−0.001	
	0.100		−0.074	
Intangible management				
Productivity culture	−0.001		F	F
	−0.048			
Family culture	−0.041	−0.051**	F	F
	−1.808	−2.766		
Efficiency culture	−0.038	−0.035	F	F
	−1.787	−1.780		
Harmony culture	−0.011		F	F
	−0.502			
Employee culture	−0.052*	−0.050**	F	F
	−2.248	−2.797		
Effective structure	E	E	−0.055	
			−1.070	
Open structure	−0.039	−0.041*	−0.048	−0.041
	−1.804	−2.086	−1.739	−1.982
Mechanisms	−0.021		−0.016	
	−1.041		−0.699	
Systems	E	E	0.000	
			0.002	
Rsq	0.680	0.653	0.551	0.450
Adjusted Rsq	0.463	0.525	0.336	0.343
F	3.123	5.089	2.558	4.222
df	15,22	10,27	12,25	6,31
p	0.008	<0.001	0.023	0.003

$0.05 < p < = 0.10$; *$0.01 < p < = 0.05$; **$p < = 0.01$; E: Variable omitted: low tolerance; F: Variable omitted.
Note: For each variable, the data reported are the un-standardized coefficients (first row) and t values (second row). Models 1 and 4 contain all of the predictor variables; Models 3 and 6 are the final backward stepwise estimated model (with probability to remove = 0.10). Models 1 and 3 start with all variables, but management systems and effective structures are eliminated because of low tolerance; Models 4 and 6 omit the five enterprise culture variables.

Table 4.   Models of productivity in 38 enterprises, 2003.

	Logarithm of productivity, 2003			
	1	3	4	6
(Constant)	4.391**	4.565**	1.336	1.144
	3.352	5.557	1.074	1.024
Initial conditions				
Log sales 1998	0.048		0.059	0.110*
	0.744		0.856	2.400
Log productivity 1998	0.561**	0.620**	0.818**	0.754**
	4.126	8.604	7.054	8.380
Contextual variables				
Young, DPEs	0.043		−0.135	
	0.309		−1.026	
China market, low comp	0.412**	0.351**	0.170	0.209*
	3.283	4.458	1.606	2.340
Provincial, DPEs	0.015		0.138	0.144
	0.164		1.613	1.796
Old industrial cities	−0.118		0.024	
	−0.945		0.188	
Predicted satisfaction				
with benefits	−0.146		0.647*	0.555*
	−0.796		2.548	2.673
With responsibilities	0.015		−0.029	
	0.338		−0.674	
Intangible management				
Productivity culture	−0.139	−0.135	F	F
	−1.298	−1.861		
Family culture	−0.190	−0.214**	F	F
	−2.055	−3.112		
Efficiency culture	−0.196*	−0.165*	F	F
	−2.267	−2.322		
Harmony culture	−0.092		F	F
	−1.072			
Employee culture	−0.241*	−0.210**	F	F
	−2.551	−3.011		
Effective structure	E	E	−0.417	−0.427*
			−2.020	−2.569
Open structure	−0.203*	−0.220**	−0.334**	−0.300**
	−2.317	−3.041	−3.038	−3.252
Mechanisms	−0.048		−0.009	
	−0.573		−0.101	
Systems	E	E	0.057	
			0.917	
Rsq	0.892	0.874	0.855	0.844
Adjusted Rsq	0.818	0.845	0.786	0.807
F	12.066	29.784	12.317	23.125
df	15,22	7,30	12,25	7,30
p	<0.001	<0.001	<0.001	<0.001

0.05 < p < = 0.10; *0.01 < p < = 0.05; **p < = 0.01; E: Variable omitted: low tolerance F: Variable omitted.
Note: For each variable, the data reported are the un-standardized coefficients (first row) and t values (second row). Models 1 and 4 contain all of the predictor variables; Models 3 and 6 are the final backward stepwise estimated model (with probability to remove = 0.10). Models 1 and 3 start with all variables, but management systems and effective structures are eliminated because of low tolerance; Models 4 and 6 omit the five enterprise culture variables.

Table 5.   Models of percentage growth in productivity in 38 enterprises, 1998–2003.

	Percentage growth in productivity, 1998–2003			
	1	3	4	6
(Constant)	0.970**	1.009**	0.303	0.248
	3.360	5.553	1.122	1.017
Initial conditions				
Log sales 1998	0.010		0.012	0.024*
	0.672		0.809	2.428
Log productivity 1998	− 0.095**	− 0.084**	− 0.039	− 0.053*
	− 3.183	− 5.243	− 1.565	− 2.724
Contextual variables				
Young, DPEs	0.008		− 0.030	
	0.266		− 1.058	
China market, low comp	0.091**	0.077**	0.037	0.045*
	3.297	4.411	1.633	2.323
Provincial, DPEs	0.006		0.032	0.033
	0.299		1.700	1.880
Old industrial cities	− 0.030		0.002	
	− 1.087		0.072	
Predicted satisfaction				
with benefits	− 0.033		0.140	0.120*
	− 0.828		2.541	2.653
With responsibilities	0.004		− 0.006	
	0.439		− 0.671	
Intangible management				
Productivity culture	− 0.033	− 0.032	F	F
	− 1.414	− 1.992		
Family culture	− 0.040	− 0.046**	F	F
	− 1.953	− 3.027		
Efficiency culture	− 0.043*	− 0.036*	F	F
	− 2.259	− 2.302		
Harmony culture	− 0.018		F	F
	− 0.968			
Employee culture	− 0.050*	− 0.043**	F	F
	− 2.399	− 2.817		
Effective structure	E	E	− 0.091	− 0.093*
			− 2.040	− 2.573
Open structure	− 0.041*	− 0.045**	− 0.070	− 0.063**
	− 2.111	− 2.807	− 2.957	− 3.140
Mechanisms	− 0.011		− 0.003	
	− 0.606		− 0.155	
Systems	E	E	0.014	
			1.027	
Rsq	0.681	0.627	0.588	0.549
Adjusted Rsq	0.464	0.540	0.391	0.444
F	3.137	7.206	2.978	5.224
df	15,22	7,30	12,25	7,30
p	0.007	<0.001	0.010	0.001

$0.05 < p < = 0.10$; *$0.01 < p < = 0.05$; **$p < = 0.01$; E: Variable omitted: low tolerance; F: Variable omitted.

Note: For each variable, the data reported are the un-standardized coefficients (first row) and t values (second row). Models 1 and 4 contain all of the predictor variables; Models 3 and 6 are the final backward stepwise estimated model (with probability to remove = 0.10). Models 1 and 3 start with all variables, but management systems and effective structures are eliminated because of low tolerance; Models 4 and 6 omit the five enterprise culture variables.

relatively stable across the models. The significance and sign of coefficients indicate that 2003 sales are higher in enterprises which:

- Started with higher sales and lower productivity in 1998;
- Are in the new private economy or are in the old protected economy; and
- Possess open structures, or cultures of family and employee.

Less consistent or marginally significant relationships with sales in 2003 are exhibited by: enterprises in the local private economy or in cities where reform is faster; efficiency cultures; and employees' satisfaction with benefits and responsibilities.

Four models of the percentage increase in sales over the period 1998–2003 are presented in Table 3. The values of Adjusted R^2 are naturally lower than those reported in Table 2, but are still high, ranging between 0.34 and 0.53. All the models are significant at $p < 0.05$ and the coefficient estimates are stable across the models. The significance and sign of the coefficients indicate that the percentage rate of growth of sales between 1998 and 2003 depended principally on:

- High sales and low productivity in 1998;
- Being in the new private economy or are in the old protected economy; and
- Open structures, or cultures of family and employee.

Less consistent or marginally significant relationships with growth in sales 1998–2003 are exhibited by: enterprises in the local private economy or in cities where reform is faster; efficiency cultures; and employees' satisfaction with benefits and responsibilities. These results closely mirror the models of sales in 2003 reported in Table 2.

Table 4 presents four models that estimate the logarithm of productivity (sales per worker) in 2003. The values of Adjusted R^2 are high, ranging from 0.79 to 0.85, and all the equations are significant at $p < 0.01$. However, there is some discrepancy between the coefficient estimates in Models 1 and 3 and in Models 4 and 6 (the five variables that measure enterprise culture are omitted from the latter models). There is strong evidence that levels of productivity in 2003 depend on:

- Levels of productivity in 1998;
- Being in the old protected economy;
- Having open structures, cultures of family, efficiency and employee;
- Satisfaction with benefits.

There is weaker evidence that having an effective structure enhances productivity; and slight evidence that sales in 1998 also are associated with higher productivity in 2003.

Finally, Table 5 contains the estimates of four models of percentage growth in productivity per worker, 1998–2003. As would be expected, the values of Adjusted R^2 are lower than those reported in Table 4, ranging between 0.39 and 0.54. Still, the equations are all significant at $p < 0.10$ and the coefficient estimates are reasonably stable across the models. The results indicate that growth in productivity 1998–2003 depended principally on:

- Initial (1998) productivity per worker;
- Being in the old, protected economy;
- Having an effective structure, an open structure, cultures of family, efficiency and employee.

There is also evidence that growth in productivity is affected by the initial level of sales and satisfaction with benefits.

In general, these four tables provide evidence that the initial conditions and the contextual variables influence the target measures of success. The 1998 level of sales is strongly and positively associated with sales in 2003 and with the growth in sales; it is more weakly associated with 2003 productivity and growth in productivity. The 1998 level of productivity is negatively associated with 2003 sales and the growth in sales, as well as with the growth in productivity; it is strongly associated with 2003 productivity levels. Being in the new private economy contributes to sales, but not productivity; being in the old protected economy contributes to both productivity and sales; the local private economy has weak effects on sales and productivity; and the old industrial cities in which reform is lagging have even weaker effects. However, none of these variables has much effect on employee satisfaction (Table 1); their effects on success are therefore confined to these direct relationships.

Enterprise cultures are associated with success. Cultures of workplace as family and of employee satisfaction are strongly associated with all four measures of success. Cultures that stress efficiency are also associated with success, especially with productivity and the growth of productivity. By contrast, cultures that stress productivity are weakly associated with only productivity and its growth (and with satisfaction with responsibilities); and cultures of harmony with none of the measures of success. The effects of enterprise culture on success are principally direct rather than mediated through employee satisfaction.

The structures of management also have direct influence on success. Effective management structures are associated with higher productivity and higher rates of growth of productivity (though not with sales); they also have a strong influence on satisfaction with benefits. Open management structures are correlated with all four measures of success; though more weakly with satisfaction with benefits. Management structures have direct and indirect (through employee satisfaction) associations with success.

Neither the management mechanisms nor the management systems variables have significant effects on sales or productivity (or their growth). Unlike enterprise cultures and management structures, management mechanisms and systems have no direct effect on success. However, management mechanisms are correlated with satisfaction with responsibilities, and so may influence success through this indirect route.

Employee satisfaction (that is, the values estimated from Models 1 and 4, reported in Table 1) is also associated with success. Satisfaction with benefits is strongly associated with levels of productivity in 2003, and less strongly with the other measures of enterprise success. Satisfaction with responsibilities is only associated with the level of sales in 2003.

Discussion and implications

Forms of management in China have changed substantially since the economic reform process began in the late 1970s and, more particularly, since enterprise reform was hastened in the 1990s. Now, most of the management practices, forms of organizational culture, management structures and management systems that are common elsewhere are at least present to some degree in Chinese enterprises.

Employee satisfaction was divided into two components. The first aspect reflected satisfaction with promotion opportunities, pay, overtime pay rates, workload and job security – that is, it reflected employee satisfaction related to benefits. The second aspect reflected employees' responsibilities and accountabilities, which we termed employee satisfaction with responsibilities. The majority of employees expressed satisfaction with both benefits and responsibility; however, levels of satisfaction with responsibility were significantly higher than satisfaction with benefits. In other words, enterprises appeared to have been more successful in developing employee satisfaction with the intangible rather than the tangible characteristics of the job.

Hypothesis 3 states that contextual factors related to the progress of transition influence intangible management, employee satisfaction and enterprise success. The evidence we have presented fails to identify any relationship between the contextual conditions and any of the intangible management and satisfaction measures. On the other hand, there is evidence that enterprise success is strongly influenced by some contextual variables. Being in the new private economy contributes to sales, but not productivity; being in the old protected economy contributes to both productivity and sales. However, the effects of provincial market orientation, being an FIE and being in a city where reform is lagging are all hard to discern (see also Tan and Tan [2005], Ralston *et al.* [2006] and Zhu and Warner [2004] on the impact of WTO accession on the development of management in general, and HRM in particular, among enterprises with different ownership forms). This finding provides an additional complexity compared with previous research (see, for example, Tan and Tan 2005 and Ralston *et al.* 2006). These results provide only partial support for hypothesis 3; they indicate that the conditions represented by the transition have direct influences on enterprise success but little effect on employee satisfaction and intangible management.

Hypothesis 2 proposes that intangible management variables indirectly influence enterprise success through their effect on measures of employee satisfaction. On the one hand, satisfaction with benefits and responsibilities does appear to translate into success, as measured by sales and growth in sales; and satisfaction with benefits translates into productivity. The relationships between satisfaction and success are not all that strong, but they persist across the variety of models and measures of success. On the other hand, both components of employee satisfaction are related to particular forms of intangible management, though not all the relationships are strong. Of the measures of organizational culture, only culture of productivity was strongly related to satisfaction (with responsibilities). Other measures of enterprise culture are not correlated with satisfaction. Effective management structures appeared to promote satisfaction with benefits, as did open structures (though more weakly); they had no effect on satisfaction with responsibilities. The presence of mechanisms such as participation schemes, information sharing, individual grievance channels, empowerment and employee commitment schemes was associated with levels of satisfaction with responsibilities, which suggests that perhaps these mechanisms do gain some level of commitment from employees (though clearly they do not translate into satisfaction with benefits). Management systems had little relationship to satisfaction with either benefits or responsibilities. In other words, there is evidence that (some forms of) intangible management have an influence on employee satisfaction and in turn that satisfaction influences enterprise success. This research finding fills the gaps in the current literature identified earlier; on the one hand, it makes a complementary contribution to the existing research on the direct interaction between intangible elements and organizational performance (i.e. that ignores the intermediate variable of employee satisfaction), such as Dess and Beard (1984), Carmeli and Tishler (2004) and Tzafrir (2005), in particular by specifying which forms of intangible management contribute most to enterprise success. On the other hand, it develops further the argument based on the research on the psychological contract by illustrating the relations between organizational performance and employees' commitment and satisfaction (e.g. Shore and Tetrick 1994, Rousseau 1995, Kalleberg and Rogues 2000, Guest 2004). Our finding indicates that employee satisfaction does influence organizational performance in a positive way through the linkage to intangible elements (this is the reverse of the common argument that enterprise success influences employee satisfaction).

Thirdly, the direct impact of intangible management on enterprise success specified in hypothesis 1 – as measured by level and growth of sales and level and growth of productivity – has been estimated in conjunction with the effects of satisfaction on success. Neither the management mechanisms nor the management systems variables have significant effects on sales or productivity (or their growth). Open management structures are associated with all measures of success, and decentralized structures with productivity and its growth. Success was also found to be strongly related to elements of management culture, especially cultures of workplace as family and of employee satisfaction (and, more weakly, cultures that stress productivity). In other words, we have demonstrated that some intangible management variables have a direct influence on enterprise success, even after the effects of employee satisfaction on enterprise success are accounted for.

Together, these second and third sets of results are consistent with hypothesis 2 and therefore hypothesis 1. This interpretation is summarized in Figure 2. However, it does need to be emphasized that not all the intangible management elements performed well: some enterprise cultures influenced satisfaction with responsibilities and enterprise success; some structures influenced satisfaction with benefits and enterprise success; management mechanisms only influenced satisfaction with responsibilities; and management systems influenced neither employee satisfaction nor enterprise success. It also needs to be emphasized that quality of management, satisfaction and success were all measured concurrently rather than sequentially: the data are consistent with our hypotheses, but also with hypotheses in which the directions of causality are reversed.

Conclusion

The forms of management in China have changed substantially since the beginning of the economic restructuring period, and most of the innovative management practices, the forms of organizational culture, management structures and systems that are common in advanced economies are now present, at least to some degree, in Chinese enterprises. Our research confirms that the success of Chinese enterprises is due to similar kinds of intangible management variables, employee satisfaction and contextual variables that appear to drive the success of Western enterprises.

The impact of changing intangible management elements on employees' satisfaction is significant. However, the 'soft' oriented managerial style, such as better communications, participation and provision of information, is more effective than the 'hard' oriented managerial restructuring of systems or structure. In addition, the effect of the internal-oriented clan culture is more profound than that of the external-oriented market culture. Furthermore, employees' satisfaction is more associated with autonomy and individual rights than benefits, though both components are important.

The effects of changing managerial intangible elements and employee satisfaction on overall organizational survival/performance were also significant. Managerial intangible elements including certain aspects of management culture, such as references to cooperation and unity and open and decentralized management structures, were found to have a significant effect on sales (compare also the arguments of Hitt *et al.* [2001]). In addition, employees' satisfaction as measured by their level of responsibility had a positive effect on sales in enterprises.

Finally, a number of contextual variables related to the transition correlated with outcomes. Our data showed that enterprises in the new private economy and in the old

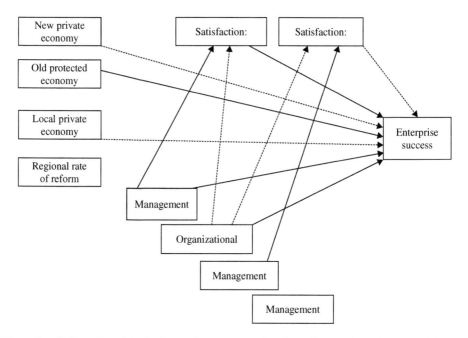

Figure 2.   Estimated model of sales performance as a function of external, environmental factors, satisfaction and management.
Note: The relationships between the initial conditions and measures of success are not shown for reasons of clarity. Solid lines indicate stronger relationships; dashed lines, weaker.

protected economy both enjoyed faster growth compared with other enterprises. However, other measures of transition (the local private economy or locational variations in the pace of reform) do not have much impact on organizational performance. None of the measures of transition have a significant influence on employee satisfaction or on the adoption of forms of intangible management.

The study has significant practical and theoretical implications. In practice, the results provide an improved understanding about which intangible elements have significant impact on employee satisfaction and how both intangible management and employee satisfaction work together to influence the success of organizations. These findings also contribute significantly to the literature. The major contribution of this study is to provide an evaluation of the role of intangible elements in enterprise performance in the context of the emerging economy of China. Little work has been done in this area, and the use of a more holistic approach, one that uses multiple predictor, outcome and control variables, has been able to advance previous research that focused on single elements and examined each variable separately. In doing so we have confirmed that intangible management influences employee satisfaction and enterprise success and have identified the most important of those variables. Nevertheless, the research was limited by the relatively small sample size and the focus on two industries, notwithstanding the use of multiple respondents to collect enterprise data. We would, therefore, suggest that future research should include a range of industries and cover a more representative sample of enterprises in China and other non-Western countries. Ultimately, if research is to identify the factors that affect improved performance or success, a longitudinal survey is required. These suggestions would require a major funding initiative that was well beyond the scope of our project. What is possible, however, is for researchers to adopt a more holistic approach to their research and modelling that would enable more accurate predictions about the key influences on enterprise success.

References

Benson, J. and Zhu, Y., 1999. Markets, enterprises and employees: the transformation of HRM in Chinese state-owned enterprises. *Human resource management journal*, 9 (4), 58–74.

Cabrera, E., 2008. Participation. *In*: S. Clegg and J. Bailey, eds. *International encyclopedia of organization studies*. Los Angeles and London: Sage, 1225–1229.

Canals, J., 2000. *Managing corporate growth*. New York: Oxford University Press.

Carmeli, A. and Tishler, A., 2004. The relationships between intangible organizational elements and organizational performance. *Strategic management journal*, 25 (13), 1257–1278.

Chatterjee, S. and Wernerfelt, B., 1991. The link between resources and type of diversification: theory and evidence. *Strategic management journal*, 12 (1), 33–48.

Child, J., 1994. *Management in China during the age of reform*. Cambridge: Cambridge University Press.

Cliff, N., 1987. *Analyzing multivariate data*. New York: Harcourt Brace Jovanovich.

Desarbo, W.S., *et al.*, 2005. Revisiting the Miles and Snow strategic framework: uncovering interrelationships between strategic types, capabilities, environmental uncertainty, and enterprise performance. *Strategic management journal*, 26 (1), 47–74.

Dess, G.G. and Beard, D.W., 1984. Industry effects and strategic management research. *Journal of management*, 16 (1), 7–27.

Dupuis, J., 2008. Organizational culture. *In*: S. Clegg and J. Bailey, eds. *International encyclopedia of organization studies*. Los Angeles and London: Sage, 1035–1039.

Guest, D.E., 2004. The psychology of the employment relationship: an analysis based on the psychological contract. *Applied psychology: an international review*, 53 (4), 541–555.

Hitt, M.A., *et al.*, 2001. Direct and moderating effects of human capital on strategy and performance in professional service enterprises: a resource-based perspective. *Academy of management journal*, 44 (1), 13–28.

Huang, S.J., 1996. *Guoyou Qiye Chanquan Zhidu Biange (The reform of state-owned enterprises' ownership and management system)*. Beijing: Economic Management Press.

Iaffaldano, M.T. and Muchinsky, P.M., 1985. Job satisfaction and job performance: a meta analysis. *Psychological bulletin*, 97 (2), 251–273.

Itami, H. and Roehl, W.T., 1987. *Mobilizing invisible assets*. Cambridge, MA: Howard University Press.

Judge, T.A., *et al.*, 2001. The job satisfaction–job performance relationship: a qualitative and quantitative review. *Psychological bulletin*, 127 (3), 376–407.

Kalleberg, A. and Rogues, J., 2000. Employment relations in Norway: some dimensions and correlates. *Journal of organizational behavior*, 21 (3), 315–335.

Koys, D.J., 2001. The effects of employee satisfaction, organizational citizenship behaviour, and turnover on organizational effectiveness: a unit-level, longitudinal study. *Personnel psychology*, 54 (1), 101–114.

Mahoney, J.T. and Pandian, J.R., 1992. The resource-based view within the conversation of strategic management. *Strategic management journal*, 13 (5), 363–380.

Marceau, J., 2008. Innovation. *In*: S. Clegg and J. Bailey, eds. *International encyclopedia of organization studies*. Los Angeles and London: Sage, 671–673.

Michalisin, M.D., Smith, R.D., and Kline, D.M., 1997. In search of strategic assets. *The international journal of organizational analysis*, 5 (4), 360–387.

Muchinsky, P.M., 1996. The correction for attenuation. *Educational and psychological measurement*, 56 (1), 63–75.

Pfeffer, J., 1998. *The human equation: building profits by putting people first*. Cambridge MA: Harvard Business School Press.

Ralston, D.A., *et al.*, 2006. Today's state-owned enterprises of China: are they dying dinosaurs or dynamic dynamos? *Strategic management journal*, 27 (9), 825–843.

Rao, C.R., 1993. *Linear statistical inference and its application*. New York: Wiley.

Rousseau, D., 1995. *Psychological contracts in organizations*. Thousand Oaks, CA: Sage.

Shore, L. and Tetrick, L., 1994. The psychological contract as an explanatory framework in the employment relationships. *In*: C. Cooper and D. Rousseau, eds. *Trends in organizational behavior*, vol. 1. Chichester: Wiley, 91–109.

Soper, D., 2008. *Post hoc statistical power calculator for multiple regression* [online]. Available from: http://www.danielsoper.com/statcalc/calc09.aspx [Accessed 29 July 2008].

Strati, A., 2008. Organizational structure. *In*: S. Clegg and J. Bailey, eds. *International encyclopedia of organization studies*. Los Angeles and London: Sage, 1185–1188.

Tan, J. and Litschert, R.J., 1994. Environment-strategy relationship and its performance implications: an empirical study of Chinese electronics industry. *Strategic management journal*, 15 (1), 1–20.

Tan, J. and Tan, D., 2005. Environment-strategy co-evolution and co-alignment; a staged model of Chinese SOEs under transition. *Strategic management journal*, 16 (2), 141–157.

Teece, D.J., 2000. Strategies for managing knowledge assets: the role of enterprise structure and industrial context. *Long range planning*, 33 (1), 35–54.

Tischler, A. and Lipovetsky, S., 2000. Modelling and forecasting with robust canonical analysis: method and operation. *Computers and operations research*, 27 (3), 217–232.

Tzafrir, S.S., 2005. The relationship between trust, HRM practices and firm performance. *International journal of human resource management*, 16 (9), 1600–1622.

Waldman, D.A., *et al.*, 2001. Does leadership matter? CEO leadership attributes and profitability under conditions of perceived environmental uncertainty. *Academy of management journal*, 44 (1), 134–143.

Warner, M., 1987. China's managerial training revolution. *In*: M. Warner, ed. *Management reforms in China*. London: Frances Printer, 73–85.

Warner, M., *et al.*, 2005. *Management in transitional economies: from the Berlin Wall to the Great Wall of China*. London and New York: Routledge-Curzon.

Wernerfelt, B., 1984. A resource-based view of the firm. *Strategic management journal*, 5 (1), 171–180.

Wright, M., *et al.*, 2005. Strategy research in emerging economies: challenging the conventional wisdom. *Journal of management studies*, 42 (1), 1–33.

Zeller, R.A. and Carmines, E.G., 1980. *Measurement in the social sciences*. Cambridge: Cambridge University Press.

Zhang, W.Y., 2000. *Qiye Lilun Yu Zongguo Qiye Gaige (Theory of enterprise and Chinese enterprises' reform)*. Beijing: Peking University Press.

Zhu, Y. and Warner, M., 2000a. Changing approaches to employment relations in the People's Republic of China. *In*: G.J. Bamber *et al.*, eds. *Employment relations in the Asia-Pacific: changing approaches*. Sydney: Thomson Learning, 117–128.

Zhu, Y. and Warner, W., 2000b. An emerging model of employment relations in China: a divergent path from the Japanese. *International business review*, 9 (3), 345–361.

Zhu, Y. and Warner, W., 2004. Changing patterns of human resource management in contemporary China: WTO accession and enterprise responses. *Industrial relations journal*, 35 (4), 311–328.

Intensity of competition in China: profitability dynamics of Chinese listed companies

Neng Jiang and Paul A. Kattuman

Judge Business School, University of Cambridge, Cambridge, UK

How intense is market competition in the Chinese economy? We extend to China, the literature that measures the intensity of market competition in terms of the persistence of firm profitability from year to year. The fundamental notion is that intense competition will quickly evaporate any short run quasi-rents enjoyed by any company, and force each to revert to its own 'normal' level of profitability, as determined by its command over various strategic resources. We examine the extent to which deviations from their expected values of profitability tend to be corrected among quoted companies in China. Our estimates, based on Chinese listed companies over the 11-year period to 2005, find that the rate of mean reversion in profitability is 55%. This suggests an intensely competitive market. We also find that the state owned enterprises (SOEs) have a higher propensity to revert to their expected profitability, at the average rate of 76%, suggesting that they are subject to more intense competitive pressure.

Introduction

In the Economics textbook formulation of competitive markets, rates of return cannot remain persistently dispersed. Competitive pressures catalyse internal and external business restructuring. The prospects of failure or takeover encourage firms with below-normal returns to restructure internally and improve performance through more efficient production and organization. External restructuring occurs through the process of market selection: transferable resources gravitate to firms that can offer better returns. Laggards presenting poorer performance are more likely to be eliminated and replaced by entrants who have prospects of better performance; at the same time better managed incumbents are more likely to gain market share and attract imitators.

The view from strategic management is more sceptical of the efficiency of markets. The mission of a firm is to pursue competitive advantage. The 'resource based view' traces sustained competitive advantage of firms to (tangible and intangible) capabilities, and to resources that are 'rare, valuable, difficult to imitate, non-substitutable' (Barney 1991), and non-transferable in that they cannot be easily purchased in resource markets (Dierckx and Cool 1989). Firms pursue such resources and capabilities, and are constantly engaged in renewing and reconfiguring them as competition, and the business environment, diminish their value (Rumelt 1984).

In its essentials, the resource-based view is not inconsistent with the Schumpeterian view of dynamic competition (Schumpeter 1943). Innovations of different types can be characterized as augmenting resources that confer competitive advantage and are sources of dominance and quasi-rents. In practice, they are imitable to varying extents, and are eroded by competition in the long run. Profitability differences between companies will have some element of persistence and, conversely, some element of transience. With competition, the tendency of profitability to revert to normal should be stronger, and to that extent changes in profitability and in earnings will have some element of predictability.

Our primary motivation is to explore the competitive process in the context of an important, large, emerging market with a limited market history – China. State-owned enterprises (SOEs) still dominate the Chinese economy in size share, though not in numbers but the private sector has expanded its role considerably and rapidly, bringing competition. Despite its significance, there has been, notably, no empirical study of the intensity of competition in China, though there is a significant empirical literature on profitability dynamics in other developing countries, and a large literature covering developed countries. We seek to redress this gap, with a research question focused on the degree of mean reversion in profitability among Chinese listed companies. It is useful to understand the extent to which competition is a force in this important socialist market economy. Does the relative immaturity of market, the existence of state-owned monopolies and administrative intervention weaken the effectiveness of competitive forces? Did WTO membership make a difference to the intensity of competition?

The predictable component in earnings is also an interesting question. Since the pioneering work of Ball and Brown (1968), the information content and timeliness of accounting income numbers have been explored in the context of capital markets. The informativeness of earnings, such as their (lagged) effects on equity price (Ou and Penman 1989), suggest that its predictability would be of value to financial markets. At a scholarly level, the efficient market hypothesis (EMH) (Fama 1970, 1991) and equity valuation models (Campbell and Shiller 1988, Ohlson 1989, 1995, Feltham and Ohlson 1999) relate to earnings expectations. These provide further motivation to determine the predictable component in earnings (Kothari 2001).

This study is organized as follows: the next section reviews previous work relating to profitability and earnings; the third section outlines the way we employ Fama and French's partial adjustment model (2000); the fourth section presents estimates of the model with the Chinese sample, and discusses results in the light of findings from mature economies; and the final section concludes.

Literature

In this section we review the theoretical, methodological and empirical literature on persistence of profitability, to provide the context of our research question, and rationalize our chosen methodology.

There is a lineage of studies in Finance on the persistence and predictability of corporate profitability and earnings, following both time series and cross section methodologies. On the time series front, early research focused on the behaviour of corporate earnings, around the hypothesis that earnings changes form a random walk (Little 1962, Little and Rayner 1966, Ball and Watts 1972). Later branches in this literature have explored different forms of predictability, such as moving average models with an underlying pure mean reverting process (Beaver 1970), sub-martingale and similar processes (Lookabill 1976), and trend models with non-linear mean reversion conditioned on book rates of return (Brooks and Buckmaster 1976, Freeman *et al.* 1982). Furthermore, motivated by the appetite of capital markets for information, earnings research in accounting and finance literatures have explored the predictability of equity prices or returns (Collins and Kothari 1989, Collins *et al.* 1997, Kothari 2001).

In economics, initiated by Mueller (1986), Jacobsen (1988) and Geroski (1990), there is an empirical literature focussed on characterizing the degree of persistence of profits. The motivating proposition is that: *ceteris paribus*, the more intense the competition in a market, the lower the persistence of corporate profitability over time. The starting point was Mueller's (1986) time series model of profitability with three unobserved components: competitive return on capital in the market, permanent 'rent' specific to the firm, and short run 'quasi rent' of the firm which may vary over time but tends to zero in long run. Under some assumptions, the dynamics of the short run quasi-rent could be translated to an autoregressive model of profitability. Geroski (1990) provided structural underpinnings to this model, making explicit the competitive forces that drive the dynamics of profitability: excess profitability of any firm depends on 'entry' – which includes all activities of market participants targeting the firm's niche, conditioned on the observed and anticipated profitability of the firm. Potential 'entrants' targeting the firm can be expected to make their decisions based, not only on observed past excess profits but also on profits they 'rationally' expect after entry. This will depend partly on the equilibrium response of the targeted firm, and partly on the risks carried by the business environment. This structural view is conceptually useful but not so much from an estimating point of view. Entry, broadly defined, is profoundly unobservable, incorporating strategic entry prevention and contestability.

However, the reduced form of the model encapsulates the feedback between entry and excess profitability into a general autoregression for excess profitability. And on this basis it is possible to estimate a persistence (autoregressive) coefficient for each individual firm. Essentially, this approach examines whether the evolution of profitability is a unit root process. Empirical time series analysis of profitability dynamics in emerging markets – Brazil, India, Korea, and Malaysia among others (Glen *et al.* 2001) and Turkey (Yurtoglu 2004) – find that, contrary to general opinion, profitability is less persistent in emerging markets than in developed markets (Geroski and Jacquemin 1988, Schwalbach *et al.* 1989, Cubbin and Geroski 1990, Mueller 1990).

There are a number of acknowledged limitations to the time series approach. First, many studies have found a significant proportion of companies marked by non-stationarity in profitability (see in particular, Goddard and Wilson 1999, on the finding of transient non-stationarity) violating one of the requirements for estimating long run profitability. Second, long histories are necessary for power in inference, and this requirement tends to produce survivor bias. Usually less than 30 observations can be retrieved at the annual frequency for all but a few companies. Third, the longer the time series, the greater the probability that the data generating process (the competitive business environment) has changed and less likely is persistence to be constant. Gschwandtner (2004) reports evidence of different profit dynamics in different sub-periods in the US in the second half of the last century. High persistence observed in profitability could be an artifact of misspecification of the data generating process (Cuaresma and Gschwandtner 2006). Time series tests may not be reliable unless profitability is in steady state dynamics, or observed values do not deviate far from the limiting distribution so that sample moments are still representative of the population (Bernard and Durlauf 1996). Recent time series models of profitability have employed structural time series methods (Cable *et al.* 2001), and time-varying persistence models (Cuaresma and Gschwandtner 2008).

The conceptual basis of an alternative approach that uses cross section/panel methods and builds on Fama and MacBeth (1973), is the simple Galtonian regression. This route circumvents some of the difficulties with the time series approach. The larger sample size enhances the power of inference, and reduces potential survivor bias.

Mean reversion is when a firm's abnormal profit rate reverts to the normal, but it is restrictive to assume that the normal is captured by the cross-sectional mean of the profitability distribution. Firms command strategic resources (for example, reputation, closer relationships to the government, apart from knowledge assets), which generate their permanent firm specific rents (Roberts and Dowling 2002, Hoopes et al. 2003). The question we ask is whether, if in one year firms earn above (below) their own normal rate of profit, then in the following year does their rate of profit fall back (rises towards) their own normal rate of profit. In this view, only the short run 'quasi rent' of the firm is affected by competition from other firms, and is consistent with Mueller's unobserved components model of profitability.

We follow Fama and French (2000) in allowing each firm to revert to its own conditional mean profitability. In the next section we set out the profitability model that is estimated for each cross section, and from which each firm's mean, or normal, profitability is predicted. This seeks to capture the sum of the 'rent' specific to the firm, on top of the competitive return on capital in the market. This cross section approach is robust to firms deviating from their steady states. A rich set of explanatory variables can be included as controls (Freeman et al. 1982, Collins and Kothari 1989, Easton and Zmijewski 1989, Ou and Penman 1989, Elgers and Lo 1994, Fairfield et al. 1996, Basu 1997).

The panel structure of the data was exploited by Fama and MacBeth (1973) through a series of cross-sectional regressions, one for each year, yielding a time series of coefficient estimates which is then averaged to yield the panel coefficient. The standard error is obtained from the time series of estimates assuming that they are independent of each other. This takes account of the year-to-year variation in regression coefficients due to cross-sectional residual dependence, that is the correlation across companies in current changes of profitability or earnings, other than that captured by explanatory variables, due to random shocks at the macroeconomic or industry level.

Until recently, the econometric theory underpinning the Fama and MacBeth methodology (1973) was not known. Ibragimov and Müller (2007) have shown that the Fama-MacBeth method of inference – estimating the regression model separately for each year, and testing hypotheses about the coefficient of interest by the t-statistic relating to the set of yearly coefficient estimates – is efficient. The Fama and French (2000) method provides efficient estimate of parameters in situations where data is correlated and heterogeneous in unknown and possibly pronounced ways. Building on the results of Bakirov and Székely (2006, cited in Ibragimov and Müller 2007) on the small sample properties of the t-test they showed that the Fama and French (2000) method results in valid inference even for a short panel that is heterogeneous over time.

Fama and French (2000) find the average rate of mean reversion at around 38% per annum in the profitability of US firms. The convergence process appears to be non-linear as well as asymmetric. The convergence rate is higher when profitability is below the mean, and also when it is in the outer zone of either side. They also find that much of the predictability in earnings could be attributed to mean reversion in profitability, though there is still significant autocorrelation in earnings left unexplained. Allen and Salim (2005) replicated Fama and French's work on a sample of 987 UK listed companies from year 1982–2000. Ahmed (2005) extends the analysis to all registered UK companies. They obtain similar results with the average rate of mean reversion around 25% per annum, though without significant non-linearity in either mean reversion of profitability or autocorrelation of changes in earnings.

To recapitulate, our research question is centred on mean reversion in profitability among Chinese companies. The authors wish to understand the extent to which competition plays a role in this socialist market economy. Are state-owned enterprises subject to competitive forces? Did WTO membership increase the intensity of competition?

Methodology

Mean reversion in profitability

In order to estimate the degree of mean reversion among Chinese listed companies, we adopt the Fama and French approach. In the first step, we determine expected profitability for each company. This acknowledges that companies are likely to differ in their 'normal' profitability. While competitive forces will have some influence in directing changes in profitability, so will systemic differences in risk, (unobservable) quasi rents, and accounting procedures. Fama and French (2000) used three variables to estimate the level of profitability for US companies:

- The ratio of dividends to book value of common equity: If companies tend to pay out dividends proportionally to earnings, dividends should be positively correlated with profitability and earnings (Miller and Modigliani 1961).
- The market-to-book ratio (a variant of *Tobin's q*): To capture the variation in expected profitability uncaught by the dividends signal. According to the EMH, a company's market value is the present value of its future net cash flows, and expected earnings derived from the current information set are useful in predicting equity prices (Kothari 2001). Market price should thus reflect expected earnings (Ou and Penman 1989, Elgers and Lo 1994). This has been empirically verified in capital markets research, such as the three-factor model (Fama and French 1996) and earnings response coefficients (Collins and Kothari 1989). In the case of Chinese stock market, the diminution of state-ownership (restructuring through discounted sales, normally in the form of stock dividends) is ongoing, and most companies who are engaged in this reform, still have some temporarily non-tradable shares outstanding, not amenable to valuation at the contemporary market price of tradable shares. Given the nascent corporate governance system and lack of transparency in the Chinese stock market, *Tobin's q* may not be as effective in reflecting systematic differences in profitability as in mature market economies.
- Dividend dummy – 0 for dividend payers and 1 for non-payers: is to capture the extreme non-linearity in the relation between dividends signal and expected profitability.

On account of relative youth of the Chinese stock market, particularly in accounting and regulatory systems (Su and Fleisher 1998, Chen *et al.* 2001, Sami and Zhou 2004, Gao and Kling 2006), and the reform process underway in shareholding structures, ownership and corporate governance (Zhou 2001, Levi and Diao 2005), and the fact that our sample covers all listed companies,[1] these three factors may be inadequate to explain the cross-sectional variation in expected profitability. We augment the model and bring in variables that are relevant in determining the rent specific to each firm, taking note of the local context:[2]

- Size: denoted by the log of net sales: In view of lack of proper impairment accounting until 2001 in China (China Accounting Standards Committee 2001), sales are considered more accurate than total assets as a proxy of size effect.
- Capital intensity: represented by log of the ratio of depreciation to total assets: Higher capital intensity may push up productivity and thus lead to a higher profit margin (Burmeister 1980), especially in a developing country, though a large portion of growth in productivity may be attributed to technology and human capital.
- Gearing: calculated as log of debt to equity ratio (total liability/shareholders' equity). This reflects the risk profile of capital structure, and also differences in corporate governance.
- Ownership structure dummy: 1, when the state owns more than 50% of the company's shares and zero otherwise. This differentiates SOEs from other privately or publicly owned companies. Under socialism, ownership position would translate to profitability intrinsically. Policies that favour SOEs in business development, government procurement, finance and direct taxation, would proffer competitive advantage and thus higher profitability in expectation (Wei *et al.* 2003, Lin and Rowe 2006). On the other hand, due to the lack of strict accountability and surveillance, and soft budget constraints, managements of SOEs may have less incentive to adapt to competition and changes in business environment, effectively jeopardizing SOEs' advantageous positions (Xu and Wang 1999, Schipani and Liu 2002).
- Share marketability dummy: 1, when more than 50% of the company's outstanding shares are tradable, zero otherwise. This is intended to capture the discipline that the capital market exerts on company performance (Liu 2006). The possibility of being taken over should enhance managerial motivation to maximise the company's market value, in particular, through earnings growth. However, share marketability also induces various agency problems arising from wide dispersion of ownership[3] (Xu and Wang 1999, Chen *et al.* 2006).
- Industry dummies: this marks out companies in specific industries – mining, utility, transportation or commerce sectors.[4] Industry effects can be large and significant (Schmalensee 1989, Conyon and Machin 1991, Mueller and Raunig 1999). From the nature of these industries, we would expect mining, utilities and transportation to enjoy higher profitability in general, and commerce to return lower profitability.

Thus, our regression model for predicting normal profitability for company i in year t is:

$$E_{it}/A_{it} = \alpha_{0,t} + \beta_{1,t}D_{it}/BE_i + \beta_{2,t}\ln(MV_{it}/A_{it}) + \beta_{3,t}DD_{it} + \beta_{4,t}\ln(SALE_{it})$$

$$+ \beta_{5,t}\ln(CAPIN_{it}) + \beta_{6,t}\ln(GEAR_{it}) + \beta_{7,t}D\_SOE_{it} + \beta_{8,t}D\_TV_{it}$$

$$+ \sum \beta_{9-12,t}\text{Industry effects} + \varepsilon_{it} \tag{1}$$

where E_{it} is earnings before interest and extraordinary items but after taxes; A_{it} is the company's total assets at year end; D_{it} is the dividends paid out during the year; BE_{it} is the book value of common shareholders' equity at year end; MV_{it} is the company's market value at year start; DD_{it} is a dummy that is 0 for dividend payers and 1 for non-payers; $SALE_{it}$ is net sales; $CAPIN_{it}$ is capital intensity (=depreciation/total assets); $GEAR_{it}$ is leverage (=debt/equity); D_SOE_{it} is a dummy that is 1 when the state owns more than

50% of the company's shares and 0 otherwise; D_TV_{it} is a dummy that is 1 when more than 50% of the company's outstanding shares are tradable and 0 otherwise; and industry dummies mark out industry sectors; ε_{it} is an error term (residual) assumed to be IID; $\alpha_{0,t}$ and $\beta_{1,t}$ to $\beta_{12,t}$ are parameters to be estimated.

The second step involves using predicted and observed profitability to explain profitability change. As mentioned earlier, this is fundamentally rooted in the Galtonian regression. The simple partial adjustment model has been widely applied to research on economic growth (Barro 1991), income growth (Barro et al. 1991, Barro and Sala-i-Martin 1992) and productivity (Baumol 1986, Oulton 1998), as also to the study of corporate earnings and profitability (Whittington 1980, Freeman et al. 1982, Elgers and Lo 1994). Fama and French (2000) explained change in profitability (from year t to $t + 1$) in terms of the deviation of profitability from its expected value (in year t), and a first-order autoregressive component:

$$E_{it+1}/A_{it+1} - E_{it}/A_{it} = \alpha_{1,t} + \gamma_{1,t}[E_{it}/A_{it} - E(E_{it}/A_{it})] + \gamma_{2,t}[E_{it}/A_{it} - E_{it-1}/A_{it-1}] + \varepsilon_{it+1}$$

$$CP_{it+1} = \alpha_{1,t} + \gamma_{1,t}DFE_{it} + \gamma_{2,t}CP_{it} + \varepsilon_{it+1} \tag{2}$$

where $E(E_{it}/A_{it})$ is the expected profitability from Equation (1); $CP_{it} = E_{it}/A_{it} - E_{it-1}/A_{it-1}$ is change in profitability from year $t - 1$ to t; $DFE_{it} = E_{it}/A_{it} - E(E_{it}/A_{it})$ is the deviation of profitability from its expected value; $\alpha_{1,t}$, $\gamma_{1,t}$ and $\gamma_{2,t}$ are parameters to be estimated; with $\gamma_{1,t}$ representing the speed of mean reversion, and ε_{it+1}, an IID error term. Under the extreme assumption that all companies converge to an economy-wide profit rate, that is the cross-sectional mean profitability, Equation (2) could be simplified to:

$$CP_{it+1} = \alpha_{1,t} + \gamma_{1,t}E_{it}/A_{it} + \gamma_{2,t}CP_{it} + \varepsilon_{it+1}$$

In addition, Fama and French (2000) do not restrict E/A and E(E/A) to have the same coefficient in Equation (2); so the unrestricted model is:

$$CP_{it+1} = \alpha_{1,t} + \lambda_{1a,t}E_{it}/A_{it} - \lambda_{1b,t}E(E_{it}/A_{it}) + \gamma_{2,t}CP_{it} + \varepsilon_{it+1} \tag{3}$$

In this specification, mean reversion is constrained to be linear. Brooks and Buckmaster (1976) and Elgers and Lo (1994) suggest that reversals in earnings were stronger for extreme changes in either direction, and strongest for extreme negative changes. Since the predictability in earnings could be traced to mean reversion in profitability, the third step expands the simple partial adjustment model to accommodate potential non-linear and asymmetric behaviour as follows:

$$CP_{it+1} = \alpha_{2,t} + \delta_{1,t}DFE_{it} + \delta_{2,t}NDFE_{it} + \delta_{3,t}SNDFE_{it} + \delta_{4,t}SPDFE_{it} + \delta_{5,t}CP_{it}$$

$$+ \delta_{6,t}NCP_{it} + \delta_{7,t}SNCP_{it} + \delta_{8,t}SPCP_{it} + \varepsilon_{it+1} \tag{4}$$

where $NDFE_{it}$ equals to DFE_{it} when DFE_{it} is negative, and 0 otherwise; $SNDFE_{it}$ equals to the square of DFE_{it} when DFE_{it} is negative, and 0 otherwise; $SPDFE_{it}$ equals to the square of DFE_{it} when DFE_{it} is positive, and 0 otherwise; NCP_{it} equals to CP_{it} when CP_{it} is negative, and 0 otherwise; $SNCP_{it}$ equals to the square of CP_{it} when CP_{it} is negative, and 0 otherwise; $SPCP_{it}$ equals to the square of CP_{it} when CP_{it} is positive, and 0 otherwise. The coefficients $\delta_{2,t,}$, $\delta_{3,t,}$ and $\delta_{4,t}$ capture the non-linearity and asymmetry in mean reversion, whilst $\delta_{6,t}$, $\delta_{7,t}$ and $\delta_{8,t}$ capture the non-linearity and asymmetry in profitability change. It is likely that multi-collinearity may make the above full specification difficult to estimate. If so, it will be necessary to reduce the model using appropriate diagnostics.

We use the Fama-MacBeth protocol to draw a series of cross-sectional pictures of mean reversion in profitability for Chinese listed companies, building on the assumption that competition drives a partial adjustment, error correction mechanism.

Mean reversion and predictability in earnings

To examine whether change in earnings is predictable, and whether its source of predictability rests with mean reversion in profitability (Freeman *et al.* 1982, Lev 1983), we again follow Fama and French and replace change in profitability with scaled change in earnings, $CE_{it} = (E_{it} - E_{it-1})/A_{it-1}$:

$$CE_{it+1} = \alpha_{3,t} + \delta_{1,t}DFE_{it} + \delta_{2,t}NDFE_{it} + \delta_{3,t}SNDFE_{it} + \delta_{4,t}SPDFE_{it} + \lambda_{1,t}CE_{it}$$

$$+ \lambda_{2,t}NCE_{it} + \lambda_{3,t}SNCE_{it} + \lambda_{4,t}SPCE_{it} + \varepsilon_{it+1} \tag{5}$$

We use the same specification as in Equation (4), where: NCE_{it} equals to CE_{it} when CE_{it} is negative, and 0 otherwise; $SNCE_{it}$ equals to the square of CE_{it} when CE_{it} is negative, and 0 otherwise; $SPCE_{it}$ equals to the square of CE_{it} when CE_{it} is positive, and 0 otherwise.

Data

Our sample covers almost the entire population of Chinese companies (including 'special treatment' and 'particular transfer' companies but excluding those from financial sector[5]) listed in Shanghai and Shenzhen Stock Exchanges (A-shares) for the years from 1995–2005. The sample period is determined by the availability of data.[6] The data were compiled from the CSMAR® (China Stock Market and Accounting Research)[7] – a financial and market database covering Chinese listed companies, and supplemented and verified by Thomson ONE Banker® (including Worldscope®, Thomson Financials® and Datastream®) where accounting or market data for some firms were missing or their local definitions did not match (such as depreciation) generally accepted international principles. Unlike some other studies, we do not censor our sample on the basis of firm size (total assets or book value of shareholders' equity), but we examine the influence of outliers. This dataset has 10,584 company years in total, with 962 companies observed per annum on average. The panel is unbalanced due to the increasing trend in IPOs in a growing market: the numbers of companies increased from 307 in 1995 to 1343 in 2005.

The size and inclusiveness of our dataset are expected to enable robust inferences about profitability performance of Chinese listed companies.[8] And yet the short history of Chinese stock market (established first in Shanghai on 19 December 1990), makes the data set smaller and the sample period necessarily shorter than desirable. The relatively small coverage of the economy by listed companies during our sample period does raise a question about its representativeness with regard to the economy as a whole. In coming years, further analysis with richer datasets as they become available will be fruitful.

Some prior studies have suggested that managers in China are prone to manipulating earnings (Aharony *et al.* 2000, Liu and Lu 2003, Zou and Chen 2002). Indeed, in the early years after the inception of the Chinese stock market the accounting and regulatory system was somewhat specific to the country and arguably encouraged earnings management, for example, prior to initial public offering (IPO), to reduce the risk of delisting, or being

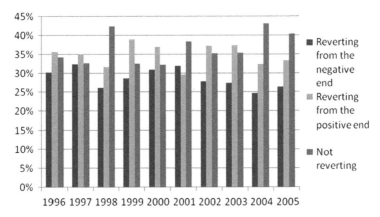

Figure 1. Proportions of firms reverting to expected profitability from the positive and negative ends.

placed under special treatment, and so on. However, at the end of 2001, the Ministry of Finance substantially tightened enterprise accounting principles, and the stock market authority in China (the CSRC) has been firm in enforcing accounting rules. Kam *et al.* (2005) suggest that Chinese accounting data are more reliable than generally thought.

Year-to-year reversion can be claimed when the deviation from expected profitability is less in one year relative to the previous year, that is positive deviation turns less positive or indeed negative; and negative deviation turns less negative, or even positive. Figure 1 below provides a summary characterization in terms of the percentages of companies reverting to expected profitability. On the whole, reversion from the positive end appears more marked in the later years relative to reversion from the negative end. This may relate to the accounting policy changes introduced in 2001, which will be detailed in a later section. By a large margin, more companies converge (from either end) than diverge. In particular, SOEs account for about one-third of the sample, and there appears to be very little to differentiate them from other firms.

We note the suggestion in Figure 1 that the proportion of firms not reverting to mean in 2004 and 2005 are higher than prior years. This might be seen to be somewhat contrary to the expectation that competition should have intensified after China's entry into the WTO in 2001. It is important to bear in mind that WTO accession gave large internationalized Chinese companies the opportunity to take advantage of the most favoured nation clause in their exports and increase their returns. At the same time, for some domestic companies, the early years were marked by deeper threats to their domestic niches from foreign entrants, worsening returns. The decrease of mean-reversion in the early post-WTO years is not incompatible with intensified competition.

Empirical results and discussion

Mean reversion in profitability

Table 1 presents the averaged coefficients from year-by-year regressions for expected profitability and mean reversion in profitability. While the Fama-Macbeth t-statistic approach avoids estimation bias due to the cross-sectional correlation of regression residuals, it is necessary to rule out autocorrelation in the series of coefficients from the year-by-year regressions. There is no significant autocorrelation in our data at either first- or higher-orders. The results of Ibragimov and Müller (2007) reassure us that the small number of yearly

Table 1. Expected profitability and mean reversion in profitability: 1995–2005.

Panel A: Expected profitability E_t/A_t

	α	D/BE	ln(MV/A)	DD	ln(SALE)	ln(CAPIN)	ln(GEAR)	D_SOE	D_TV	D_Ind1	D_Ind2	D_Ind3	D_Ind4	R^2	N
Mean	−0.274	0.218	0.023	−0.013	0.014	−0.007	−0.015	−0.003	−0.005	0.013	0.017	0.017	−0.011	0.34	10303
t(Mn)	−14.18	8.13	4.35	−3.37	13.85	−7.83	−7.88	−2.19	−2.97	3.29	9.35	6.47	−6.86		

Panel B: Means and standard deviations of variables

	E/A	D/BE	ln(MV/A)	DD	ln(SALE)	ln(CAPIN)	ln(GEAR)	D_SOE	D_TV	D_Ind1	D_Ind2	D_Ind3	D_Ind4
Mean	0.04	0.03	0.45	0.45	20.12	−3.09	−0.15	0.32	0.15	0.01	0.04	0.04	0.08
Std.	0.07	0.04	0.71	0.50	1.31	1.03	0.94	0.47	0.36	0.12	0.20	0.19	0.28

Panel C: Mean reversion in profitability $CP_{t+1} = E_{t+1}/A_{t+1} - E_t/A_t$

	α	E_t/A_t	$E(E_t/A_t)$	DFE_t	$NDFE_t$	$SNDFE_t$	CP_t	NCP_t	$SNCP_t$	R^2	N
Mean	−0.009			−0.557	0.571	5.296	−0.008	0.155	−5.525	0.14	7663
t(Mn)	−1.56			−3.42	0.90	1.15	−0.077	0.19	−0.95		
Mean	−0.032	−0.322	0.771		0.412	5.381	0.031	−0.138	−5.783	0.15	7663
t(Mn)	−1.81	−3.00	2.58		0.73	1.17	0.28	−0.17	−0.99		

Panel D: Means and standard deviations of regression variables

	CP_{t+1}	E_t/A_t	$E(E_t/A_t)$	DFE_t	$NDFE_t$	$SNDFE_t$	CP_t	NCP_t	$SNCP_t$
Mean	−0.020	0.025	0.043	0.000	−0.016	0.002	−0.019	−0.041	0.115
Std.	0.373	0.330	0.040	0.057	0.046	0.023	0.379	0.336	3.606

Notes: Panel C reports the means (across years) of the intercept (α) and slope coefficients relating to Equation (4). T-statistics for these coefficient means t(Mn), are also reported. Panel D reports averages (across years) of the means and standard deviations (SD) of these regression variables.

Panel A variables are as follows: E_{it} is earnings before interest and extraordinary items but after taxes; A_{it} is the company's total assets at year end; D_{it} is the dividends paid out during the year; BE_{it} is the book value of common shareholders' equity at year end; MV_{it} is the company's market value at year start; DD_{it} is a dummy that is 0 for dividend payers and 1 for non-payers; $SALE_{it}$ is net sales; $CAPIN_{it}$ is capital intensity (= depreciation/total assets); $GEAR_{it}$ is leverage (= debt/equity); D_SOE$_{it}$ is a dummy that is 1 when the state owns more than 50% of the company's shares and 0 otherwise; D_TV$_{it}$ is a dummy that is 1 when more than 50% of the company's outstanding shares are tradable and 0 otherwise; and industry dummies mark out when the company is in mining, utility, transportation or commerce sector; ε_{it} is an error term (residual) assumed to be IID; We take the logarithm of those explanatory variables showing considerable heterogeneity.

Panel C variables are as follows: $CP_{it} = E_{it}/A_{it} - E_{it-1}/A_{it-1}$ is change in profitability from year $t - 1$ to t; $E(E_{it}/A_{it})$ is the expected value of profitability; $DFE_{it} = E_{it}/A_{it} - E(E_{it}/A_{it})$ is the deviation of profitability from its expected value; $NDFE_{it}$ equals to DFE_{it} when DFE_{it} is negative, and 0 otherwise; $SNDFE_{it}$ equals to the square of DFE_{it} when DFE_{it} is negative, and 0 otherwise; NCP_{it} equals to CP_{it} when CP_{it} is negative, and 0 otherwise; $SNCP_{it}$ equals to the square of CP_{it} when CP_{it} is negative, and 0 otherwise.

estimates do not negate precise estimation. The log transformations (on *MV/A, SALE, CAPIN, GEAR*) eliminate only 45 observations in total, less than 0.5% of the entire sample.

As a prelude to the analysis of how changes in profitability are driven by deviations from expected profitability, we explore the extent of reversion to the simple cross-sectional mean in Equation (6). With ND_{it} and SND_{it} relating to negative deviations, and SPD_{it} relating to positive deviations from the cross-sectional mean profitability, we find significant reversion to the cross-sectional mean only from extreme deviations to either side (t-statistics in the parentheses). Note that the only significant coefficients are on squared deviations from the cross-sectional mean, and that reversion from the extreme positive end is at a much higher rate than reversion from the extreme negative end.

$$CP_{it+1} = -0.020 + 0.324\,E_{it}/A_{it} + 0.086\,ND_{it} + 1.380\,SND_{it} - 3.140\,SPD_{it}$$

$$\phantom{CP_{it+1} = } (-1.38) \quad (1.02) \qquad\quad (0.14) \qquad\quad (1.78) \qquad\quad (-2.18)$$

$$-0.212\,CP_{it} + 0.131\,NCP_{it} - 0.513\,SNCP_{it} + 1.290\,SPCP_{it}; \quad R^2 = 0.24, F(8, 8) = 17.69$$

$$(-2.01) \qquad\quad (0.59) \qquad\quad (-0.46) \qquad\quad (1.64)$$

$$(6)$$

Panel A of Table 1 shows the average coefficients from the models for annual expected profitability (*E/A*), where all t-statistics reported are well above 2.00 in absolute value. The positive average coefficients (more than 5 standard errors from zero) on both *D/BE* and *ln(MV/A)* underscore the significance of *Tobin's q* in explaining the variation in profitability, in addition to the portion explained by dividend information. *Ceteris paribus*, higher market-to-book ratio and scaled dividends would signal higher expected profitability. The highly significant negative coefficient on *DD* confirms a non-linear relationship between dividend policy and profitability; so no dividends signal the prospect of lower profitability.

Variables that contextualise the model for China and capture more of the firm specific rents, reduce the potential for omitted variable biases. They have significant ability to explain variation in profitability. As a proxy for size effect, the positive coefficient on *ln(SALE)* has a convincingly large t-statistic of 13.50, which may indicate above normal profitability arising from quasi-rents rooted either in scale (and scope), and/or dominance. The significant negative coefficients on both *ln(CAPIN)* and *ln(GEAR)* (with -5.55 and -7.73 standard errors respectively) suggest higher capital intensity and leverage detract from profitability. The minute, but significant, negative effect of capital intensity on profitability may reflect the scarcity and, thus, the high cost of capital relative to other resources. Higher leverage ratio indicates higher risk and arguably reduces managerial flexibility in seizing emerging opportunities or manoeuvring around unpredictable adversity. The small negative coefficient on *D_SOE* (-0.003), also found by Xu and Wang (1999), reflects the adverse effect of state ownership on profitability. Similarly, the negative coefficient on *D_TV* (-0.005) implies that share marketability bringing with it enhanced risk of being acquired/merged, in fact reduces profitability, perhaps by quenching risky but profitable initiatives: the low penetration of performance-related incentives (such as lack of share-option schemes) arguably leaves managers somewhat indifferent to share prices, while wide dispersion of ownership hinders monitoring (Xu and Wang 1999); non-tradable portion of shares is largely owned by the state which retains a long reach. Thus, combining the effects from *D_SOE* and *D_TV*, we find that privately-owned companies with smaller proportion of marketable shares are the most profitable, followed by stated-owned companies with smaller proportion of marketable shares, then by privately-owned companies with larger proportion of marketable shares and, finally, state-owned companies with a larger proportion of marketable shares.

There is considerable sectoral heterogeneity in profitability – as expected, mining, utilities and transportation (not subject to as much competition) are more profitable than the other industries; commerce is less profitable. The structural conditions in these four industries suggest that entry barriers – institutional control, capital requirement – play a significant role in determining profitability. The correlations among the explanatory variables[9] are not high. The average R^2 is a respectable 0.328.

Panel C of Table 1 presents the estimates of mean reversion from the partial adjustment model. Diagnostic tests show significant correlations between the variables. This leads to loss of significance of individual coefficients when all variables are introduced together. We eliminate irrelevant variables, using diagnostic tests to ensure that model reductions are valid, in order to arrive at the specification in panel C.

The mean reversion to company-specific level of profitability proves to be notable. When we do not constrain the coefficients on expected and observed profitability to be the same, the coefficients are opposite in sign as expected. They are, however, discrepant in absolute values. The coefficient on observed profitability, E/A, is -0.322. The coefficient on $E(E/A)$ is 0.771, over twice the coefficient on E/A. Fama and French (2000) conjectured that if there were little error in the prediction of $E(E/A)$, then its coefficient should be equal to that on E/A. Our model for profitability explains at least as much of the variation in profitability for China as the Fama and French (2000) model does for the US. It would appear that expected profitability is less dispersed across companies, and as estimates of expected profitability lie closer to their mean, the smaller variance of $E(E/A)$ raises its coefficient: in Panel D of Table 1, the standard deviation of $E(E/A)$ is only 0.04 compared to 0.373 of CP_{t+1}. The average of the coefficients on E/A, and on $E(E/A)$ is 0.55, and this is the same as the coefficient on DFE_t in the first equation in Panel C, when coefficients on expected and observed profitability are constrained to be the same. There is no evidence of any significant non-linearity or asymmetry in mean reversion.

We find that lagged CP (the first-order autoregressive term), has no linear, non-linear, or asymmetric explanatory power for the cross-sectional variation in profitability, over and above the partial adjustment process. Therefore, mean reversion seems to be the sole source of predictable variation in profitability among Chinese listed companies.

State owned enterprises

The most distinctive sub-population among the Chinese listed companies are of course, the SOEs. Until early 1990s, SOEs were responsible for a significant proportion of urban jobs and more than half the industrial output, tax revenues and exports. Rising productivity among SOEs in the 1980s and 1990s made gradual reform possible. Notwithstanding this, there is the view that governance problems are rife among SOEs. SOEs have been highly profitable in recent years. According to the 'Financial Statistics for Central Government controlled SOEs for fiscal year 2005' released by the State-owned Assets Supervision and Administration Commission (SASAC), the profits of 169 SOEs under Central Government jurisdiction rose by 27.9% between 2004–2005. A small number of large SOEs – China National Petroleum Corporation (CNPC), China Petrochemical Corporation (Sinopec), and China National Offshore Oil Corporation (CNOOC) and Shenhua Group Corporation Limited turned in outstanding performances. There are 19 Chinese SOEs among the Fortune 500. It is widely perceived that in the light of their special connection to the government, and

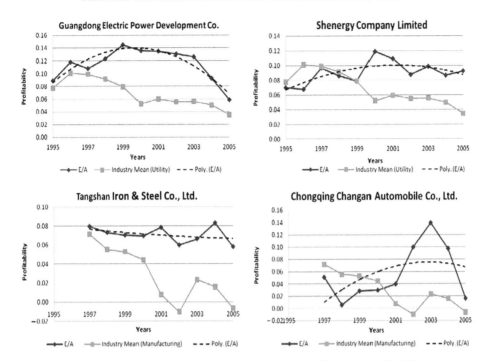

Figure 2. Profitability of selected large SOEs and industry-specific mean profitability.

their governance mechanism, their profitability dynamics may well be unmarked by competition and be characterized by persistence (Lin *et al.* 1998, Lo 1999, Sun *et al.* 2002).

Figure 2, which presents the profitability of selected large SOEs vis-à-vis mean profitability of the industries to which these enterprises belong, shows that they have generally turned in higher than average profitability. There is an evident tendency to revert to mean when the deviation is large. The regression results for SOEs alone, in Equation (7) below characterizes the extent of reversion to the simple cross-sectional mean. We find significant reversion to the cross-sectional mean from extreme negative deviations. Comparing these results with the pooled results in Equation (6), the message is that SOEs turn around from underperformance relative to the SOE cross-sectional mean at a faster rate. The lack of significance of the term relating to extreme positive deviations suggests that SOEs tend to sustain high profitability to a greater extent.

$$CP_{it+1} = -0.014 + 0.454\,E_{it}/A_{it} - 0.793\,ND_{it} + 4.010\,SND_{it} - 3.134\,SPD_{it}$$

$$\phantom{CP_{it+1} = }(-0.54)\quad(0.76)\quad\quad(-0.78)\quad\quad(2.81)\quad\quad\quad(-0.90)$$

$$-0.041\,CP_{it} - 0.227\,NCP_{it} - 5.156\,SNCP_{it} + 0.303\,SPCP_{it}; R^2 = 0.41, F(8,8) = 59.40$$

$$(-0.32)\quad\quad(-0.58)\quad\quad(-1.96)\quad\quad(1.00)$$

$$(7)$$

The results in Table 2, which again relate only to SOEs, suggest that relative to their own individual expected profitability, SOEs are marked by a higher rate of mean reversion: the constrained coefficient on DFE_t (and the average between the coefficients on observed and expected profitability) is -0.76, compared to -0.56 for the pooled sample. It is interesting that the profitability dynamics of listed SOEs is more pronounced

Table 2. Mean reversion in SOEs' profitability: 1995–2005.

Panel A: Mean reversion in SOE profitability $CP_{t+1} = E_{t+1}/A_{t+1} - E_t/A_t$

	α	E_t/A_t	$E(E_t/A_t)$	DFE_t	$NDFE_t$	$SNDFE_t$	CP_t	NCP_t	$SNCP_t$	R^2	N
Mean	−0.003			−0.761	0.635	3.272	0.160	0.254	0.597	0.22	2353
t(Mn)	−0.71			−2.80	1.10	1.13	1.28	0.60	0.23		
Mean	−0.011	−0.674	0.838		0.598	3.742	0.134	0.162	0.125	0.24	2353
t(Mn)	−0.96	−3.27	2.09		0.99	1.13	1.23	0.42	0.05		

Panel B: Summary statistics of variables

	CP_{t+1}	E_t/A_t	$E(E_t/A_t)$	DFE_t	$NDFE_t$	$SNDFE_t$	CP_t	NCP_t	$SNCP_t$
Mean	−0.014	0.045	0.045	−0.001	−0.016	0.001	−0.004	−0.018	0.002
Std.	0.169	0.059	0.038	0.047	0.035	0.010	0.093	0.038	0.013

Notes: Panel C reports the means (across years) of the intercept (α) and slope coefficients relating to Equation (4). T-statistics for these coefficient means t(Mn), are also reported. Panel D reports averages (across years) of the means and standard deviations (SD) of these regression variables.

Panel A variables are as follows: E_{it} is earnings before interest and extraordinary items but after taxes; A_{it} is the company's total assets at year end; D_{it} is the dividends paid out during the year; BE_{it} is the book value of common shareholders' equity at year end; MV_{it} is the company's market value at year start; DD_{it} is a dummy that is 0 for dividend payers and 1 for non-payers; $SALE_{it}$ is net sales; $CAPIN_{it}$ is capital intensity (= depreciation/total assets); $GEAR_{it}$ is leverage (=debt/equity); D_SOE_{it} is a dummy that is 1 when the state owns more than 50% of the company's shares and 0 otherwise; D_TV_{it} is a dummy that is 1 when more than 50% of the company's outstanding shares are tradable and 0 otherwise; and industry dummies mark out when the company is in mining, utility, transportation or commerce sector; ε_{it} is an error term (residual) assumed to be IID; We take the logarithm of those explanatory variables showing considerable heterogeneity.

Panel C variables are as follows: $CP_{it} = E_{it}/A_{it} - E_{it-1}/A_{it-1}$ is change in profitability from year $t-1$ to t; $E(E_{it}/A_{it})$ is the expected value of profitability; $DFE_{it} = E_{it}/A_{it} - E(E_{it}/A_{it})$ is the deviation of profitability from its expected value; $NDFE_{it}$ equals to DFE_{it} when DFE_{it} is negative, and 0 otherwise; $SNDFE_{it}$ equals to the square of DFE_{it} when DFE_{it} is negative, and 0 otherwise; NCP_{it} equals to CP_{it} when CP_{it} is negative, and 0 otherwise; $SNCP_{it}$ equals to the square of CP_{it} when CP_{it} is negative, and 0 otherwise.

in the tendency to revert to conditional mean. What is evident is that expected profitability is driven by, and takes into account, the various entry barriers that apply to protect their dominant positions, and preferential treatment they receive from the government. It is relative to this benchmark, that the SOEs exhibit this high degree of mean reversion.

WTO accession

Structural changes in business environment may of course greatly influence the intensity of competition, and the effects can be expected to be evident in terms of mean reversion. China's entry into the WTO after 11 December 2001 entailed opening up its economy to foreign competition. This should have intensified competition from the global market. The opening up of the market was phased over five years to give Chinese firms the opportunity to adjust to competition. Tariffs fell by more than 50% in five years, and many non-tariffs measures were phased out over the same period. Protected sectors such as financial services and telecommunications were also opened up to foreign ownership over time. We divided the sample into the two sub-periods: pre-WTO (1995–2001) and post-WTO (2002–2005), and re-estimated the model separately. However, the period after WTO accession appears to be too short, and we found no evidence of any significant change in mean reversion due to changes in the competitive climate post-WTO.[10]

It is also conceivable that firmer accounting principles may have been responsible for this negative finding. At the end of 2001, the Ministry of Finance amended the enterprise accounting principles.[11] It stipulated that incomes from debt restructuring and non-cash transactions should be recognized as capital reserves but not profit. This provision reduced the scope of earnings management in relation to assets restructuring. Later that year, the Ministry of Finance issued a related temporary regulation on assets deals involving related parties, in which the portion above fair price could only be entered into capital reserves, but not profit or capital equity. This prevented companies from dealing with related parties to polish their accounts through, for example, sale of goods or assets, transfer of receivables or liabilities, and formation of business coalitions. In 2000, for example, there were 992 listed companies reporting extraordinary items in their P/L accounts, accounting for 97% of all listed companies (2% up from 1999). Among them, 111 companies had more than half of their net incomes from extraordinary items, and 57 traced all their profits to extraordinary items. Since 2001, earnings management under the cover of restructuring has become less practicable due to these policy changes. 'Turnarounds' from adversity is likely to have decreased after these institutional changes.

Mean reversion in earnings

Following the same protocol as above, Panel A in Table 3 summarizes the regressions on mean reversion in earnings. We find that the negative deviations from expected profitability drive the predictable mean reversion in earnings. The coefficients on $NDFE_t$ and $SNDFE_t$ have expected signs (−0.44 and 1.05 respectively) and are highly significant ($t > 3$), whereas the linear mean reversion coefficient is less significant. Companies underperforming in terms of profitability are more likely to reverse their earnings – particularly those in the extreme negative end. The coefficient on CE_t is significant and positive, revealing that serial correlation hold explanatory power for change in earnings, in addition to mean reversion in profitability.

In summary, we find that patterns observed in the variation in earnings is due to the strong reversal tendency of (extreme) negative deviation from expected profitability and

Table 3. Changes in earnings: 1995–2005.

Panel A: Changes in earnings $CE_{t+1} = (E_{t+1} - E_t)/A_t$

	α	E_t/A_t	$E(E_t/A_t)$	DFE_t	$NDFE_t$	$SNDFE_t$	CE_t	NCE_t	$SNCE_t$	R^2	N
Mean	− 0.005			− 0.168	− 0.404	1.064	0.0665	0.281	0.135	0.19	7663
t(Mn)	− 2.59			− 1.82	− 3.34	3.25	2.14	1.73	0.22		
Mean	− 0.009	− 0.123	0.193		− 0.444	1.059	0.0681	0.230	0.0451	0.19	7663
t(Mn)	− 1.93	− 1.17	1.98		− 3.42	3.17	2.10	1.52	0.08		

Panel B: Summary statistics of variables

	CE_{t+1}	E_t/A_t	$E(E_t/A_t)$	DFE_t	$NDFE_t$	$SNDFE_t$	CE_t	NCE_t	$SNCE_t$
Mean	0.008	0.039	0.039	0.000	− 0.018	0.003	0.008	− 0.02	0.004
Std.	0.206	0.073	0.04	0.057	0.049	0.025	0.157	0.063	0.057

Notes: Panel A reports the means (across years) of the regression intercept (α) and slope coefficients from Equation (5). T-statistics for these coefficient means t(Mn), are also presented. Panel B reports averages (across years) of the means and standard deviations (SD) of the regression variables. The variables are: $CE_{it} = (E_{it} - E_{it-1})/A_{it-1}$, is scaled change in earnings; $E(E_{it}/A_{it})$ is expected profitability; $DFE_{it} = E_{it}/A_{it} - E(E_{it}/A_{it})$ is the deviation of profitability from its expected value; $NDFE_{it}$ equals to DFE_{it} when DFE_{it} is negative, and 0 otherwise; $SNDFE_{it}$ equals to the square of DFE_{it} when DFE_{it} is negative, and 0 otherwise; NCE_{it} equals to CE_{it} when CE_{it} is negative, and 0 otherwise; $SNCE_{it}$ equals to the square of CE_{it} when CE_{it} is negative, and 0 otherwise.

linear autocorrelation in earnings. These results are different from those reported by Fama and French (2000), who find significant linear autocorrelation (the coefficient on CE_{it}) as well as non-linear autocorrelation of changes in earnings (the coefficients on NCE_{it}, $SNCE_{it}$ and $SPCE_{it}$).

Conclusions

Perspectives on competition ranging from mainstream economic theory to the Schumpeterian view agree that under competition profitability will tend to move towards what is 'normal'. While economists would tend to define normal profitability at the level of the market, the resource-based view suggests that normal profitability should properly be defined at the firm level. With either definition, the intensity of competition can be expected to determine the rate of this process of mean reversion, and thus make for a degree of predictability of variations in profitability and in earnings. We apply this profitability partial adjustment model to an important emerging market, China, and find evidence for remarkably intense competition. Our contribution is the finding that, though institutions of the market economy have only emerged recently in China, and transactional frictions of many types yet hinder market process and business conduct, the mean reversion process is both salient and significant.

Based on the Fama and French (2000) model, our estimates for the period 1995–2005 suggest that the 55% of any deviation from expected profitability was reversed within a year. This compares very favourably with the 38% that Fama and French (2000) report for the US over the period 1963–1996, and the 25% that Allen and Salim (2005) report for the UK over the period 1982–2000. The profitability behaviour of listed SOEs suggests that they are subject to more intense competition than other listed companies, notwithstanding their relationship with the government. We reiterate the fact that the higher rates of mean reversion experienced by the SOEs are towards their individual levels of company-specific expected profitability. Thus the benchmark for each SOE factors in the likelihood that it is operating in a protected industry, enjoying benefits of monopoly, and/or receiving subsidies from the government. China's entry into the WTO in 2001 opened out the Chinese market in a gradual way to global competition. That has not had a significant impact in terms of further intensifying competition faced by Chinese listed companies.

We find profitability mean reversion contributes significantly to the predictability in earnings, notably reversion from negative deviations in profitability. It has been claimed that earnings management and government subsidies and support may explain reversion for loss-making companies (Burgstahler and Dichev 1997, Zou and Chen 2002). However, our finding is that predictable variation in earnings is driven by the mean reversion process, as it is related to negative deviations of observed from expected profitability (even when observed profitability is not negative).

The fact that there is no evidence of non-linearity – in the sense of more pronounced tendencies of reversion from the far positive end and/or the far negative end of deviations from the firm specific expected profitability – could be attributed to the high rate of growth of the Chinese economy. It would appear that companies falling far short of their own expected or normal profitability are not under any greater pressure to restructure than others deviating less; and companies doing far better than expected are not under any greater competitive threat from incumbent competitors or entrants than other companies. This situation is likely to change if the rate of growth of the economy were to slow down or decline.

Acknowledgements

We are grateful to seminar participants at Cambridge, and to Mark Fagan and Mike Scherer for useful comments.

Notes

1. In Fama and French's sample, financial and utility companies are not considered, and moreover, companies with less than $10 million in assets or $5 million in book equity are excluded as influential observations. In our sample, all listed companies (except those from financial sector) subject to data availability are included.
2. Fama and French found that size (log of total assets) and capital intensity (the ratio of depreciation to total assets) were statistically insignificant in their US sample. In addition to the explanatory variables eventually included in our model, current ratio (current assets to current liability), labour intensity (number of employees to net sales) and exports dummy were also considered in the first instance, but excluded due to lack of significance.
3. For the most part, state-owned shares were non-tradable during the sample period, so there would be some overlap between the dummies: D_SOE and D_TV.
4. This is based on the industry classification 2001 from the Chinese Security Regulation Commission (CSRC); a more specific classification than the 1999 one, with 14 alphabet-level industries.
5. Special treatment companies are those which have failed to comply with regulations or have suffered negative net incomes for two consecutive years. Particular transfer companies are those which have made losses for three consecutive years. Financial companies are excluded from the sample because their regulation and patronage that they are subject to is likely to determine the behaviour of profitability.
6. Chinese stock market consists of much fewer companies pre-1995, and relevant data are not fully retrievable or verifiable from extant databases.
7. This system is developed by GTA information technology Co., Ltd according to the international standards to meet the requirements of business and investment research, and it encompasses data on the China stock market and the financial statements of China's listed companies. There are several databases: Trading, Financial Statement, Trade and Quote, Mutual Fund, IPO, Event Dates and the like: some of them can be found in Wharton Research Data Services (WRDS).
8. There was no precedent of delisting in both exchanges until the end of year 2001, and since then up to 2006 about 30 companies have been delisted. This reduces the survivor bias in our sample.
9. Yearly correlation coefficients among explanatory variables in the model are available on request.
10. Results are available on request.
11. Relating to intangible assets, loan expenses, leasing, cash flow statement, debt restructuring, investment, the alteration of accounting estimation and error correction, and non-cash transaction.

References

Aharony, J., Lee, J., and Wong, T.J., 2000. *Financial packaging of IPO firms in China* [online]. Available from: http://ssrn.com/abstract=201093 [Accessed 1 August 2007].

Ahmed, S., 2005. Forecasting profitability, earnings, and corporate taxes: evidence from UK companies. *In*: S. Ahmed, ed. *Essays in corporate tax modelling*. Thesis (PhD). University of Cambridge.

Allen, D.E. and Salim, H.M., 2005. Forecasting profitability and earnings: a study of the UK market (1982–2000). *Applied economics*, 37 (17), 2009–2018.

Ball, R. and Brown, P., 1968. An empirical evaluation of accounting income numbers. *Journal of accounting research*, 6 (2), 159–178.

Ball, R. and Watts, R., 1972. Some time-series properties of accounting income. *The journal of finance*, 27 (3), 663–682.

Barney, J., 1991. Firm resources and sustained competitive advantage. *Journal of management*, 17 (1), 99–120.

Barro, R.J., 1991. Economic growth in a cross-section of countries. *Quarterly journal of economics letters*, 106 (2), 407–443.

Barro, R.J. and Sala-i-Martin, X., 1992. Convergence. *Journal of political economy*, 100 (2), 223–251.

Barro, R.J. *et al.*, 1991. Convergence across states and regions. *Brookings papers on economic activity*, (1), 107–182.

Basu, S., 1997. The conservatism principle and the asymmetric timeliness of earnings. *Journal of accounting economics*, 24 (1), 3–37.

Baumol, W.J., 1986. Productivity growth, convergence, and welfare. *American economic review*, 76 (5), 1072–1085.

Beaver, W.H., 1970. The time series behavior of earnings. *Journal of accounting research*, 8 (Suppl.), 62–99.

Bernard, A.B. and Durlauf, S.N., 1996. Interpreting tests of the convergence hypothesis. *Journal of econometrics*, 71 (1–2), 161–173.

Brooks, L.D. and Buckmaster, D.A., 1976. Further evidence of the time series properties of accounting income. *The journal of finance*, 31, 1359–1373.

Burgstahler, D. and Dichev, I., 1997. Earnings management to avoid earnings decreases and losses. *Journal of accounting and economics*, 24 (1), 99–126.

Burmeister, E., 1980. *Capital theory and dynamics*. Cambridge: Cambridge University Press.

Cable, J., Jackson, R.H.G., and Rhys, H., 2001. *Profit cycles: the dynamics of corporate earnings revisited*. Mimeo. School of Management and Business, University of Wales.

Campbell, J.Y. and Shiller, R.J., 1988. Stock prices, earnings, and expected dividends. *The journal of finance*, 43 (3), 661–676.

Chen, C.J.P., Chen, S., and Su, X., 2001. Is accounting information value-relevant in the emerging Chinese stock market? *Journal of international accounting, auditing and taxation*, 10 (1), 1–22.

Chen, G., Firth, M., and Rui, O.M., 2006. Have China's enterprise reforms led to improved efficiency and profitability. *Emerging markets review*, 7 (1), 82–109.

China Accounting Standards Committee, 2001. *Accounting system for business enterprises*. Beijing: The Ministry of Finance.

Collins, D.W. and Kothari, S.P., 1989. An analysis of intertemporal and cross-sectional determinants of earnings response coefficients. *Journal of accounting and economics*, 11 (2–3), 143–181.

Collins, D.W., Maydew, E.L., and Weiss, I.S., 1997. Changes in the value-relevance of earnings and book values over the past forty years. *Journal of accounting and economics*, 24 (1), 39–67.

Conyon, M.J. and Machin, S., 1991. The determination of profit margins in UK manufacturing. *The journal of industrial economics*, 39 (4), 369–382.

Cuaresma, J.C. and Gschwandtner, A., 2006. The competitive environment hypothesis revisited: non-linearity, nonstationarity and profit persistence. *Applied economics*, 38 (4), 465–472.

Cuaresma, J.C. and Gschwandtner, A., 2008. Tracing the dynamics of competition: evidence from company profits. *Economic inquiry*, 46 (2), 208–213.

Cubbin, J.S. and Geroski, P.A., 1990. The persistence of profits in the United Kingdom. *In*: D.C. Mueller, ed. *The dynamics of company profits: an international comparison*. Cambridge: Cambridge University Press, chap. 9, 147–168.

Dierckx, I. and Cool, K., 1989. Asset stock accumulation and sustainability of competitive advantage. *Management science*, 35 (12), 1504–1511.

Easton, P.D. and Zmijewski, M., 1989. Cross-sectional variation in the stock market response to accounting earnings announcements. *Journal of accounting and economics*, 11, 117–141.

Elgers, P.T. and Lo, M.H., 1994. Reductions in analysts' annual earnings forecast errors using information in prior earnings and security returns. *Journal of accounting research*, 32 (2), 290–303.

Fairfield, P.M., Sweeney, R.J., and Yohn, T.L., 1996. Accounting classification and the predictive content of earnings. *The accounting review*, 71 (3), 337–355.

Fama, E.F., 1970. Efficient capital markets: a review of theory and empirical work. *The journal of finance*, 25 (2), 383–417.

Fama, E.F., 1991. Efficient capital markets II. *The journal of finance*, 46 (5), 1575–1617.

Fama, E.F. and French, K.R., 1996. Multifactor explanations of asset pricing anomalies. *The journal of finance*, 51 (1), 55–84.

Fama, E.F. and French, K.R., 2000. Forecasting profitability and earnings. *The journal of business*, 73 (2), 161–175.

Fama, E.F. and MacBeth, J.D., 1973. Risk, return and equilibrium: empirical tests. *Journal of political economy*, 81 (3), 607–636.

Feltham, G.A. and Ohlson, J.A., 1999. Residual earnings valuation with risk and stochastic interest rates. *The accounting review*, 74 (2), 165–183.

Freeman, R.N., Ohlson, J.A., and Penman, S.H., 1982. Book rate-of-return and prediction of earnings changes: an empirical investigation. *Journal of accounting research*, 20 (2), 639–653.

Gao, L. and Kling, G., 2006. Regulatory changes and market liquidity in Chinese stock markets. *Emerging markets review*, 7 (2), 162–175.

Geroski, P.A., 1990. Modelling persistent profitability. *In*: D.C. Mueller, ed. *The dynamics of company profits: an international comparison*. Cambridge: Cambridge University Press, chap. 2. 15–34.

Geroski, P.A. and Jacquemin, A., 1988. The persistence of profits: a European comparison. *Economic journal*, 98 (391), 375–389.

Glen, J., Lee, K., and Singh, A., 2001. Persistence of profitability and competition in emerging markets. *Economics letters*, 72 (2), 247–253.

Goddard, J.A. and Wilson, J.O.S., 1999. The persistence of profit: a new empirical interpretation. *International journal of industrial organisation*, 17 (5), 662–687.

Gschwandtner, A., 2004. *Evolution of profit persistence in the US: evidence from four 20-years periods*, Working paper No. 0410. Department of Economics, University of Vienna.

Hoopes, D.G., Madsen, T.L., and Walker, G., 2003. Guest editors' introduction to the special issue: why is there a resource-based view? Toward a theory of competitive heterogeneity. *Strategic management journal*, 24 (10), 889–902.

Ibragimov, R. and Müller, U.K., 2007. *T-Statistic based correlation and heterogeneity robust inference* [online]. Harvard Institute of Economic Research, Discussion Paper No. 2129. Available from: http://ssrn.com/abstract=964224 [Accessed 8 March 2008].

Jacobsen, R., 1988. The persistence of abnormal returns. *Strategic management journal*, 9 (5), 415–430.

Kam, A., Citron, D.B., and Muradoglu, Y.G., 2005. *The characteristics of corporate distress in an emerging market: the case of China* [online]. Cass Business School Research Paper. Available from: http://ssrn.com/abstract=690181 [Accessed 23 August 2007].

Kothari, S.P., 2001. Capital markets research in accounting. *Journal of accounting and economics*, 31 (1–3), 105–231.

Lev, B., 1983. Some economic determinants of time-series properties of earnings. *Journal of accounting and economics*, 5 (3), 1–48.

Levi, M.D. and Diao, X., 2005. Stock ownership restrictions and equilibrium asset pricing: the case of China [online]. Available from: http://ssrn.com/abstract=687583 [Accessed 23 August 2007].

Lin, J.Y., Cai, F., and Li, Z., 1998. Competition, policy burdens, and state-owned enterprise reform. *The American economic review*, 88 (2), 422–427.

Lin, S. and Rowe, W., 2006. Determinants of the profitability of China's regional SOEs. *China economic review*, 17 (2), 120–141.

Little, I.M.D., 1962. Higgledy piggledy growth. *Oxford bulletin of statistics*, 24 (4), 387–412.

Little, I.M.D. and Rayner, A.C., 1966. *Higgledy piggledy growth again: an investigation of the predictability of company earnings and dividends in the UK*. Oxford: Basil Blackwell.

Liu, Q., 2006. Corporate governance in China: current practices, economic effects, and institutional determinants. *CESifo economic studies*, 52 (2), 415–453.

Liu, Q. and Lu, J.Z., 2003. Earnings management to tunnel: evidence from China's listed companies [online]. The European Financial Management Association 2004 Basel Meetings Paper. Available from: http://ssrn.com/abstract=349880 [Accessed 23 August 2007].

Lo, D., 1999. Reappraising the performance of China's state-owned industrial enterprises: 1980–96. *Cambridge journal of economics*, 23 (6), 693–718.

Lookabill, L.L., 1976. Some additional evidence on the time series properties of accounting earnings. *The accounting review*, 51 (4), 724–738.

Miller, M.H. and Modigliani, F., 1961. Dividend policy, growth, and the valuation of shares. *The journal of business*, 34 (4), 411–433.

Mueller, D.C., 1986. *Profits in the long run*. Cambridge: Cambridge University Press.

Mueller, D.C., 1990. *The dynamics of company profits: an international comparison*. Cambridge: Cambridge University Press.

Mueller, D.C. and Raunig, B., 1999. Heterogeneities within industries and structure-performance models. *Review of industrial organization*, 15 (4), 303–320.

Ohlson, J.A., 1989. Ungarbled earnings and dividends: an analysis and extension of the Beaver, Lambert and Morse valuation model. *Journal of accounting and economics*, 7 (2–3), 109–116.

Ohlson, J.A., 1995. Earnings, book values, and dividends in equity valuation. *Contemporary accounting research*, 11 (2), 661–687.

Ou, J.A. and Penman, S.H., 1989. Accounting measurement, price-earnings ratio, and the information content of security prices. *Journal of accounting research*, 27, 111–144.

Oulton, N., 1998. Competition and the dispersion of labour productivity amongst UK companies. *Oxford economic papers*, 50 (1), 23–38.

Roberts, P.W. and Dowling, G.R., 2002. Corporate reputation and sustained superior financial performance. *Strategic management journal*, 23 (12), 1077–1093.

Rumelt, R.P., 1984. Toward a strategic theory of the firm. *In*: R.B. Lamb, ed. *Competitive strategic management*. Englewood Cliffs, NJ: Prentice-Hall.

Sami, H. and Zhou, H., 2004. A comparison of value relevance of accounting information in different segments of the Chinese stock market. *The international journal of accounting*, 39 (4), 403–427.

Schipani, C.A. and Liu, J., 2002. Corporate governance in China: then and now. *Columbia business law review*, (1), 1–69.

Schmalensee, R., 1953. Intra-industry profitability differences in US manufacturing 1953–1983. *The journal of industrial economics*, 37 (4), 337–357.

Schumpeter, J.A., 1943. *Capitalism, socialism and democracy*. London: Allen and Unwin.

Schwalbach, J., Graβhoff, U., and Mahmood, T., 1989. The dynamics of corporate profits. *European economic review*, 33 (8), 1625–1639.

Su, D. and Fleisher, B.M., 1998. Risk, return and regulation in Chinese stock markets. *Journal of economics and business*, 50 (3), 239–256.

Sun, Q., Tong, W.H.S., and Tong, J., 2002. How does government ownership affect firm performance? Evidence from China's privatization experience. *Journal of business finance & accounting*, 29 (1–2), 1–27.

Wei, G., Zhang, W., and Xiao, Z., 2003. *Dividends policy and ownership structure in China* [online]. The European Financial Management Association 2004 Basel meeting paper. Available from: http://ssrn.com/abstract=463924 [Accessed 1 August 2008].

Whittington, G., 1980. The profitability and size of United Kingdom companies: 1960–74. *The journal of industrial economics*, 28 (4), 335–352.

Xu, X. and Wang, Y., 1999. Ownership structure and corporate governance in Chinese stock companies. *China economic review*, 10 (1), 75–98.

Yurtoglu, B.B., 2004. Persistence of firm-level profitability in Turkey. *Applied economics*, 36 (6), 615–625.

Zhou, X., 2001. *The improvement of the structure of corporate governance of Chinese listed companies* (translation from Chinese). Beijing: The symposium for corporate governance of Chinese listed companies 2001.

Zou, X. and Chen, X., 2002. Earnings management of Chinese listed companies: a survey of empirical studies. *China world economy*, 4, 38–43.

Managers, markets and the globalized economy in China: epilogue

Chris Rowley[a] and Malcolm Warner[b]

[a]Centre for Research on Asian Management, City University, London, UK; [b]Judge Business School, University of Cambridge, Cambridge, UK

In this Epilogue to the Symposium, we look at the conclusions we can draw from our *tour d'horizon* of managers, markets and the globalized economy in the People's Republic of China. We have seen that, since the late 1970s, industrial ownership has significantly opened-up and become more fragmented, that the state-owned enterprises are arguably no longer the dominant mode in the economy and indeed neither is their management model. Managing, we also noted, has become more complex and diversified, as well as more professional. This edited collection has thus shown how China's managers now have to operate in a more market-driven context if somewhat bounded by the parameters of the 'harmonious society'.

Introduction

In this Epilogue, we ask what conclusions can be drawn from this *tour d'horizon* of the field. We have, for example, seen that much has transpired since *Deng Xiaoping* introduced his economic reforms in the late 1970s, with the 'Open Door' (*kaifang*) and 'Four Modernizations' (*sige xiandaihua)* policies (see Child 1994, Bergsten *et al.* 2008, Rowley and Cooke 2010a). However, the restructuring process which involved reforming the state-owned enterprises (SOEs) and the accompanying more or less lifetime employment system, the 'iron rice bowl' (*tie fan wan*), was not without controversy. Many of the reforms were clearly unwelcome to the Communist Party hardliners (see Korzec 1992).

By adopting a pragmatic approach, *Deng* persuaded the *middle ground* that his reform programme was to be the most feasible way of modernizing the nation's economy. The most urgent priority was to achieve a *balance* between boosting the efficiency and competitiveness of enterprises on the one hand, and protecting social rights on the other. Management, in turn, became more professionalized and less ideological; privately-owned enterprises (POEs), joint ventures (JVs) and wholly foreign-owned enterprises (WOFEs) were now numerous; a wide range of business schools appeared (Warner and Goodall 2009). A new form of people management, '*renli ziyuan guanli*', literally meaning 'labour force resources management', became – for better or worse – a *synonym* for what was understood as human resource management (HRM) (see Warner 2009, 2010). As China now had to face the challenges of globalization, it adapted its system to promote institutional and organizational characteristics more appropriate to a greater reliance on markets (see Garnaut *et al.* 2005).

Having survived the 1997 Asian financial crisis and the later 2003 SARS epidemic without a major upheaval, China now had to come to terms with the global downturn of 2008–2009. Although the Beijing Olympics symbolically confirmed China's claim to be a super-power status, the boost to the economy was temporary; the leadership then announced a recovery package of US$586 billion to stimulate the domestic market and cope with the unemployment that by the Spring Festival in 2009 had rung alarm bells. Happily, there now seems to be an upswing of economic activity, with a projected annual growth-rate just above the danger-threshold, namely the level where the problem of absorbing the new school-leavers and university graduates, let alone the flow of migrant workers from the countryside, would be problematic.

'Modernization' meant learning from abroad but in Chinese eyes still holding on to indigenous values. A fashionable notion at the time – 'linking up with the international track' *(yu guoji jiegui)* – had emerged in China in the late 1980s (Wang 2007, p. 13ff) – and may be seen as an key feature of how it had sought to adapt to 'globalization', on the one hand, but at the same time stressing socialism with 'Chinese characteristics' *(juyou Zhongguo tese)* in order to be seen as respecting its own values, on the other hand, vis-à-vis the new economic, political and social environment it faced. These developments were said to link directly into the current President Hu Jintao's and Premier Wen Jiabao's drive for a more 'harmonious society' *(hexie shehui)*, first articulated in 2005 (Hawes 2008, p. 39). A key report 'A Resolution on the Major Issues Concerning the Building of a Socialist Harmonious Society' was adopted at the Sixth Plenum of the Sixteenth CCP Central Committee, 2006 and spelt out more explicitly the new social model to which the new Chinese leadership aspired.

A seasoned observer of Chinese affairs (Lam 2005, p. 1) commented that:

> China's 11th Five Year Plan (FYP) has laid out a grandiose roadmap for the country's 'scientific development', a euphemism used by the country's leadership for economic growth that takes into consideration the welfare of disadvantaged sectors as well as environmental concerns. Given the track record of China's supercharged economy, there are relatively few doubters regarding the just-announced goals of attaining a GDP of US$4 trillion ..., and a per capita GDP share of $3000, by 2020. Yet more ambitious objectives such as curtailing pollution and energy waste – and in particular, 'constructing a harmonious society' – could remain illusory given the Chinese Communist Party's (CCP) refusal to entertain comprehensive structural and political reforms.

The latter observation emphasized the gravity of the dilemma facing the nation's leadership.

There was however, a possible way of 'squaring the circle', built into this proposed policy of 'harmony', we would argue, involving a sometimes contentious trade-off between 'economic' goals and 'social' ones. Some of the contributions to this Symposium have in their turn stressed, or at least implied, the importance of the one vis-à-vis the other. At one extreme, a paper might be high on both Economic and Social axes (H, H), or low (L, L) alternatively. Most are, in reality, a mixture (H, L or H, L) but in different degrees, as can be seen from say, the contributions here on labour-management relations, trust relations, corporate social responsibility, as well as others such as the contribution on banking relationships, amongst others.

Contributor conclusions

What do the contributions to this volume conclude about Chinese management per se? First, 'Labour and management in the People's Republic of China: seeking the "harmonious society" ' concludes that economic reforms have moved quickly, with China no longer the same society it was. While not a 'pluralist' society, there is more 'social space' than there was. Once a 'command economy', it is now a 'socialist market' one, even becoming a 'consumer society'. Again, its trade unions have attempted to respond to the new *status quo* if with difficulty. Yet, rapid development has generated a more unequal society and the sources of potential conflict and crisis may be hard to contain. Therefore, developing a 'harmonious society' as a 'coping mechanism', as initially hypothesized, has become a priority, in particular to enhance 'harmony' in labour-management relations, between different interest groups, between human and natural environments, between China and the international community and between current and future generations, as the official line puts it. However, some events indicate the need to tread most carefully.

The second study, 'Business relationships in China: lessons about deep trust', interprets the interpersonal nature of this important construct which many scholars believe to be a major linchpin of Chinese business behaviour (see Child and Warner 2003). 'Trust' has been identified in literature as being a critical construct, however, an indigenous definition and understanding of both *guanxi* and *xinren* is an important step in closing a gap in the literature on trust-relationships. China is now said to be a global powerhouse, but it remains a country in a state of flux when it comes to institutional or systemic trust. An in-depth understanding of such social-cum-business constructs appears pivotal to the future of Sino-Western inter-relationship.

In the third entry, 'Small and medium-sized enterprises in China: a literature review, human resource management and suggestions for further research', the authors conclude that SMEs have become recognized as important to business development around the world. China appears to be no exception to this generalization. This review was conducted to enhance the understanding of HRM development in such firms in China. The emphasis was on highlighting the depth and breadth of research that has occurred and to identify the gaps. There is a need, it concludes, for the development of more longitudinal research, with more rigorous empirical studies. Of course, this is a 'clarion call' for more difficult and long-term, but more meaningful, research in an always difficult area – dealing with employment matters. This conclusion is also 'against the grain' and current pressures in academia to churn out 'salami-style' publications to meet whatever the latest rankings are.

The fourth entry, 'Employees' satisfaction with HRM in Chinese privately-owned enterprises', concludes that although the literature recognizes that employees in different sectors expect and respond to reform differently and that while HRM in such firms is problematic, less is known about how employees in the private sector perceive specific policies and practices. This study investigated employees' satisfaction with HRM and the differences in satisfaction between groups. It revealed new trends in employees' acceptance of, and attitudes toward, HRM reform, indicating the diminishing influence of socialist egalitarianism ideology. This was evidenced by general acceptance of modern HRM concepts, such as labour contracts, need for training and development, performance appraisals, and performance-based reward and compensation. Currently, Chinese employees in POEs appear to have a moderate to high level of satisfaction with HRM policies and practices except for training and development. Also, the level of satisfaction with policies and practices varies according to demographic variables. These findings have significant practical implications for developing more effective and harmonious workplace relations in China's private economy.

The fifth piece, 'Corporate social responsibility and HRM in China: a study of textile and apparel enterprises', revealed views of managers on issues related to corporate social responsibility (CSR) and its accompanying practices. It suggests firms are only now beginning to realise the full importance of CSR, despite many not having written policies or obtaining standards. The study argues that legal compliance remains the main source of pressure and public statements of commitment to CSR may be little more than lip-service. While firms recognize employees as stakeholders, they pay less attention to labour-standards issues than other aspects of the CSR. They also score poorly on other HRM issues such as employee involvement in decision-making and work-life balance. There is little evidence of strategic involvement of employees in delivering CSR activities. Nevertheless, the study provides evidence that effective employee involvement schemes do have a positive impact. It also suggested that external bodies and value chains are not the main drivers for CSR activities. Based on this evidence, pressure, both internal and external, for firms to assume CSR is limited. Without tangible benefits, as well as effective measures for non-compliance, firms are unlikely to shown much interest in engagement with CSR. While many of the findings reflect those found in other studies outside China, suggesting some universal patterns in adoption, it also reveals a number of unique characteristics and institutional weaknesses specific in the Chinese context. These include, for example, the role of the government and the types of incentives that may prove effective to motivate firms and employees to engage in CSR activities. The limited power of non-government led pressure groups is evident and a voluntary approach to CSR is unlikely to have much effect in the current business environment in China.

The sixth entry, '*Hukou*-based HRM in contemporary China: the case of Jiangsu and Shanghai' tested the hypothesis that Chinese HRM is *hukou*-(residence-permit)-based due to the rural-urban separation found in contemporary China. This system, it finds, has ossified into socially shared normative and cognitive templates and consequently, continues to have a major impact on HRM, even though many of the regulations that previously ensured the system discriminated against off-the-farm workers had weakened. This situation ensured that rural migrant workers were managed in ways different from their urban counterparts. The study clearly indicated HRM is clearly *hukou*-biased, even though moving towards a Western model. Therefore, even if firms are utilizing Western HRM practices, these practices might be *hukou*-based as they are primarily used for urban employees only. The findings show that this system has shaped not only the HRM of domestic firms but also that of foreign firms. Therefore, ignoring the influence of the *hukou* system and assuming that the HRM policy and practice of Chinese firms covers all employees is problematic.

The seventh entry, 'The antecedents and consequences of commitment in bank–corporate relationships: evidence from the Chinese banking market' used a model of what motivates corporate customers to continue their relationships with their banks. This study had several implications, including around the ideas of shared values and creation of trust, while arguing that affective commitment is importantly influenced by service quality. The study concluded that service-quality in China is a significant precursor of affective commitment, which in turn leads to cooperation and continuance intentions. Management should be aware of the importance of quality in contributing to the development of good bank–corporate relationships. Banks will benefit from focusing efforts on this. To foster calculative commitment management, they should concentrate more on its service-portfolio and other technical quality matters, that is, what is provided, rather than the functional quality issue, how the service is provided. However, management in China should also try to avoid those relationships where corporate customers only demonstrate calculative commitment, as the results identify calculative commitment as positively associated with opportunistic behaviour and negatively correlated with cooperation, reducing expectations of relationship continuation. Without a genuine attempt to develop affective commitment, it argues, efforts to develop relationships with corporate customers will be ineffective.

The eighth contribution looked at 'The influence of western banks on corporate governance in China'. The findings suggested that while there has been rapid change in the formal legislative environment in which banks operate, the informal normative and cultural-cognitive realms are changing more slowly. Components of Western models of corporate governance (Board of Directors, diversified ownership structures, and technical assistance in areas such as credit rating and risk management) had been widely adopted. However, the over-riding perception was that the motivation for these changes was legitimacy seeking by Chinese banks in the global financial environment. Enduring cognitive and normative institutions, including a 'who you know' credit culture and the importance of informal institutions, such as *guanxi*, meant that the influence of foreign banks on corporate governance reforms is perceived as ineffective. Given the serious failures of Western credit-rating systems in the post-2008 sub-prime crisis, it is likely that this perception will increase in the future.

The ninth investigation, 'Intangible management and enterprise success in the Chinese transitional economy' concludes that the forms of management in China have changed substantially with economic restructuring, and that most of the innovative management practices, the forms of organizational culture, management structures and systems that are common in other economies are now present, at least to some degree, in its enterprises. This study confirmed that the success of Chinese enterprises is due to similar kinds of intangible management variables, employee satisfaction and contextual variables that appear to drive the success of Western enterprises. The impact of these intangible factors on employees' satisfaction is significant. A 'soft' oriented managerial style, such as better communications, participation and provision of information, appears to be more effective than a 'hard' oriented managerial restructuring of systems or structure. In addition, an internal-oriented clan culture is more profound than that of the external-oriented market culture. Furthermore, employees' satisfaction is more associated with autonomy and individual rights than benefits, though both components are important. The effects of changing managerial intangible elements and employee satisfaction on overall organizational performance were also significant. Managerial intangible elements, including aspects of management culture, such as references to cooperation and decentralized management structures, have significant effects on sales. In addition, employees' satisfaction as measured by their level of responsibility had a positive effect on sales. Finally, a number of contextual variables related to the transition correlated with outcomes. However, other measures of transition (the local private economy or location variations in the pace of reform) do not appear to have much impact on performance. None of the measures of transition, it seems, had a significant influence on employee satisfaction or on the adoption of forms of intangible management or social harmony.

The tenth entry, 'Intensity of competition in China: profitability dynamics of Chinese listed companies' concluded that different perspectives on competition agree that under competition profitability will tend to move towards what is 'normal'. This study found evidence for remarkably intense competition and that though institutions of the market economy have only emerged recently and transactional frictions of many types hinder market process and business conduct, the mean reversion process is both salient and significant. The profitability behaviour of listed SOEs suggests that they are subject to more intense competition than other listed companies, notwithstanding their relationship with the government. China's entry into the WTO (2001) gradually opened up the market to global competition. This step has not, however, had a significant impact in terms of further intensifying competition faced by Chinese listed companies. It would appear that companies falling far short of their own expected or normal profitability are not under any greater pressure to restructure than others deviating less; and companies doing far better than expected are not under any greater competitive threat from incumbent competitors or entrants than other companies. This situation may be likely to change if the rate of growth of the economy slows down or declines.

Discussion

Where do the above findings lead the reader? What is the cumulative upshot of such investigations? Is there a specifically *Chinese* theoretical framework that be adduced? There is undoubtedly an ongoing, as yet unresolved, debate at the time of writing at least, as to whether the field needs a '*Chinese theory of management*' anyway, as opposed to a '*theory of Chinese management*' in order to fully understand what has been happening since the reforms were implemented (see Editors Forum 2009, Tsui 2009).

Here, we can say that the Chinese institutional framework which emerged was clearly '*Chinese*' in its characteristics and it was also true that the resultant management model was consonant with these features. However, it is more contentious to assert that there exists or needs to be an *indigenous* Chinese theory of management (see also Poon and Rowley 2007, 2008). We can here furthermore argue that a specifically 'Chinese' theory of economics did *not* in fact arise in past time and this in itself did *not* present major problems (Trescott 2007) and that therefore, as a generalization, an indigenous theory of management may be *neither* a necessary nor a sufficient condition for an understanding of how national systems of management work. The contributions to this volume, in their respective ways, may nonetheless be seen as 'building blocks' towards a Chinese model of management. Many of the contributors do have Chinese roots, even though perhaps researching and/or teaching overseas. In this sense, their 'theories' are Chinese but it is clear that the theoretical frameworks they are using, we would argue, are *Western* in origin, whether or not they are '*context-embedded*'. Child (2009) in fact argues that it is necessary to:

> [...] investigate Chinese management in a way that takes account of its context, in order to assess the extent to which its features are context-specific or context-bounded. The first requirement, therefore, is to develop a way of conceptualising and measuring that context. A framework articulating material, ideational and institutional contextual features is offered to that end. Second, [the author] argue[s] that both 'outside in' and 'inside out' approaches to the study of Chinese management require comparison between China and other countries. Even a theory that claims uniqueness for China needs to have that claim tested through external comparison. We, therefore, have to employ a methodology that allows for valid comparisons between context and management in China and other countries.

[The author] then focuses on:

> these two issues of context and methodology ... [and] ... examines them in turn and closes by arguing that the choice ... between a Chinese theory of management and a theory of Chinese management – needs to be reframed within a more dynamic evolutionary perspective. (Child 2009, p. 57)

This approach has a good deal of *prima facie* plausibility.

There is also the specific *focus* that should be considered as a *contingency*, that is, say, the size, ownership, or location of firms. As far as the latter is concerned, there is however a difference between firms enjoying an apparently similar macro-cultural background, whether Confucian or neo-Confucian, in say, Mainland China or the Overseas Chinese (*Nanyang*) economies, such as Hong Kong, Singapore or Taiwan. A large SOE in Beijing will be dissimilar in management culture from say, a family business in Macao. A diverse wealth of 'real-life' case examples across all sorts of organizational types indicate this as well as the changing face of management in China, as seen in recent studies (see Rowley and Cooke 2010a for example). These include those in the areas of performance management (Poon *et al.* 2010) and SME management (Cunningham and Rowley 2010) as well as areas such as marketing, accounting, SOEs, mergers and acquisition and Hong Kong (Rowley and Cooke 2010b, Cooke and Rowley 2010)

Again, the cultural context may be perceived negatively, with *guanxi* and corruption being seen as inter-linked (see Luo 2008, p. 731):

> Despite the enormous economic progress it has made over the past thirty years, China is increasingly demoralized, manifested in part in the intertwinement between *guanxi* and corruption. This change has fundamental repercussions on business culture, practices, and performance, and even more so in the years ahead if corruption continues to be ubiquitous there... [The author]... explain[s] why and how *guanxi* and corruption are intertwined, define the level of intertwineability that differs between weak form and strong form, and provide the taxonomy along the level of power abuse and the strength of intertwineability. This taxonomy can be used as a reference framework by future research within which to analyze the dynamics of *guanxi*-corruption interrelationships as well as organizational responses to such dynamics.

So, we can see that there are many open questions on such trust relationships here yet to be resolved.

Concluding remarks

Summing up, we can clearly assert that Deng's reforms unleashed a sequence of events which reshaped the Chinese economy, with a wide range of behavioural, institutional, and organizational outcomes, after 1978. Enthusiasts for globalization believe there is little reason to believe that these steps towards the 'marketization' process will possibly seriously regress in what is now a mixed economy and that fully mature markets will not eventually emerge in China. The forces shaping convergence, driven by globalization in general and WTO membership in particular, will no doubt, they might agree, extend contemporary trends albeit with the constraints of economic circumstance, residual ideological factors, political pressures and so on (see for example, Huang 2008, Scissors 2009). Yet, as always, a certain degree of critical caution is called for, as there are always unintended consequences and outcomes possible.

Another related question is whether they will be a convergence of management models either between China and the West or between Asian economies (see Zhu *et al.* 2007). We have seen that there are constraints of values and policies, such the neo-Confucian attempt to build a 'harmonious society' (see Bell 2008). There is little doubt, whatever happens, that '*Chineseness*' will remain a major characteristic, whether in managerial behaviour or in the more general context.

Last, there are still storm clouds on the horizon and nothing is certain in matters economic. If the severity of the crisis further intensifies, the State/Party may have to go further than just advocating the 'harmonious society' to cope with deep social fissures that might ensue, indeed in varying degrees to re-regulate both external trade, as well as internal factor-markets, as far as these are needed (see Scissors 2009). The dialectical relationship between state control and market forces in the Chinese context is always a dynamic one. Again, as we move into possible further systemic turbulence, with all the complex political and social repercussions this may have, we must keep all analytical options open.

References

Bell, D., 2008. *China's new Confucianism*. Princeton, NJ: Princeton University Press.

Bergsten, C.F., Freeman, C.F., Lardy, N., and Mitchell, D.J., 2008. *China's rise: challenges and opportunities*. Washington DC: Peterson Institute of International Economics.

Child, J., 1994. *Management in China during the era of reform*. Cambridge: Cambridge University Press.

Child, J., 2009. Context, comparison, and methodology in Chinese management research. *Management and organization review*, 5 (1), 57–73.

Child, J. and Warner, M., 2003. Culture and management in China. *In*: M. Warner, ed. *Culture and management in Asia*. London and New York, NY: Routledge, 24–47.

Cooke, F. and Rowley, C., 2010. Setting the scene for the changing face of management in China. *In*: C. Rowley and F. Cooke, eds. *The changing face of management in China*. London and New York, NY: Routledge, 1–27.

Cunningham, X.L. and Rowley, C., 2010. The changing face of SME management in China. *In*: C. Rowley and F. Cooke, eds. *The changing face of management in China*. London and New York, NY: Routledge.

Editors' Forum, 2009. Editors' forum: the future of Chinese management research. *Management and organization review*, 5, 1–166.

Garnaut, R., Song, L., Tenev, S., and Yao, Y., 2005. *China's ownership transformation*. Washington, DC: IFC.

Hawes, C., 2008. Representing corporate culture in China: official and academic perspectives. *The China journal*, 59, January, 31–62.

Huang, Y., 2008. *Capitalism with Chinese characteristics: entrepreneurship and the State*. Cambridge: Cambridge University Press.

Korzec, M., 1992. *Labour and the failure of reform in China*. London and New York, NY: Routledge.

Lam, W., 2005. China's 11th five-year plan: a roadmap for China's "harmonious society?" *China brief*, 5 (1). Available from: http://www.jamestown.org/single/?no_cache=1&tx_ttnews[tt_news]=31019 [Accessed 26 November 2009].

Luo, Y., 2008. The changing Chinese culture and business behavior: the perspective of intertwinement between guanxi and corruption. *International business review*, 17, 731–750.

Poon, I. and Rowley, C., 2007. Contemporary research in management and HR in China. *Asia pacific business review*, 13 (1), 133–153.

Poon, I. and Rowley, C., 2008. HRM best practices and transfers in the Asia Pacific region. *In*: C. Wankel, ed. *21st century management*. Newbury Park, CA: Sage, 209–220.

Poon, I., Wei, Q., and Rowley, C., 2010. The changing face of performance management in China. *In*: C. Rowley and F. Cooke, eds. *The changing face of management China*. London and New York, NY: Routledge.

Rowley, C. and Cooke, F., eds, 2010a. *The changing face of management China*. London and New York, NY: Routledge.

Rowley, C. and Cooke, F., 2010b. Revisiting the changing face of management in China. *In*: C. Rowley and F. Cooke, eds. *The changing face of management China*. London and New York, NY: Routledge.

Scissors, D., 2009. Deng undone: the costs of halting market reform in China. *Foreign affairs*, 88 (3), 28–42.

Trescott, P.B., 2007. *Jingji Xue: the history of western economic ideas into China, 1850–1950*. Hong Kong SAR: Chinese University Press.

Tsui, A.S., ed., 2009. Editor's forum: 'the future of Chinese management research'. *Management and organization review*, Special Issue, 5, 1–166.

Wang, H., 2007. Linking up with the international track: what's in a slogan. *The China quarterly*, 189, March, 1–24.

Warner, M., 2009. "Making sense" of Chinese human resource management: setting the scene. *International journal of human resource management*, 20 (11), 1–25.

Warner, M., ed., 2010. *Making sense of HRM in China: economy, enterprises and workers*. London and New York, NY: Routledge.

Warner, M. and Goodall, K., 2009. *Management training and development in China*. London and New York, NY: Routledge.

World Bank, 2009. China's stimulus policies are key for growth in 2009 and an opportunity for more rebalancing. *World Bank Update*. Available from: www.web.worldbank.org/WBSITE/EXTERNAL/COUNTRIES/EASTASIAPACIFICEXT/CHINAEXTN/0,contentMDK:219 89619~pagePK:1497618~piPK:217854~theSitePK:318950,00.html [Accessed 26 November 2009].

Zhu, Y., Warner, M., and Rowley, C., 2007. Human resource management with "Asian" characteristics: a hybrid people-management system in East Asia. *International journal of human resource management*, 18, 745–768.

Index

For Product Safety Concerns and Information please contact our EU representative GPSR@taylorandfrancis.com Taylor & Francis Verlag GmbH, Kaufingerstraße 24, 80331 München, Germany

Batch number: 08158847

Printed by Printforce, the Netherlands